The Business of Leadership

To my dear
colleague, scholar,
and friend

[signature]

The Business of Leadership

An Introduction

Karen Dill Bowerman
and Montgomery Van Wart

M.E.Sharpe
Armonk, New York
London, England

Library of Congress Cataloging-in-Publication Data

Bowerman, Karen Dill.
  The business of leadership : an introduction / by Karen Dill Bowerman and Montgomery
Van Wart.
    p. cm.
  Includes bibliographical references and index.
  ISBN 978-0-7656-2140-5 (pbk. : alk. paper)
  1. Leadership. 2. Management. I. Van Wart, Montgomery, 1951– II. Title.

HD57.7.B688 2011
658.4′092—dc22   2010040043

Printed in the United States of America

The paper used in this publication meets the minimum requirements of
American National Standard for Information Sciences
Permanence of Paper for Printed Library Materials,
ANSI Z 39.48-1984.

EB (p)   10   9   8   7   6   5   4   3   2   1

Contents

Introduction

Every day you are influenced and you influence others. When you combine that influence with accomplishing an organizational goal, you have the ingredients for leadership. We enjoy leadership from every angle—teaching it, writing about it, developing it in others, and doing it! This book is designed to introduce "the business of leadership" to students, especially in upper-division business courses; the course could be singularly devoted to leadership or it could have professional leadership development as one of several learning goals. Faculty teaching graduate classes will appreciate that the book includes both theoretical and competency-based approaches. Wherever programs in graduate management education are criticized for ignoring the "soft skills," this text can become the basis for guided discussion on development of leadership competencies to erase that criticism.

Many schools of business now subscribe to schoolwide student learning goals—consistent with accreditation needs—and have established a leadership component as one of the overarching goals of the business curriculum. This textbook could become immensely helpful for working with students to achieve and then assess the desired learning outcome. It serves as a compass to guide students to the leadership principles that are to be gleaned; the understanding of these principles can be easily measured for purposes of outcomes assessment. Schools that establish an experiential base for developing leadership competencies (e.g., through service learning requirements) need an academic grounding for the experiences; this textbook is the base that serves as a continual academic compass for the students' varied experiences. Experiences in isolation, or by themselves, do not carry the learning of leadership principles that is possible when linked with a basic text such as this.

Cases are sprinkled in every chapter to give you the opportunity to have as much applied discussion as you wish in order to help students develop leadership competencies. We thank the subjects of many cases who agreed to interviews to describe a particular leadership situation for this text; these real situations provide a rich base for classroom discussion. Other cases are derived from our own leadership experience, and additional cases are classic stories from the media. If you do case updates by covering more about the company or the latest outcome of those cases presented in the text, you will find that persuasive lecture material follows effectively after classroom case discussions.

The team of authors work at the same academic college, but one has academic credentials emphasizing public sector leadership, and the other emphasizing private sector leadership. Knowing that the career pathways of our business students follow both public and private forks in the road, we wrote this text with sensitivity to both paths. The architecture for this book emanated from Van Wart's *Dynamics of Leadership in Public Service*, which was named an Outstanding Academic Title 2005 by *Choice*. Although this business text is entirely new, the important core that remains is the causal-chain model that is used for comparing approaches to leadership and leadership theory, and the sixty-item leadership assessment questionnaire that students may submit to others in 360-degree fashion for feedback about themselves as a leader.

We wish to acknowledge Dr. Ya (Anna) Ni, of California State University, San Bernardino, whose work on public-private partnerships was used in Chapter 11 to explicate a leadership imperative that is too frequently overlooked in introductory texts. Unless both public and business sector leaders appreciate the mutual benefits of partnering, communities cannot become as advanced as their citizenry envisions.

Further, we gratefully acknowledge contributors to the Instructor's Manual whose enthusiastic work will assist adopters of *The Business of Leadership*. Three associates have supplemented test questions and provided auxiliary lecture materials: Barry Manembu, Fernando Huang, and Christina Sumingyue Wang. Barry's multiple-choice questions give a sufficient sampling so that professors may assemble two or more versions that examine the same text material. Fernando's design of PowerPoint slides to accompany the text may be used in multiple ways, such as posting them to assist students in focusing on highlights before exams or adapting them for use during lectures. Christina's contribution to "Business Profiles in the News" can be used creatively to supplement classroom needs for cases that help students apply textbook principles to current business situations that they have been reading about in the news.

Special appreciation is given to Paul Suino for masterful editing that wove together as one the contrasting styles of two writers from related but different disciplines. His touch is responsible for the book's reader-friendly style, and we shall remain indebted to him for taking on the huge task with apt vitality. In addition, we thank Harry Briggs, executive editor at M.E. Sharpe, for his talent in helping to ensure this project's success. Leadership challenges of administration and life itself bring interruptions to the ideal project flow, and his confidence in the venture was essential for sustaining momentum.

The **Business** of **Leadership**

1 Approaches for Motivating Followers, Achieving Results, and Inspiring Change

If your actions inspire others to dream more, learn more,
do more and become more, you are a leader.
—John Quincy Adams, U.S. president, 1825–1829

What is the business of **leadership**? It is a business of delegation and direction. It is a business of energizing and compelling. It is a business of encouragement and influence and collaboration. It is the art of leading followers. Leaders are found throughout the strata of the business organization, and they act in varying capacities. They base these actions on a long history of theories and behaviors. From the depths of the basement stockroom to the heights of the penthouse boardroom, the behaviors of leaders are exercised. They inform us and bind us together. They challenge and motivate us to be our best. They inspire and cause us to dream, and they assist in our endeavor to achieve the satisfactory results for which our organizations strive. This is the business of leadership.

The epigraph at the beginning of this chapter is attributed to John Quincy Adams, a leader on many fronts, including the international front as a diplomat and the domestic front as one who helped formulate the Monroe Doctrine. But one need not be a U.S. president in order to be a leader or to know what a leader is. In fact, after Adams lost his second bid for the presidency, he served seventeen years in the House of Representatives where he led strategic initiatives to abolish slavery—many years before adoption of the Thirteenth Amendment. His quotation above, markedly similar to our twenty-first-century views of business leadership, frames a definition that will be used throughout this book.

As stated above, being a president or a CEO is not a prerequisite for being a leader. Leadership and the formal roles or titles one holds are different. We sincerely hope that CEOs and others in executive positions are indeed leaders, but leadership unfortunately is not always bestowed upon those who happen to end up in important or high-ranking positions. Just because corporate executives carry a title does not mean that they are able to inspire others to dream or do or become anything more than they currently are. Similarly, high formal positions are not always bestowed upon those who do inspire others or even those who may possess the qualities desired in leaders.

DESCRIPTION AND OPERATIONAL DEFINITION OF "LEADERSHIP"

One definition of "leadership" for the business arena is the art of motivating people to achieve a common goal. A related definition is that "leadership" is the process of social influence to enlist the support of others to achieve a desired goal. How does that common or desired goal come about? Is it necessarily the leader's vision? Is it the leader's vision that has been imposed on followers? Rarely in today's complex business environment does a business leader have such unilateral power! More commonly, the goal is formed by the leader's multifaceted influence on the organization to face its challenges and identify its opportunities. Note that the components in these descriptions involve clearly articulated motivation and inspiration for the purpose of achieving results. To paraphrase President Dwight Eisenhower, leadership is the art of getting troops to do what you want done because they want to do it. It is not a process of pushing people, but rather of pulling them along to a desired goal.

Sam Walton, founder of Wal-Mart, the largest retailer in America, always said that good leaders do whatever they can to boost the self-esteem of the people with whom they work because if people believe in themselves, it is amazing how high expectations and accomplishments can soar. In setting high expectations, leaders may have to swim upstream—one of Walton's ten rules for success in business—while clearly communicating their vision, even if it ignores conventional wisdom. When he began, well-meaning individuals constantly told Walton that his fledgling business was headed in the wrong direction because a town with a population of less than 50,000 could not sustain a discount store. But Sam Walton's operational description of leadership remained consistent with the more formal definition of motivating people to achieve common goals.

There is a conclusive link between *efficiency and effectiveness* and *management and leadership*. There is a pithy saying in the leadership literature that goes "management is doing things right; leadership is doing the right things." When you relate efficiency (using resources well) to management, and effectiveness (achieving goals) to leadership, it would imply that a parallel adage would be *efficiency is doing things right; effectiveness is doing the right things*. In other words, a leader must take the correct and appropriate course of action in order to be effective at achieving the desired results. Achieving results is the special focus of Part III of this text. It examines leadership, especially at the **executive** level, which is most responsible for developing vision and bringing to clarity an understanding of "the big picture." It also discusses motivating the organization in order to achieve its common or desired goals. A simple, imagined vision is not good enough; the successful execution of that vision depends, in part, on both its quality and accuracy. The example of Sam Walton demonstrates how a qualitative vision can lure followers even though people may initially regard the vision as ill-fated.

From an operational perspective, business leaders tend to maximize human capital as they inspire others with a clear purpose and a vision that undergirds the tasks at hand. Leaders seek innovative, creative approaches in order to get the business of leadership, as well as the job itself, done. Leaders are willing to take calculated risks rather than become immobilized by challenge. Inspiring and innovating and taking risks may sound straightforward and undemanding, but are not necessarily either fun or idealistic. Ronald Heifetz, a psychiatrist and co-founder of the Center for Public Leadership at the Kennedy School of Government, Harvard University is clear that real leadership requires individuals to understand that leading change may take them out of their comfort zone because of resistance generated when change is mobilized. He noted that we must think of leadership as independent of authority, and that even leaders such as Marie Foster or Margaret Sanger, who did not have formal authority commensurate to the change they led, experienced calculated risks. "People such as these push us to clarify our values, face hard realities, and seize new possibilities, however frightening change may be" (1994, 183–184).

When a person is challenged with the difficult decision of whether to bother to lead when the process can be painful, Heifetz establishes parameters that "Shouldering the pains and uncertainties of an institution particularly in times of distress comes with the job of authority" (251). A leader must believe that motivating others for vital change is worth shouldering the burden of the organization's problems for a time.

There is not one distinct leadership profile. Rather, leadership profiles are quite often found to possess a conglomeration of characteristics. Business leaders can be charismatic or they can be boring. They can be predominantly results-oriented or predominantly people-oriented. They can be male or female. Business leaders can bring change incrementally or they can effect change transformationally. They can live with simplicity or in luxury. They can be from any academic major or they may not be a college graduate at all. They can rise up through the ranks of the organization, or they can be hired from outside the organization. They can be old or young. They can be unquestioned or, more commonly, controversial. But to be successful business leaders, they need to motivate followers, achieve results, and inspire change.

Mark Zuckerberg, born in 1984 and founder and CEO of Facebook, is an example of a young, controversial business leader who has changed people's everyday habits with his vision for social networking. He was named by *Time* magazine as one of the world's most influential people of 2008 and by *Forbes* as one of the 500 richest people in the United States. Not only did Zuckerberg inspire those at Facebook with his vision, but also his company inspired people around the world to participate in social networking. According to Nielsen ratings the average Facebook user spent more than four hours, thirty-nine minutes on Facebook for the month of June 2009, just five years after the company was founded. Zuckerberg's forward-looking vision of social networking cannot be diminished, but despite the founder's obvious success in implementing an Internet vision, the origin of Facebook was subject to controversy following complaints filed by former classmates suggesting that he stole their idea. The purpose of citing this dispute here is not to render an opinion, but rather to affirm that business leaders who are profoundly successful are frequently controversial, often merely by virtue of their success.

Again, there is not just one leadership profile. In fact, leadership profiles are complex, varying greatly from one situation to another. Nevertheless, given the definition of leadership that opens this section, there are integral qualities of leadership upon which most researchers agree: "vision and integrity, perseverance and courage, a hunger for innovation, a willingness to take risks . . . an ability to read the forces that shaped the times in which they lived—and to seize on the resulting opportunities" (Breen 2005).

Examples of the types of behavior that demonstrate the attributes of integrity and perseverance can, at times, be difficult to pinpoint. But Ford Motor Company's president and CEO Alan Mulally clearly exhibits those qualities. When the U.S. automobile industry plummeted in 2008, GM and Chrysler positioned themselves to receive federal bailout funds in order to sustain losses and remain in business. Ford Motors, however, took the risk of bypassing federal funds. Mulally would have found an easier road through a changing automobile industry had Ford accepted bailout funds, but the market, at least in the short term, rewarded his firm stance; Rasmussen Reports (2009) found that 46 percent of Americans said they were more likely to buy from Ford because it did not take bailout money. Likewise, prior to the federal bailout, 41 percent of consumers had a positive perception of Ford, but after Ford declined bailout money, the positive perception increased to 63 percent (Aloft Group 2009). Ford Motors turned an immediate third-quarter profit, gained market share, and saw sales jump 33 percent in December 2009 (Durbin and Krishner 2010). The company has now found itself on a road lined with unique opportunity in a changing and competitive market and some have alleged that CEO Mulally is in auto overdrive because Ford's quarterly profits continued through the midst of the 2010 recession.

While the main focus of this book is on business leaders who are also managers, some of these leaders have neither much formal power stemming from a formal position, nor do they have the ability to reward or punish; nonetheless, they do have a strong influence over others. There are many such examples. A small group of people who are thrown together for the first time in order to get a project done quickly will find that one or two people emerge as leaders. Such leaders rely primarily on their expertise or force of personality alone. On a broader scale, some leaders without organizations actively encourage specific social change by some combination of reason, passion, and personality. Think of the influence of Mahatma Gandhi, Ralph Nader, or Rachel Carson (author of *Silent Spring* [1962] and a philosophical founder of the environmental movement). Finally, some leaders focus on the newness of ideas rather than on the specific policies that might need to be changed; examples in this category include philosophical zealots (e.g., historical figures such as St. Francis of Assisi, Adam Smith, and Karl Marx) and social trendsetters (e.g., Michelle Obama in fashion or the Beatles in musical tastes in the 1960s). Exhibit 1.1 identifies these different types of leaders.

Of course, leaders often cross the conceptual boundaries suggested in Exhibit 1.1 because they carry out several types of leadership simultaneously or change their leadership roles over time. Political executives who may emphasize both employees and constituents are an excellent example of dual leadership types. A corporate leader may have moved into the role over time by first exercising leadership with adherents in small groups and later in development of policy for social responsibility. Presidents and governors are the putative heads of enormous organizations who at the same time recommend legislative initiatives and enact laws by signing them.

Exhibit 1.1   **Examples of Different Types of Leaders**

		Types of work		
		Execution	Policy	New ideas
Types of followers	Employees	Managers	Executives with policy responsibilities	Transformational leaders
	Constituents	Community leaders of volunteer groups	Legislators and advisory board members	Policy entrepreneurs
	Adherents	Small group leaders	Organizational leaders who value social responsibility	Leaders of social movements

President George H.W. Bush was himself a bureaucrat by training, kept a close eye on the morale of the federal bureaucracy, and was personally responsible for several personnel initiatives. Ten years later, President George W. Bush relied more heavily on his legislative background and focused almost solely on his constituents and policy. In terms of changing their type of leadership over time, leaders of social movements often acquire formal status. Famous examples in the twentieth century include Nelson Mandela (known initially as anti-apartheid activist from South Africa), Lech Walesa (trade-union organizer in Poland), and Kim Dae-jung (owner of a shipping company formerly Japanese-owned during the Japanese occupation of Korea from South Korea), who ended up being the leaders of their respective nations. Cindy Lightner (Mothers Against Drunk Driving) started out as an outraged parent and ended up heading an organization that influenced legislative agendas across the country. Jimmy Carter left the presidency and became a moral and civic leader in the fight for affordable housing in this country and fair elections around the globe.

The reason for making these distinctions, despite the fact that the lines can get blurred and that some leaders practice multiple types, is that different competencies are involved. Good leaders for social change do not necessarily make good managers, and good managers frequently do not have the skills necessary to influence social or legislative agendas. Managerial executives may have little taste or ability to stimulate social action, and leaders of social movements may find themselves much criticized for their awkward management style when they do successfully create formal organizations. In this book, our focus on organizational business leaders allows us to be more specific in our analysis and leadership guidelines than if the text were focused on all types of leaders.

The recipe for good leadership cannot be learned from a simple "cookbook" because leadership is not a programmed activity that people can learn by rote. Although we talk about techniques and methods, they are not the heart of leadership. The business of leadership is about inspiring others to a shared vision and effectively bringing about organizational change. And so is this text.

There is a distinction between leadership and management, although the two can overlap, as shown in Exhibit 1.2. In fact, the more overlap of the two concepts, the better.

Exhibit 1.2   **Relative Importance of Task, People, and Organizational Competencies at Different Career Levels**

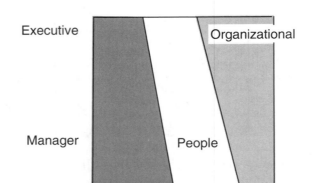

WHAT IS "MANAGEMENT"?

A manager is a person who holds a separate and distinct title with inherent authority for carrying out particular assigned responsibilities. Accordingly, we think of **management** as the functions of planning and organizing in order to achieve given results through the deployment of resources, including human resources. Management is a process of achieving results both efficiently and effectively. **Efficiency** is a measure of the process of achieving results, referring to resource utilization in terms of the ratio of outputs to inputs, or the cost of inputs for each unit of output produced. In contrast, **effectiveness** refers to the extent to which actual results mirror targeted results. Efficiency is a measurement of productivity, while effectiveness is a measurement of quality. Doing the wrong things (i.e., being ineffective) is a waste of time, and doing the right thing poorly is not really doing the right thing at all. Doing something efficiently that should not be done at all is futile, and similarly, tackling that which should be done with methods that waste resources or take one in circles is ineffectual.

A good business manager should be both effective and efficient. But that ideal is not always the case. A manager can be efficient but not effective. However, a manager must be efficient *in order* to be effective. For example, if the sales manager of a service organization had a goal of $400,000 per month in sales with a budgeted staff of four salespersons, but achieved $405,000 per month with an increased and overbudget staff of five full-time salespersons, we would say that the manager was inefficient. Because efficiency is a requirement for effectiveness, we cannot conclude that the manager was effective just because the staff had sales greater than the goal. Was the sales manager a good or successful business leader? Probably not, but all we know for sure is that he or she was a *manager*, by virtue of the title, the inherent authority over sales staff, and the responsibility for achieving a particular result.

Workers must understand the different responsibilities and levels of authority for different positions. Management is fundamentally different from hourly work, and some people are happier with hourly work or skilled blue-collar work rather than with the responsibilities and accountabilities of management. People who have developed the competencies to move into management may have to consider critically if "moving up" is what they personally want to do. If someone in a relatively low-paying job is offered a significant salary increase along with assumption of managerial responsibility, the decision may be easier for that individual to make than for a highly-paid physician or attorney or academic who is offered almost no salary increase for assumption of managerial responsibility and accountability. Many physicians, for example, seek "lower-paying" positions in an HMO because of benefits such as predictable work hours and having an employer who provides expensive insurance coverage and a facility in which to work, rather than becoming the entrepreneur, executive, and manager of their own business practice. Similarly, many professors prefer to remain in teaching roles rather than move into administration because of the benefits of flexibility in faculty work hours and the joy that comes from a direct influence on student learning. (In both cases, the "lower-paying" position may actually pay more on a per hour basis because the exempt physician or administrator, who receives an annual salary and no overtime, may invest many extra hours for the success of the unit.) However, other professions may implicitly push employees toward greater authority because it is the only way for them to get additional income and status over time. Such industries may set up a parallel track for nonmanagerial advancement, as does a university or the military, to divert those who seek advancement solely to attain lifestyle improvements. In this manner, nonmanagerial advancement can entail a greater assumption of responsibility without movement into management per se, similar to the system available for noncommissioned military officers.

Management requires continuous skill development, hard work, and self-discipline to be effective. Managers must be willing to understand the needs of the job and to undertake the requisite accountability, time, and other personal sacrifices in order to merit the level of authority given to them by virtue of the role they play in the business.

The main focus of this book is organizational (business) leaders who have a primary or sole concentration on motivating and inspiring others in order to achieve results. The best examples of leaders who focus on execution and implementation are managers. Managers have programs to run, projects to complete, and deadlines to meet. The organizational leader focused on new ideas is a transformational leader who could be found at any level in the organization where the planned change efforts are being attempted.

This book focuses on formal or appointed leadership, although much of the discussion applies equally to informal or emergent leadership, too. For the purpose of this book, all those who lead others, no matter whether they are frontline supervisors or the heads of organizations, are considered leaders. Indeed, even lead workers can assume important leadership roles. However, the type of leadership practiced will normally vary. The frontline supervisor will tend to focus on task completion while, at the other extreme, the executive will focus on intellectual tasks such as policy planning and systems design. The frontline supervisor will need good one-on-one interpersonal skills while the chief executive may need good communication or public speaking skills for explaining vision and goals (Katz 1955).

OVERVIEW OF THE LITERATURE ON ORGANIZATIONAL LEADERSHIP

Although the modern scientific study of leadership dates only from the turn of the twentieth century, interest in leadership defines history from its earliest writings. Indeed, one can even go back further by examining the biological antecedents of leadership.

Most higher-level animals exhibit patterns that can be recognized as rudimentary to advanced behaviors related to leadership. The popular reference to the "pecking order" comes from Murchison (1935), who investigated social status in *Gallus domesticus* (roosters). By placing roosters in successive pairings and establishing their relationships, he identified a clear and consistent pattern of dominance—a primitive form of leadership. Douglis (1948) found that hens follow suit and that they can recognize exact status differentials among a group of up to twenty-seven individuals. With primates, the similarities of human conceptions of leadership become more pronounced. Early studies of primates established strict pecking orders or dominance hierarchies. Dominant males eat sooner and better, thus maintaining their strength and status. They also have preference in mating, thus ensuring a Darwinian selection bias. The presence of dominant males reduces intragroup fighting while leadership succession temporarily increases it. Significantly, a strong dominant male substantially increases the group's territory, establishes the direction that the group takes in its meandering, and regulates the group's interactions with outside groups.

Although the scientific approach to leadership study is only about 100 years old, interest in leaders and leadership dates back thousands of years. Leadership is referred to many times in the Bible, for example. The father-in-law of Moses tells him to

> teach them the statutes and the laws and make known to them the way in which they are to walk, and the work they are to do. Furthermore, you shall select out of all the people able men who fear God, men of truth, those who hate dishonest gain; and you shall place these over them as leaders of thousands, of hundreds, of fifties, and of tens. And let them judge the people at all times; and let it be that every major dispute they will bring to you, but every minor dispute they themselves will judge. So it will be easier for you, and they will bear the burden with you. (Exodus 18:20–23)

In this excerpt from Exodus, leadership is described through specific principles, qualities, training, and the managerial notion of delegation through a hierarchy so that leaders would develop at various levels.

Most of the great early stories of the world—the Babylonian *Gilgamesh*, the Homeric *Iliad*, the Norse *Beowulf*, the French *Chanson de Roland*, and the more recent Spanish classic, *Don Quixote*—are about the virtues and weaknesses of leaders. Greek and Roman philosophers focused a great deal of attention on leadership. Plato, in *The*

Republic, examines the traits of the ideal philosopher king, Aristotle examines the need to cultivate virtue and encourage education for good leadership, and Plutarch takes pains to show the similarities of great Greek and Roman leaders in *The Parallel Lives*. Writing about leadership in his military campaigns in Gaul, Julius Caesar explains that it is important *both* to be highly task-oriented and simultaneously to be concerned for the well-being of the troops, a finding that was empirically reestablished in the human relations leadership theories of the 1960s. *The Prince* (1513), Machiavelli's fascinating study of leadership, is still a must-read in leadership studies because of its complex blend of idealism and practicality. According to the medieval commentator, leaders need to maintain order, continuity, and political independence, preferably through fairness and the esteem of the people, but they should also be willing and able to use guile, threats, and violence as necessary.

For centuries, discussions of leadership followed the great military, religious, and political leaders. Leadership was regarded as an innate art—not an approach to organizational life that could be developed nor a competence beyond a personal gift. Even into the twenty-first century, some say that leadership and artistry are more closely linked than leadership and management. The "science of leadership" really did not emerge until the twentieth century. It moved from the "Great Man" perspective in the late 1800s to trait theories in the first half of the twentieth century. Leaders were supposedly born with certain traits such as decisiveness, and then later it was thought that leaders had magnetism over followers. This tactic of listing traits to prescribe leadership had two problems. First, the lists became longer and longer as research continued. Second, and more important, the traits and characteristics identified were not powerful predictors across situations. For example, leaders have to be decisive but they must also be flexible and inclusive. On the surface, these traits are contradictory. Without situational specificity, the endless list of traits offers little prescriptive assistance and descriptively becomes nothing more than a long laundry list of "attributes that are nice to have." In 1948, Ralph Stogdill published a devastating critique of pure trait theory, which subsequently fell into disfavor as being too one-dimensional to account for the complexity of leadership.

The study of leadership moved to behavior theory in the 1950s, evaluating the behavior of people thought to be successful leaders, and then to situational and contingency theory in the 1970s, focusing in part on different styles that achieve good results in different situations. This major thrust looked at the situational contexts that affect leaders and attempted to find meaningful patterns for both theory building and useful advice. One early example was the work that came out of the Ohio State Leadership Studies (Hempill 1950; Hempill and Coons 1957; Shartle 1950). These studies began by testing 1,800 statements related to leadership behavior. By continually distilling the behaviors, researchers arrived at two underlying factors: consideration and initiation of structure. **Consideration** describes a variety of behaviors related to the development, inclusion, and good feelings of subordinates. The **initiation of structure** describes a variety of behaviors related to defining roles, control mechanisms, task focus, and work coordination both inside and outside the unit. Coupled with the humanist and human relations revolution that was occurring in the 1950s and 1960s, these (and similar studies) spawned a series of useful, if often simplistic and largely bimodal, theories. Argyris's maturity theory (1957), Likert's motivational approach (1959), and McGregor's Theory X and Theory Y (1960) implicitly encourage more consideration in all leadership behavior. Maslow's eupsychian management recommends that leadership be assigned based on the needs of the situation so that authoritarian tendencies (excessive structure) can be curbed (1967). This line of thinking was further advanced and empirically tested by Fiedler, who developed a contingency theory and related leader-match theory (1967; Fiedler, Chemers, and Mahar 1976). Blake and Mouton's (1964, 1965) managerial grid recommends leaders be highly skilled in both task behaviors (initiating structure) and people-oriented behaviors (consideration). Hersey and Blanchard's life-cycle theory (1969, 1972) relates the maturity of the followers (both in terms of willingness to do the job and ability to do the job) to ideal leader behavior—whether telling, selling, participating, or delegating, depending on the situation.

These early situational theories were certainly useful as an antidote to the excessively hierarchical, authoritarian styles that developed in the first half of the twentieth century with the rise and dominance of large organizations in both the private and public sectors and with the importance of scientific management that sought "the one best way" to get a job done. The situational theories were also useful as teaching tools for beginning and practicing managers who appreciated the uncomplicated, simplistic models as development tools. As a class, however, these theories failed to meet scientific standards because they tried to explain too much with too few variables. Of the major theories, only a decision-making model by Vroom broke out of this pattern somewhat because it self-consciously focused on a single dimension of leadership style—the role of participation—and identified seven problem attributes and two classes of cases (group and individual) (Vroom and Jago 1988; Vroom and Yetton 1973). Although the **situational perspective** still forms the basis of most leadership theories today, it has largely done so either in a strictly managerial context (i.e., a narrow level of analysis) on a factor-by-factor basis or it has been subsumed in more comprehensive approaches to leadership at the macrolevel.

Despite modern efforts to curb excessive powers of leaders, whether political, financial, or religious, many leaders around the world continue to wield incredible amounts of power. In countries where democratic institutions are weak, political leaders may be as powerful as in ancient times. Ayatollah Ali Khamenei, known as the Supreme Leader of Iran, shaped both religious and political forces. Nor have leaders in wealthy democratic states been deprived of their power; they simply must use it more deftly. Billionaire Sam Walton changed the face of rural commerce, while Bill Gates dominates the world of computers as powerfully as Charlemagne ruled Europe.

The conventional wisdom was that employees with high technical skills were promoted to supervisory roles. Supervisors with good interpersonal skills were promoted to management. Managers with good conceptual skills were promoted to executive roles to "lead" the organization. In reality, this pattern is oversimplified. The idea was that an outstanding employee at one level of the organization would be outstanding at the next level. Leadership ability varies at different levels of the organization, however, and an individual who leads on the front line does not necessarily provide the vision for guiding the organization's future.

Exhibit 1.3　**Overall Priority Given to Task, People, or Organization Behavioral Competencies by Federal Supervisors and Executives Based on Ranking of 150 Discrete Competencies** (in percent)

	Top 20 competencies		Top 100 competencies	
	Supervisors	Executives	Supervisors	Executives
Task-oriented competencies	43	35	34	31
People-oriented competencies	39	26	26	22
Organization-oriented competencies	17	39	40	47
	99	100	100	100

Note: Based on an analysis of OPM data of 1,763 executives and 3,516 supervisors. Behaviors (i.e., task, people, or organization) were based on percentage of those rating specific competencies related to that behavior as very important or crucial and whose position involved that competency.

How do managers at various levels actually spend their time and to which responsibilities do they assign importance? In a U.S. Office of Personnel Management (OPM 1992b) content analysis of 150 narrowly defined competencies that supervisors, managers, and executives identified as crucial or important, we obtain a concrete sense of priorities of managers in the public sector that parallels most business organizations. High priorities are captured by looking at the top 20 discrete competency preferences, medium priorities by looking at the top 100, and low priorities are ranked 101 and below. Supervisors divide their attention quite equally between people (39 percent) and tasks (44 percent), while organization-oriented activities get a scant 17 percent. This focus shifts significantly when the top 100 competencies are analyzed to capture medium-range priorities. It is observed here that supervisors' attention becomes quite balanced, with task-oriented behaviors (34 percent) now slightly behind organization-oriented behaviors (40 percent) and slightly ahead of people-oriented ones (26 percent).

As expected, the profile is different for executives. Their top priority attention goes to organization-oriented behaviors (39 percent), followed closely by task-oriented behaviors (35 percent). Exhibit 1.3 illustrates the results of the task competency study comparing supervisory to executive priorities.

Exhibit 1.2 takes a look at similar information, showing relative importance of task, people, and organizational leadership competencies at the supervisory, managerial, and executive levels. Assume for a moment that you will move up a career ladder from supervisor to manager to executive; Exhibit 1.2 shows that organizational leadership competencies become proportionately more important while task- and people-oriented leadership competencies remain critical. In fact, the three leadership competencies become relatively balanced in their importance as your career moves into the executive level. In the course you are currently taking, the belief is that you will be a better employee or supervisor if you understand all levels of organizational activity.

The organization of this text mimics the development of leadership competencies needed as a person's career advances—from task- and people-oriented to **organization-level competency**. Exhibit 1.4 analyzes the types of actions that a leader engages

Exhibit 1.4   **Summary of the Three Behavior Domains**

	Leader actions: Behavior domains		
	Task	People	Organizational
Assessment and evaluation	1. Monitor and assess work	1. Consult	1. Scan the environment
Formulation and planning functions	2. Operations planning	2. Plan and organize personnel	2. Strategic planning
Implementation functions	3. Clarify roles and objectives	3. Develop staff	3. Articulate the mission and vision
	4. Inform	4. Motivate	4. Network and partner
	5. Delegate	5. Build and manage teams	5. Perform general management functions
"Change" functions	6. Problem-solving	6. Manage conflict	6. Decision-making
	7. Manage innovation and creativity	7. Manage personnel change	7. Manage organizational change

in at each behavioral domain in order to be well-rounded. Organization-level behavior domains (right column) are covered in Part III.

There are two major explanations for enduring interest in the topic of leadership. First, the effect of leaders is omnipresent. Second, society is enthralled with leaders and their successes and failures.

Leaders affect the nation on a grand scale in that they determine the success or failure of our societies, countries, and localities. Hitler destroyed Germany. Churchill saved Great Britain. The leaders of Arthur Anderson destroyed a highly successful company with their unwise profiteering. CEO Lee Iacocca saved Chrysler from economic implosion in the 1980s. Social leaders as disparate as Jerry Falwell, Ralph Nader, Gloria Steinem, and Jesse Jackson fight for, or against, deeply held convictions. Leaders affect a business just as much in the firm's daily settings. A bad supervisor sends us scurrying for a new job. A good team leader makes a difficult assignment seem easy because of strong organization and encouragement. Personal problems or lack of parental discipline cause a father to be a poor role model for his children.

Second, our society is one of many that are compulsively fascinated by people in leadership positions or those who assume the roles of leaders. Whether the leader is a spiritual saint like Joan of Arc or a despot like Stalin, a great success like the Duke of Wellington, who defeated Napoleon at Waterloo, or a flawed ruler like the mythical Oedipus, people are equally mesmerized.

There are a number of reasons why it is critical to study leadership. Since leaders affect us so profoundly on both a grand as well as a personal scale, it is important to understand how leadership functions. We should be able to recognize the different types of leaders we have in terms of their strengths and deficiencies. We must assess the various types of leaders we need for different and changing situations and the particular competencies they should possess. Another important reason for studying leadership is that all of us function as leaders from time to time. For their professional success, managers need to be good leaders, and the study of leadership can help all of us be at least marginally better—and in some cases can have a dramatic impact. Indeed, because of the complexity of leadership and the myriad situations in which leaders are found, the study of leadership cannot help but improve the rate and degree of success. Great leaders often start with great talent, but these abilities rarely find expression without study, mentoring, and practice. It is an explicit purpose of this book to help readers become both better analysts of leadership as well as better practitioners in organizational settings.

CONSTRAINTS ON LEADERSHIP

It is true that all behavior is constrained in some way by practical factors such as information capacity, physical reality, or even by personal preference. Take, for instance, the behavioral constraint felt by a leader, determined to act by her own ethical credo of truthfulness and honesty, when faced with temptation. Suppose that the leader is asked by an employee why he was not given a salary increase. If the reason was the worker's poor performance, the temptation to say "there wasn't enough money" is prohibited by the leader's ethic, so her behavior is constrained. Some constraint, including that imposed on leaders, is natural and normal.

There are times and situations, when constraints prohibit the expression of real leadership. Just because an individual seems to have every potential to become a leader does not mean that the situation encountered will foster his emergence as a leader on the job. Sometimes the high school student voted "most likely to succeed" assumes an early managerial role in business, yet does not end up leading corporate activity. Perhaps the current supervisor is not impressed by his work, or unfortunate political alliances in the organization try to build themselves up by putting him down. Perhaps he is the subject of litigation that forces him to defend his past actions rather than allow him to look ahead with vigor. Perhaps he was not educated in business or lacks the confidence or energy needed for dealing with the reality of an economic downturn, or perhaps poor health limits that energy. There can be an endless number of constraints that interfere with the emergence of leadership in a person's career.

Constraints are relatively structural or long-term environmental elements that set parameters or limitations on the leader's range of choices or results. While almost never immutable, they are generally substantial and need considerable time, energy, or luck to change.

LEGAL OR CONTRACTUAL CONSTRAINTS

Legal or contractual constraints affect organizations because of myriad requirements concerning corporate governance, discrimination, the environment, safety, pricing, contracts, taxation, labor relations, financing, workers' compensation, dispute resolution, regulations, family and medical leave, interest rates, public heath, transportation infrastructure, and so on. "Managerial values of efficiency, economy, and internal organizational effectiveness retain importance, but they are augmented by and sometimes subordinate to representativeness, participation, openness, responsiveness, procedural safeguards, and public accountability" (Rosenbloom 2000, xi).

How can leaders deal with these constraints to minimize their negative effects? First, an understanding of the law and regulations applicable to an individual's industry is fundamental. In a study of innovative managers who had been successful at implementing substantial change, legal constraints were cited less than 10 percent of the time (Borins 2000, 504). Second, managers can be more optimistic and steadfast at changing rules and laws that are outdated, contradictory, vague, or ineffective. Managers must proceed cautiously and patiently when recommending policy changes at any level, but it is their professional duty to do so. For example, the American Institute of CPAs (2010) begins its code of professional conduct by stating that a

> distinguishing mark of a profession is acceptance of its responsibility to the public. The accounting profession's public consists of clients, credit grantors, governments, employers, investors, the business and financial community, and others who rely on the objectivity and integrity of certified public accountants to maintain the orderly functioning of commerce. This reliance imposes a public interest responsibility on certified public accountants. The public interest is defined as the collective well-being of the community of people and institutions the profession serves.

LIMITATIONS OF POSITION POWER

Limitations of position power can place substantial constraints on the emergence of leadership. **Position power** refers to the authority inherent within a position, regardless of who happens to be holding the position. Thus, the authority or limitation on authority stems from the position itself rather than from the unique leadership qualities of an individual in the role. As established above, a leader need not be on the executive team, in management, or in any other high-authority role. However, forces of authority, or position power, can be used to hold back the expression of leadership by lower-ranking employees. Similarly, leaders' abilities to act may be constrained by organizational structures, job descriptions, and various types of organizational policies having to do with specific business functions such as purchasing, human resources, and budgeting. Exhibit 1.5, for instance, describes a case in which limitations of position power are imposed and consequently an employee's visionary thinking is not allowed to emerge. Constraints from organizational policies overlap with legal and rule-based constraints, but also extend to organizational practices not necessarily rooted in law. For example, organizational leaders may be given an additional unit to manage, or a job description may be changed due to new needs. Formal means to resist leader actions are often used by employees or their representatives. For informal constraints, culture figures prominently along with the informal organization.

Responses to these internal constraints are similar to those imposed by external factors. It is imperative for leaders to know their position power, both formally and informally, and to act confidently. Leaders can affect changes in position power over time. Leaders can also request temporary adjustments or waivers for specific situations. The greatest informal constraint will generally be both the lack of trust and the lack of a sense of shared interests.

Exhibit 1.5

Limitations of Position Power

Katie holds the position of marketing analyst in the marketing department of a medium-sized firm, Af-Mark, which deals with imports from Africa. Her job description calls for her to design and implement marketing campaigns and to recommend actions stemming from marketing impact by customer segment and client research. Her dreams are big—to position Af-Mark with programs for social responsibility to bring economic improvement to the villages where the imported products are made. Trilingual, with five years' experience in retail and a BA in marketing from Tri-State University, Katie is new at Af-Mark and is confident that she meets all qualifications for her job.

Katie is eager to help lead the organization to new growth from her position in marketing. Having completed an assessment of the strengths and weaknesses of Af-Mark's number one competitor, she clearly sees the opportunity for offensive strategic pricing relative to a particular import. She gives her supervisor, Chakide, a position paper on the opportunity, saying, "I'd like to give a presentation to our company's strategy group, and of course, if you want to be there with me, I'd like that." After not hearing from him for a week, she asks to meet with him for follow-up. He replies only by email, saying they can meet, but that he will not entertain further schemes from her on changing the corporation's strategic pricing because, after all, this is not in her job duties.

Katie thinks about his reply all night. Is Chakide intimidated by her forwardness in stepping outside of what a marketing analyst is responsible for? Does he simply disagree with her position? Are there cultural or gender issues that explain why he does not want her to receive credit for her idea? Does she need to squelch ideas for company improvement that are not within the authority level of her position? Should she just turn over her ideas to Chakide so that he can fly solo with them? The bottom line for Katie is that she does not want to overstep her position with Chakide or jeopardize her future in Af-Mark just because she feels there would be a missed strategic opportunity at this moment. After all, he "knows Africa" better than she, and she knows that she has a long career ahead of her.

LACK OF SUFFICIENT RESOURCES

Lack of sufficient resources is a chronic concern at some level for many managers and an acute concern when faced with a decline in the business environment, such as that discussed in Chapter 11. While start-up enterprises often find resources highly constrained, they may not be better or worse off than older bureaucratic enterprises.

Because of the demands of operations management, employee development, and strategic planning, few leaders have the luxury of spending an adequate amount of time in all areas. Another resource scarcity is the number or quality of subordinates; rarely are there ideal numbers of employees in the right positions. In addition to human resource limitations, these resource scarcities might include budget, equipment, and facilities shortages. Even in the face of scarce budgetary resources, which would make hiring a possible solution, the problem of scarce human resources may be mitigated by improving delegation, training, and mentoring employees or by prioritizing the work. In terms of financial and physical resources, the leader may need to make compelling requests, borrow resources that are needed only for peak demand or for a crisis, creatively find new resources, or reengineer processes or needs so that resource demands are lessened. Leaders who are unable to address these demands will generally find that they have significantly less leverage.

One key resource for the leader is time. Though the problem of insufficient time for the leader can never be solved, it can be managed. Leaders must be astute in their planning at various levels and monitor their progress in each through goals, objectives, and timelines. Short-term, close-at-hand issues can easily dominate a leader's schedule. Therefore, time management becomes a critical tool with which to carve out needed attention in advance of the flurry of interruptions, activity, and daily crises in order to ensure long-term goal achievement. As important is the conservation of energy, which can be enhanced by bundling certain activities and setting aside adequate time for large operational, personnel, or strategic projects, as well as for the consideration of any problems.

LEADERSHIP ABILITY

Leadership constraints and limitations on ability are inevitable because of the chaotic environment in which we conduct organizational life, even with leaders who are, overall, successful and effective. Mitigating this constraint is a particular theme of this book.

One aspect of the leadership ability constraint is having the right traits, skills, and behavioral competencies for the job. Some jobs may require a great deal of flexibility, decisiveness, operational creativity, delegation, problem-solving, and long-term planning. Others may emphasize operations excellence and strong monitoring competency, or an ability to clarify roles and objectives and manage conflict. Because leaders may not possess the necessary strengths, successful leaders frequently fail when given entirely new assignments. A second, related aspect of leadership capacity involves having *enough* skill or ability. A leader may, for example, have rather good interpersonal skills for one-on-one situations, but lack sufficient skills to handle intractable, long-term feuding within a department.

Knowing the leadership demands of a job is the preliminary means of dealing with the capacity issue. Leaders' detailed assessments of the organization, business environment, and constraints, as well as an appraisal of how their own personal skills and abilities do or do not match the situation, is critical. This knowledge can be obtained through introspection, self-observation, and feedback. It can be accomplished through a formal assessment process or through less structured discussions. When leaders know how their skills and abilities match up to the job, they are better able to detect their own weaknesses.

A list of possible strategies to deal with leadership constraints can be found in Exhibit 1.6. Certain constraints may be brought to light by a leader's own abilities. However, there are also constraints caused by legal or contractual situations, the position itself, or a lack of resources. When leaders diagnose what is constraining their circumstances, appropriate strategies can be adopted in order to turn the situation around over time.

LEADERSHIP PASSAGES: DEVELOPING LEADERSHIP SKILLS OVER TIME

Just as an infant gradually progresses though an expected course of physical, social, behavioral, and intellectual development, a young leader matures in stages. Celebrated

Exhibit 1.6

Possible Strategies to Deal With Leadership Constraints

By definition, leadership constraints tend to be structural and long-term. However, effective leaders can mitigate, improve, or even turn around some leadership constraints over time.

When leaders are constrained by substantial or excessive legal or contractual limits, consider:

- Learning about the nature of those legal or contractual matters in detail so that it is possible to work within them confidently and fully, and perhaps more freely
- Gaining the confidence of those who set policy in order to gain the full latitude of legal discretion
- Requesting policy changes through appropriate channels as a long-term project

When leaders are constrained by substantial or excessive position constraints, consider:

- Learning about the details of the position and its power so that it is possible to work within them confidently and fully
- Gaining the confidence of those who set policy in order to gain the full latitude of management discretion
- Requesting (or making) rule changes and seeking appropriate waivers of policy

When leaders are constrained by a lack of resources, consider:

- Using more delegation, training, mentoring, and planning, depending on the type of resource constraint
- Reconfiguring the organization if resource constraints are chronic
- Enhancing the leaders' own time management and planning to conserve the leaders' valuable energy and focus

When leaders are constrained by a lack of certain leadership abilities, consider:

- Analyzing the leadership demands of the position to determine the critical leadership competencies required
- Analyzing strengths and weaknesses through a thorough assessment process
- Addressing some of the leadership gaps by additional training, structured experiences, or a team model of leadership

Saturday Evening Post cover illustrator Norman Rockwell's 1966 painting for *Boys' Life* titled *Growth of a Leader* well depicts this step-by-step transition through the profiles of four men in uniform, ranging from the young Cub Scout to the mature Scout Leader.

The advancement or maturation of a young leader is not unlike the coming of age. To examine these **leadership passages** brings to the foreground a self-awareness that allows for continuous growth. *Leadership Passages* (Dotlich, Noel, and Walker 2004) looks at the personal and professional transitions in a person's life. The authors identify thirteen passages that constitute choice points for the leader and offer an opportunity for growth by acknowledging the adversity or diversity of experiences. These points include both personal and professional exigencies that demand a response—from dealing with a first leadership assignment to dealing with the death of a loved one, and much in between.

Changes or growth in the ability to affect good leadership can also be observed as an individual's career typically evolves over time. That is the approach taken in this text. Leadership skills are developed over time as a worker moves from the position of employee to supervisor to manager. The venue for the development of leadership skills is usually conceived as the career setting, as reflected in the terminology used in this book, but the experience could just as easily occur in a different organizational setting where one volunteers, such as Boy Scouts or church. The evolution of leadership remains similar. Exhibit 1.7 provides an overview of the skills at each phase.

The need to nurture and develop young, new professionals over time is strong. Although the previous exhibit does not reflect the age of workforce participants during any particular stage of leadership, many industries realize that they will be faced with an ever-increasing majority of executives who plan to retire within a few years. The generation of young professionals between the ages of twenty-five and forty who are now in supervisory roles will then provide the pool from which new leaders in these businesses will emerge. With time and experience, these individuals will move into managerial or executive roles in their current organizations, transition into others, or even create their own.

Not everyone moves lockstep through these stages, as we know from the unusual example of Mark Zuckerberg, the twenty-year-old founder of Facebook, who served as its executive leader from the organization's beginning through its growth to 700 employees and $300 million in revenue by its fourth year. It is not unusual for a worker to use start-up funds to invest in a venture in which he can be his own boss; by default, he immediately assumes the visionary role and, subsequently, as he hires other employees, the supervisory role. This entrepreneur might therefore jump from employee to the executive role and back to supervisor (a difficult move for some entrepreneurs as different levels call for different leadership emphasis). Or, in some cases, the business owner may hire one or more managers to take care of the day-to-day supervision in order to free him for activities more akin to the executive role. When this occurs, the entrepreneur will have jumped from employee to executive while permanently skipping the supervisory stage.

There are other exceptions to the general evolution of leadership. For example, few military or noncommissioned officers move up the hierarchy to become general or sergeant major of their branch of service, and few licensed vocational nurses move up the hierarchy to become hospital directors. Not every employee has that meteoric rise as a goal, nor should they, so not every supervisor reaches the top of the hierarchy where visionary leadership is essential. Nevertheless, for the majority of employees who move into successively higher positions during their career, they will experience the progression of passages through leadership. Supervisors always have the need to understand and appreciate the complete spectrum of leadership phases at work in their organizations. Those who are now executives have a great responsibility to mentor employees or those in a supervisory capacity in order for them to be able to move with ease into higher-level leadership roles.

Despite exceptions in the passage through various levels of leadership, business graduates should clearly understand these stages of the organizational experience. This textbook is organized to reflect the natural evolution of leadership through maturing stages of organizational participation. In other words, the major sections of the book

Exhibit 1.7   **Leadership Passages**

	Employee	Supervisor	Executive
Purpose of leadership behavior	Gain experience through innovative performance	Motivate those who report to you for organizational results	Create vision to inspire change as needed with all stakeholders
Emphasis of leadership behavior	Appreciate effective leadership	Task- and people-oriented, with increasing range of experience	Continuous leadership development with increasing depth of experience
Role of management	Respond appropriately to management	Develop managerial skills in order to use authority well	Maintain managerial excellence including fiduciary responsibility

echo the phases of leadership. At each stage, readers are exposed to leadership that has wider and deeper impact throughout the organization and its environment. The text is organized into three primary sections—managerial behaviors that motivate followers, executive behaviors that help the organization achieve results, and the factors involved with human capital.

This textbook follows the general career pattern described in the previous paragraphs. In Part I, which encompasses Chapters 2 and 3, the overview of traditional theories of leadership provides a foundation on which we build.

In Chapter 2, the causal-chain model is introduced as a framework to analyze different approaches to different theories of leadership. Within the confines of this framework, we can better and more readily analyze an onslaught of otherwise confusing information and put it into perspective. Ten styles commonly used in leadership theories are presented and discussed in the overview. Contingency factors are also included in the chapter as intervening or moderating variables. Finally, performance results are discussed as outcomes that are desired in order to affect a greater degree of accomplishment or function over the long term.

In Chapter 3, we examine early leadership theories, starting with the three classical approaches to management: scientific management, administrative theory, and bureaucracy. We then move on to examine in greater detail more recent trait, behavioral, and contingency theories. We conclude this chapter by touching on the strengths and weaknesses of interaction and interactive process theory, which includes the path-goal method and leader-member exchange relationships.

Part II (Chapters 4 through 6) deals most directly with *managerial leadership behaviors* carried out by those in supervisory positions or those who are promoted to management positions. We focus specifically on those behaviors that contribute to leader effectiveness.

In Chapter 4, we present the traits and skills that contribute to leader effectiveness. Personality characteristics and the classic motivational drives are placed in this grouping. Also to be considered here are value orientations and more general leader proficiencies, including, among others, communication and social skills and the need for continual learning.

Chapter 5 presents the task-oriented behaviors of leaders. The discussion takes us through monitoring, assessing, and planning. We also discuss role clarification and the distinctions between informing, delegating, and problem-solving. The chapter ends with a focus on the management of technical innovation and creativity.

Chapter 6 brings the people-oriented behaviors of leaders to light for leaders at every organizational level. We explain why leadership behaviors like consulting and motivating must not suddenly stop when a leader is promoted to an executive level, even though they are primarily a focus of the supervisory and managerial levels. We discuss the art of motivating and how good leaders are adept at managing not only teams, but conflict and personnel changes as well.

In Part III, comprising Chapters 7, 8, and 9, we look at *executive leadership behaviors* that encompass a wider scope in terms of stakeholders affected. Effective executives and members of the top management team may not cast aside the task- and people-oriented competencies that were discussed in the prior parts of this text, but they will also develop new competencies. What is the importance of charisma in achieving organizational change? How is transformational change brought about? We examine the need for vision to guide organizational activity. The section ends with a discussion of the importance of goals and how to assess leadership in order to understand its effectiveness.

Chapter 7 discusses the charismatic behaviors of leaders, which can often help an organization achieve vast change. The unique leadership behaviors that can foster transformational change within an organization demonstrate both a deeply rooted motivation for change and an orientation toward the achievement of results.

Chapter 8 embodies the vision-oriented behaviors of leaders. From scanning the environment to planning, networking, and articulating, executive leadership involves opportunities for the implementation of vision because this level of decision-making brings strategic and overarching direction.

Chapter 9 involves assessments of effectiveness and the goal approach, or behavior, as one important method for determining effectiveness. We look at sources of information for goal-setting. Emphasizing the need for assessing the organization and environment, we discuss the science and art not only of setting goals, but also of selecting the goals themselves.

Although the chapters in Part III present competencies that are of extraordinary importance for effective executives, they are competencies that supervisors and managers should begin to build, as we saw in Exhibit 1.2. Young people who are just beginning their careers benefit from understanding the jobs of those at higher levels of the organization who are using vision-oriented behaviors or attempting to bring change in order to adapt to environmental pressures. With understanding comes improved performance.

In Part IV (Chapters 10, 11, and 12), we study the notion of human capital. The background and principles of human capital theory are presented. We see how it is quantified, how it can be monitored, and how it is a beacon of hope and inspiration for the future. This section moves through leadership imperatives and concludes with strong reasoning for training, education, and experience that will enhance the development of leaders for years to come.

Chapter 10 introduces the aspects of gender, ethnicity, and culture to the dialogue. What are the impacts of gender and ethnicity that leaders experience today, either personally or indirectly? How does culture play into the equation?

In Chapter 11, we analyze leader imperatives. We discuss how to lead wisely and consider the possibilities of beneficial partnering. We discuss the need for ethical behaviors and how to cope in suboptimal environs. And we stress the need to think outside of borders, be they organizational or global in scope.

In the final chapter, Chapter 12, we cover the topic of leader development—that is, the ability to expand the strengths and quality of leadership through introspection, education, and structured experience. We speak of the tools for evaluation and of developing others to carry on the roles of leadership.

Throughout the book, the qualities and behaviors of leadership that have great importance for guiding thought processes in the twenty-first century have been examined. It is most appropriate for the final discussion of the text to center on leadership development. To continually keep leadership up-to-date on general and specific industry issues, to personally stay refreshed and current in the field is to forever be focused and forward-thinking. Leadership is about motivating followers. It is about achieving results and it is about inspiring change. When it comes to great leaders, this is the stuff of which they are made. This is the correct approach. After all, it is not just about doing, or even doing things right—it is about doing the right things. And *that*, pure and simple, is the business of leadership.

KEY TERMS

consideration

effectiveness

efficiency

executive

initiation of structure

leadership

leadership constraints

leadership passages

legal or contractual constraints

management

organization-level competency

position power

situational perspective

RESOURCES

For rich discussions in class, students or teams of students may be assigned resources on the Internet that complement topics covered in each chapter. Outside reading adds depth to many of the concepts presented in the text, bringing them alive and aiding in their application. Although sites that tend to be enduring have been selected for the Resources sections of all chapters, please note that sites are often changed and it may be necessary to search for similar online articles.

Take the personal quiz at the first website listed below to gain feedback on what type of leader you are. Then go to the second site to compare your own natural tendencies to those of the leader discussed in the article who is designated most like your style. Do you see similarities in your style? Would you like to develop the skills that accompany that style? Be prepared to discuss your findings in class.

- Anthony J. Mayo, "Which Type of Leader Are You?" Fast Company, August 23, 2005. www.fastcompany.com/articles/2005/08/quiz.html.
- Bill Breen, "The Three Ways of Great Leaders," Fast Company, September 1, 2005. www.fastcompany.com/magazine/98/open_3ways.html?page=0%2C0.

Visit the current issue of the *Journal of Leadership & Organizational Studies*. Select three or four articles with titles that interest you and view the abstracts, which can be done at no cost. (If you find no particular topic that stimulates your curiosity, explore the archives, select a few articles, and view the abstracts.) What did the authors find? Be prepared to give an overview of your impressions of the types of research that are currently being conducted about leadership.

- *Journal of Leadership & Organizational Studies*, Sage journals online. http://jlo.sagepub.com/current.dtl.

SCORE counselors—executives, CEOs, and other retired businesspersons—give tips on effective leadership. What do you think of these tips in light of the introductory chapter on leadership? What organizational level are these tips geared to in light of the general information on leadership passages in Exhibit 1.7?

- SCORE, "5 Tips on Effective Leadership." www.score.org/5_tips_1_4.html.

DISCUSSION QUESTIONS

1. How can it be that one can be a leader without position power, and yet position power can be a constraint on leadership emergence?
2. To what degree does the information in Exhibit 1.3 and Exhibit 1.2 bear out the conventional belief that supervisors focus most on tasks, and executives on conceptual skills (e.g., strategic planning)? Provide some examples of where the focus on task, people, or organization would vary based on the type of professional position.
3. How do leadership passages parallel the typical growth and development of leadership skills?
4. What leadership constraint have you seen in action in the last couple of years, either by reading the newspaper or from personal experience? Could the recommendations from Exhibit 1.6 have made a difference in the impact of constraints?
5. Go online to read about the educational and experience background of Alan Mulally before he became president and CEO of Ford. Would you have predicted that he would become a successful leader in the automotive industry? Why or why not? Do you see leadership skills as transferable between industries? Why or why not?
6. Summarize the difference between management and leadership.
7. Give an operational definition of leadership.
8. What is the difference between efficiency and effectiveness, and what do those characteristics have to do with management and leadership?

9. Describe leadership passages and how one might move over one's career through each phase.

CLASSROOM ACTIVITIES

1. At the site below, read about "antiheroes who turned their backs on what they knew was right" according to *Fast Company*. Get into teams and adopt one of the individuals cited. Research the person's background and the circumstances of the event presented on the site. Then compare the person's behavior to the information in this chapter on what constitutes leadership. All the individuals who are listed and discussed in the article had at one time been identified as corporate leaders. Are these individuals correctly classified as antiheroes according to your research? If so, what changed, or was there a misreading of their status as a leader from the beginning?
   - *Fast Company*, "Cowards of the Year," September 1, 2005. www.fastcompany.com/magazine/98/open_cowards.html.
2. *Leadership Passages* (Dotlich, Noel, and Walker 2004) seeks to prepare organizations for effective leadership development. The book calls for more than a series of work challenges to which the leader is exposed; it also calls for personal introspection and the opportunity to learn from personal failures and tragedies. The authors claim that both diversity of experiences and adversity of experiences in people's personal lives and careers can shape them as leaders. For this activity, reflect on the diversity of your personal life experiences that may shape you as a leader. Be prepared to join a discussion group in class and describe their anticipated effect on you as a leader. For example, have you lived in a unique place, studied a different culture in depth, developed a personal plan for an ethical life, raised a sibling, worked to pay for your own education, or had other experiences that contribute to the diversity of your life?
3. You are supervisor of the call center of a manufacturing organization in the high-tech industry. Parts produced at your factory are subject to ISO 9001:2000 quality management system certification, and administration of the system must be very strict. Recently, because of the economic slowdown, demand for your product has significantly decreased and several people in manufacturing have been laid off, leading to a few quality defects. Customers calling in to the call center are not patient because they were led to believe they had purchased top-quality items. Customers have begun to complain to your supervisor in marketing about the call center's lack of service. Unfortunately, the marketing department feels that "anyone" should be able to handle these calls without difficulty. You have asked your supervisor if you can attend general marketing meetings for the purpose of increasing communication; his response was "No, not until you learn how to improve customer service." As the call center supervisor who has an interest in developing your leadership ability, what would you do? Leave the organization, or stay? If you remain with the organization, what strategy will you use to mitigate constraints on leadership development? Be prepared to explain your approach to the class.

CASE ANALYSIS

Johnson & Johnson (2009) has a history of expressing its responsibility to produce high-quality products and services for the medical community, its patients, and everyone who may use the company's products and services. The link of leadership competency with the company's culture and credo forms the basis of an "ethical decision-making process" with these steps:

1. Recognize the moral issue
2. Discern the "right thing"

   - Review the credo for guidance
   - Review policy for guidance
   - Examine the ethical issues

3. Test the alternatives
4. Make the decision
5. Revisit and reflect on the decision

If you were a Johnson & Johnson manager in China at a time when your baby products were charged with containing formaldehyde and p-dioxane (according to National Institutes of Health, a toxic and carcinogenic substance that irritates mucous membranes on inhalation or ingestion), how would you handle the situation in general terms? Given the corporate credo, what would guide your decision-making? Note that companies have developed ethical guides for their employees because of imperfect situations that may arise; also note that product development is not a perfect process devoid of challenges. This case could just as easily be about a food-processing company that retails organic lettuce for all the right reasons but is dealing with an outbreak of E. coli, or about a toy manufacturer that develops flame-resistant toys that are found to contain a toxic chemical that could impair learning if ingested.

TRADITIONAL THEORIES OF LEADERSHIP

Traditional theories of leadership provide the backdrop for understanding other approaches that have developed over time. Traditional theories are not only about "using power," but also about different leader styles and finding a style that yields performance results. Traditional theories are not about "holding positions of authority," but about gaining followers toward a particular goal. Traditional theories are expansive, even going as far as acknowledging the importance of various aspects of leader relationships themselves—relationships with followers and relationships to the situation.

The influence people are afforded through traditional leadership theories comes from a wide range of varying leader styles. In turn, each style gives particular insight into the manner or approach used for providing direction, implementing plans, and motivating people. The most basic of the styles, devised by Kurt Lewin in the 1930s, were directive, participative, or delegative. Whereas today a good leader may use all three styles depending on what forces are involved between the followers, the leader, and the situation, this was not the emphasis when the traditional theories were formed during the mid-1950s.

These traditional leadership theories go beyond mere leader style to the concerns of the follower and the leader as they work toward mutual benefit. In transactional theory, employees are given incentives—including moral rather than tangible rewards—in return for their acceptance of authority. In the 1930s, James MacGregor Burns pioneered a shift in analysis, away from the leader traits of "great men" to today's more familiar interaction of leaders and followers in a reciprocal exchange. Traditional theories led to the behavioral approach in the early 1960s, with the managerial grid model identifying leadership styles based on the constructs of leader concerns for people, tasks, or production. Finally, traditional theories led to the contingency approach in the early 1970s, as situational leadership suggested that leaders adapt their styles to the willingness and ability of their followers to do the task at hand.

How much have we learned about leadership since the zenith of traditional theories? Leaders are most highly observed, but leadership itself remains an ever-changing and adapting phenomenon. From the 1900s through the current age of technology, leaders have been examined with close personal scrutiny. Yet the field is forever unfolding as new leaders emerge and as new causes and crises and contingencies arise. Theories are stretched and tweaked, combined and separated as situations change over time and as new opportunities to lead followers are met in an always evolving business environment. This section of the text provides an overview of those theories.

2 Understanding Theories of Organizational Leadership

In theory there's no difference between theory and practice.
In practice there is.
—Yogi Berra

Because leadership is a highly complex social phenomenon, it is not surprising that many theories have been advanced in an effort to explain different aspects of it. For example, some theories emphasize a psychological study of personality such as the trait approach, some theories emphasize leader attitude and leader behavior, some emphasize the relationship between leaders and followers, some emphasize task or goal accomplishment, and others emphasize vision achievement through motivating others. Leadership is variously presented as an influence process, an attribute, or an exchange. Most researchers do not recommend wholesale attempts to organize all approaches to understanding leadership together under one general theory, but rather they advise pulling together the web of approaches and perspectives on leadership (Ciulla 2004).

How can a student clearly understand this web of approaches to leadership? In this chapter, we review basic approaches to the study of leadership and give you a framework to apply to any theory of leadership. This generic framework will help you diagnose its specific components and broad purpose for a comparative perspective between theories.

Consider the famous fable of the ten blind men who had never seen an elephant. Each tried to discover the nature of the beast by investigation. After feeling the side of the animal, one blind man asserted that the elephant was like a wall. A second man, touching the leg, stated that the elephant was really like a tree. A third blind man touched the trunk and announced it was like a snake; a fourth stroked the ear and said it was like a fan, and so on. The men could not agree on a simple general description, yet they had not even begun to address the questions of the elephant's strength, endurance, speed, or use. Similarly, a bewildering number of theories have been advanced to explain a variety of aspects of leadership, each with its own partial wisdom or advantages. Leadership is like the elephant in that it is a complex system that cannot be examined or understood or appreciated completely from any single perspective. The contributions and limitations of various theories of leadership must be examined in an effort to explain the "whole elephant" and more fully understand the phenomenon that is leadership. The framework best utilized for comparing the various theories and aiding in the diagnosis of their varying contributions and limitations is called the causal-chain framework.

The **causal-chain framework** helps identify the answer to a key question of leadership study: What performance goals tend to be achieved, with what leader approaches, and under what conditions? This framework readily allows for a comparative understanding. Additionally, for each theory we shall discuss the following aspects:

- What is the background of the theory and what have researchers tried to explain?
- What type of performance goals does the theory emphasize?
- Which contingency factors does the theory emphasize, if any?
- Which style or approaches does the theory emphasize?
- What are the strengths and weaknesses of the theory for explaining leadership in general?

Finally, this chapter identifies ten overall styles that have been recommended by the various theories. Different theories use different styles to explain leadership effectiveness, and they define each style in significantly different ways. With these theoretical building blocks in place, the following chapters examine specific leadership theories in more detail.

THE CAUSAL-CHAIN FRAMEWORK

The causal-chain framework is a model for comparing leadership theories. Theories of leadership come in all shapes, sizes, and formats. Some attempt to be elegant; that is, they try to explain a good deal with as few variables as possible. Particularly notable for this type of analysis are so-called universal theories, which attempt to explain leadership in a uniform fashion regardless of the situation. Sometimes we call these the "one best way" approaches to leadership, assuming that there is "one best way" to lead in any situation. Other theories attempt to be more comprehensive; they try to consider all significant factors. Some theories try to explain a narrow aspect of leadership well—for example, the causes and effects of leader attribution process on followers. Other theories try to explain a broader array of leadership functions simultaneously, so that not only are production and employee satisfaction explained, but so is the need for external alignment and organizational change. Sometimes leadership styles are experimentally treated as independent variables, sometimes as dependent variables, and at other times as contingencies. In order to provide a consistent basis for comparison, however, all theories will be discussed in this book in terms of the causal-chain framework. The model gives a consistent framework for comparing leadership theories. Generally speaking,

- **descriptive theories** explain approaches typically taken in reality,
- **prescriptive theories** identify the approach to be taken for ideal effectiveness in a situation,

- **universal theories** identify the "one best way to lead," applying in all situations, and
- **contingency theories** (Fiedler 1967) identify aspects of leadership that apply only in limited or particular situations.

The causal-chain framework is certainly not the only basis for comparison of leadership theories. For example, whether theories are "descriptive" or "prescriptive" can be meaningful for classifying different approaches to leadership. Whether theories are "universal" or "contingency" can be used as a means to classify different approaches. However, the causal-chain framework allows for an organized, consistent way to analyze and see the relationships of various components for each leadership theory. It then becomes apparent how each theory contributes a partial perspective to the whole and has its own partial or unique advantages, parallel to the descriptions of the elephant in the fable about the blind men.

The causal-chain framework is similar to a Malcolm Baldrige performance management model[1] that is designed to bring an organization to higher overall quality. Those management models identify causal linkages between multiple external results and multiple internal performance metrics (Evans and Jack 2003). Using the Malcolm Baldrige causal linkage framework, databases can be established with hypothesized linkages between various external quality results, such as market performance, and internal performance metrics, such as employee satisfaction, which can then be tested for statistical correlation. These correlations can then validate or disprove certain linkages using the scientific model to help explain how to achieve quality results. The similarity between the two causal-chain models is that relationships between variables are hypothesized, and linkages to performance results can be tested.

The causal-chain framework also has elements in common with David McClelland's leadership chain (Spencer 2007). The leadership chain establishes the impact of several variables on organizational effectiveness. Specifically, a causal chain is established from individual motives, leadership style, and organizational climate in order to hypothesize and measure the impact on organizational effectiveness. McClelland's leadership chain attempts to provide a reasoned tool for explaining how leaders with different approaches, called "needs," are motivated in different organizational conditions to achieve effectiveness.

The causal-chain framework that is used here incorporates three different types of factors: leader behaviors, intervening and moderating variables, and performance results. *Leader behaviors* are at the beginning of the causal chain because they are the first demonstrable action toward the follower, the organization, and the environment. From a social science perspective, leader behaviors include leadership style and all of the behavioral variables exhibited by the leader. They also lead the chain in terms of applied interest in the important question to managers: What leader actions lead to what performance?

The next elements considered are the *contingency factors*, which can be of two types—intervening variables or moderating variables. Some contingency factors affect which behavior or style would be selected to enhance the desired outcome. In other words, what are the ideal conditions for a specific leadership style to be used?

These factors are sometimes called **intervening variables**. Associated theories are often called either contingency or situational theories.

Other contingency factors affect the impact of the leadership behavior or style in terms of its strength, quality, or success. They are sometimes thought of as strategies for success in lay terms, or **moderating variables** in scientific terms. Common types of moderating variables have to do with leader expertise in executing the desired style. For example, the ideal behavior in a given situation may be supportive, but the leader may demonstrate this supportive behavior in such a clumsy fashion that it makes followers feel as if the attention they receive is micromanagement, thus affecting the success of the desired result. Other types of moderating variables have to do with follower readiness. For example, even if the ideal leader behavior in a given situation may be diagnosed to be supportive, the follower may be psychologically unwilling to accept guidance, thus again affecting the success of the desired result.

The third part of the causal-chain framework is *performance results*. Performance results can refer to goals or specific outcomes that are desired over the long term. They can relate to both organizational efficiency and effectiveness. Originally, performance was seen almost exclusively from an organizational perspective as "production efficiency" or as "organizational effectiveness" in coordinating business activities for goal achievement. Over the years it has morphed to become a more focused result for an organization that wants to be high-performing in the long term. Performance results or goals can involve production efficiency, follower satisfaction and development, external alignment, and organizational change, among others.

Exhibit 2.1 displays the causal-chain framework. To review, how a leader behaves influences performance. The behaviors or styles that the leader uses affect how much is accomplished, how followers feel, how well the organization adapts, and so forth. However, important factors influence this relationship. Some contingency factors, or intervening variables, are so important that they determine what styles will work most effectively in a given situation. For example, in some cases a directive style is most effective, while in others an inspirational style may better lead to the desired results. Other factors, or moderating variables, affect the impact of a style. For example, a leader who correctly assesses that an inspirational style is called for and attempts to employ it, but who lacks the trust of his followers and who has weak motivational speaking skills (moderating variables), is likely to have limited success in achieving performance results. Finally, depending on the interaction of leader behavior in light of intervening or moderating variables, we see the end result on performance. The remainder of this chapter takes the student through each major component of the causal-chain framework—leader behaviors and styles, intervening and moderating variables, and performance results.

LEADER BEHAVIORS AND STYLES

What are the best and most predominant leader styles? Not surprisingly, different theories have somewhat different answers. Many use similar concepts but provide a different vocabulary. Some use the same name for different concepts. Many theories do not try to comprehensively capture all aspects of the major leader functions.

Exhibit 2.1 **The Causal-Chain Framework**

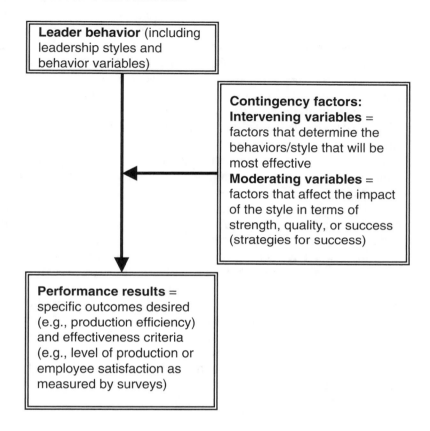

This analysis aims to provide an overview of "generic" styles as discussed in the literature. The ten styles identified are distinct enough to be separate categories and are relatively comprehensive of leader functions. Nonetheless, three warnings are in order. First, the ten styles identified do overlap. Second, few leaders use a single style all or even most of the time; most leaders adapt their styles to different situations or contingencies, including how they feel at the time. Third, some "ideal" styles that are recommended by researchers are really fusions of two or more of the other styles; these conglomerates are called combined styles for this taxonomy.

LAISSEZ-FAIRE STYLE

The **laissez-faire style** is not an absence of style. It occurs when the leader exhibits passivity or indifference about tasks and subordinates or purposely neglects what could be seen as an area of responsibility. The French term "laissez-faire" (literally "to let do") means "let it be"—or to let people do as they choose. Originally, the term referred to an economic belief that government should not interfere in society except when government action is essential for the free enterprise system to regulate itself. In reference to leadership, the term refers to a hands-off style or, on occasion, a conscious strategy when competing demands necessitate overlooking some areas of responsibility. The laissez-faire style tends to be identified in universal hierarchical approaches to leadership as the least desirable or worst style. Many contingency approaches do not discuss a laissez-faire style. However, this does not mean they do not assume that such a style exists. Because contingency theories focus on the most effective styles of leadership, rather than a survey of all leader styles, they simply do not address what are seen to be suboptimal styles in most situations.

Laissez-faire is the style most frequently considered a poor choice. Nevertheless, all leaders may occasionally resort to a laissez-faire style when they are overwhelmed by excessive job demands or when the situation does not call for action from the individual in their particular role. For example, a leader may consciously neglect a low-priority responsibility for a limited period of time while attending to other more pressing concerns. Certainly, other styles can sometimes be poor or ineffective as well.

A laissez-faire style is typified by low leader control, low leader goals and performance expectations, and little or no motivational stimulation for followers. It can mean that the leader is not focusing on either the internal or external aspects of the organization, or it is possible that the leader's focus on external matters leads to a laissez-faire style internally. The leader's lack of response may lead to situations that should have been prevented or to needless negative public relations. But lack of response by one individual may also result in action being taken by a more appropriate individual.

An example of the laissez-faire style is given to illustrate how a leader can be known for accomplishments on many fronts, but also for a hands-off approach in other areas. Every leadership style throughout this chapter can have both positive and negative applications and variations in results, depending on factors such as the appropriateness of the style for the given situation and the expertise of the leader in using the style. The example below involves top military medical officers whose laissez-faire leadership style on one important concern became synonymous with negligence in the press.

In February 2007, the *Washington Post* exposed outpatient failures at Walter Reed Army Medical Center and shocked a nation that had believed *all* medical care at the center was top-notch. The exposé (Hull and Priest 2007) centered on Building 18, where wounded soldiers were brought "home" from Iraq and Afghanistan to a facility that was infested with mold, mice, and cockroaches. There was reportedly a lack of heat and water in the winter. Soldiers were known to be lost, literally, in hospital bureaucracy. The *Post* reported that these conditions were known by top management, but were not addressed. As far back as 2004, Beverly Young, the wife of Rep. Bill Young (R-FL), had complained, first to a nurse and then to Army Surgeon General Kevin Kiley, about the lack of care for a soldier she visited who was reportedly lying in filth. In October 2006, a friend of Joyce Rumsfeld, the wife of then-Defense Secretary Donald Rumsfeld, brought her to a meeting of the supporters of soldiers; despite the friend being a frequent volunteer at Walter Reed, she was told that she could no longer come on the hospital grounds presumably because Mrs. Rumsfeld questioned that her husband was being given too idealistic an understanding of hospital conditions and treatment. After the newspaper depiction was published, George W. Weightman, acting commander of the U.S. Army's top hospital, told the *Washington Post* that repair orders and mold removal for the fifty-four rooms at the building in question were being completed. On February 20, 2007, Weightman said that "Walter Reed and Army officials have been 'meeting continuously for three days' since the articles began appearing" (*Washington Post* 2007).

The medical care of veterans may or may not have been negatively impacted by the command culture of the military, but a change in the laissez-faire leadership style of the officers in charge of Walter Reed would have certainly changed the results. Their hands-off style did not solve anything.

It is not uncommon for those who use the laissez-faire style much of the time to experience significant difficulty. Leaders who use a predominantly laissez-faire style often consider their job to involve fixing problems, crises, and scandals after subordinates have failed to properly carry out their duties. Therefore, when negative events occur, the leaders are often quite unapologetic, spring to action, and may even take decisive, firm steps to correct other people's failings. In some instances, an inattentive laissez-faire leader can appear to be the hero by seizing the initiative, fixing the problem, and punishing the innocent. That is, inattentive leaders may fail to do their job of preventing problems through proper monitoring and then place the blame on someone else as they belatedly fix a mess of their own making.

DIRECTIVE STYLE

A **directive style** is exhibited when a leader lets subordinates know what they are expected to do, gives directions and guidance, asks subordinates to follow rules and procedures, and schedules and coordinates work activities. Behaviorally, the directive style of leadership emphasizes task skills such as monitoring, operations planning, clarifying roles, informing, and delegating in relation to the assignment of work projects. At the organizational level, it also involves general management functions, such as human resource management as an extension of coordinating and scheduling functions. A directive style assumes high leader control, average (or above average) performance expectations, a formalistic notion of motivation based on legitimacy of command, reward, and punishments, and an internal focus. It is also known as task-oriented (Fiedler 1967; Fiedler, Chemers, and Mahar 1976), authority-compliance (Blake and Mouton 1965), autocratic decision-making (Vroom and Jago 1988; Vroom and Yetton 1973), strongman (Manz and Sims 1989, 1991), top-down leadership (Locke 2003), and the one-best-way in scientific management (Taylor 1911). Here is a look at the directive style of leadership in action.

Jace (whose name is changed for this "real life" example) was supervisor in the paint department of a home improvement store. He taught employees in the department that new goods had to be entered into inventory in a certain way and tagged in a uniform manner for scanning at the time of purchase. If new employees departed from these instructions, Jace would remind them of expected procedures privately. On one occasion, Jace wrote up an experienced employee for violating procedures by selling goods to a customer directly from a new shipment of paint that had not yet been entered into inventory. The employee explained that she had been practicing good customer service, as the sale would have been lost since "the customer would not have wanted to wait while I tagged the paint." Jace, in turn, replied, "There are other ways to avoid losing a sale, but you cannot sell merchandise that is not yet in inventory. If employees do that, then paint could be sold, the money could be pocketed, and the company would think that merchandise missing from the back room had been an error in shipping. I told you to follow procedures, and because you did not, you are being written up." The employee said she felt as if she were not trusted.

In this example, Jace used the directive style of leadership. He gave directions, told the subordinate to follow rules and procedures, and took personnel action when the subordinate did not do as he said. It is unusual for a company not to have clear-cut procedures for inventory management. A supervisor must follow such procedures, but employees who fail to understand the need for such procedures may react negatively to the directive style. While Jace could have communicated the same direct message in a less accusatory manner or found a better method for defending the company's required inventory procedures, such guidelines are carefully crafted and must be routinely followed in order to prevent known problems in business, such as employee theft. Normally, a directive style that is well administered is the most clear-cut way to ensure compliance with policy. Additionally, the leadership style that typically enforces the uniform use of procedures can be described as directive in style.

A variety of subtypes can be identified that have distinctly different connotations. Several of the prominent subtypes point to the fundamental importance of the leader making sure that the work of the organization is done properly. An *instructive style* emphasizes the telling, informing, and clarifying aspects of directing. Followers need instruction on what they do not know how to do, what they are doing improperly, or what will be done differently because of changes in mandate or technology. They also need to know what the rules are, what rule infractions mean, when exceptions are allowable, and how to interact with others. Finally, they need help with their questions and problems. Followers who do not get this task support may be untrained, error prone, and frustrated. A related subtype is *structuring*. Structuring means that work activities are arranged in advance, work schedules are coordinated, and contingency plans have been developed. There is always much behind-the-scenes work that managers and leaders must do to make sure operational problems do not occur and that resources are properly received and allocated. Structuring also includes a good deal of task monitoring, whether that is reading reports, analyzing data trends, or managing by walking around. The absence of good structuring can mean a substantially higher incidence of problems and crises.

A directive style often has negative connotations, which are generally identified by a term like "authoritarian." Telling may be interpreted as commanding or being bossy, informing becomes dictating, clarifying becomes threatening, and planning becomes micromanagement. At its worst, this substyle is typified by actual or perceived characteristics such as rigidity, complete lack of input from others, leader centeredness, and the treatment of subordinates as replaceable parts. A directive style was more commonly accepted in the first half of the twentieth century in an era of manufacturing when there was more frequently "one right way" to do a job with narrow job scope.

Since then, it has become less popular or acceptable for a leader to adopt the directive style as a dominant style. Nonetheless, in times of crisis or when major change is imperative, people often expect a stronger style to emerge in a leader. An authoritarian style may be considered appropriate as a short-term approach during such periods in order to avoid employee confusion and uncertainty. Yet even then, the general rule of thumb is that the need for quick response time for safety or for major change must be present for this substyle to suit the circumstances and gain acceptance.

SUPPORTIVE STYLE

A **supportive style** is demonstrated by showing consideration toward followers, displaying concern for their needs, and creating a friendly work environment for each worker. It focuses exclusively on people-oriented behaviors: consulting (especially the listening modality), coordinating personnel, developing staff, motivating, and, to a lesser degree, building and managing teams and conflict. The job of planning and coordinating personnel is different from operations planning; it refers to matching the talents, interests, and preferences of employees to the work, rather than vice versa. A supportive style does not directly imply a lack of leader control if a leader can both direct and support at the same time. However, if doing so distracts a leader, then it does imply low control. Supportive behavior typically assumes at least average performance, and many researchers assert that its absence negates the prospect of high performance. In terms of motivation, this style, which was highly influenced by the human relations school (e.g., Argyris 1957; McGregor 1960), emphasizes human compassion and dignity. It assumes an internal approach to the organization that specifically focuses on followers. Below is an illustration of the supportive style of leadership.

A company rule in a retail store required that all incoming checks be processed "same day." In other words, if a check came in when the business closed at 8 P.M., it was to be bundled for deposit that same night. The bundle of checks would be placed by the night manager into a safe and checked early in the morning before being picked up for deposit at the bank. One evening near closing, Yvette, the night manager, received a call from her junior high school daughter requesting permission to go out to a movie. "No, Shelly, on school nights, I expect you to stay home." Yvette prepared everything for closing earlier than usual because the store had emptied. Moreover, she wanted to return home as early as possible since her daughter had a history of disobeying the rules and getting into trouble. As luck would have it, another customer walked in near 8 P.M., vacillated about the final purchase until after 8:15, and paid by check. Rather than reworking the deposit and refiguring the totals, Yvette locked up the additional check with an explanatory note for her supervisor and hurried out the door. When she came in the next day, the supervisor asked if her daughter was okay and said that he understood why the checks had not been properly bundled for deposit, but cautioned that this must not become common practice for dealing with late purchases.

In this "real-life" example, the supervisor could have used different approaches to deal with Yvette's improper handling of funds, yet chose to use a supportive style. Yvette was relieved by her supervisor's approach, understanding that he likely believed her to be a conscientious employee who was torn between the conflicting needs to follow known proper procedure and to be responsive to family concerns. Still, the caring that the supervisor showed for the night manager's situation was coupled with an asserted recognition of the need to follow procedure in the future. If the supervisor's supportive style resulted in Yvette repeating procedural violations, then the style used would need to become more directive in order to ensure clarity of communication with Yvette.

The predominant subtype of supportive behavior is a caring model. Leaders first make sure that subordinates or followers feel socially connected and that they are part of a group. This may be demonstrated by a cheerful tone of voice, friendly body language, and inclusiveness in the social aspects of work. Leaders also ensure that followers feel both good about themselves and valued in the work context—for example, by providing individual attention, soliciting information, and offering praise. Second, supportive leaders are attuned to followers' personal and career needs; a leader may adjust a schedule for the parent of a newborn or recommend a management training class for an employee who wants to advance. When used appropriately, these behaviors should lead to an atmosphere of trust in the workplace (because the employees' interests are considered along with work interests) and increased liking and respect for the leader. A negative subtype also exists, as when a supportive style squeezes out proportionate concerns for production. Blake and Mouton (1964) call this the country club style (a 1, 9 style in their grid approach). In this style, the emphasis on personal satisfaction, interpersonal relations, and personal development becomes overweening, while the tougher demands of trying to achieve high standards, fix short-term problems, and confront vexing long-term issues are overlooked.

PARTICIPATIVE STYLE

Leaders who use a **participative style** consult with subordinates and take their opinions into account, provide suggestions and guidelines rather than regimented direction, and establish a friendly, creative work environment for the team as a whole. Behaviors include consulting, coordinating personnel, developing staff, motivating, building and managing teams, managing conflict (especially as it arises out of constructive disagreements and creative tensions), managing personnel change by including followers in change decisions, and a modest amount of delegating in the task domain. Supportive and participative styles are indeed similar. However, supportive style emphasizes listening, caring, and empathy, whereas participative style emphasizes discussion and inclusiveness in work decisions and problem-solving. The participative style assumes only moderate control, at least average performance goals, and appreciation of competence and involvement as motivators. The following vignette illustrates the appropriate application of participative style.

The corporate website was out of date in both technical capacity and content. The executive team realized that the site needed upgrading for a more integrated sense of corporate identity. They assigned the upgrade to the IT Division, requesting a new design showing an appropriate connection between the first two levels of the hierarchy online by the end of the month. The IT Division successfully followed through on the timetable, but when departments saw how they were represented, there were howls of discontent: "Our page is insensitive to our mission!" "Our page has no artistic flair!" "Ours has none of the online features that we want!" The unanticipated vexation was heard by an executive team that quickly became defensive. Why were the departments not pleased with the improvement in integration? The executives finally decided to bring in department heads for consultation. It soon became apparent that changing the look and feel of the website required more than a quick fix and that honest discussion and inclusiveness in decision-making were essential. The executive team regrouped, abandoned its implicitly directive approach, and moved toward a more participative style of leadership. The process of design-to-implementation took longer, but departmental insights were heeded and incorporated into the new design. The IT Division interacted with the departments to accomplish what they envisioned, all within the constraints of an integrated corporate identity. Whereas the first approach got new but unacceptable pages posted efficiently, it was only the second participative approach that resulted in acceptance and effectiveness. (This particular example is not lifted directly from just one consulting experience, but has taken place in many organizations—particularly around the same issue of new website design which, by its nature, demands consultation with departments represented online.)

One subtype is an *inclusive style* of leadership. The leader seeks to discuss surface problems with individuals and get a broad base of information and input, coordinates the needs of the group such that individual needs are not neglected, and motivates by providing a robust inclusiveness. A second subtype is a *self-conscious team* approach. The leader facilitates team discussions, provides relatively wide decision parameters, and tends to implement team decisions as recommended, given the range of decision-making that the leader has established for the group. This subtype focuses on interactive meetings, group learning, and managing complex group processes. There is not a negative subtype of participative leadership per se. However, contingency theory makes clear that a participative style is only one of several and that circumstances may not be ideal for this style much of the time. Leaders who are always in a participative mode may be inefficient a good deal of the time even though they are blessed with a good team. For example, an executive mode (i.e., a directive style) may be more effective in some cases, while a delegative style would better conserve group resources in others. Stated differently, sometimes the group wants the leader to handle business unilaterally because it does not want to be bogged down by details, and at other times the assignment of a problem to an individual makes more sense than a more time-consuming group process.

DELEGATIVE STYLE

A **delegative style** is defined as one that allows subordinates relative freedom for decision-making and from daily monitoring and short-term reviews. The main behavior of this style is the designation of responsibility and allocation of authority. Providing additional responsibility is similar to job enlargement. Allocation of authority means greater decision-making independence and thus is a form of power. It is the latter element that is considered especially critical to true delegation. Additional behaviors involved in this style involve developing staff and motivating. A delegative style assumes low leader control and at least moderate performance goals. The motivational assumption is that followers seek independence as a form of self-fulfillment. In addition, they often perceive delegation as recognition of professional mastery and superior competence. The style does not necessarily assume either an internal or external focus on the part of the leader. Delegation should free up the leader's time for other activities, which can include other production-people issues, public relations, strategic issues, or even personal pursuits.

Theory on leadership substitutes indirectly, but powerfully, addresses the delegative style (Kerr and Jermier 1978), begging the question: When can you reduce the imposition of leadership? It identifies primary situations in which leadership delegation can be increased:

- Followers have ample education, training, or experience in their jobs.
- Followers have a professional orientation and have internalized work standards and ethical norms.
- The work itself is somewhat structured so that relatively few substantial issues arise. The roles and procedures are clear.
- Feedback is provided as a part of the job.
- The work is intrinsically satisfying—which is, of course, a self-referential perception.
- The work group is cohesive so that there is support for peer training and inter-member routine problem-solving.

In other words, when these types of situations exist, less directive leadership or more delegation is realistic to explore, assuming that other moderating factors do not contravene to complicate the leadership situation.

There are two forms of delegating. In the first, subordinates are given *additional duties*, functions, or tasks to perform. The leader maintains the same level of monitoring, clarifying, and review. In the second form, subordinates are given *additional decision-making authority* over processes, problems, exceptions, and the like. The latter granting of authority is closer to what is generally considered true delegation and is often referred to as **empowerment**. Under the right conditions, such as those specified by the leadership substitutes theory, empowerment can be helpful to the efficiency of both the subordinate and the leader and can enhance motivation. However, with greater empowerment also comes greater accountability and—generally—shifts in the types of accountability. The subordinate who is assigned a project (responsibility) and given responsibility to handle it in whatever way seems most appropriate without prior approval (authority) must be accountable for the quality of decisions made under the circumstances. Greater empowerment and authority generally mean that accountability shifts from a prior-approval approach using an item-by-item method to a postperformance review on an aggregate basis, perhaps for an entire project or series of projects. Greater empowerment and authority usually signal a shift to more internalized control mechanisms, such as professional norms and a sense of virtue or character regarding the organization's interests. Exhibit 2.2 is a good example of a manager who has difficulty with accountability and the notion of "letting go."

Exhibit 2.2

The Broker as Delegator

When George Smith completed his degree in real estate and development, he obtained a broker's license and was determined to open his own real estate firm within five years. He put aside 25 percent of his earnings on each residential sale toward the eventual down payment on his own office. He networked constantly in order to find the best salespeople for his future firm. Four and a half years after graduation, he was ready to open the doors of George Smith Realty. A group of residential realtors and brokers made up half of the organization, and commercial realtors and brokers made up the other half. George felt he had identified a winning team.

For quality, George enforced the requirement that he personally would approve all final transactions of the firm. Realtors and brokers would handle deals of differing levels of complexity, and George himself would then close all deals. George sent commercial buyers nice arrangements of fruit and chocolate, and residential buyers less expensive arrangements of chocolate-dipped biscotti. Customers were happy, and his business grew by word of mouth. His realtors and brokers were rewarded generously. Generally, people appreciated the personal attention that George gave to every transaction.

In the community George quickly gained a reputation for personal commitment to his customers and for attention to detail. His business continued to grow. Many realtors and brokers in his firm were responsible for over $1 million in annual sales.

Occasionally, when George's family convinced him to go on vacation, brokers in his firm jokingly told him not to leave because they might lose hot deals that could not be closed until he returned. George turned off his cell phone and did not check email, so he could not be reached while on these outings. Realtors in his firm suggested that when he was away they would like to close deals with George Smith brokers. George restated his rule to the realtors, saying any deal could wait and would be handled when he returned.

Several brokers eventually left the firm, explaining that they had opportunities for personal growth elsewhere and thanking George for the successful environment he had provided. Business was still good, but there was no growth. George learned the meaning of the word "plateau." With his attention to detail, George Smith had envisioned a real estate firm that would forever prosper, eventually handling most of the residential and commercial transactions in the region. Instead, his former employees now provided competition.

George Smith clearly held tight reins on his company. If he changed his style of leadership to that of a delegator, what specific differences would there be in his behavior and approach to decision-making? What would be the likely result, and why? How would accountability have to change?

ACHIEVEMENT-ORIENTED STYLE

With an **achievement-oriented style**, a leader sets challenging task goals, seeks task improvements, emphasizes excellence in follower performance, and shows confidence that followers will perform well. The primary behaviors involve a combination of both people- and task-domain types. The task focus includes clarifying roles, informing, delegating, problem-solving, and managing innovation and creativity. The people focus includes consulting, developing staff, and building and managing teams. This achievement-oriented style assumes a medium level of leader control and an internal organizational focus on the part of the leader. The achievement-oriented and inspirational styles (discussed next) are the two styles that focus specifically on challenging goals and high expectations. The primary motivational base of the achievement-oriented style is individual commission and accomplishment, which will be contrasted with inspirational style, a more group-achievement approach.

The theoretical basis for the achievement-oriented style is anchored in the social-exchange literature that emerged in the 1950s (Homans 1958), which emphasized the transactional basis of most social behavior. The achievement factor was much advanced by McClelland (1965, 1985), who studied the achievement characteristic or "need" in leaders more than the leadership style, but whose insights are nonetheless important to the study of leadership. In particular, he points out the limitations of an achievement-oriented approach: the excesses to which it is prone and the potential problems caused by overly obsessed and selfish leaders and by followers who feel exploited and distrustful. Although this style was not included in the original formulation of path-goal theory (House 1971), House did include it in his later formulation (House and Mitchell 1974). Bass (1985) refers to what is essentially an achievement-oriented style as contingent reward, which is then contrasted with elements of an inspirational approach. That is, normally in an achievement-oriented style there are specific, individual payoffs (contingent rewards) for high achievement levels. Mintzberg's (1973) entrepreneurial function also implies an achievement style; similarly, the style has loose ties to the excellence and goal-setting literatures. Management by objectives strongly encourages an achievement style, although it allows for a more directive or participative approach as situations demand. Recognition of the importance of achievement motivation is shown in this example of the manager of a computer store.

The manager for a high-end ladies clothing and accessories store, Eva, realized that sales were stable at best, as competition from both local stores and virtual vendors had increased. In this "real life" company, prices and product were competitive, much time and advertising money had been poured into aggressive marketing, and there was no shortage of customers circulating through the store. Nonetheless, salespeople were not energetically trying to close sales, and some of the best salespeople showed relatively high turnover. As manager, Eva initiated new monthly sales bonuses targeted at high-performing sales personnel. She called a meeting of the sales staff before store opening one Monday morning, explained the new bonus plan, and assured the employees that she knew they could meet the challenge. Eva also believed that with the store's strong customer service orientation, they could be competitive against Internet sales. Within a week, volume began to increase as salespeople focused on both customer service and closing sales. Eva thought briefly to herself that the sales staff should have been making high sales all along. But then she stopped herself, realizing that the staff was motivated by achievement and that when she said she knew they could do the job, and when a positive reward structure was put in place, they came through for the company.

Because it is wedged in fairly tightly among other styles, there really are no subtypes of achievement-oriented style other than a negative version. As McClelland's (1965, 1985) research indicates, excesses of competition that are not well integrated can lead to self-serving behaviors, egotism, and insensitivity. Manz and Sims (1989, 1991) discuss the dynamics of this style: interactive goal-setting, contingent personal reward, contingent material reward, and contingent reprimand. However, they point out that the result can be followers who are "calculators." The followers can quickly become accustomed to relying on external motivation (the what's-in-it-for-me syndrome), and when that motivation does not exist, they may become obstinately passive. Another aspect of this problem is the divisibility and immediacy of rewards implied by this style. While a highly reward-driven style may work well most of the time in sales or mass-production jobs because of the ability to tie results to specific individuals, it is less appealing in jobs when there is a group product that does not tie clearly to the achievement of a particular individual.

INSPIRATIONAL STYLE

An **inspirational style** uses intellectual stimulation to produce new ideas, gain acceptance for new approaches, and arouse contagious enthusiasm for the achievement of group goals. It relies heavily on acceptance of the leader's wisdom and/or integrity by followers, and it draws on many behaviors. In the task domain, it includes managing innovation at the operational level. In the people domain, it includes managing personnel change because the style often implies significant attitudinal changes in followers. At the organizational level, it includes scanning the environment, strategic planning, articulating a vision, networking and partnering, decision-making, and managing organizational change. Note this style's emphasis on rising to the challenges of all types of change. The style generally assumes high goal levels, but the goal is often a "change" goal as opposed to a strictly quantitative performance objective more common to the achievement-oriented style. The degree of leader control varies among the substyles. The leader is largely divided between an internal focus on tasks and people and external needs for new structures and production reconfiguration. The motivational base focuses on group achievement through acculturation ("oneness" with the group), intellectual engagement, and trust of and excitation by the leader.

The inspirational style was introduced employing a distinctive approach with the transformational-charismatic school of thought, which itself covers a wide array of perspectives. Different transformational models imply slightly different types of inspirational style. When the transformational approach is directed at the operational level, a process improvement approach or a reengineering approach can be recommended. The former emphasizes change and innovation coming from the line and espouses a learning-organization environment; the latter encourages top-down analysis of dysfunctional processes in which significant improvements are possible, largely based on leader direction, if follower implemented (Hammer and Champy 1993). Transformational leadership often encourages organizational change and thus vision, strategy, and mission articulation are featured. It is possible for this to be an inclusive, evolving process with an egalitarian tone, such as in a visioning process. It may also be driven by a strong-willed leader with a sharply defined vision, a crisp timeline, and a willingness to make some hard decisions. Overlapping with these different approaches is the charismatic aspect of change leadership. Charismatic leaders are viewed as having a "special gift," insight, or wisdom and an especially appealing personality (at least to most people). Not all exceptional transformational leaders are charismatic (Bennis and Nanus 1985).

The leadership literature is also well attuned to the negative aspects of the inspirational style, especially the overreliance on charisma and overly powerful leaders. For example, Manz and Sims (1989, 1991) point out that the common, leader-driven transformational style encourages communication of the leader's vision, emphasis on the leader's values, exhortation, and inspirational persuasion. This type of leader, they assert, tends to create followers who are "enthusiastic sheep." The dark side of charisma is well known among researchers (Bass and Steidlmeier 1999; Conger 1989; Sandowsky 1995), and the general public is familiar with cult charismatics such as Adolf Hitler, David Koresh, and Jim Jones. Yukl points out some of the many problems that can occur with inspirational leaders: "Being in awe of the leader reduces good suggestions by the followers; desire for leader acceptance inhibits criticism by followers, adoration by followers creates delusions of infallibility; excessive confidence and optimism blind the leader to real dangers; denial of problems and failures reduces organizational learning; risky and grandiose projects are more likely to fail; taking complete credit for successes alienates some key followers" (2006, 260). The subsequent example embodies the inspirational style.

Football coach Vince Lombardi was known for nine phenomenal winning seasons with the Green Bay Packers, earning five NFL championships and two Super Bowl trophies. In 1969, after one year of retirement, he became the head coach of the Washington Redskins, leading them to their first winning season in fourteen years. Through his golden career of ever trying to get the best out of people, Vince Lombardi became known as an inspirational leader. He is credited with saying, "Leadership is based on a spiritual quality: the power to inspire, the power to inspire others to follow" (2007). Both his passion for creating a team bound together with a shared purpose and his long winning record were achieved by virtue of his inspirational style: "Coaches who can outline plays on a blackboard are a dime a dozen. The ones who win get inside their players and motivate." His ability to communicate and build a shared passion in his players established a culture of inspiration.

STRATEGIC STYLE

The **strategic style** focuses attention on external organizational matters in the environmental context. It involves all organizational behaviors: environmental scanning, strategic planning, vision articulation, general management functions, networking and partnering, decision-making, and managing organizational change. Sometimes the magnitude of change is small, with incremental changes made in technical updates, process redesign, or market expansion. At other times the magnitude of change is radical, with major realignments made in closing down divisions, acquiring talent globally, or merging with other corporations.

A number of the common style dimensions do not apply to external leadership because of its external focus. In other words, this approach does not really suggest much about control of followers, goal levels, or motivational factors used to stimulate followers. It is often most clear in large organizations when there is a sharp demarcation between internal and external functions, with the chief operating officer handling internal affairs and a chief executive officer handling the external affairs.

Frequently, an organization that has had a long period of stable leadership with an internally focused leader but is increasingly out of touch with its environment may seek a leader who possesses the special skills of strategic style and can discover new external opportunities or make calculated changes to prevent organizational decline.

The strategic leadership style is more than how one particular leader anticipates the environment in order to prepare for the future. It is also a management model that involves that leader training and encouraging employees and managers to mobilize the business for its future, including its regional and global relationships. These leaders take responsibility for the deep-laid future of the business, but they acknowledge that the best results may be achieved by involving thinking individuals throughout the hierarchy. The strategic style, in other words, provides an umbrella under which the organization overall devises tactical procedures that will provide a road map for reaching the vision in a turbulent environment.

Although the strategic style tends to be most linked to the top management team because of its responsibility for organizational strategy, the style is rightly associated with leaders at all levels of the hierarchy. Any leader involved in shaping personal responsibilities to broad corporate strategy or conveying goals and objectives in a form that is appealing to employees and investors is practicing the strategic style. Here is an illustration of strategic style leadership.

Donald J. Trump is a developer and executive known for showmanship, whether in memorable "You're fired!" pronouncements to apprentices on his television show or in staged announcements about property development. Over the years, his company has been on a financial yo-yo, reportedly going in and out of bankruptcy. Yet through it all, Trump remained personally protected because of his external strategic focus. In 1988, Trump financed the $1 billion construction of the Taj Mahal Casino in Atlantic City with high-interest junk bonds. By 1991, facing $900 million in personal debt, he was forced to declare business insolvency; the *New York Times* stated, "Mr. Trump will give up half his ownership in the casino in exchange for lower interest rates on its junk bonds" (1991). Nevertheless, by 2004 he was ranked the seventy-forth-richest American by *Forbes* magazine. In 2005, Trump Entertainment recovered from its second round of bankruptcy. Still, Trump remained chair and CEO, collecting a $2 million salary. Analysts (Sanders 2005) affirmed that Trump protected himself by being externally involved rather than personally involved and by filing for *corporate* bankruptcy while protecting his personal finances. Even when embroiled in proceedings on smaller projects, Trump sent representatives to hearings or meetings rather than attend himself (Vizard 1999). Overall, Donald Trump demonstrates an external strategic style of leadership that focuses strategic attention on large-scale organizational challenges in his external environment.

Collaborative Style

Both strategic and collaborative styles of leadership have an external focus, with the distinction that the collaborative style is not competitive. The **collaborative style** focuses on external networking for a sense of collegiality, contacts, and enhanced trust that comes from long-term interaction; civic-mindedness or philanthropic activity from participating in the community without specific payoffs in mind, except perhaps to the nonprofit arena; partnering for cooperative projects in which there is mutual gain; and "expanding the pie" for an external win-win collaboration, including community-building for mutual gain.

There is a dysfunctional version of this style that focuses on external challenges to the neglect of internal issues. Although most executives know better than to neglect internal issues, they can get considerable psychic reward from civic-minded activity, and if others within the organization fail to make up for the deficit, administrative processes will suffer. In contrast, midlevel managers often suffer from the reverse problem: a neglect of the collaborative style. It is easy for midlevel managers to ignore community concerns in favor of operations and their specific responsibilities, especially when those internal concerns are constantly evident and demanding.

Discussion of the collaborative style with an external focus began to appear in the mid-1990s in response to the leadership imperative for formation of long-term, public-private partnership contracts to rebuild public infrastructure (discussed in Chapter 11). In application, the focus is frequently on public problems that are too big for any one organization to solve alone, such as the 2010 Winter Olympics in Vancouver or the Big I (Interstate junction of I-25 and I-40), known as a transportation megaproject in New Mexico. The Big I project entailed redesign for safety of the tenth most congested interchange in the nation at that time; the project included fifty-five bridges on an Interstate highway that handled more than ten times the traffic volume for which it was designed and was plagued by almost two accidents daily. Collaborations and partnerships were needed between public entities such as the City of Albuquerque and the Federal Highway Administration, and private engineering firms and companies specializing in a range of products such as concrete, rebar, bearings, expansion devices, post-tensioning materials, casting forms and epoxy.

In the second decade of the twenty-first century, there is important discussion on sustainable communities as solutions to a healthier lifestyle. The collaborative leadership style is needed to address such inclusive challenges. Education about eating low-calorie foods does not achieve comprehensive results unless communities also have bicycle lanes and alternative food choices in the school cafeteria. The phrase that Hillary Rodham Clinton popularized in her book by the same name, "It takes a village," is applicable to the long-term partnerships and collaborative leadership needed between and within public health entities, private business, local schools, and city planning in order to build sustainable communities.

Chrislip and Larson (1994, 5) coined a good early definition of collaboration as a "mutually beneficial relationship between two or more parties to achieve common goals by sharing responsibility, authority, and accountability for achieving results. . . . The purpose of collaboration is to create a shared vision and joint strategies to address concerns that go beyond the purview of any particular party." Rosabeth Moss Kanter (1994, 97) discusses leaders who understand the critical business relationships "that cannot be controlled by formal systems but require [a] dense web of interpersonal connections." Noting that business relationships cannot be controlled by formal systems is an important introduction to the notion that hierarchical authority relationships do not work either internally or externally when collaboration is needed.

Archer and Cameron (2008, xv) also go beyond hierarchical relationships in saying that collaborative leaders with a passion for a particular cause "have to learn to share control, and to trust a partner to deliver, even though that partner may operate very differently from themselves." The collaborative leadership style is challenging because not every successful manager in business wishes to share knowledge externally to the extent necessary for real collaboration. Nor does every successful manager wish to share credit with others externally. Furthermore, feeling as if they are stripped of power and authority brings most managers out of their comfort zone into a complex system of synergy, and yet that is an inescapable requirement of partnerships that work well. Well-founded trust, in addition to any legal contracts, can be a firm base on which a partnership thrives.

Examples of the collaborative style abound when meaningful public-private partnerships are formed (presented in Chapter 11). Take, for instance, the case of R&R Development, a company that is aware of Roxbury's interest in building a metro station near property that the company currently owns (imaginary company and city names for purposes of confidentiality). The property is currently zoned for large single-family homes because that is R&R's specialty. John Risis, president of R&R Development, meets with Roxbury city planners in the belief that he will find a cooperative spirit and the support of city hall to help him submit plans based on mutual interests. He knows, however, that he will have to venture into a new business model. He begins the discussion by stating that both parties share an interest in the metro station being well-utilized, surrounded by mixed-use development with low-density housing, commercial, office, institutional, and other land uses. He insists that although his reputation in the community has been made as a builder of homes no smaller than 4,000 square feet, he shares the city planners' vision of a city with high walkability. He adds that he has the business contacts to realize such a vision and potential funding for the development, including the metro station itself, in exchange for revenue-sharing when the city enjoys a profit in future years. Having established a common basis in which mutual interests will be best served by partnering, John is successful in understanding the goals and plans of the city planners to such depth that he leaves the meeting confident he will be the successful bidder for at least part of the development. A city employee meets him at the elevator and says, "John, we thought we were going to have to buy your property and find a developer from another region of the country where mixed-use development is ahead of us here. So it comes as a pleasant surprise that R&R right here at home may have the willingness to partner with the city."

COMBINED STYLE

A **combined style** is the use of two or more styles simultaneously in a single fused approach, such as directive and supportive together. The behaviors will vary according to the styles that are fused, as will the dimensions of the combined style. It is natural, of course, for good leaders to rotate from one style to another, depending on the situation; however, rotating behaviors is not part of the combined style of leadership. It is also natural for good leaders to have a preferred style that they use instinctively and secondary styles that they use consciously, depending on the situation; however, simple conscious use of a behavior that is different from what is usual for the leader is not considered combined style.

A variety of combined styles can be cited as examples. Many of the taxonomies in the literature with fewer categories are simply combinations of various styles having similar characteristics. A directive style will not only include the narrower definition used here, but may also include aspects of delegative, achievement-oriented, and inspirational styles. A supportive style may implicitly include aspects of participative and inspirational styles. Thus, a combined style can simply be a cluster of styles with similarities.

However, some combined styles purposely integrate divergent elements or perspectives in order to achieve an overall balance. One of the most famous examples is team leadership, as defined by Blake and Mouton (1964, 1965) in their grid leadership theory. According to Blake and Mouton, universally ideal leaders are both supportive and directive, two conceptually distinctive styles. Likert's System 4 style is similar in its approach (1981). Later iterations of leader-member exchange theory implicitly recommend a combined directive, supportive, and participative style (Graen and Uhl-Bien 1995). Locke (2003) calls a combined style "integrated," which is defined as elements of top-down, bottom-up, and shared styles that are blended as circumstances dictate. Lipman-Blumen (2000) calls a combined style "connective," although she envisions it as a variety of alternating styles that match organizational needs.

The most inclusive combined style is the transformational style. For example, Bass's (1985) highly articulated transformational style explicitly includes all those discussed (although participative and delegative are implied rather than stated). In his hierarchy of leadership styles, leaders essentially begin by successfully employing directive behaviors (shedding a slothful laissez-faire style), next integrating achievement-oriented behaviors, and ultimately overlaying supportive and inspirational behaviors, informed by an external perspective. Such an approach to style has many merits. When well done, as Bass describes, it has intuitive appeal and brings a great deal of knowledge together in a single-style hierarchy. It implicitly acknowledges the complexity and artistry of using leadership style. The weaknesses are also substantial. Because of the breadth of the style, which ultimately becomes a universal approach, the advice for practicing managers becomes extremely abstract. Just when and how are various elements of a transformational style used in various concrete situations? To overcome this problem, Kouzes and Posner (1987) focus on inspirational behaviors (challenging the process, inspiring a shared vision, enabling others to act, modeling the way, and encouraging the heart), though then they are no longer really discussing transformational style with its style diversity, but rather some of its critical elements. The transformational approach is also highly biased in favor of change and inspirational behaviors, although often a more stable approach with a more mundane style may be appropriate.

This raises the question of whether a combined style is really a fused style or a series of rapidly alternating styles. It is easy to think of a supervisor who rotates a directive style in instructing and informing employees, concern and warmth in frequent consultations, participation in staff meetings and ad hoc problem discussions, and delegation with senior employees. The gentle manner the supervisor uses with employees causes followers to label this a supportive style overall, even though it is actually a more complex style. On the other hand, a supervisor may have a recalcitrant employee whom he must reprimand and direct (command performance improvement), while he simultaneously shows concern, empathy, and support (i.e., a truly fused style). Similarly, it is easy to imagine a transformational leader alternating between directional, supportive, and external foci as she proceeds through the days and weeks. It is also possible to imagine a transformational leader commanding followers but nonetheless inspiring them and stimulating their own personal sense of achievement. Think of a general just before battle, commanding, but exciting the troops with images of group success and individual valor and honor. In answering the question, then, depending on context, a combined style can be either a fused style or a rapidly alternating series of styles.

More important than settling questions of theoretical issues of style, however, is simply being able to analyze the different types of styles that are put forward by different researchers and being able to think of styles coherently as a practicing manager. Exhibit 2.3 (see next page) gives a summary of leader styles.

Some Examples of Pure Styles

Whereas combinations of intervening variables may call for a combination of styles, it is easier to understand the effects of intervening variables on leadership styles when a primary contingency situation dominates. Below are examples of situations in which the primary intervening variable would generally call for a relatively pure leadership style (shown at the end in parentheses).

1. Sam, a frontline supervisor, has an employee who has become increasingly schizophrenic in the past six months. The employee refuses to acknowledge the problem, which is probably due to a biochemical imbalance, and is becoming highly disruptive due to extreme paranoia and mood shifts (*directive*).
2. Susan, also a frontline supervisor, has a new employee who has tremendous potential but is a slow learner and highly insecure. The employee has the right social skills and disposition for the job, but is currently overwhelmed by the extensive technical demands of certifying clients and denying benefits (*supportive*).
3. Steve is the director of information technology not because he is a technical expert but because he has first-rate management skills. The last three directors all failed because of their general lack of management skills and their tendencies toward autocratic micromanagement, regardless of the situation. Steve's company has to change its backbone database management system. Although each of Steve's subordinates has an opinion about the best system to use, Steve has learned by talking with them that they do not agree on the same system. Steve is also aware that no one has consulted with the other departments that would be users of the system, such as finance and human resources (*participative*).
4. Sylvia is the director of an agency. Because of her position, she receives many legitimate, routine requests that must be channeled to departments to handle (*delegative*).
5. Sean is a manager in charge of a group of lawyers. To keep productivity up,

Exhibit 2.3 **Styles Commonly Described by Leadership Theories**

Leadership style	Narrative description	Behavioral competencies
Laissez-faire	Showing passivity or indifference about tasks and subordinates or purposely neglecting what could be seen as an area of responsibility	Tasks and people: a hands-off approach
Directive	Letting subordinates know what they are expected to do; giving specific guidance by utilizing task-oriented behaviors; asking subordinates to follow rules and procedures; scheduling and coordinating	Tasks: monitor, plan operations, clarify roles, inform, delegate Organizational: general management functions
Supportive	Showing consideration to the needs of followers; displaying concern for their needs; creating a friendly work environment for each worker	People: consult (listen), support, coordinate personnel, develop staff, recognize and motivate, build and manage teams, manage conflict
Participative	Consulting with subordinates and taking their opinions into account; providing advice rather than direction; establishing a friendly and creative work environment for team	Task: delegate People: consult (discuss), support, coordinate personnel, develop staff, recognize and motivate, build and manage teams, manage conflict, manage personnel change
Delegative	Allowing subordinates relative freedom for decision-making and from daily monitoring and short-term review	Task: delegate People: develop staff, motivate
Achievement-oriented	Setting challenging task goals; seeking task improvements; emphasizing excellence in follower performance; showing confidence that followers will perform well	Task: clarify roles, inform, delegate, problem-solving, manage innovation and creativity People: consult, develop staff, build and manage teams
Inspirational	Using intellectual stimulation (for new ideas or processes); using inspirational motivation (for group goals); use of charisma	Task: manage innovation People: manage personnel change Organization: scan the environment, strategic planning, vision articulation, network and partner, decision-making, manage organization change
Strategic	Focusing attention on organizational matters in the environmental context	Organization: scan the environment, strategic planning, vision articulation, network and partner, decision-making, manage organization change
Collaborative	Focusing on representation, external partnering, external networking in order to build a positive image and create goodwill, and enhance the professional or local community	Task: inform internally and externally People: consult (externally) Organization: network and partner
Combined	Using two or more styles simultaneously in a single fused style	Effective in complex situations when one single style does not match the situation

Notes: (1) Styles are not mutually exclusive categories; substantial overlap exists. (2) Styles examined here are generally based on relatively holistic assessments. Leadership theories looking at "styles" from a relatively narrow perspective (e.g., risk aversion, change style, communication style, planning style, etc.) are not included.

he must appeal to their sense of personal accomplishment and provide bench-mark standards they can customize to their specialized jobs (*achievement*).

6. Shelly is in charge of fleet maintenance for a state university that is under intense pressure to reduce costs. The large fleet maintained by the university provides convenience and control for the institution, but currently at a premium price. If fleet maintenance is not to be privatized, Shelly will need to dramati-cally change the business model, work routines, and performance standards. Her employees are only vaguely aware of the threat and she believes they are likely to become less motivated if they are not convinced that a positive change is likely and can be attractive to the group (*inspirational*).

7. Scott is the public affairs and legislative liaison. He is the "eyes and ears" of the organization. When he interacts with the top management team, he finds that others are generally unaware of the public affairs and legislative details to which he is accustomed (*strategic*).

8. Stedman, a marketing director in his small public relations firm, recently sought an appointment by the governor to work on a state commission dealing with trade because he has realized the importance of continually expanding external relationships. Stedman has already led his own firm to partner with the county economic development planners to stimulate additional export trade from businesses in the county, including some that might have been considered competitive in the past (*collaborative*).

INTERVENING AND MODERATING VARIABLES

Both intervening and moderating variables are considered contingency factors that affect outcomes. As touched upon briefly at the beginning of this chapter, an *intervening variable* is a factor that surfaces to explain the relationship between other variables. The intervening variable is not measured when testing the relationship between the variables because it has not been identified in a precise manner for its effect. The intervening variable can throw off interpretation of results in a study because it was not accounted for and was not measured. A factor such as employee willingness might influence leadership outcome, but willingness is an ambiguous factor typically not measured.

A *moderating variable* is known to have such a strong affect on the relationship between the independent and dependent variables that if the moderating variable itself is controlled, it will control the effect relationship that the independent variable has on the dependent variable. Moderating variables are measured, and the presence of this third variable modifies the original relationship between the independent and the dependent variables. For example, the statistical association between directive leadership style and productivity needs to be explained because just being directive does not make productivity change. Other variables intervene between style and productivity. The nature of the task being done, for example, surfaces to explain the relation between directive leadership and productivity and would therefore be studied in empirical research. Therefore, the task being done is an intervening variable.

An immense number of intervening variables affect a leader's preferred modes of action, or leadership styles, and the degree of effectiveness of those actions. What does the leader think the overall goals should be? What are the task skills of the followers? What is subordinate effort like? How well is work organized or structured, and how does this align with performance strategies? What types of constraints do leaders have to incorporate, including their own abilities such as traits, skills, and behavioral competencies? People studying leadership want to know not only which contingencies or intervening variables are important, but how important they are. For example, a researcher may test the common assumption that emergencies (one type of contingency) require a directive leadership style. Ideally, the investigator can examine situations in which identical emergencies are handled with and without a directive style. Further, the researcher would compare different types of emergencies using experimental and control groups. Alternatively, for example, the researcher may wish to test an intuitive assumption that lack of goal achievement (another type of contingency) is best dealt with by an achievement-oriented leadership style. Likewise, the investigator would wish to examine similar situations with lack of goal achievement, through experimental and control groups that are handled with and without an achievement-oriented style.

The range of intervening and moderating variables is extensive and includes contingencies such as the following:

1. leadership characteristics (traits and skills, behaviors, and leader perceptions of followers),
2. task characteristics (role, task, and organizational clarity and complexity),
3. subordinate characteristics (follower traits and skills, task commitment, and follower perceptions of leader),
4. organizational characteristics (power relationships, organizational design, external connectedness, and environmental uncertainty), and
5. other characteristics, such as ethics and gender. Exhibit 2.4 lists examples of these variables.

Leadership theories in the first half of the twentieth century tended to emphasize contingency variables pertaining to leader characteristics; task and subordinate characteristics were most heavily emphasized in the 1950s through the 1970s; and organizational and other characteristics were emphasized from the 1980s to the present. These intervening and moderating variables are discussed at length in the theory chapters. As seen by reviewing the individual theories, the more factors we want to incorporate, the more complex—and general—the theory inevitability becomes. To really understand theories well, it is important not only to know what factors are being considered, but also to be aware of the factors that are *not* being considered.

PERFORMANCE RESULTS

Performance goals for leadership results include specific outcomes desired to bring change needed for long-term effectiveness. Possible outcomes include a wide range of results involving development of a vision, communication of the vision, and

Exhibit 2.4

Variables Frequently Included in Major Leadership Theories

A. Leader characteristics
    1. Traits and skills
    2. Gender
    3. Ethics
    4. Leader attributions of followers
B. Task characteristics
    1. Role and task clarity
    2. Task ambiguity
    3. Complexity
    4. Task interdependence
C. Follower characteristics
    1. Traits and skills
    2. Team behavior
    3. Task and organizational commitment
    4. Follower attributions of leader
D. Organizational characteristics
    1. Power relationships
    2. Organizational and system design
    3. External connectedness
    4. Environmental uncertainty

motivation to attain the vision (Kotter 1990). Vision may include a wide variety of outcomes such as employee satisfaction, increased customer service, an improved environmental record, or a better OSHA rating. It should be noted that performance goals for management are also established in most organizations, such as goals for efficiency or process reliability. In contrast to performance goals for leadership, management performance goals tend to revolve around the more traditional functions of management—goals for planning, organizing, staffing, and controlling. Performance goals for both management and leadership are integral to overall organizational success; one without the other is not sufficiently balanced for practical, purposeful innovation and change. Performance goals for both management and leadership may be negotiated for the same individual when he or she is responsible for both the visionary aspects of long-term organizational accomplishment and the traditional functions of management.

In successful businesses, goals are often encouraged by leaders. These companies set goals for new products or services to account for a substantial percentage of sales each year. Incremental improvement of existing products is sometimes thought of as a long-term formula for decline. Learning from primary product users can be a formula for epic change and innovation. A classic example from the 1990s highlights how the 3M Dental Products Division set goals that would bring products introduced within a rolling five-year period from 12 percent to 45 percent of total annual sales. In five years, the division doubled its rate of profit, and over ten years doubled global sales. Having met its innovation goals, the division realized benefits in nearly all facets of its business.

CONCLUSION

This chapter provides a background and reference system to allow readers to assess and evaluate the contributions of major leadership theories. It describes a causal-chain framework that gives students a tool with which they can examine leadership theories through important components of leader behavior and styles, intervening and moderating variables, and performance results and goals.

We identified ten leadership styles. A leader using the laissez-faire style exhibits passive behavior or indifference about tasks and subordinates. A directive style is indicated when a leader lets subordinates know what they are expected to do, gives directions and guidance, asks subordinates to follow rules and procedures, and schedules and coordinates work activities. A supportive style is demonstrated by showing consideration toward followers, displaying concern for their needs, and creating a friendly work environment for each individual. Leaders using a participative style consult with subordinates and take their opinions into account, provide suggestions and advice rather than direction, and create a friendly and creative work environment for the team as a whole. A delegative style is defined as one allowing subordinates relative freedom for decision-making and from daily monitoring and short-term reviews. In an achievement-oriented style, a leader sets challenging task goals, seeks task improvements, emphasizes excellence in follower performance, and shows confidence that followers will perform well. An inspirational style uses intellectual stimulation in order to produce new ideas or to gain their acceptance for new approaches, inspirational motivation to achieve group goals, and heavy reliance on acceptance of the leader's wisdom and/or integrity by followers. A strategic style focuses attention on organizational matters and the environmental context. A collaborative style is noncompetitive and relies heavily on external networking, collegiality, trust, civic-mindedness, and partnering for the greater good. A combined style is the use of two or more styles simultaneously in a single fused style, such as directive and supportive styles melded together as one. It has been argued that although these ten styles are not mutually exclusive, they are distinctive enough to be conceptually useful because of the patterns they imply and because of their utilization by researchers and popular writers on leadership.

The intervening and moderating variables, or contingencies, affecting the business of leadership are extensive. Five clusters of commonly used contingencies have been discussed. One group deals with leader characteristics. When leader characteristics vary, how do and how should styles vary? Another group focuses on task characteristics. Task clarity, project ambiguity, and task interdependence are issues that affect style substantially. A third group encompasses characteristics of subordinates—their traits and skills, their commitment to task, and their attributions of leaders' ability and trustworthiness. Still another category of variables is organizational in nature. Power relationships, organizational design, external connectedness, and environmental uncertainty all affect the type of style that a leader uses. A fifth and final group comprises other characteristics such as gender and ethics.

While performance goals for management involve traditional functions such as staffing or planning, performance results and goals for leadership include any outcomes that are specified or implied in a theory. Traditionally, efficiency and effectiveness are implied, but possible outcomes include a range of items such as follower development, organizational alignment and change, and an increased dedication to customer service. Without question, to achieve change or reach the desired results in the business arena, performance goals for both the management and leadership spectrum can be, and are, important inspirational and motivational forces.

KEY TERMS

achievement-oriented style
causal-chain framework
collaborative style
combined style
contingency theories
delegative style
descriptive theories
directive style
empowerment

inspirational style
intervening variables
laissez-faire style
moderating variables
participative style
prescriptive theories
strategic style
supportive style
universal theories

RESOURCES

This Department of Transportation site contains success stories about transportation mega-projects. Become familiar with one of the stories, and explain how the collaborative leadership style worked and how it made the outcome possible.

- U.S. Department of Transportation, Federal Highway Administration, and University of Maryland University College, "Collaborative Leadership: Success Stories in Transportation Mega Projects," Fall 2004. www.fhwa.dot.gov/programadmin/mega/collaborative.cfm.

The media story about Major General George W. Weightman, charged with inappropriate use of laissez-faire leadership at Walter Reed Army Medical Center, has multiple dimensions, as do most events. Read more about Weightman in supplemental articles such as the following, and discuss the example from the textbook again.

- Tom Philpott, "Exclusive Interview: Maj. Gen. George W. Weightman," Helmets to Hardhats, March 6, 2007. http://info.helmetstohardhats.org/content/wounded-warriors/exclusive-interview-general-george-weightman.
- *Washington Post*, "Not 'a Good News Story': Why Is Gen. Kiley Back in Charge at Walter Reed?" Editorial, March 2, 2007. www.washingtonpost.com/wp-dyn/content/article/2007/03/01/AR2007030101516.html.

Find out more about the Thematic Apperception Test (TAT). Resources are readily available on David McClelland's achievement theory.

- NetMBA, "McClelland's Theory of Needs." www.netmba.com/mgmt/ob/motivation/mcclelland.

Innovation goals are felt to be important for performance results. However, if that is the case, how can the inertia cited in this *Harvard Business Review* blog be overcome?

- Andrew O'Connell, "Why I Don't Innovate at Work (or Watch Cooking Shows at the Gym)," *Harvard Business Review* blog, February 11, 2010. http://blogs.hbr.org/research/2010/02/why-i-dont-innovate-at-work-or.html.

DISCUSSION QUESTIONS

1. What are the major types of contingency factors considered in most leadership theories?
2. What differentiates the laissez-faire and delegative styles?
3. What is a directive style? What are the important differences among directive style subtypes?
4. What is a supportive style called when the approach is excessive and pushes out legitimate organizational concerns?
5. What are some other names that are used for a participative leadership style?
6. What leadership styles specifically focus on challenging goals and high expectations? How do the styles differ?
7. What types of leaders are likely to use an external style frequently?
8. What is a combined style and how is it conceived in significantly different ways?
9. Analyze the styles of a leader whom you either know well or whom you can interview. What is his or her style range? What are his or her strong or weak styles? When the leader uses a combined style, is it a fused style or a rotating style?
10. What is your opinion regarding the ability and willingness of leaders and managers to adjust from one leadership style to another? What is your opinion regarding the appropriateness of universal theories?

CLASSROOM ACTIVITY

Place the following components onto the causal-chain framework shown in Exhibit 2.1 and discuss in class how the framework supports clear analysis of leadership behavior. This is the same example, by the way, that was used earlier in the chapter to illustrate a primary intervening variable that would generally call for relatively pure directive leadership style.

- Leader behavior: The leader uses a directive style, clearly explaining to the subordinate what type of behavior is allowed and why disruptions will result in negative personnel action up to and including termination.

- Intervening variables: The employee refuses to acknowledge his highly disruptive behavior, which is probably due to a biochemical imbalance that is causing mood shifts.
- Performance results: When mood shifts begin to appear, the employee responds to the supervisor's ever-so-slight acknowledgment and stops to think through his behavior; highly disruptive behavior ceases.

CASE ANALYSIS

Julie Roehm graduated in engineering from Purdue University, where she had experience in the co-op program as a member of a package engineering team. It was there she discovered that she enjoyed the business side of marketing. In 2006, at age thirty-five, she was recruited to Wal-Mart headquarters in Bentonville, Arkansas, away from Chrysler's marketing communications directorship, where she was known for unconventional marketing campaigns while keeping an astute business eye on the bottom line. The vice president of marketing offered Roehm an alluring package to head up consumer advertising, replete with signing bonus, restricted stock, stock options, and bonuses beyond her base salary. She was tasked with helping to update the Wal-Mart brand. Wal-Mart's top managers wanted to bring in a colorful change agent to upgrade their gray, lackluster image and "everyday low prices" culture in order to attract more upscale buyers.

Upon arrival, she painted her corporate office chartreuse and brown (Berner 2007), a vivid contrast to the building's neutral interior. Rapidly, some relationships were reported to become strained, both within and outside of her department. External analysts thought it was, in part, because she was *doing more* rather than *listening more*. For example, she missed several Friday morning meetings with the chief executive and top 300 managers as she planned skits for the annual meeting (against tradition) and collected bids from ad agencies that were vying for a dazzling Wal-Mart contract. However, she failed to convince the merchandising department to follow fashion trends recommended by marketing and to remove what she felt was store clutter. In-store signs for "everyday low prices" actually seemed to increase. As weeks passed, top management gathered data showing that upscale buyers were not buying from Wal-Mart.

To make matters more contentious, Draftfcb, the creative ad agency that won the Wal-Mart contract, placed a celebratory ad in an industry publication. The ad said "It's good to be on top" and showed a lion on top of its mate. It was not long before Roehm was called to a meeting that reportedly took only seven minutes during which she was challenged first by the marketing vice president as to how the ad agency had been chosen, and then by a representative from the legal department about accepting gifts from the agency and about having an alleged affair with a subordinate. Julie Roehm was then fired after ten months on the job.

After her termination, David Kiley (2006) wrote critically about both sides. As if he were addressing Julie Roehm, he says: "You were part of a team, not the Chief Marketing Officer. And you weren't there long enough to justify the high profile you were creating for yourself. Remember: It's the whale that comes to the surface that gets harpooned. Wal-Mart has a very conservative culture. You can't ram change through a place like that. . . . You'll get another gig. But your brand has gone from '*provocative*' to '*notorious*.'"[2]

DISCUSSION QUESTIONS

1. How would you characterize Julie Roehm's leadership style?
2. What moderating variable is most dominant in affecting the impact of her style?
3. To what extent did Wal-Mart's organizational culture impact Roehm's overall performance results? Is there a different kind of organizational culture in which she could be more effective? Defend your position.

NOTES

1. The Malcolm Baldrige performance management model encourages quality judgments to be made about an organization in seven areas: leadership; strategic planning; customer and market focus; measurement, analysis, and knowledge management; human resource focus; process management; and results. Annual Malcolm Baldrige Quality awards have been given by the president of the United States ever since Congress established the award program in 1987, named after the 26th Secretary of Commerce Malcolm Baldrige who was an advocate of quality management. Following an application process, organizations are judged on all criteria by examiners, and then finalists are visited by examiners. All applicants receive from the examiners a comprehensive evaluation of strengths and weaknesses, designed to help the organization continue to improve its organizational performance and its value to its customers or clients.

2. Students are encouraged to read online U.S. District Court documents for greater depth of understanding. As an example, see U.S. District Court in the Eastern District of Michigan Southern Division, Case No. 07-CV-10168, *Julie Ann Roehm v. Wal-Mart Stores, Inc.*, http://online.wsj.com/public/resources/documents/walmart-roehm20070525.pdf.

This case is summarized from the three sources cited in this section and is shared for the sole purpose of providing an in-depth opportunity for learning about the influence of different cultural environments on leadership and what constitutes effective leadership in different environments.

3 From Early Managerial to Transactional Theories of Leadership

Strong management alone can create a bureaucracy without purpose, but strong leadership alone can create change that is impractical.
—Gary Yukl, *Leadership in Organizations*, 6th ed.

This chapter progresses from the classical Western perspectives on administrative and management theory, through the trait theory, and on to the more detailed transactional approaches for leadership theory today, including both situational or behavioral, and contingency. Yet before focusing on modern Western approaches, we begin with a very brief discussion of collectivism and individualism in connection with leadership so that the biases (preferences) of the Western tradition are placed in a global context.

COLLECTIVIST VERSUS INDIVIDUALIST APPROACHES TO LEADERSHIP

To know that the study of management is deeply rooted in history, we need only study water management in ancient Greece, construction of the pyramids in ancient Egypt, or control and recycling of building materials for quality construction of public projects in ancient China. In postindustrial Asia, the study of leadership continues to be not a study of individualism, but of collectivism. **Collectivism** in this application refers to how people of a culture think about the importance of group relationships and economic systems of ownership by the people as a whole, as opposed to the importance of acting independently. Consistent with cultural values, the work group is central to an individual's identity with his or her organization, and is coupled with the notion that cooperation and competition coexist effectively. Although collectivism and consensus decision-making are not synonymous, when consensus is practiced, there is low value placed on individualism. The Iroquois Confederacy Grand Council used consensus-style decision-making as early as 1142. In fact, the self-proclaimed name "Iroquois" means "people of the longhouses," the narrow, linear homes that collectively held more than twenty families. Quakers, too, in seventeenth-century America were known for their consensus decision-making approach, characterized as having the goal of "unity, not unanimity."

In the preindustrial United States, a variety of collective approaches to leadership

59

can be explored. For example, the Nez Perce Leadership Council is one early example of an approach to leadership that differs from a focus on individual leadership styles (Humphreys et al. 2007). The Nez Perce were known for diverse accomplishments, including breeding the spotted Appaloosa horse, offering peace and assistance to Lewis and Clark in 1805 when the explorers were desperate, and being clever and successful in battle. These accomplishments were reached through a leadership approach that involved extended families living in bands under the watchful eye of a headman. For lack of an overall tribal structure, the Leadership Council, consisting of the headmen, elders, shamans and war leaders, would meet to reach consensus on major tribal decisions. A global understanding of leadership is truly possible only with a thorough examination of both the collectivist and individualist approaches.

Academic study of management and leadership emerged in the United States around the turn of the twentieth century with a focus on the individual, as a reflection of U.S. culture. A systematic scientific study of leadership was fully under way in the early 1930s. The eclectic approach that emerged, bringing together research from economics, sociology, psychology, and statistics, was termed "classical management theory." Both management and leadership developed paradigms that guided researchers for nearly fifty years. Calls for a shift in the fields began to be heard in the late 1940s (Dahl 1947; Simon 1947; Stogdill 1948; Waldo 1948). Although work from this era is often characterized as simplistic, a fairer assessment is that the frameworks proposed tended to be narrow in scope and purpose.

Today, the field of leadership research is increasingly sensitive to collectivist approaches in its "postmodern" stage. Postmodern here refers to seeing theory-building from a multifaceted, less hierarchical approach that looks more critically at traditional power structures. Some postmodern approaches emphasize the leader as a part of the leadership process (i.e., a relational approach; Uhl-Bien 2006), rather than the leader as dominant factor. Increased emphasis on the roles of followers in the leadership process is one result (Kellerman 2008). Other contemporary work incorporates complexity theory, which emphasizes the many factors impinging on leadership, of which the leader is but one (Schneider and Somers 2006). Still other researchers emphasize chaos theory, which pays special attention to "tipping points," "butterfly effects," and radical incidents in relation to leadership (Osborn and Hunt 2007). Chaos theory is helpful in understanding dramatic events that seem to suddenly emerge, such as the collapse of the world financial system in 2008. Nonetheless, we start our review with the American tradition that emphasized individuals as leaders for the most part until the last twenty years, when team approaches and empowerment began to reinvigorate an appreciation of collectivist approaches.

THREE CLASSICAL APPROACHES TO MANAGEMENT

The first half of the twentieth century is considered the classical management period. Three approaches dominated most management thinking and writing: Taylor's scientific management, Fayol's administrative theory, and Weber's theory of bureaucracy. Though all three remain in the common management wisdom today, they are not the basis for most of today's research or the basis of leadership studies.

SCIENTIFIC MANAGEMENT

In the United States, the **scientific management** movement was a reaction to major changes that had occurred in the national economy, which was becoming an industrial power. Manufacturing and business operations—emerging from a period of cottage industries that were small and randomly ordered—were frequently poorly organized because they failed to change practices as their industries matured and new technologies emerged. Scientific management authorities such as Taylor (1911), Gantt (1916), and Gilbreth and Gilbreth (1917) advocated the use of analytic tools with which to design efficient management practices. One powerful analytic tool was the **time-and-motion study**. Experts would study a process (such as laying bricks) and the workers' patterns of activity to determine (1) the most efficient way for individuals to do the work and (2) the most efficient way to use factory design or overall organization to coordinate the workers' activities. It was during this period in history that training became professionalized through standardization, and work specialization resulted in enormous advances in assembly-line technology.

The term "scientific management" is still in frequent use today; the tools of scientific management and its focus on work analysis and efficiency at the worker and unit level, originally advocated a century ago, are integral to standard management practices. The decreased cost of goods and therefore increased sales, increased employment at higher-level positions, and increased wages from higher-level jobs still remain valid reasons today for the use of analytic tools in order to achieve greater efficiency.

United Parcel Service (UPS) is a 100-year-old company that has continued its focus on *The Principles of Scientific Management* (the name of Frederick Taylor's 1911 publication). Whether early time-and-motion studies were done by supervisors holding clipboards, or later by workers utilizing handheld technology to enter tracking data on every package, efficiency remained a key business goal. Because UPS employs automated route-planning, automated truck-packing, and bar code tags, the company can track the precise location of 16 million packages delivered each business day, whether in a truck or on a plane. Therefore, it was a logically progressive business step to introduce a new service called "Delivery Intercept" for customers who send out the wrong product to the wrong person or need to "intercept" delivery at any point prior to reaching the receiver. In part because of its important emphasis on efficiency through scientific management principles, UPS was voted by business-people in *Fortune*'s 2007, 2008, and 2009 polls as one of the thirty most admired companies overall.

ADMINISTRATIVE THEORY

Administrative theory is a cornerstone of classical management. Even when managers have instructed workers in efficient protocols and have clarified best practices, they still have substantial responsibilities in staffing, planning, and communicating with superiors on productivity and planning issues. This approach emphasized the role of mid- and senior-level managers in organizing rationally at a high level of organizational activity. Henri Fayol, a French mining engineer, was an administrative theorist with considerable influence in the early twentieth century. **Fayol's administrative theory** was built on personal observation of what worked (1917). His desire for an "administrative science" with a consistent set of principles that all organizations must apply in order to run properly was realized in his writings on administrative theory that emphasized fourteen Management Principles and Five Elements of Management. His Management Principles outlined the most basic guidelines such as "unity of command," which stated that each worker should have only one boss, and the "scalar chain," which delineated the hierarchical line of authority, from the top management on down, necessary for unity of direction, and which allowed for lateral communication as long as superiors know that the communication is occurring. His **Five Elements of Management** are more akin to what other theorists call their principles of management: plan (prevoyance for forecast and strategy), organize (build material and human structure), command (maintain activity among personnel), coordinate (bind and harmonize all activity), and control (actions are in conformity with established rule).

During the early twentieth century, management theorists devised slightly different lists of the functions of management. Gulick's (1937) summary of the principles of management has become an acronym in the management literature referred to as POSDCoRB, which stands for planning, organizing, staffing, directing, coordinating, reporting, and budgeting. Just as scientific management focused primarily on the study and efficient design of worker and unit systems, the principles approach focused on the study of what managers do within organizations. Important concepts such as unity of command and span of control (the number of subordinates that report to each manager) emerged. Just as scientific management experts argued for expert analysis of line workers' job functions and unit coordination, advocates of the principles approach encouraged analysis of manager functions to ensure that responsibilities were reasonable and not excessively fragmented. Although some of the specific prescriptions that were relevant for their time are obsolete, the general ideas behind a principles approach are still valid. That is, what managers do needs to be analyzed by experts and studied by organizational constituents, which requires self-conscious rationality and extensive training.

Today, the list of the functions of management is often modified to cover planning, organizing, staffing, directing, and controlling. But just like the first classical approach of scientific management, the principles of management originally brought to light by Fayol remain in use today as an outline for introductory management textbooks because they cover generally "what managers do."

BUREAUCRACY

The third classical approach, **Weber's theory of bureaucracy**, also remains in current use, although it is not in vogue to point out the benefits or virtues of bureaucracy. This classical management approach described how a bureaucracy should be established and even cautioned against potential excesses of bureaucracy that are now taken to be its nemesis. Max Weber, a German sociologist and political economist, concentrated on power and authority in large-scale organizations (1921). He wrote about an efficient organizational form that specified jobs with detailed rights, obligations, responsibilities, and scope of authority. The importance of unity of command was highlighted, just as it was by Fayol. There was to be training in job requirements and extensive use of written documents for the consistent application of rules. Although these notions seem natural today, Weber wrote at a time when favoritism was rampant and job appointments were not based on merit, competence, or experience. Bureaucracies were to be impersonal (thought to be positive, in contrast to personal favoritism not based on merit) and always rational. Business during Weber's time was not characterized by rapid technological change; he wrote about bureaucracy as an enterprise that was well adapted to the operational routine in organizations that surrounded him.

Weber also wrote about dysfunctions of bureaucracy carried to the extreme, which can become too impersonal and stultifying in dealing with individual cases if rules are followed, particularly in an overly centralized manner and to the exclusion of reason. In essence, he warned about the very excesses of bureaucracy that concern today's management theorists. At best, elements of bureaucracy in organizations today should avoid the excesses about which Weber cautioned, lest the chapter's opening quotation from Yukl be realized. When well executed with centrality of purpose, elements of bureaucracy can support purposeful organizational activity.

Although classical management theory did much to propel management into a science and profession by emphasizing careful analysis, planning, and implementation at all levels, its contributions to leadership theory were more modest. Classical approaches assume high leader control, high use of formal authority and extrinsic incentives, and an internal focus. The only style assumed is directive and the only kinds of outcomes of interest are unit or organizational production and efficiency improvements. An important moderating factor is the use of analytic and management tools. This results in a simple causal model: The more that a directive style relying on analytic tools is used and used well, the better unit and organizational performance will be. The logic is summarized in Exhibit 3.1.

The uncomplicated classical approaches to management are not without virtue. First, a particularly important tacit statement we can infer today is that the authoritarian management style of individuals so popular in the first half of the twentieth century was different from a directive style. The directive style, properly engaged, is employee-centered and uses analysis and rationality before implementing formal authority; it has an important role among the commonly used leadership styles. The authoritarian style is manager-centered and uses formal authority based on tradition.

Second, classical management theory helped establish crucial aspects of what has long been considered pivotal for successful leaders. For example, without classical management we would not have as strong a foundation for efficiency of operations. It keeps our eye on the ratio of outputs to total inputs. It is quite possible the more modern approaches emphasizing leader behaviors that enhance vision and effectiveness may have been employed at the expense of also emphasizing efficiency as a component of management.

The limitations of classical management approaches are also apparent. The focus is narrow, thus leaving a great deal out of the management and leadership equations. At times, too, it may appear that the classical approaches focus more on management

Exhibit 3.1   **Classical Management Theory Causal-Chain**

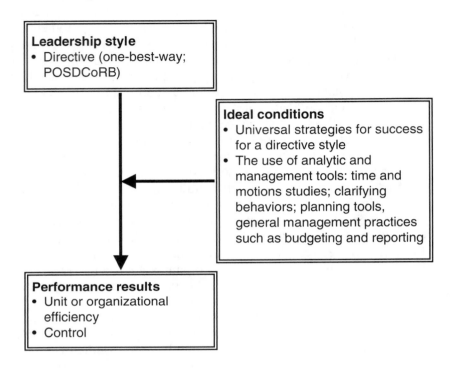

or operations than on leadership. There are styles other than directive, there are tools other than analytic and management-oriented ones that affect performance, and there are types of performance results other than efficiency. The weaknesses of overextending the theory in the first half of the twentieth century were less noticeable in a climate in which organizations utilized more routine processes and in which management experience was largely sufficient for all design and problem-solving. Today, an exclusively directive style is generally dysfunctional because it prevents necessary worker contributions and frustrates the educated workforce that drives services.

TRAIT THEORY

The **trait theory** is examined in Chapter 4 through a listing of personality characteristics, classic motivational drives, and value orientations. Here it is presented in terms of its contribution to early managerial approaches to leadership. Influence from psychology on management theory has been seen in many ways over the years because of the eclectic nature of the study of management. For example, Carl Jung, the famed Swiss psychologist who wrote on the collective unconscious, was an early colleague of Sigmund Freud. Although they ultimately split because of differences in emphasis and hypothesis, both began writing during the 1920s of the classical approaches to management. Jung highlighted what he called "temperaments," or genetically determined traits that shape one's manner. He created the familiar classifications of "introvert" and "extrovert," depending on the individual's relationship to the external world (Corbett 2009).

Another psychologist, Gordon Allport, was interested in the study of personality and wrote in the mid-twentieth century about the importance of an individual's "central traits," which are those that make up the bulk of personality. If there is one trait that dominates, Allport theorized, it can become the individual's "cardinal trait." Interestingly, Allport claimed that these traits were environmentally influenced until they become integral to the individual (Pettigrew 1999).

A mother-daughter team, Katharine Cook Briggs and Isabel Briggs Myers, who were students of Jung's theory in the 1920s developed a personality test based on his temperaments, called the Myers-Briggs Type Indicator, published in the 1940s. When scored, the instrument describes sixteen distinctive personality types that result from various combinations of Jung's temperaments. Beyond extrovert-introvert temperaments were individual preferences for sensing versus intuition information processing, thinking versus feeling, and judging versus perceiving structures relative to the outside world. The Myers-Briggs instrument is still used today as an introduction to management development workshops to help attendees identify their own traits and understand more about their own personality in relation to others (Myers and Briggs Foundation 2010).

Since the study of management and leadership is eclectic, it is no surprise that at the same time in history that the field of psychology emphasized the study of traits, the focus spilled over to management theory. Following from the period of classical approaches to management theory, the trait theory bridged to a new era prior to the mid-twentieth century.

The theory attempted to identify traits that were particularly suited to leadership and then to identify individuals with those traits or combination of traits. Since Jung and other psychologists of the era taught that people are born with inherited traits, the focus of this approach was not on *teaching* behaviors that would result in effective leadership. The underlying assumption of trait theory in management study was that leaders have certain *inherent* characteristics that are utilized across time to enhance organizational performance and leader prestige. The notion was that traits affect behaviors and behaviors influence effectiveness. In other words, as was often stated, "leaders are born, not made."

Prior to the mid-twentieth century, the **Great Man theory**—which in today's world appears sexist, but was probably not consciously so—emerged to distinguish natural leaders based on inherited traits and accomplishments (Carlyle 1840). The notion was that a particular condition at a particular time brought about the emergence of the particular "great man" who was needed to deal with it. In political-social terms, Napoleon Bonaparte, William Lloyd Garrison, or Abraham Lincoln would be proof of the theory for those who believed that such individuals rose to greatness not for reasons of inherited position, wealth, or physical attractiveness, but by being the right person for the time. Fate was believed to play a major role in the course of history, so it was widely accepted in the Great Man approach that a few individuals were born to lead and the masses were born to follow. The theory is highly relevant to the business world, where innumerable self-made business magnates have had great influence—for example, Andrew Carnegie, Leland Stanford, Sam Walton, Bill Gates, Oprah Winfrey, and Warren Buffet. Lest we think self-made business moguls are only an American phenomenon, international examples of successful leaders who also happened to be self-made billionaires include Carlos "Slim" Helu (Mexico—CEO of Telmex, Telcel and América Móvil and thought to be the wealthiest person in the world as of 2010), Amancio Ortega (Spain—fashion entrepreneur), Theo Albrecht (Germany—CEO of the Aldi Nord discount supermarket chain and owner of Trader Joe's in the United States), Vladimir Lisin (Russia—chairman of Novolipetsk Steel), and Yan Cheung (China—paper manufacturer Nine Dragons). The Great Man theory, however, did not explain which traits were the basis for leadership success in general, and attention turned to the investigation of specific traits such as gender, need for achievement, appearance, intelligence, and personal energy.

The ultimate hope of the trait theory was to identify a master list of traits—essentially a master style—that would prescribe the ideal leader. However, as early as 1948, Stogdill asserted two problems with this master-list approach to leadership. First, no traits were universally required for leadership. Second, leadership varied extensively according to the "characteristics, activities, and goals of the followers" (64). The field persisted by examining a wide variety of leader traits that bore a positive correlation to leadership. Many studies found that "the average person who occupied a position of leadership exceeded the average member of his or her group, to some degree, in the following respects: (1) sociability, (2) initiative, (3) persistence, (4) knowing how to get things done, (5) self-confidence, (6) alertness to and insight into situations, (7) cooperativeness, (8) popularity, (9) adaptability, and (10) verbal facility" (Bass 1990, 75). Following his reviews of the literature, Stogdill, who was the most influential scholar to address the subject of traits, concluded that traits could be studied relative to their interaction with situational factors in the future of management research.

In terms of leadership style, the underlying notion was that a master list of traits would eventually provide the basis for a combined style. That is, even though traits are not actual behaviors, they were known to guide activity (e.g., knowing how to get things done or sociability as traits may guide organizational activity effectively) and also to guide character that underlies behavior (e.g., persistence or adaptability). Bass and Stogdill's list is indeed a useful starting point for thinking about the types and qualities of behaviors that are typically significant. One limitation of this approach is that it does not indicate either when certain traits are critical or when they can be omitted, without extensive situational analysis. In fact, two leaders with different traits can achieve the same level of success, and, more importantly, the same leader could have the same traits in two different situations, only to succeed in one and fail miserably in the other. As researchers attempted to find the ideal list of traits, their lists varied widely. Evaluations of the trait literature show that "one problem with early trait research was that there was little empirically substantiated personality theory to guide the search for leadership traits" (House and Aditya 1997, 410). "As a consequence of the lack of theory and valid measurement instruments, both the traits studied and the way they were operationalized varied widely among investigators. Further, neither specific situational demands of leaders nor the degree to which the situation permitted the behavioral expression of personality inclinations were taken into account" (ibid 411).

Exhibit 3.2 **Universal Trait Theory Causal-Chain**

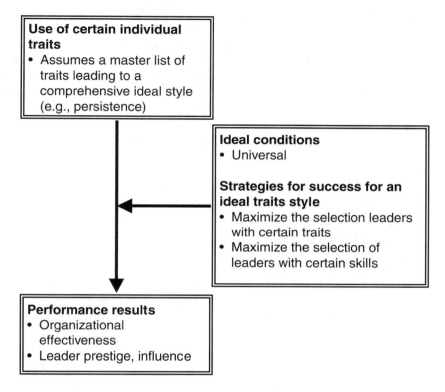

Further explanation of traits as part of leadership competency will be provided in Chapter 4, presented through discussion of six personality characteristics, two classic motivational drives, and two value orientations. The underlying causal model is shown in Exhibit 3.2.

BEHAVIORAL THEORY: BLAKE AND MOUTON

With the rise of the behavioral sciences, the trait theory fell out of favor as researchers became discouraged from lack of valid measurements and few empirical data substantiating personality theory to guide the search. Efforts were made to describe leader behaviors rather than leader traits. In addition, researchers such as Warren Bennis and Burt Nanus (1985) considered the proposal that "leaders are born, not made" as myth. They contended that leadership can be learned. Therefore, scholars have directed their focus for over fifty years primarily toward behavioral theories, contingency theories, and transactional approaches.

Behavioral approaches were under way in the 1950s. Some of the implicit leadership assumptions of the early management and trait theories were consciously challenged by the basic research conducted at Ohio State University, the University of Michigan, and other settings. Some studies focused on what managers do and others focused on what leadership behaviors were most effective.

The trait theory approach relies on personality that a leader "has." The behavioral approach emphasizes what leaders "do" and the activities that they undertake. Studies done at Ohio State used a method of winnowing a list of 1,800 behaviors down to 150, whereby the Leader Behavior Description Questionnaire was devised. Leaders were then rated by the frequency of display of each behavior. Ultimately, two dominant factors were determined to describe core leadership behavior: task-oriented behaviors (initiation of structure) and people-oriented behaviors (consideration). Task behaviors are critical to the organizational aspects of goal accomplishment, while relationship behaviors are critical to the human aspects of getting a job done through motivation. One of the first popular theories that tried to make sense of the relations-oriented and task-oriented dichotomy of leadership was the **managerial grid**, proposed by Robert Blake and Jane Mouton in 1964. It was called "grid theory" because it locates five leadership styles on a grid constructed of two behavioral axes. The managerial grid thus integrates relationship and task behaviors.

Grid theory largely fits into a universal, rather than contingency, approach to leadership. While the authors acknowledge situational factors (Blake and Mouton 1982), they do not address them as a primary focus of their model. The primary focus is instead to help leaders develop the "team" style that combines maximum concern for people and concern for results. According to Blake and Mouton, leaders should be aware of situational factors and should select ideal behaviors accordingly, always striving to achieve a combined style that they propose as ideal. The causal model implicit in Blake and Mouton's grid theory is illustrated in Exhibit 3.3.

Concern for task or *concern for production* is the horizontal axis and *concern for people* is the vertical axis in grid theory. Each axis varies from 1 (low) to 9 (high). A 1,1 leader has little concern for either subordinates or production. This is called an "impoverished" management style. A 9,1 task-oriented leader places great emphasis on efficiency and considers workers merely as vehicles of production. Because efficiency in operations is the exclusive concern, "human elements interfere to a minimum degree" (Blake and Mouton 1985, 12). This is called an "authority-compliance" or "authority-obedience" management style. In contrast, a 1,9 leader places great emphasis on people concerns, which in turn leads to "a comfortable, friendly organization atmosphere and work tempo." This is called a "country club" management style. A 5,5 leader combines both concern for production and people, but not at optimal levels. This approach, which leads to "adequate organization performance," is called "organization man" management. Blake and Mouton's ideal style is **9,9 team leadership** or the "team management" style, which combines both elements at high levels. "Work accomplishment is from committed people; interdependence through a 'common stake' in organization purpose leads to relationships of trust and respect" (Blake and Mouton 1985, 12). The managerial grid is illustrated in Exhibit 3.4.

Team management—which is based on trust, respect, and openness—calls for management objectives that are mutually determined, clarification of organizational goals in alignment with worker needs, and creative use of worker talents and skills. Many managers espouse this style and self-describe themselves as 9,9 leaders, but when provided feedback on their actual style, find that their perceptions and those

Exhibit 3.3 **Blake and Mouton's Grid Theory Causal-Chain**

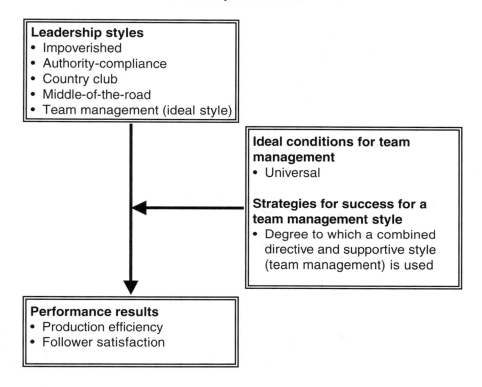

of their subordinates vary markedly (Blake and Mouton 1985), and many move to self-descriptions as 5,5 managers.

Grid theory was the first popular theory of leadership that utilized the task–people duality. Part of this success was due to the elegance and directness of the theory and its appeal at an intuitive level. Therefore, it provided an excellent heuristic framework for training purposes as well as an overarching ideal of management behavior. Yet the theory also suffers from a variety of important deficiencies. First, as a universal theory, it provides no alternative acceptable leadership style to the "team" style, and it gives little explanation about why leader behavior varies from one situation to another. Not surprisingly, empirical support has been modest because of its lack of situational discrimination (e.g., Weed, Mitchell, and Moffitt 1976). Problematic is that the 9,9 or team management style does not always seem to be ideal because correlations to subordinate performance are weak. Even though a balance of *concerns* for task and people may be preferable most of the time, it is not hard to envision many situations in which a disproportionately directive (authority-obedience) or supportive (country club management) leader behavior would be more appropriate (e.g., Miner 1982). Because Blake and Mouton were intentionally focused on *concern* for people and task rather than on *behavior* that reflects those concerns, researchers' ability to obtain reliable correlations to performance is diluted. A hardworking, perfectionist subordinate who has just discovered her own error may need a great deal of support but no

Exhibit 3.4   **The Managerial Grid**

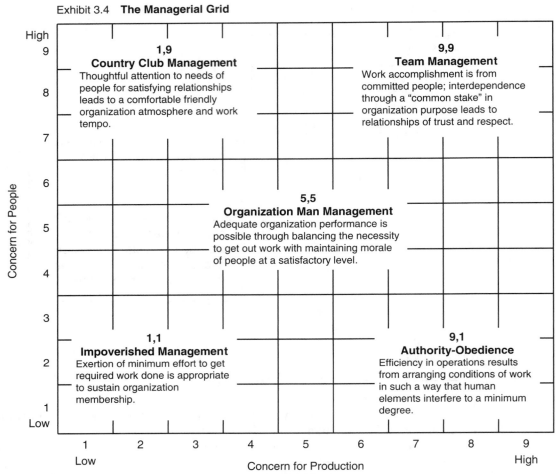

Source: The Managerial Grid figure from *The Managerial Grid III: The Key to Leadership Excellence*, by Robert R. Blake and Jane Srygley Mouton. (Houston: Gulf Publishing Company), Copyright © 1985, p. 12. Reproduced by permission.

directive behavior, while a highly selfish and destructive employee who is about to be terminated may misinterpret supportive behavior as weakness to be manipulated. Thus the 9,9 style as a one-best-way style may be a useful ideal for new managers to think about their attitude in getting jobs done, but it does not present detailed advice on leader behavior that is needed in different situations or provide a mechanism to handle the many exceptions that leaders encounter in various situations with which they must deal daily.

CONTINGENCY THEORY: HERSEY AND BLANCHARD

When a theory identifies leadership style effectiveness in terms of contingency variables, it is referred to as a contingency theory. Such a theory can be thought of as the

Exhibit 3.5 **Situational Leadership Causal-Chain**

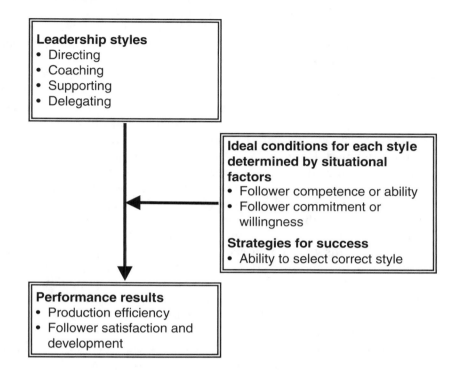

"if-then" approach: "if" X is true about the situation, "then" Y is the recommended leadership style. Thus, contingency theories help to explain the variables that determine what style is most effective.

HERSEY AND BLANCHARD'S SITUATIONAL LEADERSHIP®

Unlike the universal 9,9 approach advocated in the managerial grid, some theorists advocated a situational approach in which the recommended leadership style differed depending on a combination of circumstances. The most popular of these approaches has been **Situational Leadership®** as put forward by Hersey and Blanchard in 1969. The formative situations that they proposed were based on follower capacity in terms of ability and willingness. How able are followers and what are their levels of motivation? Depending on one's analysis of these contingencies, situational leadership can prescribe one of four different leadership styles: directing, coaching, supporting, and delegating (1969, 1972). The performance goals that they assume are primarily related to production, but they do consider follower satisfaction and development as well. The causal-chain model is illustrated in Exhibit 3.5.

As Hersey and Blanchard have responded to their critics, they have varied some minor aspects of the contingencies in discussion, but have kept the styles constant. In all versions of situational leadership there is a contingency variable called follower maturity that is composed of two elements: job maturity and psychological maturity. Job maturity is composed of experience, education, and capacity. Is the follower able to do the task or not? The progression of competence or ability can be relatively straightforward over time. Generally speaking, competence increases in a linear fashion, assuming good instruction and feedback.

The second element, which has varied slightly in different versions, is attitudinal. The focus is on the worker's willingness or commitment to do the job. In turn, willingness is based on motivation and confidence. It functions in a curvilinear manner over time. Willingness starts on a high level as new employees come to jobs full of excitement and enthusiasm. However, as the realities of the job and the challenges of reaching mastery sink in over time, motivation sags. In the long term, however, as workers become highly competent and absorb professional values, their commitment increases again. The developmental aspect of situational leadership largely depends on this pattern being a relatively universal one—high, low, high. However, it is much disputed whether this is so or whether many other common attitudinal patterns also exist such as low, medium, high (especially as related to confidence) or even high, medium, low (as when employees experience burnout). Leader styles are a combination of directive and supportive behaviors. Directive behaviors include monitoring, directing, instructing, clarifying, setting goals, establishing timelines, and so on. The emphasis is on one-way communication. Supportive behaviors include listening, various types and levels of inclusion, and encouragement. Hersey and Blanchard's "directing" style is composed of high directive behavior and low supportive behavior. A "coaching" style is composed of high directive and supportive behavior. A "supporting" style is composed of low directive and high supportive behavior. A "delegating" style is composed of low directive and supportive behavior. Their situational model is illustrated in Exhibit 3.6.

Hersey and Blanchard explain that followers who are low in competence but high in commitment, such as new employees, are eager for instruction and structure but do not need much supportive behavior. These types of situations call for a directing style. Followers who are moderate in competence but low in commitment because of a lack of confidence generally continue to need a lot of both directive behavior and supportive behavior to encourage them or a coaching style that encourages high engagement with subordinates and extensive supervision. As followers' competence continues to increase within the moderate range, enabling them to handle problems and issues, leaders should provide lower direction and maintain high support through a supporting style. Finally, highly mature followers need little direction or support, since they will seek advice and technical support as needed. The delegating style assumes that relative worker independence is both a reward and an efficiency strategy.

The strengths of this theory are significant. The first is that various aspects of the model have intuitive appeal. The job maturity aspect has tremendous face validity because it uses a widely accepted developmental learning model. When people do not know how to do something, they need direction; as they learn, they need less and less direction. In similar fashion, supportive behavior should shift with types of needs and maturity of the followers. Because of its intuitive appeal, this model has been the most widely used in applied training settings. Moreover, the principles behind the

Exhibit 3.6 **Situational Leadership Model**

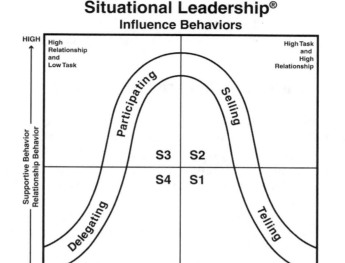

model are easy to master because leadership style is based only on follower maturity. Further, the model is highly prescriptive, providing clear diagnoses for practitioners who like answers more than abstract theories. Finally, the theory emphasizes leadership style range and adaptability. The idea that leaders have a variety of styles they use and varying skill in each of them is a valuable concept for leaders to grasp because leadership flexibility enhances overall capacity.

The weaknesses of the model are also substantial. First, the basis for determining the correct leadership style is quite narrow. Style is based only on subordinate competence and commitment, excluding other contingencies such as environmental, organizational, or leader factors. Second, the psychological maturity aspect of the theory is quite loose, and explanations have varied significantly about the pattern and connection to leadership style. Overall, the single, nonlinear pattern proposed in different versions of situational leadership is unconvincing in a tougher analysis. Why should the first flush of commitment generally decrease over time? Further, although some support has been provided (e.g., Hambleton and Gumpert 1982), overall, the level of empirical support is quite low. Indeed, generally the research community has responded with either negative findings (e.g., Blake and Mouton 1982; Fernandez and Vecchio 1997; Graeff 1997) or concerns about the fundamental explanations of the theory.

INTERACTION AND INTERACTIVE PROCESS THEORIES

It was a natural flow from early contingency approaches to explain more about the leader-follower relationships in leadership theories that followed. The theories can become complex as they are used to explain the relationship in the context of many factors pertaining to the circumstances, the leader, and the follower. These theories are still thought of as contingency approaches, with a focus on leader-follower relationships as an interactive process; how one participant changes the other is important. For example, a leader may normally assume that employees with college degrees need little direction to do the job, but if qualified followers repeatedly state that instructions are unclear, the leader will likely use a different style because of that interaction. In the two examples that follow, the path-goal theory and the LMX theory, the leader-follower relationship of mutual influence is evident.

PATH-GOAL THEORY

Path-goal theory asserts that "leaders, to be effective, engage in behaviors that complement subordinates' environments and abilities in a manner that compensates for deficiencies and is instrumental to subordinate satisfaction and individual and work unit performance" (House 1996, 323). In other words, it is the leader's responsibility to align worker and organizational goals and then to ensure that the employee's path to goal attainment is clear. The theoretical foundation of path-goal theory derives from both social exchange theory (Hollander 1958; Homans 1958) and expectancy theory (Vroom 1964). Path-goal theory assumes that workers and employers are in a mutually beneficial exchange relationship and that it is a leader's job to enhance reciprocity and shared goals. This is conceptualized more fully in expectancy theory, which states that motivation is a multiplicative function of worker capacity, reward accessibility, and reward desirability.

Path-goal theory emphasizes the two types of contingencies found in transactional leadership models—task and subordinate characteristics. Because the number of task and subordinate characteristics considered are numerous and ultimately open-ended, path-goal theory is really more a framework than a theory per se. The number of styles appropriate to most effectively deal with the contingencies identified is also open-ended and has increased over the years. The most commonly referenced path-goal articulation, by House and Mitchell (1974), has four styles and will form the basis of the current discussion.

An important contribution of the theory is its conceptualization of the need for leadership. Leadership supplies what is needed or missing for subordinates or their task environments. For example, Larry is a sales manager in an insurance company with a clearly structured product line. Employees are well trained, cooperative, and highly motivated, with ample incentives. Because little is missing for subordinates or their task environment, the need for leadership from Larry is low. Because ideal conditions are rare, however, leadership is usually needed to improve and maintain those conditions. Path-goal theory examines the many contingencies that may be deficient and suggests the type of leadership that would remedy the specified need.

The contingencies that affect the correct style to use are primarily related to either the task or followers. Although theoretically the number of task-related contingencies is endless, the research on path-goal theory has identified five major types: task ambiguity, task difficulty, the quality of the job (stressful, monotonous, etc.), interdependency (team approach), and worker control (level of autonomy). Another class of contingencies involves subordinates. These include experience and training of workers, the work preferences, and the types of fulfillment they prefer.

To attend to these contingent needs, directive and supportive styles were originally proposed (House 1971). Later, House and Mitchell (1974) added participative and achievement-oriented styles. "Directive path-goal clarifying leader behavior is behavior directed toward providing psychological structure for subordinates: letting subordinates know what they are expected to do, scheduling and coordinating work, giving specific guidance, and clarifying policies, rules, and procedures" (House 1996, 326). Such behavior is nonpunitive and nonauthoritarian. Such behavior helps to structure and clarify the work and provides extrinsic motivation where intrinsic motivation may be lacking. For example, Richard is office manager of a physical therapy organization. Office staff, hired for their undergraduate degrees in business, screen new clients for assignment to a particular therapist. Because that portion of their work is ambiguous, Richard provides specific questions to the staff to use in screening. He then provides charts of therapists' backgrounds as they match the responses given to the screening questions. Staff must ask the designated questions and then use the charts to assign patients. Although a therapist might occasionally have to reassign a patient, office staff knows that they are normally doing a good job of screening when they follow Richard's procedures. Thus Richard is meeting the needs of his subordinates, thereby guiding them to the goal.

"Supportive leader behavior is behavior directed toward the satisfaction of subordinates' needs and preferences, such as displaying concern for subordinates' welfare and creating a friendly and psychologically supportive work environment." It is a "source of self-confidence and social satisfaction and a source of stress reduction and alleviation of frustration" (House 1996, 326). Supportive behavior may also be exhibited as calming subordinates or providing them with a sense of significance and/or equality.

"Participative leader behavior is behavior directed toward encouragement of subordinate influence on decision making and work unit operations: consulting with subordinates and taking their opinions and suggestions into account when making decisions" (House 1996, 327). It has four effects. First, it clarifies the relationships among effort, goal attainment, and extrinsic rewards. Second, it increases worker and employer goal congruence through the mutual-influence process. Third, it increases worker effort and performance by having subordinates clarify intentions even as they act autonomously. Finally, it increases the involvement and commitment of peers as well as the social pressure that they can apply to enhance organizational performance. We can see the importance of participative leader behavior in Sid's window washing company, where the work itself is not satisfying. In fact, some washing is at dangerous heights, although workers' pay increases when they take on the more dangerous assignments. Sid's employees are of varying levels of experience and age; experience leads to greater knowledge of safety, but, in a bipolar manner, both youth and old age lead to higher accident rates. Typical customer interaction focuses on windows that were not cleaned to perfection, and some customers are known to complain more than others. Sid uses participative behavior when determining what assignments will be posted to which of his employees. His approach compensates for some of the negative aspects of the work itself, leading to lower stress among employees.

"Achievement-oriented behavior is behavior directed toward encouraging performance excellence: setting challenging goals, seeking improvement, emphasizing excellence in performance, and showing confidence that subordinates will attain high standards of performance" (House 1996, 327). It also tends to encourage differentiating the levels of contingent reward more sharply and to emphasize self-actualization through work goals. For example, Evlyn manages a placement service in which her carefully trained employees have control over their own work and set their own goals; they are paid on the basis of their successful placements. Evlyn's style with her employees is to set overall corporate goals that their individual goals are to mirror. She provides helpful research data on applicants' profiles and on organizations' employment needs in their service area, knowing that information helps employees become more successful. Her achievement-oriented behavior allows employees to reach high levels of performance on their own.

The causal-chain model of path-goal theory is provided in Exhibit 3.7.

Based on the contingencies present, different styles will supply what is "missing" according to path-goal theory. When job clarity and formalization are lacking, directive leadership supplies structure. When jobs are difficult because of complexity or change, participatory leader behaviors are helpful, as well as achievement-oriented behaviors when higher standards are required. Unpleasant jobs call for supportive leader behaviors. Highly interdependent jobs call for more participatory styles. When workers control their jobs more, achievement-oriented leader behaviors work better than directive ones. Lack of training and education commonly calls for a more directive style, as do situations in which subordinates have a preference for structure and order. However, when workers have a preference for high control over their work, a more participatory or achievement-oriented style tends to work better. When need for security is high, directive leadership is preferred, but when it is low, an achievement style may work better. High need for affiliation tends to call for supportive and/or participative behaviors, while directive and achievement-oriented styles become dysfunctional. Individuals with strong yearnings for individual recognition prefer supportive and achievement-oriented styles, while those interested in-group success are more amenable to participatory styles (House 1996).

One of the strengths of path-goal theory is its focus on the connection between

Exhibit 3.7 **Path-Goal Theory Causal-Chain** (1974 version)

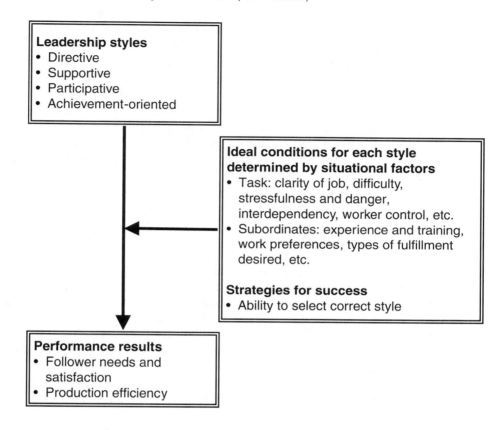

leadership and subordinate motivation in the context of the work environment. As new relationships become established regarding the contingencies that subordinate experience and the styles leaders use, they can easily be incorporated into path-goal theory. In 1996, House did just that by incorporating new styles and twenty-six new hypotheses. Further, the theory does not preclude blended leadership styles, and it assumes alternating styles as different subordinate needs evolve. While the theory or framework has become increasingly complex, it can be argued that leadership is simply a complex phenomenon and that simpler models are either much narrower in what they explain or extremely abstract and nonspecific.

The inclusive nature of the path-goal theory has given rise to several weaknesses. First, it is not an elegant theory. The propositions are widely scattered over the motivational terrain and thus must be learned one at a time. There is no reason that House's twenty-six propositions could not double or that the styles could not be enumerated endlessly. Not surprisingly, path-goal has provided little basis for leadership training programs because of its complexity. House himself wrote that his theory has led to other good approaches, including the theory of charismatic leadership and the value-based theory of leadership (House 1996, 349).

LEADER-MEMBER EXCHANGE THEORY

Leader-member exchange (LMX) theory focuses on the *ongoing* relationship that leaders and members of their group experience as they negotiate and exchange mutual perceptions, influence, types and amount of work, loyalty and perquisites, and so forth. Unlike path-goal theory, this theory examines the leader-member exchange as long-term interaction trends rather than discrete and unrelated events. Initially, this theory described the nature of **in-groups** and out-groups in the workplace; later, the theory looked more closely at the effects of the presence of in-groups and out-groups.

The initial version of the theory was called vertical dyad linkage theory (Graen and Cashman 1975) because it focused on influence processes within "vertical dyads" where one person has authority over the other. It separates followers into two member categories according to high- and low-exchange relationships. High-exchange relationships might emerge over time because, for example, the two people in the vertical dyad are compatible or because the subordinate is particularly competent. Leaders perceive high-exchange relationship members as more skilled, more hardworking, and more likable. High-exchange relationship members tend to have expanded roles and negotiated responsibilities in any kind of desired task; they tend to get more benefits, including desirable assignments, tangible rewards, better schedules, more praise, assistance with career advancement, and consultation in decision-making. In turn, to have and maintain high-relationship status, members must be willing to take on more responsibilities or work, such as administrative duties; they must be loyal or must produce more. The advantages to the leader are a core group of committed people, loyalty, and backup for special and administrative functions. However, high-relationship members expect greater inclusion and support, and avoidance of coercive or authoritarian tactics. Low-relationship members tend to stay within their defined roles and do little more than what is required; that is, they "put in their time." Further, they are less committed to either the job or the leader. Leaders perceive low-exchange relationship members as less competent, less hardworking, or less loyal. Therefore, low-exchange relationship members are less likely to be provided extra benefits, given professional or personal support, or consulted on organizational decisions.

A second version of LMX theory shifted from this descriptive approach to a more prescriptive one based on the assumption that good leaders create as many high-exchange relationships as possible. This assumption is based on research indicating that high-exchange members tend to have better attitudes, produce more, be more flexible, experience less turnover, advance more frequently, and be more willing to participate in and advance group goals. Implicitly, it proposes an ideal style; ideal leaders maintain numerous high-exchange relationships, while poor leadership produces many low-exchange relationships (Graen and Uhl-Bien 1995).

This theory does not focus on situational or intervening variables. It does look at factors increasing leader success (moderating variables)—those that affect the strength of the ideal leader style. One important characteristic is the nature of influence. In low-exchange relationships, influence is one-way or directive (from the leader to the member), but in high-exchange relationships, influence is reciprocal. Another characteristic is the nature of the roles played by the member. In low-exchange relationships, the roles are defined or scripted by procedures and protocols. In high-

Exhibit 3.8   **Leader-Member Exchange (LMX) Theory Causal-Chain**

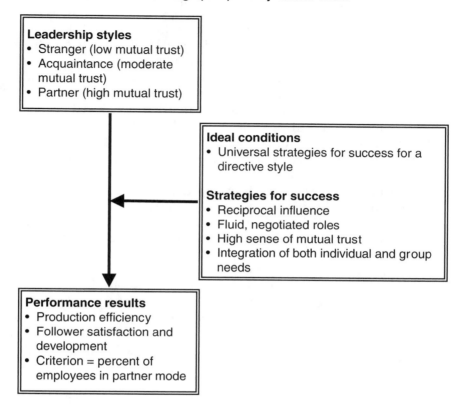

Leadership styles
- Stranger (low mutual trust)
- Acquaintance (moderate mutual trust)
- Partner (high mutual trust)

Ideal conditions
- Universal strategies for success for a directive style

Strategies for success
- Reciprocal influence
- Fluid, negotiated roles
- High sense of mutual trust
- Integration of both individual and group needs

Performance results
- Production efficiency
- Follower satisfaction and development
- Criterion = percent of employees in partner mode

Source: Graen and Uhl-Bien (1995).

exchange relationships, the roles are more fluid and negotiated. Another characteristic is the amount of respect and trust that is shared by both leaders and members, which is quite limited or formalistic in low-exchange relationships. This means that ideal leaders will frequently incorporate supportive behaviors in order to build up goodwill. Finally, there is the nature of the focus on interests. In low-exchange relationships, member interests are largely self-serving (as are the interests of management), but in high-exchange relationships, interests of both leaders and members focus on those of the group, which realistically integrates individual and organizational needs. This tends to encourage inspirational behaviors.

Styles range from the least desirable to the ideal style. The "stranger" style tends to be formal, directive, and distant. Leaders have low respect for and trust in their subordinates. The "acquaintance" style is less formal, directive, and distant, but is still cautious in monitoring and managing members. Leader confidence in members is moderate. The "partner" style is characterized by reciprocity, unconditional "favors," flexibility, high trust and confidence, and high support of member needs. The partner style is reminiscent of the ideal team management approach advocated in the managerial grid. The implicit LMX causal-chain model is illustrated in Exhibit 3.8.

One of the major strengths of the LMX theory is that it describes a commonly perceived reality—the presence of in-groups and out-groups, as well as high producers and low producers. Another strength of the theory is that it brings attention to the long-term relationship aspects of leadership. While not alone in this focus (Hollander 1958), it is in contrast to the theories that have been explored so far. Leadership is more than a series of discrete and unrelated episodes between leaders and members in which the calculus of exchange begins anew each time. Finally, the theory is practical in realizing that although the relationship is a shared one and the subordinate contributes to it, it still puts final responsibility for managing the relationship on the leader. Leaders frequently project their biases on followers or create and maintain dysfunctional first impressions of members, for which this theory places responsibility squarely on leaders' shoulders.

A major weakness of the later, prescriptive version of LMX is that it falls prey to the problems of universal approaches. It tends to be simplistic and to ignore situational variables. For example, what do you do when a member is psychotic, the unit has a history of intense self-serving behavior, or the unit has more than its share of generally untalented and incompetent employees? The other major weakness of the theory is that it does not adequately explain how high and low relationships evolve. The incorporation of attribution theory would probably assist in this regard (Yukl 2006). Attribution theory proposes that (1) leaders try to determine the reasons for effective and ineffective performance, and (2) leaders take the appropriate action according to their behavior or style.

Leaders can use the following strategies to assist low performers with performance deficiencies:

- Express a sincere desire to help and show confidence in the subordinate.
- Gather information about problem performance prior to acting and carefully avoid attributional biases.
- Provide feedback quickly and in specific terms.
- Provide feedback calmly and professionally by focusing on the behavior rather than the individual.
- Point out the adverse effect of the subordinate's behavior.
- Mutually identify reasons for inadequate performance.
- Ask the subordinate to suggest remedies and then mutually reach agreement on specific action steps.
- Summarize the discussion and verify agreement (adapted from Yukl 2006, 124–125).

CONCLUSION

This chapter has begun the in-depth review of various theories that explain aspects and perspectives on leadership. Leadership is a complex phenomenon; it is unlikely that any single theory will ever adequately explain all aspects of leadership for the many different purposes that theories fulfill (explanation, evaluation, training, etc.). To help with the task, a causal-chain model was presented in the last chapter as a useful tool to compare the different types of theories that are popular. In this model, leader styles are the independent variable and performance is the dependent variable. However, various contingencies affect the best style to use (intervening variables), and the effectiveness of style execution (moderating variables) is also important.

First, two early perspectives were reviewed. Classical management largely assumes "one best style": directive leadership. Trait theory largely assumes a combined style as a composite of an ideal set of traits, but this approach leaves too many elements and variables unexplained. Transactional approaches pay more attention to the leadership situation—either worker needs and/or contingencies. Blake and Mouton's managerial grid assumes an ideal balance of task and support in a universalist approach. Hersey and Blanchard focus on followers' development needs, varying the style according to their maturity. House and his colleagues in path-goal theory include not only follower needs, but task and organizational needs as well. This means that the calculus for deciding exactly what type of leadership style is necessary can become quite sophisticated, although in his 1974 model House proposes only four major styles. Leader-member exchange theory (LMX) focuses on the interaction of the leader with various followers and points out the possible detrimental effects of creating in-groups and out-groups. A comparison of the leader styles implied by management and transactional perspectives is found in Exhibit 3.9.

All the transactional theories tend to focus on the leadership function at the supervisory level in fairly stable conditions, bringing in the basic needs of followers, especially their basic or "exchange" needs. The next set of theories that we will examine focuses on executives in conditions requiring change (or in crisis) and bringing in "higher"-level needs (e.g., the need to make contributions to the group).

KEY TERMS

collectivism	9,9 team leadership
Fayol's administrative theory	path-goal theory
Five Elements of Management	scientific management
Great Man theory	Situational Leadership®
in-groups	time-and-motion study
leader-member exchange (LMX) theory	trait theory
managerial grid	Weber's theory of bureaucracy

RESOURCES

As suggested previously, students or teams of students may be assigned resources on the Internet that complement topics covered in the chapter to increase the richness and depth of class discussion. Although sites that tend to be enduring have been selected for the Resources sections, be aware that webpages may change so it might be necessary to search for similar online articles.

Read in the *Administrative Science Quarterly* about this experiment by Christopher Earley in which he found that participants from a collectivist culture performed best

Exhibit 3.9 **Comparison of the Leader Styles Implied by Early Management and Transactional Perspectives**

| | | | Leadership theory | | | |
Leadership style	Early management	Trait approach	Grid (Blake and Mouton)	Situational (Hersey and Blanchard)	Path-goal (House 1971)	LMX (Graen and Uhl-Bien 1995)
Laissez-faire		Impoverished				
Directive	One-best-way* POSDCoRB*		Authority-compliance	Directing	Directive	Stranger
Supportive			Country club	Coaching	Supporting	Acquaintance
Participative				Supporting	Participative	
Delegative				Delegating		
Achievement-oriented					Achievement-oriented	
Inspirational						
External						
Combined		Heroic* (multiple styles implicit in multiple traits)	Team*			Partner*

Notes: 1. An asterisk denotes a style recommendation considered superior. 2. Many style equivalencies are only "best fit."

with conditions opposite those for U.S. participants. Specifically, for collectivists from China, group-focused training (as opposed to individual-focused training) had a stronger impact on managers' estimate of their ability to perform a task as well as a stronger impact on actual performance; the opposite was true for individualists in the United States. Clearly, leadership in these opposite conditions would call for different approaches.

- P.C. Earley, "Self or Group? Cultural Effects of Training on Self-Efficacy and Performance," *Administrative Science Quarterly*, 39 (1) (1994), 89–117. www.jstor.org/stable/2393495.

Lillian Gilbreth, like her husband Frank Gilbreth, was instrumental in time and motion studies (1917). She was particularly involved with the psychological aspects of time management for better productivity. She had twelve children, two of whom wrote the famous book *Cheaper by the Dozen*. Many interesting outside resources can be found on the Gilbreths. The site shown below tells, for example, of the Gilbreth children earning extra money by being the lowest bidder to a family council that accepted sealed bids for special jobs such as painting. Lillian was the inventor of what are now everyday conveniences such as trash cans that open with an efficient foot pedal, and refrigerators that store more food because of doors with shelves.

- "Lillian Moller Gilbreth (1878–1972)," Women's Intellectual Contributions to the Study of Mind and Society, Webster University. www.webster.edu/~woolflm/gilbreth2.html.

Robert House is a professor at the Wharton School and the creator of the path-goal theory. In the *Leadership Quarterly* article listed below, written twenty-five years after his initial work, House (1996) summarizes the theory and its legacy and then reformulates his classic theory.

- Robert House, "Path-Goal Theory of Leadership: Lessons, Legacy, and a Reformulated Theory," Knowledge@Wharton, January 1, 1996. http://knowledge.wharton.upenn.edu/paper.cfm?paperID=674.

DISCUSSION QUESTIONS

1. Why is leadership theory so complex and seemingly contradictory? How can multiple theories be correct? Is leadership theory simply the sum of all the theories proposed?
2. Explain a generic framework for leadership that can be used to compare leadership models using behavioral, intervening, moderating, and performance variables.
3. What is the implicit leadership recommendation in classical management theory? Discuss the weaknesses of the approach in relation to leadership.
4. Provide an example of why an excellent leader in one case (one with a specific set of traits) might perform poorly in another situation. Include a set of leader

characteristics in which very different traits might be required in different settings.

5. Describe situations in which the managerial grid might be useful as an analytical tool. When might it not be so useful?
6. Describe the differences and similarities between the styles recommended in Situational Leadership® and path-goal theory. What are the differences in the intervening variables that they focus on?
7. Describe the recent version of LMX theory. Do you think its prescriptions are realistic? How do its prescriptions enhance the likelihood of a high-trust model?
8. Is there a place today for any of the classical approaches to management study? Explain.

Classroom Activity

Instructions

Divide into six teams, with one team assigned to each of the following leadership approaches: scientific management, trait theory, managerial grid, Situational Leadership®, path-goal, and LMX. Study the following case and then meet with your team to analyze the case from the perspective of your team's assigned leadership theory. Evaluate the leadership situation using the applicable causal-chain framework. If your assigned theory cannot be applied in depth to the case, explain why and identify what additional information you would need in order to apply the theory appropriately. All groups then present their analysis of the case. The purpose of this classroom activity is to gain practice in the application of particular theoretical approaches to a leadership situation.

The Case

When CEO Douglas Conant arrived at the Campbell Soup Company in 2001, he wanted to survey the top 350 executives on twelve questions, but reported: "I couldn't even get them to fill out the questionnaire, which was anonymous. They were concerned that I'd know who they were." Upon completion of the survey, Gallup "told me it was the worst level of employee engagement they had ever seen" (Fitzgerald 2007). Campbell's, a company founded in 1869 by a fruit merchant and an icebox manufacturer, with 2001 net sales of $6.7 billion producing earnings of $649 million, had grown complacent. We know that large, mature, sluggish corporations decline or run risk of decay unless they take charge of their life cycle. Despite lowering projected earnings and cutting the dividend by 30 percent upon his arrival, Conant led Campbell to 2006 earnings of $766 million on net sales of $7.3 billion, and a long way toward managing the tension between innovation for that which is new and adaptation of that which already exists. In contrast to Gallup's 2001 findings, the 2007 Campbell Soup Company website stated that one key goal of the company is to "achieve world-class employee engagement."

Conant—joining Campbell with an MBA and twenty-five years of food industry experience from General Mills, Kraft, and Nabisco—applied methods learned from his experience, including increased marketing, cutting total cost, acting on innovative ideas from workers, and upgrading product quality. Innovations brought earnings up substantially; for example, pop-tops on soup cans, lower-sodium soups, 100-calorie packs of Pepperidge Farm Goldfish, and functional shelving systems for retailers were all "winners."

In an in-depth article (Carter 2006), *Business Week* portrayed Conant as a "self-described introvert" who enjoys his daily commute of four hours for the "alone time" it offers. Conant is an avid reader of a wide range of books on leadership, runs a book club for top executives, and shares books with employees. He draws on books to satisfy a craving for fresh insights, and he can be heard quoting Leo Tolstoy in everyday discussion. Conant is known to have sent Campbell employees at all levels more than 16,000 handwritten notes in the spirit of celebrating "what's right." Once every few weeks he meets for lunch with about a dozen employees in order to gain feedback. He established a CEO Institute to support promotion from within. He requires that goals are clearly stated at every level of the organization and that every manager meets quarterly with all subordinates. For the next stage of planned growth, and citing a requirement that corporations grow, Conant is exploring markets such as China, where homemade soup is consumed in quantity.

Conant says, "Every day, you've got to be making deposits in the emotional bank account of your company. When people do something right, you have to celebrate it, and then you have to celebrate it again. And if they do something wrong, you have to thoughtfully call them on it, because this isn't a patronizing culture, it's a performance culture" (Fitzgerald 2007).

CASE ANALYSIS

Janice has just been promoted to unit supervisor after five years of hard work in the marketing department. She is looking forward to taking over, but is very nervous about the prospect of being a leader, given her limited experience and the challenges of the work environment. The previous boss, Ralph, had been supervisor for eighteen years before retiring. Fortunately, Janice was one of his favorites, which ultimately led to her getting the job. Workers either played Ralph's game or were not well received by him, and their assignments and raises reflected his preferences. Ralph would ask questions of his favorites, but he did not consult with anyone regarding assignments, budget priorities, or major operational decisions because that was his job. The timeliness and quality of the work in the unit have generally been quite good because Ralph insisted on it and was brutally frank about lateness or major mistakes. Brian and Roberto were also well respected by Ralph, because he perceived them to be harder working and more responsible than Yvonne, Brenda, or Larry.

Yvonne has heavy family responsibilities, works hard to fulfill her responsibilities, but does not have an extra moment to spare on the job beyond its basic requirements. She simply cannot work on special projects requiring spurts of extra time or meet impromptu with customers without extensive advance notice. She is extremely accurate in her work and excels when the task is set out before her and she can work on just one or two major projects at a time, in detail. However, she is not very flexible and is prone to discouragement and being overwhelmed, partially because she is frequently tired.

Brenda is still relatively new but is not performing very well at this point. It is hard to understand *exactly* why. She has minimal technical training in planning and was hired because of an absence of well-qualified people. Nonetheless, she has some planning courses and an internship in the area. Some of her ideas are good, but some are just terrible, and she does not seem to be able to distinguish between them. Nor does she know how to interact with the team in a constructive fashion in order to use the other members' expertise. She is very smart and sociable; she does not goof off, but she seems to be very slow in defining her projects, managing her time, and bringing her projects to closure.

Larry has been with the department for fifteen years and is the weakest performer in the group. He generally arrives slightly late, leaves slightly early, and takes a longish lunch break—but only by a few minutes. Projects rarely capture his interest and he lets people know that most of the assignments provided to him are conceptually flawed. Perhaps there are too few resources to do a great job, or perhaps the time frame is too short, or perhaps the fundamental purpose of the project is suspect. Although he can be quite pleasant and sociable—especially with a cup of coffee in his hand when he is taking one of his breaks—he can be grumpy or rude if he perceives incompetence in others, and aggressive and nasty if he perceives he is crossed. He knows the rules and ensures that management does not cross the line. His lack of interest shows in his work, which is mediocre in design and marred by small sloppy details. Janice noticed, however, that when he was assigned a client promoting "green development" last year, Larry did an exceptional job, overcoming a number of major obstacles. (Larry is often outspoken about his perception that the business is too greedy to be concerned with the future of humanity.)

Brian is probably the most well-rounded in the group, a self-starter, and even-tempered. He is quiet and work-oriented most of the time but quite articulate when asked a question. He was one of Ralph's top choices as his successor, but ultimately the job was given by the management team to Janice because of her superior effort, greater natural ability to use people-oriented style and longer-term employment with the company. Brian prefers to be given projects and to be largely left alone to complete them so he can work as efficiently and quickly as possible. Nonetheless, he works well in a team or as a mentor if requested to do so.

Roberto is anxious to move ahead in professional standing. In fact, he is the most likely to leave the unit since he has been passed over for the promotion that he wanted. He works in spurts and is at his best in the latter part of the day. He is very gregarious, which is both an asset and a liability. On one hand, he can stimulate a lot of enthusiasm and camaraderie at a human level and get a lot of perspectives out on the table. On the other hand, he is significantly slower in getting his projects completed and occasionally gets a bit carried away with a somewhat impractical idea, such as using a new but nonindustrial-strength piece of equipment (which invariably breaks down in the first six months). He loves tough projects and the accolades he wins for completing them, but gets very bored with routine marketing research projects.

DISCUSSION QUESTIONS

1. What characteristics suggest that Ralph was an old-school (classical) manager? What were Ralph's strengths and weaknesses as a manager?
2. Critique Ralph using leader-member exchange theory (LMX).
3. Assume that Janice has to choose between Brian and Roberto for promotion. List their strengths and weaknesses (their traits). Under what conditions would Brian be better and under what conditions might Roberto be better? Use your analysis to discuss the weakness of trait theory.
4. Managerial grid theory has a tendency to average out the characteristics of a group. It is quite useful as a method of looking at the group culture, but generally less so in assessing individual needs. Explain why the managerial grid is not as useful as other theories in analyzing this particular scenario.
5. Both Hersey and Blanchard's theory and House's path-goal theory have four leadership style recommendations. Three of the styles are quite comparable. Both have a directive style, both have a highly supportive style (coaching and supportive), and both have a moderately supportive style (supporting and participative). Hersey and Blanchard have a delegative style as their fourth style, while House proposes an achievement-oriented style (focusing on customizing assignments and enhancing individual incentives).
   a. Which styles should Janice as the new supervisor use with Yvonne, Brenda, Brian, and Roberto and why? (Do not worry too much about distinguishing between moderately and highly supportive styles.)
   b. Larry is a more complex case and a clear style preference is unclear. Which one or several of the situational and path-goal styles should Janice use in his case and why?

MANAGERIAL LEADERSHIP BEHAVIORS

Supervisors and managers have specific responsibilities—often called management functions or managerial leadership behaviors—that they adopt for planning, organizing, and controlling. Part II deals primarily with managerial leadership behaviors carried out by those in supervisory positions or by those promoted to a management capacity. At either of these levels within the organization, work can be done to reinforce the routine and can be accomplished with a zest that befits a leader. In this section, we are interested in those behaviors that directly contribute to managerial leader effectiveness.

Executive leaders at the top tier of their organizations are not exempt from carrying out managerial behaviors such as planning, organizing, and controlling. With learned behaviors, these functions can be fulfilled with the passion of a leader who remains steadfastly focused on visionary accomplishments.

How do these managerial leadership behaviors apply to new or young professionals? There are at least two applications that are of equal importance. First, as employees of an organization, a full understanding of the context in which they work will lead to a greater rate of success within that organization. Even if they are not initially placed at the supervisory or managerial level, to become an outstanding employee calls for a clear appreciation of what managerial leadership is attempting to accomplish within the confines of any constraints. Similarly, even when employees have not reached the executive level of an organization, they have the potential to grow and become outstanding members of the supervisory team if and when the responsibilities of executive leadership, as well as the constraints within which those leaders must execute their duties, are fully realized.

Second, many young professionals follow a common pattern in their business career. It typically begins in high school, with an hourly job, perhaps as a waiter in a restaurant or a clerk in a retail store. Opportunities for leadership exist at all levels, including such entry-level positions. Leader roles are particularly common in an environment that is open and participative, although little space for decision-making is usually given. However, a waiter may demonstrate initiative by taking the feedback he is exposed to via his direct involvement with diners and giving meaningful input on menu adjustments to management. Equally, a clerk may exercise leadership by asking to alter a retail display in light of her understanding of the customers' flair for accessories.

Following graduation from college, it is not unusual for our new or young professional to soon move into a supervisory position, with the possibility of promotion to a management position at some point in the future. For example, the high school waiter may transition into the role of a project manager in construction by virtue of his experience and/or achievements. The retail clerk may transition into the role of an accounting supervisor for similar reasons. In these new jobs, they will have ample opportunity to demonstrate managerial leadership ability. Leadership is needed in supervision and management positions in order to achieve organizational goals, particularly when administering others is a direct function of the job. Effective decision-making in day-to-day operations is critical, and a solid grasp of the role of leadership makes this possible.

From among those successful or "connected" leaders at the management level, a few will be promoted yet again, to the ranks of the top management team where executive leadership is exercised. Titles such as "partner," "vice president for administration," "director of international affairs," or "president" may be used when working at the executive level in business. Decision-making at this level of leadership is central to the job, with emphasis on strategy and the long-term effectiveness of the organization. Individuals who reach the top of the hierarchy have significant opportunity to carry out their vision and impact the future direction of the organization.

The point is clear. At all levels of organizational activity, from the entry-level position to the corner office, and from the first paycheck to the last, the business graduate should have a sound understanding of managerial leadership behaviors—whether for personal application or for better comprehension of leaders in the organizational setting. This section of the text helps to provide that understanding.

4 Traits and Skills Contributing to Leader Effectiveness

Let me tell you the secret that has led me to my goal:
my strength lies solely in my tenacity.
—Louis Pasteur, 1885

In Chapter 3, we explored how the initial hope of the trait theory was to identify a master list of essential traits in order to prescribe the ideal leader. Because Jung and other psychologists believed that people are born with certain inherited traits, the focus was that *leaders are born, not made*, and there was an effort to identify those who already possessed those characteristics. Even though trait theory per se is not the theory of choice in management research to explain leadership, it is still accepted that traits influence behaviors and behaviors influence effectiveness. Consequently, an important discussion of leadership traits continues as individual concepts (called constructs in social science), with the realization that they are not a substitute for integrated theories. We have also moved toward trying to understand to what degree traits and skills can be studied, absorbed, and refined, as the focus today is that *leadership can be learned*.

Reading about traits and skills that contribute to leader effectiveness is very helpful when attempting to develop oneself or others (such as subordinates), as discussed in Chapter 12. For example, if decisiveness traits or technical skills for the job are lacking, they would be appropriate for self-study or training. The top trait and skill lists presented here are not all-inclusive simply because there are endless traits and skills that could be listed. For example, traits such as kindness and compassion are not on our "top" list. However, such traits certainly do not preclude business success: one of the wealthiest men in the world in the 1830s, Stephen Van Rensselaer, accumulated a vast fortune (equal to that of current American billionaires) from his enormous land holdings in New York, even though he often failed to collect rent and was much beloved (*New York Times* 2007). The contemporary investing genius Warren Buffet is as much known today for his largesse, bequeathing his fortune to the Gates Foundation, as for his analytical skills, decisiveness, and other business-oriented traits. Gates and Buffett, bonded together by benevolence, sought donations for charity from persons and families listed on the Forbes 400 list of wealthiest Americans, and received pledges from 57 billionaire families by December 2010, each contributing at least half of their wealth. Van Rensselaer, and the wealthy business magnates who followed, exhibit dichotomous traits that define them as individuals.

Despite the outstanding examples of benevolence highlighted above, it is clear that traits of altruism and compassion for charities are not absolute requirements for leadership effectiveness (Karnani 2010; Trudel and Cotte 2009). For example, when business schools approach a successful business for a philanthropic gift for education and the door is closed, one reason sometimes is "declining because I will not act in the public interest against shareholder interest." Assuming that varying behavioral responses are at least in part an extension of varying traits, it is evident that there is not *one* perfect list of traits that are essential for leadership effectiveness. There is literally no end to the lists of favorable traits and skills that could be crafted. Even if a leader had *all* the favorable traits and skills needed in a *particular* situation, it would not necessarily mean that he effectively used the trait or skill. In a particular situation, the leader might use the favorable trait of decisiveness, for example, when the situation may have called for a trait of kindness.

Prominent businessman, socialite, and TV showman Donald Trump is a personality with certain traits that he projects as "bigger than life." He started with a small family fortune, grew it through the early 1980s owing to sharp analytic skills and decisiveness, and then made a series of overleveraging mistakes in the late 1980s. These mistakes (which he had the ability to foresee) were based on poor analysis or hasty decisions, and they pushed him into bankruptcies and painful restructuring in many projects. Of course, he regained his wealth and renown in the late 1990s as he used his business acumen wisely. The point here is that having favorable traits and skills does not necessarily mean that the leader applies them for a favorable outcome in every situation.

Because traits and skills are often building blocks of more sophisticated theories and are extremely useful for pinpointing areas for development, in this chapter we focus on traits and skills that contribute to managerial leader effectiveness. *Traits* are the distinguishing features of a person's character. The ten traits discussed in this chapter include *six personality characteristics:* self-confidence, decisiveness, resilience, energy, flexibility, and emotional maturity; *two classic motivational drives:* the willingness to assume responsibility and the need for achievement; and *two value orientations:* personal integrity and a service mentality. As previously stated, this is not the only possible list of appropriate traits. However, it is a good list, with its components seen frequently in the literature, and can be extremely helpful in pinpointing areas for self-development (see Chapter 12).

Skills are defined as broadly applied, learned characteristics of leader performance. We discuss six skills that contribute to leadership effectiveness. They are introduced later in the chapter.

It is important to distinguish among different types of leadership competencies. The generic term "**competency**" generally refers to discrete abilities to accomplish a job, including traits, skills, and behaviors. There are relatively innate or long-term dispositions (traits), broadly applied learned characteristics (skills), and concrete actions (behaviors).

Attempts to patch together specific lists of "best" traits, skills, and behavioral competencies face several challenges. These competencies are analytic inventions used to categorize a vast terrain. Therefore, people use different terms to define concepts that may differ only slightly. Another challenge is an operational definition. No matter how the concepts are divided and labeled, it is impossible to define exactly when one competency such as "energy" ends and another such as the "drive for achievement" begins. These are challenges not only to researchers, but also to practitioners studying leadership. Although this textbook does not adopt a single comprehensive list from one of the traditional sources (e.g., Bass 1990; Howard and Bray 1988; Kotter 1982; U.S. Office of Personnel Management 1992a, 1999; Yukl 2006), because of our purpose in providing an introduction to the business of leadership, we strive to be as consistent as possible with the various lists that are cited. In this chapter we cover ten traits and six metaskills, and in subsequent chapters we will discuss twenty-one behavioral competencies. If one adds in the various leader styles (Chapter 2), leader assessment of organizational priorities (Chapter 9), and leader evaluation (Chapter 12), the total is more than fifty competencies.

As general traits, these ten traits are all relatively stable dispositions by adulthood. Yet they are amenable to significant improvement, and a few, to substantial improvement. For example, with good education, training, and experience, the trait of self-confidence on the job is enhanced greatly. While modest and incremental improvements can be made, it is wise to remember that traits are deeply anchored in personality so radical, rapid changes are unlikely.

LEADERSHIP TRAITS: PERSONALITY CHARACTERISTICS

SELF-CONFIDENCE

Self-confidence is an attitude giving persons a positive yet realistic sense about their ability to accomplish what needs to be accomplished. Self-confidence leads people to a reasoned surety about their capacity to perform. They do not need continual external encouragement and compliments. The notion of self-confidence is composed of several subelements. Self-esteem is a positive regard for oneself and one's abilities. Good self-esteem helps during the awkward learning phase prior to mastery of a new skill set. **Self-efficacy**, the belief that one has either the specific abilities necessary or the ability to work with others who have those abilities, is the aspect of self-confidence most influenced by training and experience. Another aspect of self-efficacy is innate, having to do with feeling that one's actions make a difference (Miller, Kets de Vries, and Toulouse 1982; Rotter 1966). This means that people with high self-efficacy tend to be more optimistic about influencing their own fate. Finally, self-confidence is related to courage, which is included in the concept here but could be considered a separate factor. Without self-confidence, courage is almost impossible.

Self-confidence is important because it provides leaders themselves, subordinates, and others with a sense of order and direction. It assists leaders to encourage themselves and others to assume more challenging tasks, set higher expectations, make decisions in crises more confidently, and plan changes with more assurance. Charismatic leaders are especially adept at enhancing others' self-confidence (House 1977; Shamir, House, and Arthur 1993). Some degree of self-confidence and at least a passable facade are necessary for many other traits—particularly decisiveness, resilience, energy, and the willingness to assume responsibility. An extreme lack of self-confidence may lead to inactivity, vacillation, defensiveness, paranoia, and overcautiousness.

The negative aspects of excessive self-confidence are substantial. Excessive confidence can lead to foolish risk-taking. It can lead to micromanagement when leaders think that their skills are superior and that they must personally supervise all-important tasks. Even when leaders' skills are clearly superior, this stifles subordinates' initiative and learning. Too much self-confidence can also be perceived as arrogance when other people's ideas, perceptions, and concerns are not considered.

Guidelines for Improving Self-Confidence

1. Assess personal strengths and weaknesses in order to address them. Although lack of self-confidence is not necessarily directly related to lack of ability, in healthy people it is partially due to actual skill deficiencies. Therefore it is important to know where these deficiencies and strengths lie.

2. Seek training or experience to remedy skill or knowledge liabilities. Training, experience, and practice significantly improve effectiveness and self-confidence.

3. Practice positive self-talk and positive visualization. Much as we would all like to have a positive coach behind us all the time, it is rarely the case. Therefore, we must coach and encourage ourselves. Positive self-talk can be a healthy antidote to negative attitudes. It is even better to visualize positive outcomes. For good and readable discussions of this concept and self-management in general, see the work on "self-leadership" (Blanchard, Fowler, and Hawkins 2005; Manz and Sims 1980, 1987, 1989, 1991; Neck et al. 2006)

DECISIVENESS

Decisiveness is the ability to act relatively quickly depending on circumstances without excessively damaging decision quality. Decisiveness is a trait of firmness that brings an element of power in determining the outcome. For leaders, decisiveness is just one aspect of a larger concept: degree of follower participation in decision-making (Vroom and Jago 1988; Vroom and Yetton 1973). Follower inclusion in decision-making should embrace a range of options, from no input (directive leadership in Chapter 2), to minimal input, to substantial input but with the leader making the decision, and, finally, to subordinate decision-making individually or in groups (self-managed teams discussed in Chapter 12). This can be arrayed as a spectrum of leader options. Decisiveness emphasizes action at the directive end of the degree-of-participation spectrum, particularly in time of crisis or when there is the need for efficiency.

Exhibit 4.1

Decisiveness and Enforcement of Ethical Practices

While going through an extensive leadership development program, accountant Tom Savich was enthusiastic about trying out new managerial tactics. As chair of the internal audit committee, he was charged with implementation of measures to enforce the Sarbanes-Oxley Act in his corporation, and Tom took his responsibility very seriously. He felt that the importance of his role was to serve as the watchdog for unethical practices and to be the champion who brought ethics back into the workplace. He wanted to make a number of changes, which, given the strong authority of his position, he could easily mandate. However, he was also burdened with avoidance by some managers in the corporation. "From what I have been exposed to in the class," he noted, "I have made an effort to adjust the way I go about change within the organization. I have gone—for the most part—from the 'me' to the 'we' style of management." Yet he was also careful to point out that the transformation of styles would never—could never—be complete in his position. "There are times when the 'we' must make way for the 'me' style because of the mandates of the law. Of course it is not really me, but I must be careful to be the forceful spokesperson for the law." And almost as an afterthought he added, "And of course when we are in the midst of a major investigation, I am very decisive because that is expected of me as chair of the internal audit committee."

Ultimately, the situation dictates how much inclusion of both subordinates and external sources to utilize. Even when the situation calls for inclusion of input, the ultimate decision can still be made in a firm, resolute manner. For example, a decision on whether or not to expand to a particular new location may call for timely input from a wide range of organizational perspectives, with the final decision being made with conclusive and relative speed based on that input.

Leader decisiveness is important in crises because it gives followers a sense of confidence that matters are being taken care of and lends substantial credibility to the leader (Mulder et al. 1986; Mulder and Stemerding 1963). In noncrisis situations, decisiveness can be useful for decisions when the leader is uniquely responsible and qualified, such as employment levels or work distribution issues, when levels of agreement are low and discord would likely result, or when it is simply inefficient to consult with others. To the degree that decisiveness represents a preference for action and initiative, it relates to the drive for achievement (Spencer and Spencer 1993). Indecisiveness, also known as vacillation or hesitation, is often identified as one of the most damning traits a leader can have (Yukl 2006).

The excesses of decisiveness are serious, particularly when combined with a directive style. Leaders who employ it too often or too quickly are likely to be rash. What appears to be a crisis at first blush may be no more than a momentary problem, or the crisis may leave more time for deliberation and response than one supposes, and a hasty reaction may actually make the situation worse. This is a particular problem when a policy or order is issued, but then quickly has to be amended or countermanded. Decisiveness also has an addictive quality. Being decisive is efficient in the short run and gives the leader a great sense of power. But excessive decisiveness can quickly lead to reduced information availability and authoritarianism, resulting in worker alienation. For an example of the tricky balance that must be achieved by effective leaders, see Exhibit 4.1 on decisiveness and enforcement of ethical practices.

Guidelines for Improving Decisiveness

1. Study decision-making. The study of decision-making not only assists leaders in refining their analytic skills, but also helps in knowing when to be decisive. Discussions and analysis of the role of subordinates in decision-making are reviewed in detail in Vroom's normative decision model (Vroom and Jago 1988; Vroom and Yetton 1973).

2. Do not procrastinate in gathering information or making important decisions. It is easy to delay important decisions or data-gathering. Yet important decisions are a key function of the leader's role and should not be relegated to when-time-allows status. Leaders need to decide the time parameters of decisions, gather information with appropriate speed, and act decisively.

3. Prepare for possible emergencies and crises by developing contingency plans. Most emergencies are simply the less likely possibilities of more plausible scenarios (Boin and Otten 1996; Weick, Sutcliffe, and Obstfeld 1999). Examples for which contingency plans may be important in some industries or locations include sudden or severe budget cutbacks, loss of key personnel, service demand spikes, and loss of electricity from inclement weather.

4. Stay calm. Pressure to make important but unpleasant decisions with limited information is acute. A leader who does not stay calm is far more likely to jump to an ill-conceived "quick fix." In most complex management crises, such hasty decisions are generally suboptimal and may appear rash once the ramifications are understood. While some people are predisposed to staying calm under duress, most people must cultivate this ability. Among the best means are the advance planning discussed above, along with prior experience, or incremental roll-out of the situation with increasingly detailed levels of complexity explained so that solutions are thoughtful and responsive to the depth of the crisis.

RESILIENCE

Resilience refers to a hardiness of spirit, usually complemented by a hardiness of strength, which allows a leader to remain focused or to spring back effectively when pushed by external influences. The resilient leader invests her energy wisely in order to deal appropriately with difficult times and difficult situations. The leader is capable of a natural sort of personal revitalization, usually without dwelling on it to those around her. Having resilience means that after the weariness of long hours, distractions, conflict, or external misfortune, a person is able to recover direction, vigor, and good humor relatively quickly.

One subelement is persistence. This trait yields the ability to stay the course despite setbacks. It assumes that one is seeking to accomplish long-term goals (see achievement below). As actor and director Woody Allen said, "Eighty percent of success is just showing up." And as quoted at the opening of this chapter, Louis Pasteur, the

French biologist and bacteriologist, said, "Let me tell you the secret that has led me to my goal. My strength lies solely in my tenacity."

People who are good at persistence generally have stamina to "show up" and endure, patience to wait for opportunities, and flexibility to find new ways to achieve long-term goals. The other subelement is the ability to rebound, or stress tolerance. Circumstances themselves are only part of the equation of how much stress leaders feel; another significant component is their inner reaction to the stress with which they deal. People with **stress tolerance** can stand high levels of psychological discomfort such as uncertainty, change, and performance demands related to their jobs; they are able to thrive despite the stressful situation, quickly regaining their energy and optimism. People who have determination but no stress tolerance often accomplish great things but at personal sacrifice. People with a high stress tolerance but low determination are pleasant and hold up well, but tend to drift and to be low achievers.

Steven Jobs's personal resilience is a case study in driving his company's resilience. He was a cofounder of Apple in 1976. The Apple II computer built the company's early reputation as an inventive, rebellious, and youthful organization. In April 1983, Jobs successfully recruited John Sculley from Pepsi-Cola to fill Apple's chief executive role. However, within months their relationship became rocky to the extent that a power struggle ensued. Jobs moved to the Macintosh project, but after its introduction in 1984, business slowed. In 1985 Steven Jobs quit Apple after the Board stripped him of all operational responsibilities while planning an unsuccessful corporate takeover from Sculley. Sculley remained CEO until 1993 when the Board forced him out as product lines were mismanaged and sales dropped. In 1996, Apple bought NeXT, a company that Jobs had founded; Jobs was back at Apple. He became interim CEO and then, in 2000, assumed the position full-time once again. He overhauled the company's strategy and introduced the iPod, iTunes, and the iPhone. Jobs has been criticized for an aggressive personality, but regardless of style, he is resilient (Tirrell 2009). His resilience parallels Apple's resilience in coming to terms with redefinition from being a leading manufacturer of personal computers to being a reputed digital media organization that has redefined how Americans interface with music.

The story of Job's resilience does not stop there. Even the trait of resilience can raise angst. On a personal level, beginning in October 2003, he dealt with a rare form of pancreatic cancer, testing the question of how much health diagnosis must be given to shareholders, and when. Except for a small group of top associates, he kept his diagnosis closeted for nine months. The situation was complex because if the CEO was thought to be dying, what would that say about the company? Nevertheless, some analysts and media commentators believed it would have been wrong if shareholders had learned that the CEO died from a long-term illness that had been kept secret from them. When Jobs returned to health, the question as to whether his personal resilience had been carried too far by his unwillingness to disclose a personal matter, was set aside because no one disputed that Jobs was functioning fully as CEO of Apple throughout his health struggle.

The importance of resilience is threefold. First, resilience improves energy, long-term goal achievement, and the interest and ability to assume responsibility as a leader. Second, it contributes to leaders' good psychological and physical health. Margaret

Wheatley points out that healthy, self-renewing organizations tend to be resilient rather than rigid (1992, 88). Third, resilient leaders are considered dependable. There is more likelihood they will have the resolve to achieve goals and will not be worn down by fatigue, disillusionment, or ill health.

Guidelines for Improving Resilience

1. Know your long-term goals. Without long-term goals, resilience is nothing more than buoyancy without achievement. By determining what the long-term goals are, leaders establish articulated ideals that are more likely to be fulfilled.

2. Be patient and flexible in achieving goals. Those who are impatient in achieving goals are often considered selfish, self-centered, or even bullies. As the proverb goes, "Good things come to those who wait." Further, when there is resilience without flexibility, opportunities are lost and leaders will be accused of rigidity. Just as flexibility gives the body range of motion, flexibility gives a leader the ability to adapt to different circumstances.

3. Learn to tolerate stress but then let it go. Everyone must find his or her own strategies for accepting stress for periods of time, just as everyone should find ways to release that stress. Strategies include being organized and well prepared, rehearsing the overall importance of the task, reminding oneself of the trivial nature of many stressors, taking breaks during work to become refreshed, eating and sleeping well, accepting support, and knowing when to take a complete break or time off. Strategies for releasing stress include humor, camaraderie, regular exercise, and "leaving the job at the office." After especially high group stress has developed, group debriefings or celebrations are powerful methods of reenergizing and rededicating for long-term goal achievement.

ENERGY

To have energy is to have the physical and psychological vigor to perform. It is a better indicator of long-term leadership success, at least in terms of advancement to leadership positions, than many traits (Howard and Bray 1988). The first element of energy is physical vitality and stamina. Those with good health and physical endurance are more likely to excel. A second element of energy is mental interest. Those with mental interest can have a work focus and concentration at a technical level, and enthusiasm, commitment, or passion at an emotional level. Third, those with energy have a high activity level; that is, they do a lot so they accomplish a lot. An example of someone with both mental interest and a high activity level is Thomas Edison, who managed the business of invention so brilliantly that he became the model of the modern scientist. His mental interest was so keen that he would announce his next invention beforehand. He and his research team in Menlo Park, New Jersey, would work at least two shifts a day most of the year, and twenty-four hours a day when close to a breakthrough.

Energy contributes heavily to task accomplishment and indirectly to a drive for achievement and a willingness to assume responsibility. Those with low energy are less likely to set high goals for themselves and others or to be interested in the trappings of leadership. The importance of energy is best seen in its absence. Lethargic people are the antithesis of what most people think of when they envision leaders. It should also be noted that most people face varying levels of energy throughout the day; we cannot control the amount of time we have, but we can manage our activities and priorities in such a way as to best utilize the energy that we have at peak times of the day.

Some problems from excess energy are indeed possible. Energy without reflection, planning, or thoughtful purpose can lead to action without meaning. Empty activities can distract leaders not only from more important activities but also from contemplation. High energy coupled with a high achievement orientation and strong self-confidence can lead to dysfunctional leadership behaviors if not softened by traits such as a service mentality and emotional maturity.

Guidelines for Increasing Energy

1. Maintain good health and psychological well-being. All things related to good health invariably enhance energy. Good diet, sleep, and exercise are the foundations of long-term productivity. Further, avoidance of negative psychological syndromes—anger, jealousy, and nervousness—is indispensable for maintaining one's energy level. Energetic people are able to cope with stress well, in part because of freshness of the mind, and in part because of their ability to pace themselves well.

2. Cultivate dedication to the profession and interest in the work at hand. As the proverb states, the secret of life is not to do whatever you like, but to like whatever you do. Tom Peters's famous passion for excellence is largely based on a passion for the work itself, which he insisted could be cultivated (Peters 1992, 1994). Some of the best examples of passion for work are seen in those who practice charity.

3. Seek to eliminate "energy distracters." **Energy distracters** are almost limitless, and everyone has sources of energy drains. Although interpersonal conflict cannot always be avoided, the energy sacrificed can be enormous. Goal confusion depletes energy and task ambiguity diminishes both the speed and quality of accomplishment. While personal interaction is critical for managers and leaders, there can be a fine line between accomplishing goals and wasting time. Depending on the situation and how they react to it, anything from interpersonal conflicts, goal confusion, and task ambiguity to excess socializing, lack of exercise, and poor diet can strip their energy.

FLEXIBILITY

Flexibility is the ability to bend without breaking and to be adjustable to change or capable of modification. It has two main elements. Adaptability is a key component. Those who are adaptable are willing to use alternatives, substitutes, and surrogates. This is the attitudinal aspect; one who is flexible in this sense is not stubborn. A second aspect of flexibility is the cognitive element: alertness to the existence of alternatives and the ability to see that substitutions can sometimes be improvements. Flexible leaders do see most decisions as single yes/no choices, but as a series of options with different benefits and costs. Flexibility relates strongly to resilience (bouncing back to challenges often requires finding a new way) and achievement (accomplishments are too slow without some flexibility).

Flexibility has always been an important leadership trait (Stogdill 1974) because it is so critical to all the change functions. Flexibility is even more important in today's organizational environment, which is usually described as complex, ambiguous, and chaotic. In high-performing organizations there is a trend toward less control and more flexibility to give lower-level managers and frontline employees more discretion and autonomy. Workers are less tolerant of leaders whom they perceive to be rigid.

Guidelines for Increasing Flexibility

1. Distinguish critical objectives from noncritical means to achieve objectives. Objectives and the means of obtaining them can become erroneously fused in leaders' minds as a single concept. For example, in the drive for living up to the "Service Is Us" brand of a retail organization, leaders may identify arbitrary means to that end as critical components of the branding. One manager in the organization may see home delivery as critical service, another may see free alterations as critical service, and yet another may see no-questions-asked return policies as such. Critical components toward achieving the "Service Is Us" brand objective and reputation must be distinguished from those that are noncritical so leaders have flexibility in determining the best means for achieving objectives.

2. Appreciate the creativity of decision-making. Decision-making is not just about efficiency and speed (decisiveness) or asserting one's will as a leader (dominance). It is also about maximizing information and alternatives in order to sift flexibly through numerous permutations for the most effective resolution. This increases the likelihood of a high-quality solution.

3. Appreciate the power of innovation and change. Problem-solving and decision-making involve reacting to past problems. Flexibility helps people accept the changes that must be made to improve long-term processes or change the objectives to suit new realities. Conversely, a positive attitude toward innovation and change will invariably result in increased levels of flexibility.

EMOTIONAL MATURITY

Emotional maturity is a conglomerate of characteristics that indicate a person is well balanced in a number of psychological and behavioral dimensions. All adults like to think of themselves as emotionally mature; in reality, few people are without significant personality foibles, phobias, quirks, and other coping mechanisms that inhibit ideal interaction and leadership patterns. In fact, experts on leadership derailment have identified the top culprit as a problem in this area (McCall, Lombardo, and Morrison 1988). **Emotional intelligence** came into prominence with Daniel Goleman's (1995) book that claimed intelligence quotient (IQ) is too narrow a concept to predict success. Without emotional intelligence, smart can be dumb. With emotional intelligence, those with average IQs may be more successful than those with high IQs. Goleman makes the case that emotional intelligence is not fixed forever in the personality, but can be strengthened and allowed to grow.

Four elements are commonly associated with emotional maturity: self-awareness, self-control, responsibility for actions, and a socialized power orientation.

Self-awareness makes it possible for people to be objective about their strengths and weaknesses. Ideally people should be both proud of and humble about strengths, and cognizant and open about weaknesses. This empowers them for constant self-improvement. Similar to resilience, the element of emotional maturity also helps them accept setbacks as inevitable and learn from failures and adversity. Those who lack self-awareness tend to exaggerate strengths, overlook weaknesses, and whine when things do not go well.

Self-control leads to both evenness of emotions and balance between oneself and others. Those with good emotional self-control lack mood swings, outbursts, and tendencies toward narcissism or paranoia. As Bennis and Nanus note: "The management of self is critical. Without it, leaders may do more harm than good. Like incompetent physicians, incompetent managers can make people sicker and less vital" (2007, 53). Reactive anger (to which people are most prone when untrained or unrestrained emotionally) nearly always leads to inappropriate statements and resentment. Emotionally mature leaders are adept at avoiding cycles of interpersonal hostility, even while expressing unpleasant sentiments or taking unpopular actions.

The third element associated with emotional maturity involves taking responsibility for actions and their consequences. Those weak in this area tend to seek a scapegoat, blaming others for problems. Those strong in this area tend to share responsibility for mistakes, even when not directly at fault, and give as much credit as possible to others to encourage and reward them.

The final element is called socialized power orientation. **Socialized power orientation** means using one's formal power (especially to punish or order) as infrequently or lightly as possible. Good leaders are followed because it is known that their motives favor the "greater good," their directives make sense, and their expertise is respected in that frame of reference. On the other hand, a personalized power orientation results when power has insinuated itself into a leader's psyche and is used for the benefit of self. Leaders with a personalized power orientation draw advice from followers whose loyalty is unquestioned but who may be sycophants. Such leaders not only hold on to power, they typically try to gain more—by acquiring new authority, added resources and prestige, or additional information to use as leverage against others.

Guidelines for Improving Emotional Maturity

1. Exercise self-control and self-discipline. This is an injunction for proper channeling of emotions into productive avenues, not for repressing feelings. Although difficult to mitigate in the short term, mood swings, outbursts, and other emotional disorders such as narcissism and paranoia can be decreased over time with counseling, exercise, and self-awareness initiatives such as Covey leadership training.[1]

2. Take responsibility for your actions. A natural human reaction to problems is to "pass the buck," but mature leaders avoid that tendency.

3. Develop a socialized power orientation. The lure of power can usurp a leader's effectiveness and humanity. A socialized power mentality means that a leader always remembers from whence the power was derived, whom the power is to help, and the ultimate stewardship role that organizational leaders have.

LEADERSHIP TRAITS: CLASSIC MOTIVATIONAL DRIVES

WILLINGNESS TO ASSUME RESPONSIBILITY

Achievement and willingness to assume responsibility encompass different motivation drives. The drive for achievement is a push for accomplishment and competition. Willingness to assume responsibility means that individuals will take positions requiring decision-making duties and the use of authority. Frontline employees may have a great desire to accomplish their work, but do not want the responsibility required of supervisory positions. The need for this skill is not culture-bound, as evidenced by the fact that graduate schools of management around the world sometimes ask evaluators to rate potential students not just on intellectual capacity, but also on the applicant's willingness to accept responsibilities.

One element of willingness to assume responsibility is accepting the opportunity to learn new tasks and skills and to realign one's competencies. For example, the frontline worker who excels at work in financial planning and is promoted to unit supervisor normally stops doing financial planning work one day (or retains only the top clients) and focuses on administrative planning and divisional goals the next. Exhibit 4.2 illustrates that assuming more responsibility does not always mean moving higher up the corporate ladder, by choice. For some, there may be a call to not-for-profit service or public office, and some may find that the call for increased responsibility may mean time with a parent or child who needs concentrated attention.

Another element of willingness to assume responsibility is a willingness to use power. Power is necessary in order to direct, negotiate, and advocate. Sometimes personal power is used by leaders with an official position, usually with a managerial or supervisory title in the organization. Even if a leader has the authority of a managerial title, it does not mean that the individual in that role is ready to exercise that authority. If the individual does not fear power and has the ability to use power in forceful ways, authority can be consummated. For example, leaders sometimes have to do unpleasant tasks, such as dismiss likable but incompetent employees. Not all people are willing to exercise power, but the case can be made that a manager is not a leader when he or she keeps incompetent employees just because of inner personal fear of dealing with the task.

Exhibit 4.2

The Willingness to Serve and Sacrifice as a Leader

We often think of leadership as something to which everyone aspires and which will generally lead to greater perquisites, including financial gain. However, consider the case of José Gardenas, a successful regional account manager in a pharmaceutical firm. After earning an MBA in health care management, he moved into a lucrative position in pharmaceutical sales. José was grateful for the mentoring he had received along education's path because otherwise he would not have had the know-how to present himself with confidence in an arena that was entirely new to him.

The contrast between José's present position and his youth as a migrant worker child was enormous. He was one of the few from his community who had attended high school and the only one to earn an MBA. With hard work and a willingness to assume increasingly high levels of responsibility, he had risen within the firm from sales representative, to a territory representative, to district manager, and finally to his current role. As he rose through management ranks, he remained conscious of his roots and felt a personal need to contribute to society and to help the plight of those who remained migrant workers. He believed that equity could be achieved by migrant workers having access to quality education and quality health care. He often reflected back on his work as a district manager when he saw the inner working of hospitals in his district because it was there he saw the vision for health care that could be brought to migrant workers. He knew firsthand, as well as professionally, that migrant workers seek medical assistance less frequently than the population in general and later in the cycle of their illness. As a consequence, common diseases occur more frequently in the migrant population and tend to be more severe because they progress to advanced stages before the patient seeks medical care.

José wanted to make a social contribution. He wanted to be a role model in the health care system. However, he could not move to the not-for-profit sector without substantial financial sacrifice. After consulting with his family, he decided it was worth giving up income for the opportunity to serve for the greater good.

José worked long hours to identify sufficient county and state funding to renovate a two-story brick building that he made into an attractive clinic in a rural community, ideally located for serving the targeted population. He became known as a champion of an important cause. He obtains yearly grants from the state department of health and state department of migrant education in order to pay modestly for the services of the physicians and nursing staff. Charitable donations from his former pharmaceutical corporation help to extend the services of the clinic. As a leader who was willing to serve by sacrificing significant income, he says, "I have found that to live life richly does not mean that I earn more and more money."

Passivity is another symptom of a problem of low willingness to assume greater authority. Lack of drive can be acute for many reasons—for example, managers may be burdened with unreasonably high goals, or the organization or unit may be adrift without a meaningful strategy.

Guidelines for Increasing Willingness to Assume Responsibility

1. Understand the different responsibilities of different positions. Management and leadership are fundamentally different from hourly work, and many people are happier in the latter than in the former. The decision about whether "advancement" and willingness to assume more responsibility are appropriate for individual workers is often easier for them to make in the better-paid, more prestigious professions—medicine, law, and academe being good examples. Leadership and management require training and skill development, hard work, and self-discipline in order to be effective. Leaders must be willing to understand the needs of the job and to undertake the requisite accountability, time, and other personal sacrifices.

2. Develop a socialized power orientation. Leaders with a socialized power perspective desire power in order to benefit others. We saw this trait in action in José Gardenas in Exhibit 4.2. These leaders are less egotistical and materialistic than their counterparts who have a personal power orientation. They tend to be more emotionally mature. Their use of power is to build an organization for others to benefit. "**Servant leaders**" are at the epitome of this approach to leadership. In Robert Greenleaf's (1977) concept of servant leadership, a natural desire to serve brings a person to aspire to lead. This individual then works to ensure that others' highest priority needs are served. The personal growth of employees working together collaboratively in an ethical and supportive environment is important to the servant leader.

Because a leader's relationship to power derives from the person's core nature, this is not easy to change. Nor is it easy to self-assess because power is a great aphrodisiac. However, a socialized power orientation leads to greater long-term success (in both advancement and organizational effectiveness) and psychological well-being. Because the use of power is a social phenomenon, it is nearly impossible to study it without learning from others. Refer back to the personality characteristic of emotional maturity for a fuller discussion of socialized and personalized power orientations.

3. Learn to use a variety of influence strategies appropriately. Many have defined leadership primarily in terms of the exercise of influence—influence over people, influence over organizational culture, influence over goal attainment. Classic definitions of leadership include Katz and Kahn identification of "the influential increment over and above mechanical compliance with routine directives of the organization" (1978, 528); Rauch and Behling define leadership as "the process of influencing the activities of an organized group toward great achievement" (1984, 46). Various strategies were identified in the previous chapter. Just as important is the appropriate and ethical use of influence strategies. Those with a service mentality, personal integrity, and emotional maturity—the last three traits discussed in this chapter—are far less likely to use power inappropriately or for negative purposes.

NEED FOR ACHIEVEMENT

Leaders with a high **need for achievement** are those who have a strong drive to accomplish things and generally to be recognized for doing so. The very action and accomplishment of achieving the result is more satisfying, however, than being praised for achieving the result. The need for achievement has three elements. First, achievement is about task accomplishment. Task accomplishment for a detective might be successfully closing cases; for a managerial leader, it might be knowing that the team accomplished more than they did previously. Those high in need for achievement tend to set goals that are attainable but challenging and to stick with them. As a wit once noted, a diamond is only a lump of coal that stuck to its job. A second element of achievement is competition. What is the relative status of the achiever's level of accomplishment compared to others? This is the element most commonly associated with breaking records, a need for acknowledgment, and ambition. A third element is excellence, whether in quality, lack of errors, consistency, or innovation. How well or skillfully has the task been accomplished? Those high in need for achievement prefer to work on a problem for which they can affect the resulting excellence rather than leave it to chance.

David McClelland's classic work (1965, 1985) highlights the interaction of the needs for achievement, power, and affiliation. He defines an achievement orientation in a similar manner to that described in the previous paragraph, and he finds a curvilinear relationship with leadership. That is, a moderate drive for achievement is more likely to result in leadership advancement because those highest in need for achievement often have difficulty suppressing the competitive spirit when working in a team setting, and excellence is often defined in personal terms. Further, high achievers are sometimes loath to delegate.

The need for achievement can become extreme if not tempered with other traits such as a service mentality, personal integrity, and emotional maturity. Task orientation can become too intense. Robert Moses—known for the development of Jones Beach, beautification of the parks, and creation of the major bridges, tunnels, and highways in and around New York City—accomplished much, but accomplished it through sheer exercise of power (Caro 1975). Critics said that he lacked the ability to connect with people, in popular terms, even though he may have been the most powerful person in New York from the 1930s to the 1950s. His affinity for monumentalism, projects that required substantial space and resources, and cohesive conceptualization bequeathed the city a great legacy. Nevertheless, his leadership was considered flawed because of his ruthless tactics, penchant to micromanage, and inability to consider the needs of others—especially the poor. If measured, his need for achievement was extremely high. In contrast, a moderate amount of need for achievement is thought to be important for well-rounded success as a leader or entrepreneur.

Guidelines for Increasing Need for Achievement

1. Delineate and prioritize goals. A surprising number of managers believe that their goals are widely understood and accepted when in fact they are not because they have not been clearly delineated in writing for detailed discussion. Periodic discussions about macrogoals are important and should include opportunities for individuals to personally relate to those goals. A number of principles apply: goals must be attainable, clear, and challenging. Goals should have deadlines and not be overwhelming in number. Finally, goals should be prioritized with a clear, number one goal.

2. Strive for challenging but realistic goals. In well-managed situations, people will tend to achieve the goals that are set, especially goals they themselves have set, even if they are difficult. To be well managed, goals must generally be recorded, used as frequent benchmarks during the year, and have some type of accountability mechanism in place with rewards attached to goal achievement. This process is powerful if those doing the work have had input. Social science research has shown that generally employees as opposed to managers will set even higher standards for themselves when in charge of goal-setting (Latham and Yukl 1975).

A caveat in setting high goals is the distinction between challenging goals and unrealistic ones. Challenging goals encourage individuals to strive and work harder.

Unrealistic goals cause frustration and confusion. The careful leader does not discourage striving, yet is careful to steer subordinates away from failure. Of course, goal-setting does not always result in success; the possibility of failure, and the lessons it has to teach, are also an important part of the goal-setting process.

3. Harness opportunities for positive coordination, competition, and higher standards. Proper goal-setting is very powerful in coordinating people and activities by ensuring articulation of work elements and discussion for understanding and motivation (Earley, Wojnaroski, and Prest 1987). Group discussion and individual consultation can ensure that comparisons and competition that are fostered lead to higher standards rather than to cutthroat behaviors. Well-placed competition helps people rise to their best level. The drive for excellence ensures that standards either continue to rise or, if already high, do not drift.

4. Balance task completion goals with other types of goals. Conventional goal-setting encourages task completion and higher standards, but there are other important organizational goals that should not be left out of the mix. At least a few explicit goals should also be reserved for team building, employee development, long-term vision, collegiality, and ethical behavior so that in the quest for performance measures, balance is not forgotten (see Kaplan and Norton 1996).

LEADERSHIP TRAITS: VALUE ORIENTATIONS

PERSONAL INTEGRITY

Personal integrity serves as the foundation of sound character and requires adherence to a code of moral values and incorruptibility. The term "ethical" is frequently used as a comparable notion. The most overarching elements of personal integrity are consistency and coherence in practicing honesty and personal values. Persons who are consistent will act with the same values each time they are confronted with situations, whether or not the situations are similar. High levels of integrity require a thorough self-examination of values and an ability to express them succinctly. This is less common than is proclaimed.

The second element is honesty, which, at a minimum, refers to restraint from lying, cheating, and stealing. Those who are truthful not only avoid falsehoods or misleading information, but also are forthcoming. In other words, another person does not have to know the "right question" to ask in order to find out truthful information from the honest leader. The larger principle involved in cheating and stealing is self-dealing. Not taking things and not taking advantage of situations for selfish purposes are minimum thresholds of honor. The greater standard is placing other people's interests as high as or higher than your own. In extreme cases, this takes special moral courage, as illustrated in Exhibit 4.3 with the famous case of Marie Ragghianti.

Although the moral dimension of personal integrity is clear, the practical implication is not so obvious. In study after study, followers report that integrity and its related elements are the most important aspects of leadership—even before expertise and

Exhibit 4.3

Moral Courage

It is one thing to be honest and to maintain one's integrity in the daily routines of life; it is quite another when one's job is in jeopardy and possibly one's life. This is the story of Marie Ragghianti, whose profile in courage demonstrates how severe the test can be on rare occasions (Hejka-Ekins 1992).

In 1974, Marie was offered a position as extradition officer in Tennessee governor Blanton's administration. During this time she learned about the Board of Pardons and Paroles. She excelled at the job and, within two years, she was offered a seat on the board itself. In fact, the governor appointed her the chair of the three-person board. Yet even as she was taking over her new position, she was hearing rumors about the selling of gubernatorial pardons. She was also concerned about how energetically advisers to Governor Blanton insisted that loyalty and cooperation were important to the job and that service in the position itself was at the governor's pleasure.

Within a few months in the position, Ragghianti was sure that the accusations were true because she was constantly being pressured to approve pardons that were highly inappropriate. However, she did not know exactly who was involved. Upon meeting privately with the governor and discussing the rumors of the sale of clemency decisions, she was fairly sure that he too was involved. This was all made more obvious to her because he refused to allow the extradition of one of his chief financial benefactors, Bill Thompson, to another state. Thompson was highly involved in recommending pardons although he had no information from the Corrections Department, and he seemed to speak with the authority of the governor.

At this time she realized that she was at a critical juncture. She had been selected as a front because she was thought to be loyal, uninformed, and malleable. Indeed, she felt a loyalty to the administration that had provided such opportunities to her, but she was not uninformed and she had to decide how malleable she would be. Being loyal and malleable about management or the policy issues within the purview of the governor's authority was one thing. Acquiescing to breaking the law by approving the selling of pardons to murderers and other hardened criminals was quite another.

Ragghianti had three progressively more difficult choices. She could go along with the governor's recommendations and ignore the improprieties; she could resign and remove herself from the scandals; or she could seek to expose the scandal as an insider. She knew that life would never be the same if she blew the whistle. It wasn't.

In 1976 she secretly went to the FBI, which soon raided the governor's files and convened a grand jury. Soon she was urged to resign by the governor himself, but she refused, requiring him to officially fire her. He was unwilling to do so immediately, but Ragghianti knew that a case was being built against her. Within fourteen months the governor felt he had enough "evidence" and fired her for improper billing of the state, among other things. However, she fought the dismissal in court on grounds that the governor lacked good cause for doing so. Mysteriously the chief witness in her case, her former assistant, was murdered. Nonetheless, about a year later she won the court case, was reinstated in her job as chair of the board, and was reimbursed with a year's back pay. While she was able to complete her term, those around the governor were soon indicted, although only a few went to prison. The governor's conviction did not come until 1981 and a related scandal with better evidence, but he eventually served three years in prison also.

With the change of administration, Ragghianti—a controversial and highly publicized whistle-blower—was out of a job and also out of a career. Rather dispirited, she moved from the state. After a while she took up journalism and again had jobs related to rehabilitation in correctional systems. Eventually she found her professional stride and fully regained her peace of mind. However, like others who have called a halt to systemic corruption (such as Enron vice president for corporate development Sherron Watkins), Ragghianti paid a very high price in career and emotional torment. Although she was pleased with her boldness years later, she was uncertain that she would have had the necessary courage had she fully realized the danger and distress that her ethical convictions would cause.

competence! This makes sense when one considers the ramifications. If your leader is not honest, what good is competence? Or if your leader does not have integrity, how good will organizational success be if it is achieved? For example, in a U.S. Office of Personnel Management study (1997) of 10,000 managers with 151 behavioral categories, the first two items in all three levels of management (executive, management, and supervision) were ethics related. The first item was "models high standards of honesty and integrity" and the second was "creates a work environment where individuals are treated fairly." It is important to realize that personal integrity is not the sole criterion by which followers evaluate leaders, even if it is first among many. A classic business example of high standards of honesty is illustrated by the case of Tylenol chair Joseph Chiesa, who had a new product consultant introduce tamper-proof Tylenol Gelcaps after seven Chicago citizens died after taking Extra Strength Tylenol containing potassium cyanide poison in 1982. This was the first known case of death caused by deliberate product tampering. Despite the FBI's emphasis on trying to solve the high profile case, no suspects were ever charged with the murders, and because the case remains unsolved, no one knows the motive for the poisoning. But because of Tylenol's honesty and forthrightness with the public, the company recaptured 92 percent of sales that had been lost. Federal antitampering laws also resulted for the betterment of society.

Guidelines for Improving Personal Integrity

1. Examine and explain principles behind actions. As Mintzberg points out, leaders inevitably work in environments that are dense with interruptions, short decision time frames, and conflicting values (1973). Only by disciplined examination of one's practices, and the competing practices that frame decisions (Van Wart 1998), can one really hope to attain the high level of consistency that is expected of leaders.

2. Keep decision-making as transparent as possible. There are some cases in which decision-making must have some level of limited access related to national security, sensitive commercial transactions, and so forth. Yet in the larger scope of management, these cases are relatively few in number. Even when decisions are made in confidence, people expect the principles to be laid bare. Disciplinary actions may be executed in private (with full disclosure to the offender), but the principles of those actions must be made clear. Most employees will respect adverse decisions regarding matters such as downsizing if they see that the process was an open one.

3. Provide opportunities for candid feedback. This guideline supports the previous two. How can leaders examine their actions and principles if they do not get feedback? How can leaders be sure that decision-making is perceived as transparent if they do not receive feedback? In addition to receiving balanced feedback from a wide variety of stakeholders, good leaders integrate the feedback constantly, as both a source of problem resolution and a long-term guide to principled action.

A SERVICE MENTALITY

A service mentality is defined as an ethic of considering other people's interests, perspectives, and concerns. It has two major elements. The first is a concern for others: the public at large, customers, and employees. This is attitudinal in nature. For example, when a decision about expanding hours of operation comes up, the leader with a service mentality will tend to downplay her own needs and focus on balancing the needs of the customers and, when applicable, the employees. The second element is more behavioral: a preference for including others in decision-making to the degree that it is appropriate. A leader can have a concern for others and act on their behalf, but not directly involve them. Consistently acting on others' behalf is a type of paternalism antithetical to a robust service motivation. Decision-making inclusiveness can consist of a whole range of options, from minimal consultation prior to the decision to full delegation of authority.

A service motivation has clear, practical benefits. Many celebrated rulers in history have had a service mentality. Alexander the Great regularly consulted with his troops to keep morale high; Caesar Augustus included the public prominently in his decision-making. Equally telling is the number of rulers, such as Charles I in England and Louis XVI in France, who lost power because of insulation from the people and their concerns.

Guidelines for Improving Service Mentality

1. Adopt your professional code of ethics as your own. Most functional areas within business have a professional code of ethics that calls for professional standards. This is not new. Physicians today still take the Hippocratic Oath, pledging themselves to the ethical practice of medicine, traditionally attributed to the Greek physician Hippocrates but probably written by one of his students in the fourth century B.C. In today's business, there are relatively new acts and regulations that require certain procedures in order to avert scandals that harm the public. Sarbanes-Oxley, for example, was a federal law enacted in 2002 to prevent the kind of accounting fraud that occurred in companies such as Enron, Tyco International, Adelphia, and WorldCom. The first code of ethics in the human resources field was developed by its professional society in 1972 and has been changed over the years to adapt to the times. Accounting and law have important codes. Many companies have codes of ethics to accompany their values statements. It is important for professionals to understand what these codes call for in their behavior and why.

2. Expand decision-making to include as many people as feasible. Significant organizational decisions are generally improved with broad input and joint decision-making. Further, leaders are better able to serve when they understand other people's thought processes. An added benefit is that both leaders and followers become better educated about issues and technical challenges, and there tends to be more commitment to implement decisions.

Next we turn to leadership skills, the complementary characteristics that are especially refined by education, experience, and exposure to other leaders.

LEADERSHIP SKILLS

Stradivari had skill as a crafter of stringed instruments, and Sugar Ray Leonard had skill as a boxer. George Eliot said that God gave Antonio Stradivari the talent he needed to be the world's finest violinmaker, but that nonetheless it was Antonio himself who refined that skill and brought it to fruition. Sugar Ray Leonard reportedly quipped at about the time he won the Olympic gold in 1976, "We're all given some sort of skill in life. Mine just happens to be beating up on people." This chapter focuses on leadership skills that are particularly susceptible to refinement, albeit the skill of leading rather than the skill of beating up on people.

Skills are defined as learned characteristics that are heavily affected by training, education, and practice. Skills are similar to traits in that they are broad; they are similar to behaviors in that they are generally more directly observable than traits.

Although skills sometimes seem so broad as to be nebulous, they are immensely important. Who can imagine a powerful leader who does not have some exceptional abilities in communication, social interaction, and influence skills, for example? Six leadership skills are discussed in this part of the chapter: communication skills, social skills, influence skills, analytic skills, technical skills, and a proclivity for continual learning.

COMMUNICATION SKILLS

Whether a person is leading others, directing operations, or effecting major organizational change, communication is a fundamental part of the process and therefore a key skill in the leader's repertoire. Communication is broadly defined as the ability to effectively exchange information for meaning and shared understanding. Communication is conveyed both directly through language and indirectly through gestures, posture, and other nonverbal means. There are four main elements of communication skills in regard to leadership—oral communication, written communication, listening, and nonverbal communication—all of which shall be discussed here.

Oral communication is often considered the most prominent. Oral communication takes different forms, from speaking with individuals or small and large groups to communicating via electronic media. Some individuals are quite good at everyday one-on-one interactions, while others are better in groups. Another important distinction is the ability to relay technical versus emotive messages orally. The ability to give a clear order, for example, and the ability to inspire troops going into battle are both important but entirely different. While some leaders are blessed with both skills, most tend to be better at one type.

Oprah Winfrey is a person with extraordinary communication skills who was already successful at age thirty-two when her talk show went national and she leveraged her ability to create a media empire and business fortune. Her on-air communication style is personable instead of detached, and she might be heard confessing intimate information or crying with guests.

Written communication skills include using emails, memoranda, reports, special-purpose documents, and written public statements. Both underreliance and overreliance on written communication are common, depending on the bias of the leader. Generally, it is the written record that lasts most effectively over time, including for people not prominently in the public eye. An interesting example is drawn from Abraham Lincoln's Gettysburg Address. In writing the speech on the way to Gettysburg,

Lincoln felt pleased with the product. However, afterward he noted that it did not seem to be particularly well received. In fact, many thought his entire speech was simply the preamble. Yet history appreciated the density and clarity of the language and the speech has become one of the defining moments of American political expression.

Listening as a communication skill performs several functions. It is a source of information about facts, trends, problems, and performance. Embedded in this source is information about people's attitudes, moods, and motivation levels. Just as important, quality listening is an act of respect; therefore, it often provides a stronger bond than do speaking and writing. Despite the importance of listening as a communication skill, it is estimated that most adults listen at about one-quarter of their overall capacity. If a leader were actively listening, he would have quieted his own mind so that the other person's words and nonverbals could enter for their own impact without being evaluated. Listening communicates to the other person that "you are heard." Failure to listen effectively is a time-waster for organizations. In addition to the personal loss from employees not being heard, failure to listen effectively during professional meetings causes large amounts of organizational time to be wasted. If a manager attends the average of about sixty one-hour professional meetings per month and is "tuned out" just half of the time—daydreaming, composing his own thoughts on the subject, doing other work, judging the speaker or multi-tasking—thirty hours per month have already been compromised.

Nonverbal communication conveys a significant part of a message through immense stores of information conveyed through eye movement, facial expression, posture, gestures, and body movement. Like other aspects of communication, nonverbal communication can be done well or poorly. The leader who is about to announce how the organization will deal with a decreased budget and strides into the room with grace instills confidence; the leader who shuffles into the room and looks nervous does not.

Guidelines for Improving Communication Skills

1. Assess communication skills to identify strengths and weaknesses. Assessment of communication skills has to be discrete enough to identify the specific subcompetencies. For example, if a general perception exists that a leader's writing skills are deficient, assessment should be done to see if that perception really means (1) too little written communication, (2) the wrong type of message, or (3) poor quality in construction. Means of assessment include personal introspection, and scrutiny from workers and experts.

2. Develop a plan to address weaknesses. Perceived weakness should be addressed directly, whether by increasing the quantity of communication, using the correct medium for communication, or utilizing writing classes or communication coaches to improve quality. Some basic communication tips are included in Exhibit 4.4.

SOCIAL SKILLS

Social skills are a major pillar of a leader's skill set. They overlap with communication skills and are occasionally subsumed under them.

Exhibit 4.4

Communication Tips

Communication in General
1. In general, it is difficult to communicate too much to people in the organization. Ample communication tends to include people, inform them, and make them feel better in crises.
2. For important messages such as setting standards or recording evaluations, however, clarity is more important than quantity.
3. Less-is-more is also true for vision, mission, and inspiring statements where pithiness and symbolism count a lot.

Oral Messages

Informal
1. Do not talk just to friends, supporters, and those close at hand. Often, more important contacts are critics, competitors, and end-users.
2. It is especially important for leaders in large organizations to find opportunities to talk to people in regional and field offices on a regular basis.

Formal
3. In one-on-one communication, learn to pace your communication partner. That is, try to appreciate the person's style in the communication process. If the other person is "open," you are more likely to be heard and to be able to persuade.
4. In talking to groups, use:
   • a memorable idea, physical prop, story, symbol, etc., for all major points,
   • expressions of interest or passion for the topic,
   • a simple but clear structure such as a five-part frame (introduction, three major points, and a conclusion), and
   • one or more practice sessions to rehearse the material.

Written Messages
1. In informal writing such as emails, never say anything that you do not want passed on—because it will be!
2. In formal writing, remember that people generally have very high standards. All formal writing should have a clear purpose statement, appropriate style and structure, and flawless grammar.
3. When possible, give drafts of important documents to others to proof and critique, and reread the draft yourself after several hours have passed. If it is very important, reread it the next day. Also, it is useful to read once slowly for grammar and once for meaning.

Listening
1. There is no substitute for taking a genuine interest in what others have to say.
2. When possible, paraphrase the other person' ideas to ensure accurate understanding and demonstrate attention. Use expressions such as "So what you're saying is . . . " and "Let me see if I properly understand your meaning. You are saying that . . . "
3. Try to build on the other person's ideas. For example, good salesmen will listen to what a customer wants and then to try to sell it to the person, regardless of the product that they represent.

Nonverbal Communication
1. Remember that physical alertness and attention to task often say more than words. Attitudes such as boredom, apathy, and lack of confidence all have unmistakable physical manifestations, even though you may try to hide them.
2. If possible, watch a videotape of yourself to study your nonverbal patterns. Be sure to watch the tape at least once without the sound.

Social skills are the ability to interact effectively with others and in groups by using rule-governed learned behavior, respecting others, and satisfying your own needs without damaging the needs of others. There are three major elements of social skills. The first element is personal likability, which focuses on aspects such as optimism, kindness, tact, and respect for others. Optimism means maintaining a positive frame of mind, even when people are tired and work is not going well (H. Jennings 1943; Zullow et al. 1988). Kindness helps people trust a leader (Fleishman 1953). Tact allows people to retain their dignity. Respect for others allows leaders to cultivate people's diversity and to see others as assets rather than costs in professional settings (Fiedler 1967; Priem 1990).

A second element of social skills is expressiveness. An aspect of expressiveness is simply being sure that the right thing is said or done at the ideal time. Leaders who are strong at expressiveness are also particularly capable of putting emotions or professional passions into words. This is important in order to make people feel personally valued, infuse meaning into work, and "rally the troops" (Stohl 1986). For example, the founder of IKEA and one of the world's richest men, Ingvar Kamprad, was known for shaking hands with all 1,000 IKEA employees who attended his company's annual meeting.

Social perceptiveness is the third element of social skills (Newcomb 1961). Insight into and effective use of interpersonal dynamics are critical in demanding leadership positions (Stogdill 1948).

A special case of social skills is charisma, the natural ability to inspire devotion or allegiance. True charismatics, though rare, have intense social skills. In asking students in their twenties "what business person comes to mind when you think about charisma," the most common responses were Richard Branson, known for being Chairman of Virgin Group, and Oprah Winfrey, known for being a television host and producer of frequently uplifting and inspirational stories. Both Branson and Winfrey are known for having intense social skills. However, like any other trait or skill, charisma can lead to mistakes and evil. In Chapter 7 we shall investigate more about leaders known as charismatics, and in Exhibit 7.3 you will read about one of the famous examples of negative charisma in cult leader Jim Jones.

The importance of social skills is easy to understand. They lead directly to personal power (discussed below), enhanced communication, and increased ability to engage in team-building.

Guidelines for Improving Social Skills

1. Ask others whom you trust for feedback and take a critical look at your social skills to identify strengths and weaknesses. While most people enjoy a distinctive personality and may even find unique quirks to be interesting, untrained social skills may preclude effective leadership. Critical observation can include reviewing patterns of responses from other people, anonymous feedback instruments, and personality assessment seminars.

2. Develop a plan to address social weaknesses. Diligence and practice can turn liabilities around. Tactless people can learn discretion when they come to understand the ramifications. Verbally awkward people can refine their speaking at Toastmasters. People can learn to stop negative "self-talk" and practice positive, can-do mental routines that translate into greater optimism (Manz 1986; Manz et al. 1988).

INFLUENCE SKILLS

All leaders have various types and amounts of power that give them the potential to affect people, resources, and outcomes. **Influence skills** involve using power to produce effects on people, resources, or the course of events for purposes such as strategic or political gain.

The simplest analysis of power is based on the position, the person, or a combination of both (French and Raven 1959). Power based largely on position includes traditional authority. The power of authority stems from established law or rules, organizational structure, or custom. Control over the environment includes the ability to change the technology, physical environment, or patterns of work. Coercive power is the ability to punish, and reward power is the ability to provide financial, psychological, career, or other benefits.

Leaders exercise power over others and ultimately increase or diminish their power through the wise and effective use of concrete influence strategies. See Exhibit 4.5 for a comparison of influence strategies that are associated with differing levels of position power and personal power.

All people have both power and influence; they simply vary in type and amount. Organizational managers structurally have greater position power, but personal power can be more evenly distributed among people at all levels of the hierarchy. The corollary is that influence works both ways. While effective leaders have greater influence, at the same time they are acutely aware of and harness the process of exchange.

Guidelines for Increasing Influence Skills

1. Power is acquired over time. Highly effective leaders understand power and its importance, recognize that it is not amassed quickly, and develop the discipline to augment it over time. This is especially true of personal power.

2. The understanding and cultivation of influence tactics over time are also essential to high effectiveness. Effective leaders are able to use the least power necessary, especially formal power; use the right influence strategies for different situations; and use multiple influence strategies simultaneously for important or difficult objectives.

3. Effective leaders are very careful to guard against the corrosive effects of power and influence. While power and influence are necessary, they can lead to self-centeredness, selfishness, blind spots, manipulation, insensitivity, rudeness, arrogance, and other personal pathologies. See Exhibit 4.6 for an acclaimed example of the corrosive effects of power on Enron's CEO Kenneth Lay.

Exhibit 4.5 **Sources of Power and the Related Types of Influence** (for individuals)

Potential sources of power Position/personal power dichotomy	Subtypes[1]	Influence strategies
Largely position power	• Authority • Control over work environment • Reward • Punishment	• *Legitimating tactics:* Emphasizing the consistency of an influence attempt with established policies, procedures, or past practices, or directly asserting the right of the agent as an appropriate decision-maker to make the request or order • *Pressure tactics:* Using demands, threats, or persistence to influence; more than any other influence strategy, pressure tactics emphasize punishment • *Exchange tactics:* Mutually trading favors, either in explicit agreements or implicit, loose understandings; although emphasizing rewards, it is understood that punishment may be meted out to those who renege on agreements
Mixed position and personal power	• Expertise • Control over information	• *Rational persuasion:* Using facts and logic to convince the target that a request or proposal will be successful in achieving an objective • *Consultation:* Involving the target in the process of planning, in providing substantive feedback, or in making changes
Largely personal power	• Referent (power derived from another person liking you who is therefore willing to follow your lead)	• *Emotional appeals:* Stimulating enthusiasm and commitment by arousing certain values, preferences, or shared beliefs of the target, enabling people to feel good about making sacrifices, uniting people with shared beliefs, and enhancing self-worth and satisfaction of those targeted; also known as inspirational appeals • *Personal appeals:* Sharing "favors" based on feelings of loyalty, friendship, or human compassion; when done on a reciprocal, ongoing, and appropriate basis, introduces a culture of mutual assistance and support • *Friendliness:* Using affable behavior or praise or providing unrequested assistance in order to increase the target's responsiveness to future requests and orders

[1] Subtypes in this column are expanded from French and Raven's (1959) five sources of power: coercive, reward, legitimate, referent, and expert.

Exhibit 4.6

Power and Corruption

A variety of published lists come out annually. The Best Dressed. The Worst Dressed. The Best Companies to Work For. The Richest People in the World. The Most Corrupt. Often politicians make that particular list; but in the twenty-first century many bankers have earned that dubious distinction. Former Enron chair and CEO Kenneth Lay is one of the "most corrupt." When the Houston company declared bankruptcy in 2001, it was considered the worst case of financial corruption in U.S. history: 20,000 employees lost their jobs and investors lost literally billions of dollars.

Kenneth Lay has come to symbolize the power, greed, and corruption of the 1990s (Sunseri and Rottman 2006). With a warped belief that he was entitled to use investors' money for personal gain, he took a hefty salary of $42 million in 1999 while dumping his own company stock and stock options for $300 million as the stock fell. At the same time, he encouraged others to invest and buy what he knew was actually valueless stock. The jury further decided that Lay had lied to all stakeholders in order to disguise the worthless state of Enron. The jury pronounced him guilty on all counts of conspiracy and fraud. Although Lay died while vacationing before sentencing, he had already spent most of his accumulated wealth on legal fees. Until the end, he maintained that he was innocent and that the fall of Enron was caused by employee fraud and theft that occurred in secret deals. He never acknowledged or apologized for his corrupt behavior that led directly to others' financial demise and personal loss and suffering.

ANALYTIC SKILLS

Analytic skills are defined as the ability to structure alternatives in decision-making and to deal factually or explain different viewpoints in situations that are complex and ambiguous. Much of what people think of as intelligence is covered under analytic skills. Some elements of this skill cluster are aptly described as traits because of a large innate element. Yet analytic skills can also be improved through education and training. People may have good analytic skills in one domain, such as work processes, while having weak analytic skills in others, such as social or political situations (Streufert and Swezey 1986).

There are at least three major elements that constitute analytic skills, starting with *leadership discrimination* or the ability to distinguish between and respond uniquely to different stimuli. An example of leadership discrimination is the ability to resist contamination of personal arenas by avoiding a colleague who is delightfully gregarious in a professional setting, but whose behavior borders on vulgarity when not in his professional suit.

Cognitive complexity is another major element of analytic skills—the ability to consider and use different dimensions simultaneously or use different levels of complexity in different domains (Hunt 1996; Steufert and Swezey 1986). For a manager to do a good job in performance appraisals, some degree of cognitive complexity is an asset. Not only must the manager consider the individual dimensions of accuracy, speed, work volume, communication, record-keeping, problem-solving, creativity, collegiality, responsiveness, and flexibility, but also the cognitively complex manager will understand and address these factors as they interact with each other and the requirements of the work environment. A manager may achieve success in a low-performing division by focusing on the interactive effects of recruitment, training, and clear work protocols. But when transferred to another division that is to perform well, the manager may have to focus on the subtle dimensions involved in advanced team-building, improved reward systems, and external benchmarking.

A third element of analytic skills is *tolerance of ambiguity*—the ability to suspend judgment while new data are being gathered and to live with the lack of a decision for varying periods of time. It is considered a leadership mode reflecting different levels of thinking and different levels of development. Whereas a style of leadership refers to particular behaviors, a *mode* refers to thought processes for viewing the world. When people with extremely different modes are paired together, they need to appreciate each other's differences or there will be conflict. Suppose, for example, that a manager with a high ambiguity tolerance oversees a team of engineers with low ambiguity tolerance. As long as there is no emergency, the manager places little structure on the team and accepts broad assignments with unclear bounds, which the team finds stressful and inefficient. The manager knows that the engineers are highly talented, and therefore he purposefully does not wish to constrain them and their creativity. The manager is quite comfortable living with indecision, but the team is not. Given a relatively undefined project, the team begins to say that the manager is ineffective and does not provide "leadership" because he does not systematically and decisively resolve the ambiguous areas. In this situation, mutual understanding, through training, of tolerance for ambiguity may lead to improved analytic skills or bring both modes closer to what is needed for the type of work. On the one hand, it is true that unneeded, inefficient, and expensive billable hours should be avoided, but it is also true that some projects, even engineering projects, cannot initially be so tightly defined as to be presented in a neat box.

Guidelines for Improving Analytic Skills

1. Enhance analytic skills through targeted experience as well as extensive training and education. Experience is a useful teacher in providing basic information and data; training and education become superior teachers in enhancing the actual tools of discrimination and pointing out nuance. Conscious understanding of leadership discrimination, cognitive complexity, and tolerance for ambiguity should be developed.

2. Enhance reflectiveness. Even training and education can go only so far. Leaders must deal with unique combinations of issues and new problems. A certain amount of analytic work is the customization of knowledge, discrimination, cognitive complexity, and ambiguity tolerance through reflection. Reflection can involve sitting in a quiet room or doodling with a series of problems in order to see if there is a higher pattern and solution.

TECHNICAL SKILLS

Although leaders may do little technical work themselves, their mastery of technical skills remains important. For scores of years it has been known that even an executive "must know enough of the general field not to get lost in the labyrinth. If he does not

Exhibit 4.7

Technical Creativity Versus Leadership Ability

In an interesting set of studies about technical abilities, leadership abilities, and age, H.C. Lehman (1937, 1942) studied chemists. In the first study he found that chemists, on average, make their greatest technical contributions between the ages of twenty-eight and thirty-two. At this point the chemists were completely trained, had some experience in the field, but still had a lot of fresh ideas. That is, excessive socialization had not diminished their ability to "think outside the box." In the second study, he found that the optimal age for eminent leadership in the field of chemistry was from forty-five to forty-nine. That is, it took time for others to appreciate chemists' technical contributions, for them to rise in organizational roles, and for them to polish their social skills, which tend to increase rather than diminish over time. Additionally, in a later study Lehman found that great leaders in a variety of professional fields tend to be those whose gifts are recognized at an early age and thus who receive special attention and/or training (1953). Of course, in all his work Lehman was studying those who achieved eminent leadership status. Therefore, great technical ability early in the career certainly does not guarantee eminent leadership status later; rather, it serves as a powerful advantage that may or may not be exploited.

know the program at the onset, he must master quietly its major elements. Otherwise he will be unable to command the loyalty and respect of his specialists and weld them together as a team" (Stone 1945, 215). Exhibit 4.7 offers an insight into leadership in a functional area and its relationship to technical creativity.

It is also understood that leaders who want to have a significant impact on operations frequently have strong technical skills and involvement. This last facet, however, can be a two-edged sword in practice. Such executives are occasionally the pioneers needed to make important changes that would fail without major executive involvement. But excessive executive focus on technical issues and personal expertise is frequently a source of career derailment because of a tendency toward micromanagement and underachievement (Lombardo and McCauley 1988).

Technical skill for leaders entails the basic professional and organizational knowledge and practice associated with an area of work. Often leaders are hired or promoted based on their mastery of skills involving technical information and skills unique to the discipline. For example, managers in transportation generally have logistics or engineering degrees, in hospitals, health administration or medical degrees, and in accounting firms, accounting degrees (Carnevale, Gainer, and Schulz 1990). Even if training managers do not have a degree in human resource management or adult education, they should understand learning theory and training techniques.

A basic competence repertoire also includes information about the organization— processes, rules, employees, facilities, clients, interest groups, elected overseers, culture, and so on. External hires, people hired from outside the company, with background in the appropriate discipline may still have to spend considerable effort to understand the particular organization. However, sometimes external hires who have to master an understanding of the organization are assets in the long run because they have broader experience and can use comparative practices as a source of benchmarking.

Some leaders, in some fields more than others, have a tendency to remain technically proficient. In the field of information, for example, Bill Gates remains a knowledgeable technical leader, as evidenced in his talks about the Digital Decade, which makes digital technology central to how we live and work. He converses as only a technocratic leader on Internet storage, high-definition video, and natural user interfaces could. In contrast, companies that advertise for an "HR generalist" to fill a slot as a human resources vice president seek applicants with prior specialization in technical areas of human resources—such as compensation, benefits, safety, staffing, and employee development—who have, over time, moved out of a technical area into general supervision. However, a former benefits specialist, who may be effective as a VP, may no longer be a good source on the subtleties of current medical insurance or retirement concerns.

Guidelines for Improving Technical Skills

1. Assess your technical skills and the need for technical competence. Levels of technical competence can be assessed using a test and are much enhanced by asking candid subordinates how they would evaluate such skills or by using an anonymous survey instrument. Easily acquired competencies should be mastered as a routine aspect of ongoing personal development, as will be discussed in Chapter 12. Because professional expertise is not a critical issue for many leaders who manage programs, clusters of programs, or whole agencies, those technical skills that take considerable time to enhance must be carefully weighed against the other areas that demand attention and improvement. Increasingly, senior managers keep up technical skills on their own time or altogether delegate specialized expertise to others.

2. Develop a plan to improve select technical skills. No matter how modest or ambitious such plans may be, technical skills improve only through self-discipline. If state-of-the-art knowledge in the discipline is slipping, it may be necessary to incorporate a thorough reading of a major journal once a month or to attend conferences several times a year. If meeting skills are weak, then it may be necessary to purchase meeting software or ask for a critique of each meeting at its conclusion.

CONTINUAL LEARNING

Continual learning means taking responsibility for acquiring new information, looking at old information in new ways, and finding ways to use new and old information creatively. It relates closely to and builds on several other competencies. Cognitive complexity is required for analyzing old and new problems and developing creative solutions, emotional maturity is a competency that is important for effective relations-oriented leadership to empower others to become effective leaders themselves, and continual learning and adapting is required for effective leadership in our turbulent business environment (Yukl 2006, 444–445).

One important element is the ability to glean and use new information and data. The basic learning mode requires people to review and monitor data and trends, both internal and external to the organization. Basic learning requires using new information in standard ways.

The second element is the ability to expand knowledge. Advanced learning involves creating new knowledge that leads to application of innovation or invention for improved organizational processes.

The top two companies in the *Fortune* list of the "100 Best Companies to Work For" in 2008 had in common an emphasis on continual learning. Google, which ranked number one for two years in a row and had 761,799 applications for 3,039 new jobs in 2007, may be known for its free back massages, dog-friendly policies, and top chefs providing free food in employee cafeterias, but Google also provided 120 hours per year, on average, in professional training. The company ranked number two, Quicken Loans, is an online mortgage lender with 94,000 applicants for 1,968 new jobs in 2007. Quicken, on average, provided 250 hours per year in professional training. The hours spent learning on the job for these top companies translate to three weeks or more than six weeks, respectively. By 2009, both of those organizations slipped in ranking, and their respective rankings remained the same in 2010: Google to number four and Quicken Loans to number twenty-nine (*Fortune* 2010).

Some companies offer continual learning with indirect job benefits that may or may not have immediate application. For example, Ruiz Foods in Dinuba, California, is known for its English as a Second Language programs and for inviting the regional office of the U.S. Department of Housing and Urban Development to arrange for bankers, credit counselors, and advocates for affordable housing to present *Una Casa Para Mi Familia* to interested Ruiz employees, about half of whom do not own homes (Griswold 2003). Fred Ruiz, cofounder and chair, said, "Nurturing and educating employees is more than an after-hours benefit. . . . In short, taking extraordinary steps to help employees makes good business sense" (*Costco Connection* 2005). Many companies help employees cover the costs of returning for a degree in higher education, particularly when the degree complements the job.

Guidelines for Increasing Continual Learning

1. Focus on the benefits of learning. It is critical to keep the benefits of continuous learning in mind at all times. It provides entrepreneurial opportunities for organizational and personal advancement and it keeps people up-to-date with their business and the world, which in turn makes life more interesting.

2. Learn from surprises and problems. Dealing with surprises, problems, mistakes, and failures is the work of leaders. Leaders have a responsibility to take a proactive mental attitude toward challenges. Indeed, many problems and failures give way to unforeseen and substantial opportunities.

3. Find ways to challenge assumptions and mental models. Because leaders have the ability to change assumptions and mental models, it is their responsibility to find ways to be vigilant about questioning them. Ultimately, challenging assumptions should be a form of self-discipline that complements external competition; effective leaders constantly ask if things can be done better and whether people are achieving their best. Learning should be thought of not only as an individual activity, but also as one that is done by groups, teams, and even an entire organization.

CONCLUSION

Traits are stable characteristics or dispositions, comparatively innate or learned early, which are amenable to modest adjustment over time (either for better or worse). The traits discussed in this chapter are self-confidence, decisiveness, resilience, energy, flexibility, emotional maturity, willingness to assume responsibility, need for achievement, personal integrity, and service mentality. Exhibit 4.8 provides a summary of the traits, their definitions, and their guidelines.

Several broad assertions can be made about traits. First, despite the demise of pure trait-based leadership theories, they are enormously important. When followers judge leaders, they tend to focus on traits. Even discounting this tendency as a too-easy and unsophisticated means for quick judgments of a leader's abilities, traits are clearly powerful predictors of success or failure in very general terms.

Second, there is a good deal of synergy between certain traits. More self-confidence tends to increase and improve decisiveness. Greater resilience enhances energy, which leads to greater ability to achieve and to a greater willingness to assume responsibility.

Third, certain traits and trait sets balance each other. This is important in preventing leaders from either being denied opportunities or derailing their careers. Most notably, the value traits (service mentality, personal integrity, and emotional maturity) that have an other-oriented perspective balance all the self-oriented traits. Even among the self-oriented traits, flexibility balances decisiveness and resilience balances need for achievement.

Fourth, the traits do not have an identical pattern. For some, more is generally better (a straight-line pattern): self-confidence, resilience, energy, flexibility, service mentality, personal integrity, and emotional maturity. A moderate degree is often best for the value traits: need for achievement and willingness to assume responsibility. More than perhaps any other trait, decisiveness is highly specific to the situation, so that good leaders can both be highly decisive at times (e.g., crises) and pull back from rapid decision-making at others (e.g., when group participation or delegation is appropriate).

Finally, an authoritative or singular list of leadership traits is not possible for several reasons, including that people define the concepts differently for varying purposes. Is resilience a trait or simply an element of energy? Some authors list as few as four traits while social scientists identify dozens. Defining and operationalizing them varies significantly from study to study. For this study, ten traits that are important for leadership have been identified, as consistent with the literature.

Like the ten traits, the six broad-based skills discussed here are important and multifaceted. Exhibit 4.9 (see page 124) presents a summary of the skills, subelements, and major recommendations covered in this chapter.

Intelligence is not listed as a trait that emphasizes the innate elements of mental brilliance. Instead, cognitive skills that focus on the learned aspects of mental ability have been discussed. A cognitively well-trained, well-disciplined person of mediocre mental acuity will generally outperform an untrained, undisciplined genius (Stogdill 1948, 1974). One manager may be highly intelligent, physically robust and

Exhibit 4.8 **Leadership Traits and Recommendations**

Leadership trait	Subelement of trait	Major recommendations
Self-confidence The general (positive) sense that one has the ability to accomplish what needs to be accomplished	• Self-esteem • Self-efficacy • Courage	1. Assess personal strengths and weaknesses in order to address them. 2. Seek training or experience to remedy skill or knowledge liabilities. 3. Practice positive self-talk and positive visualization.
Decisiveness The ability to act relatively quickly depending on circumstances without excessively damaging decision quality	• Willingness to make unilateral decisions • Ability to act quickly in a crisis • Ability to remain calm under crisis	1. Study decision-making. 2. Do not procrastinate in gathering information for or making important decisions. 3. Prepare for emergencies. 4. Stay calm.
Resilience Resilience refers to a hardiness of spirit, usually complemented by a hardiness of strength that allows a leader to remain focused or to spring back effectively when pushed by external influences.	• Persistence • Stress tolerance	1. Know long-term goals. 2. Be patient and flexible in achieving goals. 3. Learn to tolerate stress and then let go of it.
Energy The physical and psychological ability to perform	• Physical vitality • Mental interest • High activity level	1. Maintain optimism and health. 2. Cultivate dedication to the profession and interest in the work at hand. 3. Seek to eliminate "energy distracters."
Flexibility The ability to bend without breaking and be adjustable to change or capable of modification	• Adaptability • Alertness to alternatives	1. Distinguish critical objectives. 2. Appreciate creativity of decision-making. 3. Appreciate innovation and change.
Emotional maturity A conglomerate of characteristics that indicate that a person is well balanced in a number of psychological and behavioral dimensions	• Self-awareness • Self-control • Responsibility for actions • Socialized power orientation	1. Assess personal strengths and weaknesses. 2. Exercise self-control and self-discipline. 3. Take responsibility for one's actions. 4. Develop a socialized power orientation.
Willingness to assume responsibility Willingness to take positions requiring broader decision-making duties and greater authority	• Acceptance of different responsibilities • Willingness to use power (in acceptable ways)	1. Understand different types of responsibility and be accountable. 2. Develop socialized power orientation. 3. Learn to use influence strategies appropriately.

Leadership trait	Subelement of trait	Major recommendations
Need for achievement Strong drive to accomplish things and to be recognized for successes	• Task accomplishment • Competition • Striving for excellence	1. Set and prioritize goals. 2. Strive for difficult but realistic goals. 3. Harness opportunities for positive competition and higher standards. 4. Balance task completion and other goals.
Personal integrity The state of being whole and/or connected with oneself, one's profession, and the society of which one is a member, as well as being incorruptible	• Consistency and coherence of values • Honesty • Fairness • Inclusiveness in decision-making	1. Examine and explain principles behind actions. 2. Keep decision-making as transparent as possible. 3. Provide opportunities for candid feedback.
Service mentality An ethic of considering other people's interests, perspectives, and concerns	• Service to the public at large • Service to clients and customers • Service to employees	1. Remember one's commitment for social responsibility. 2. Exhibit and promote professionalism. 3. Demonstrate concern for subordinates.

attractive, and come from a prestigious family, yet never get close to being a leader. When leaders work toward competencies such as the following, they will develop themselves as leaders: traits such as self-confidence, decisiveness, resilience, high energy, flexibility, and emotional maturity; classic motivations such as willingness to assume responsibility and need for achievement; values such as personal integrity and a service mentality; and communication, social, influence, analytic, technical, and continual learning skills. Although part of the leader's hand is dealt at birth and early childhood, these are areas that can be enormously affected by self-disciplined study and practice.

KEY TERMS

competency
emotional intelligence
energy distracters
influence skills
need for achievement
resilience

self-efficacy
servant leader
skills
socialized power orientation
stress tolerance

RESOURCES

These or other Internet resources can be assigned to complement topics covered in the chapter in order to increase the richness and depth of class discussion. Although sites that tend to be enduring have been selected for the Resources sections, be aware that

Exhibit 4.9

Leadership Skills and Recommendations

Leadership skill	Subelements of skill	Major recommendations
Communication skills • The ability to effectively exchange information through active and passive means	Oral skills Writing skills Listening skills Nonverbal skills	• Assess communication skills to identify strengths and weaknesses. • Develop a plan to address weaknesses (see Exhibit 5.1).
Social skills • The ability to interact effectively in social settings and to understand and productively harness one's own and others' personality structures	Personal likability (an extreme form is charisma) Expressiveness Social perceptiveness	• Assess social skills and identify those that are weak. • Develop a plan to address social weaknesses that are critical.
Influence skills • The actual use of sources of power through concrete behavior strategies	The effectiveness with which one uses influence strategies (see Exhibit 5.3) The range of influence strategies that one has to use (see Exhibit 5.3)	• Assess sources of power and ability to use influence tactics. • Develop the discipline to augment power. • Understand and cultivate influence strategies. • Guard against the corrosive effects of power.
Analytic skills • The ability to remember, make distinctions, and deal with complexity	Memory Discrimination Cognitive complexity Ambiguity tolerance	• Assess cognitive abilities. • Enhance analytic skills through targeted experience, training, and education. • Enhance reflectiveness.
Technical skills • The basic professional and organizational knowledge and practice associated with an area of work	Technical information and skills of the profession Information about the organization Basic management knowledge and skills	• Assess level of technical skills and the skills actually necessary for position. • Develop a plan to improve select technical skills.
Continual learning • Taking responsibility for acquiring new information, looking at old information in new ways, and finding ways to use new and old information creatively	The ability to glean and use new information and data The ability to expand knowledge (knowledge creation)	• Focus on benefits of learning. • Learn from surprises and problems. • Find ways to challenge assumptions and mental models. • Invest in learning despite turbulent or difficult times.

in some cases webpages are changed, and it will be necessary to search for similar online articles.

Retired general Colin Powell speaks from his *Leadership Primer* with eighteen Lessons of Leadership. Discuss how his lessons relate to the traits and skills discussed in this chapter.

- Oren Harari, *A Leadership Primer from General (Ret.) Colin Powell*, The Chally Group, 2007. www.chally.com/enews/powell.html.

Some persons who succeed as leaders also stutter. Look at this long list of such individuals named by the Stuttering Foundation, and identify skills and traits from the chapter that may overcome any concerns the individuals themselves may have.

- "Famous People Who Stutter," The Stuttering Foundation. www.stutteringhelp. org/Default.aspx?tabid=128.

Andrew Carnegie is credited with saying "The first one gets the oyster, the second gets the shell." Search for background facts about Andrew Carnegie, and draw conclusions about his leadership traits that may have led to the statement.

DISCUSSION QUESTIONS

1. Which two leadership traits are your best ones, in your opinion? Provide examples. Discuss how you use these strengths to your advantage.
2. Which two leadership traits are your weakest, in your opinion? How and when are they a problem? How might you mitigate them over time?
3. Critique a leader you know using the ten leadership traits discussed in this chapter.
4. Discuss the differences between traits and skills. How does the term "competency" relate to these terms?
5. What do you consider your strongest skills as defined by this chapter? Why? Provide an example.
6. What do you consider your weakest skills as defined by this chapter? Why? Provide an example.
7. This chapter identifies eight influence strategies. Name the two that you think you are strongest at and give examples in each case. Name your two weakest and tell why. Are you interested in improving the weakest? Do you know how you could improve them?
8. Sometimes in a skill domain one subelement is used to compensate for another. For example, it is not uncommon for people who are strong at oral communication to overrely on it and to neglect written communication. Provide an example of skill substitution in which there are negative ramifications.
9. What do you think about the argument regarding technical skills for executives? Discuss the issue with regard to (1) the level of management, (2) the

type of discipline, profession, or industry, and (3) the current environment of the organization (e.g., stable or dynamic).

CLASSROOM ACTIVITY 1

Imagine that in a "360-degree" review, you received the following information about your leadership skills from subordinates, colleagues, and your boss, following your own self-evaluation.

Leadership skill area	Leader's effectiveness at skill (5 = high; 1 = low)		
	Subordinates	Colleagues	Superior
Communication: oral	2	4	4
Communication: written	3	4	5
Social skills	2	4	5
Influence skills	2	3	4
Analytic skills	3	4	4
Technical skills	2	5	5
Continual learning skills	2	4	5

1. In groups, analyze what this information means. Looking at the data, how would you describe your leadership?
2. Describe what actions you would take.

CLASSROOM ACTIVITY 2

It is the time of year for evaluations. You are the parks director of a large park and are evaluating the superintendent, Hal Bettendorf. You use a behaviorally anchored approach to employee appraisal. The "hard" indicators are all down this year: park usage, gate and concession revenue, turnover (increased), aesthetics of maintained (nonforested) areas, and improvements (decreased). As the park superintendent has pointed out, general fund support has barely kept pace with inflation, capital improvement has been sufficient for only one new project, drought has increased fire warnings, and gas prices have dampened summer travel. These same complaints have occurred for the past three years. However, several parks in similar circumstances have increased usage and revenue and used this local money to augment small capital improvements and targeted marketing. Bettendorf has complained that these parks are stealing his clients and points out that overall park usage has not increased faster than the population increase. Your hunch is that Bettendorf is already beginning to look toward retirement (which is five years off) and that he does not work as hard as the more successful managers.

Strictly using a trait approach, critique Bettendorf. Select the three guidelines that you think would be most useful for him. As his boss, how would you urge these guidelines on him?

Case Analysis

You are a division head with three direct reports and a personal staff of two (a secretary and an assistant). Each of the people who report to you has different developmental leadership needs. Right now you are considering one of the regional assistant directors, who needs some help. Katherine Jacobs feels that she has been successful in a man's world. Most of her direct reports are men, and they are indeed a bit more critical of female leaders than of male leaders. She gives terse verbal orders that she has carefully thought about in advance. She invariably precedes or follows with a written directive or summary. She keeps personal interactions to a minimum so that the work setting can be as "professional" as possible. Her influence tactics are position-based strategies with some rational persuasion in writing. She rarely uses consultation or person-based influence strategies; in fact, she considers them inappropriate. She remains relatively up-to-date but you have noticed that the only new ideas are her own. Generally, she likes to do things "by the book," which is a strength in terms of consistency but a weakness in terms of fresh ideas. Most of her subordinates respect her but do not like her. A few have transferred out in order to serve under a different leader. In her development plans, she has outlined attending a week-long technical training course and "tightening up several messy procedural areas" in the office.

Discussion Questions

1. Use a skills approach to discuss how Jacobs is overcompensating. What does she need to work on?
2. How would you suggest that she change her developmental plan for the upcoming year in order to broaden her leadership abilities?
3. How could you model the behavior that she needs to emulate?

Note

1. Stephen Covey's leadership training, whether taught by Covey himself or by the Franklin Covey consultants, is based on his 1989 book, *The 7 Habits of Highly Effective People.*

5 | Task-Oriented Leadership Behaviors

A small daily task . . . will beat the labors of a spasmodic Hercules.
—Anthony Trollope, 1883

Leaders behave differently not only because different individuals have different traits and skills, but also because of what they need to do to accomplish tasks, motivate people, and improve the organization. Behaviors can be very broadly defined so that there are few categories, or they can be very discretely defined with hundreds of items. As Chapter 3 showed, early behavioral studies of the 1950s focused on condensing hundreds of items into a few major categories, with emphasis on either the task at hand or on the people doing the work. These two categories—*task-oriented* and *people-oriented* behaviors—are the basis of this chapter and the next. Whereas behavioral theories, such as the managerial grid, integrate task and relationship factors, we now separate them from each other in order to study each category in greater depth. A third category of *organization-related* behaviors will be examined in Part II of this text. Organization-related behaviors involve neither micro task-oriented nor people-oriented issues, but instead focus on macro organizational issues such as organizational mission, vision, and strategic planning.

When it comes to the business of leadership, behaviors vary in more ways than one within the levels of an organization, as explored in the beginning of this book. Leadership behaviors also vary across industries, organizations, and situations. James Barrie's comic stage play *The Admirable Crichton*, written over a century ago (Barrie 2006 [1902]), shows Lord Loam and his butler Crichton swapping roles when they find themselves on a desert island where the butler's survival skills are the leadership skills needed, compared to the lord's knowledge of British politics. We also see leadership behaviors vary in the extreme during war in the 1949 film *Twelve O'Clock High*. A people-oriented leader brings losses to his bombing squadron in World War II, until a dictatorial bully tightens discipline, refines technical flying skills, and ultimately restores the squadron's pride.

Whether in *Twelve O'Clock High* or in your own organization, leaders need task-oriented behaviors. But no organization thrives over the long term with task-orientation exclusively. There is no "one best way" to lead in every situation, and task-orientation needs a proper balance with people-oriented and organization-oriented behaviors.

It is known that a task-oriented focus tends to increase, normally with positive results, when there are technical problems, when there is a crisis needing immediate attention, when employees are new or training is deficient, and when customers' or clients' interests are relatively stable and understood. The reverse is generally true as well; a leaders' task-oriented focus tends to decrease when operations are running smoothly, when employees are well trained and self-managed, when customer and client demands are shrill or changing, or when a long-term crisis requires a fundamentally different approach.

There is a fundamental logic to each behavior domain that is well established in the action research literature. Before leading, people should have information and knowledge. This is called the **assessment phase**. In the **task domain**, it is referred to as monitoring and assessing tasks. Leaders have to decide what to do—the formulation and planning function. In the task domain, this is operations planning. Leaders have to get results—implementation. In the task domain, examples of these behaviors are clarifying roles and objectives, informing, and delegating. Finally, leaders must ensure that the unit of organization is responsive to operational challenges and to shifts in needs, technologies, or tastes. This is the change function. This rationale is repeated in the other behavioral domains. In sum, the typical behaviors in the task domain are monitoring and assessing work, operations planning, clarifying roles and objectives, informing, delegating, problem-solving, and managing innovation and creativity. Each one of these specific task behaviors is presented below.

In contrast, typical behaviors in the people-oriented domain are consulting, planning and organizing personnel, developing staff, motivating, building and managing teams, managing conflict, and managing personnel change. These people-oriented behaviors are presented in detail in the next chapter. Yet another key aspect of leadership, organizational behaviors, follows in Chapters 7 through 9.

MONITORING AND ASSESSING WORK

Monitoring and assessing work *involves gathering and critically evaluating data related to subordinates' performance, service or project qualities, and overall unit or organizational performance.* It involves using both quantitative and qualitative indicators and is exhibited in a wide range of discrete behaviors. Supervisors tend to focus most on the work of individual employees, work standards and procedures, and individual cases of problem identification; executives focus on overall program effectiveness and efficiency, fund balances and resource levels. However, midlevel managers often have special responsibility for monitoring and assessing the details of organizational performance.

Monitoring has three important aspects. The first aspect involves defining what is important to monitor and observe. Indicators should be strategically selected and defined because unnecessary routine data-gathering is expensive and sometimes perceived as intrusive. Different indicators are often needed to track different qualities: timeliness, accuracy, presentation, cost, effectiveness, and so forth. Some are needed for different levels of analysis: (individual vs. group vs. organization), and others are needed for areas that only indirectly affect service or production (e.g., absenteeism and turnover). Recent emphasis on the appropriate selection of critical indicators has led to the popularity of the "balanced scorecard" approach to quality control (Kaplan and Norton 1996).

A second aspect of gathering data is the consistent and disciplined review of the information. Managers, especially as they become more senior, are bombarded with so much information that it can be a full-time job to review and analyze it. Yet the liabilities of not maintaining a rigorous review of data can be enormous. Emerging crises may be missed, and weak review of data may result in poor understanding of problems.

The third aspect of data-gathering is the integration of qualitative sources. Valuable information can be gleaned from direct observation and casual conversations. Inspections of various types—for example, work samples and site visits—are helpful in paying attention to the details of production and facilities. Various types of review meetings can be used to monitor project progress or evaluate results after the fact.

While monitoring the work implies a relatively passive set of activities, assessing the work refers to the more active decision-making that occurs once the information has been collected. If the data indicate performance standards or organizational health factors within an acceptable range, managers will generally integrate minor adjustments and follow-up on a low-priority basis. However, monitoring occasionally results in surprising data. (Exhibit 5.1, for example, explores the problems that a lack of adequate monitoring and assessing caused the highly prestigious Barings Bank.) These issues receive high priority and are put at the top of the action queue for interventions.

Careful monitoring and assessing of unit or organizational work are important as the basis of planning, clarifying, delegating, problem-solving, developing, and, indirectly, most other behavioral competencies. The task can be tedious and time-consuming, but it serves as the basis for leadership accountability.

GUIDELINES FOR MONITORING AND ASSESSING WORK

1. *Define and measure key indicators of progress and performance.* Leaders need accurate, carefully selected, and timely data. Process indicators allow leaders to detect problems early. Performance indicators assist leaders to plan, make decisions, and make changes in the organization.

2. *Compare progress with plans.* One of the primary tools for problem recognition is the comparison of data with plan specifications. The detailed comparison of data and plans becomes particularly important with large, complex projects, for example, or when there has been a lot of organizational upheaval or change.

3. *Maintain a variety of sources of information.* Data should be both quantitative and qualitative. Quantitative data should include a variety of quality measures for progress and final performance, as well as financial data, customer data, and employee and customer surveys. Qualitative data are gleaned by "walking around," providing an open-door policy, and making site visits including those that are unannounced.

Exhibit 5.1

Bringing Down England's Oldest Investment Bank

Early in its long history, Barings Bank brokered the Louisiana Purchase between France and the United States even though it was a British firm. Later, it was the personal banker for generations of Britain's royal family. Nick Leeson started at Barings at the age of twenty-five as a junior manager, but was quickly promoted upon demonstrating his understanding of the derivatives market, an area poorly understood at the stodgy, traditional bank. He was sent to Singapore to be Barings's chief trader for Asia. He immediately made a large profit for the bank, a handsome bonus for himself, and was given wide latitude in his distant office, becoming the head of settlement operations. Since the head of settlement operations ensures fiscal accountability, the fusion of the two jobs would allow for fraud by a clever individual. Leeson was not a crook, but he had become addicted to market betting. After his first round of success had earned him a positive reputation in the bank, most of his following bets failed. Leeson hid his losses in special "error" accounts. Yet he continued trading, hoping to move the market by buying huge sums of futures contracts. Leeson ran liabilities of US$1.3 billion—more than the entire capital and reserves of the bank. In 1995 the 233-year-old bank was declared insolvent. The foible of a moderately clever but very foolish young man is not the point of this story. Rather, the question to be asked is this: where was bank management in monitoring and assessing this very young and brash neophyte? Indeed, the bank was subsequently uniformly condemned by the Singapore and British governments, as well as by Leeson himself—from prison. Leeson's activities were not monitored, much less assessed, despite his dual responsibilities and exceptional visibility. Bank managers assumed Barings was not experiencing loss because they failed to question Leeson's claim that his purchase orders were done with a client's backing. Leaders who do not ensure monitoring and assessment will, at a minimum, run into quality control problems and more ominously, as the story shows, may bring down whole corporations.

Source: This case is adapted in part from information provided on the Nick Leeson website (www. nickleeson.com). *Rogue Trader* (Granada Film Productions 1999) is a movie based on this story from interviews with Leeson while he was still serving a six- and a half-year-prison term in a Singaporean jail. He was released from prison in 1999 during treatment for colon cancer, one month after the movie had already premiered.

4. *Ask clarifying questions.* Walking around is not enough. Leaders talk to a variety of people. They must engage people by asking discerning questions and probing for information.

5. *Encourage open and honest reporting.* Quality data are likely only in an organizational climate that encourages accuracy and honesty. Leaders must be careful not to "punish the messenger"; they should respect those who criticize in a positive manner and should reward those who are willing to step forward regarding undetected problems.

6. *Conduct review meetings.* There should be a constant exchange of data about progress and performance among leaders and workers, as well as peers. Such meetings provide an opportunity to compare data with plans, identify problems, brainstorm solutions, and adjust plans.

OPERATIONS PLANNING

Operations planning focuses on coordinating tactical issues into a detailed blueprint. In operations planning, organizational directions have already been set, policies established, and overarching strategies selected. Similar but not identical are tactical planning, action planning, program planning, implementation, and project management. Contingency planning is a special type of operations planning that takes into account unexpected crises as well as the problems most likely to disrupt operations.

Operations planning involves deciding on a planning model, determining what logistical elements are necessary, coordinating the plan with others, and implementing the plan. Formal elements of operations planning result in schedules, memoranda, and work orders, as well as coordination with budgets and strategic, emergency, or other official plans. Informal elements include individual consultations, group meetings, and leader reflection. Operations planning functions vary enormously by position. Some management and expert positions are defined largely by their operations responsibilities (e.g., buyers in retail, or the senior staff charged with writing policy manuals), while others, at all levels, have few operations functions because of the nature of the work or because operations functions have been specialized.

Some organizations become victims of overplanning, especially centralized planning that leads to rigidity and lack of regionalization. Likewise, some managers spend all their time in an operations mode. However, far more dangerous for an organization or leader is a lack of operations planning. Glitches that occur because of poor operational planning infuriate employees, clients and customers, and organizational partners. Although good operations planning is little noticed, poor operations planning is typically glaring. Glitches in operational planning in retail, for example, can be matters as simple as how shopping carts are made available in the store, to matters as complex as a steady supply of product lines.

Many tools are used in operations planning. Some focus on scheduling elements. Most common are deployment charts, ranging from Gantt charts to planning grids, to show the flow of the steps, people involved, and time schedules. Critical path analyses such as PERT (program evaluation review technique) charts examine the shortest time frames for complex projects in order to ensure that bottlenecks are anticipated and that when multiple actions are possible, they are executed at the same time and in the proper sequence. Other tools focus on making the work efficient. Workflow plans show the physical progress of work through the organization, and flowcharts detail process steps, allowing for better analysis and improvements. Still other tools include mapping techniques, task analysis, unit-cost analysis, performance measurement, and time-and-motion studies.

All in all, while good ideas are important, they cannot succeed without good implementation, which is ultimately founded on operations planning. The case of the wealthiest man in the world in Exhibit 5.2 is an example of the essential nature of successful operations planning.

GUIDELINES FOR OPERATIONS PLANNING

1. *Identify the type of action planning necessary.* "Operations planning" is the term used for ongoing prioritization and scheduling activities, while "program planning" is the term for setting up a new ongoing operation. Special or unusual programs are subsumed under the term "**project management**." These are all tactical-level opera-

Exhibit 5.2

Achieving Opulence Through Good Operations Planning

Although Sam Walton became the world's wealthiest man through many strategies such as popularizing stock options for franchise managers, it was his brilliance in the mundane area of operations planning that made him a multibillionaire. He started with a franchise Ben Franklin variety store in Arkansas in 1945 and gained experience and equity until he opened his first Wal-Mart in 1962. From the beginning, Walton ensured that shelf stocking and merchandise options—operations issues—were priorities. As his stores grew in number, he negotiated directly with companies rather than distributors, further enhancing his ability to be a price leader while maintaining profit margins. Eventually, Wal-Mart became so prolific and powerful that he required many of his vendors to stock the shelves themselves, a relatively common practice today but one that he largely invented. His final operations planning coup was to require many of the vendors to own merchandise on his shelves until it was sold, thus shifting the burden (and challenges) of inventory control to them.

tions in which policy issues have largely been settled and the detailed logistics need to be worked out.

2. *Determine the logistics that need to be planned.* The most common elements include how, when, who, how much, and how well. The more complex the planning (of whatever type), the more critical it is to document such requirements in condensed planning grids and to remind people of responsibilities, deadlines, problems, and standards.

3. *Consult and coordinate to ensure planning accuracy and buy-in.* Consultation and coordination should occur before, during, and after operational planning as necessary. Major planning issues should be resolved before scheduling-type activities occur. After plans are drafted, it is useful to review them in order to detect errors before implementation. Entirely new or different operations plans may require extensive review or even public relations-type promotion to "sell" them to those implementing them.

4. *Implement the plan.* Implementation includes transmitting or posting the plan, explaining the details of the plan as they arise, and evaluating its effectiveness. Even though problem-solving gets *much* more attention as a critical leader competency, it is important to remember that the number, severity, and tenacity of problems is highly correlated with the quality of the operations planning done in the first place. Good operations planning anticipates or prevents most problems before they arise.

CLARIFYING ROLES AND OBJECTIVES

Clarifying roles and objectives refers to working with subordinates to guide and direct behavior by communicating about plans, duties or responsibilities, policies, and specific expectations. It is primarily directed at subordinates, whereas informing—the next task behavior to be discussed—focuses equally on supervisors, colleagues, clients, and outsiders. Clarifying roles and objectives involves more active feedback and performance loops than informing. It is also related to developing staff, but it is more short-term and position-specific in focus.

In the 1980s, the "**fishbone diagram**" was developed by Kaoru Ishikawa (1990) in Japan to get to the root of operational glitches in organizational activity so that the root problem of various issues could be analyzed. The technique, which is also called **causal mapping** or cognitive mapping, aims to help users simplify complex data into a usable form. The saying was that, typically, the root cause of organizational problems was employees not understanding their exact role in getting the job done correctly. When individuals did not understand what their contribution was supposed to be, then accomplishments as a whole were disjointed and would quickly break down. The remedy emerges clearly when a problem such as this is mapped.

More recently, the Six Sigma approach, credited to Motorola, has utilized similar techniques for the purpose of reducing variation and making customer-focused, data-driven decisions. Six Sigma works to eliminate defects by driving toward six standard deviations between the mean and the nearest specification limit as defined by customer specifications. The key to Six Sigma is providing feedback directly to employees on their role in quality. The process that became known as Six Sigma was proposed in 1986 by a Motorola engineer who envisioned setting an ambitious goal for error-free product 99.9997 percent of the time, knowing that the key to achieving the goal was clarifying to employees their role in achieving quality. By training employees to control against variation around the mean, the statistically driven process has had significant effect over the years throughout all functional areas of Motorola (Crockett 2006). General Electric, the next large company to adopt Six Sigma, presented it to employees as a metric, a methodology, and a management system for clarifying expectations. Twenty-five years after its introduction, Six Sigma has come to be a business unto itself for training other companies and their so-called Black Belt management teams in the approach.

Whether fishbone diagrams or Six Sigma or another approach is used, there are three subelements of clarifying roles and objectives: (1) defining job responsibilities to ensure that job occupants know the major duties they are expected to accomplish; (2) setting performance goals to ensure that job occupants know what standards they are expected to attain; and (3) providing instruction to ensure that job occupants fully understand the tasks, processes, and knowledge to execute each major function and perform at the required standard.

Clarifying roles and expectations is always important, but most important when subordinates are new and when roles and expectations are changing or not clearly articulated in policies, procedures, and formal training programs.

Problems resulting from too little or poor clarification of roles and objectives are a major cause of employee frustration, confusion, and turnover (Buckingham and Coffman 1999). Although much less common and generally less problematic, it is possible to focus too much on role and objectives clarification, which can lead to role rigidity, lack of creativity, and micromanagement, problems that sometimes occur in large public bureaucracies and large corporations with stable production.

GUIDELINES FOR CLARIFYING ROLES AND OBJECTIVES

1. *Mutually define job responsibilities.* When job incumbents are new or changing positions, it is critical for the superior to meet with them in order to define their ma-

jor job responsibilities and the results they are expected to attain. The review should cover a position description or generate some sort of mission statement for the job. This guideline is useful for ongoing employees when the supervisor is new or when the agreement about work priorities seems unclear. It is important to listen to subordinates' ideas carefully and to consider them genuinely, even though the superior is ultimately responsible for the final selection of roles and objectives.

2. *Establish priorities among job responsibilities and establish a scope of authority.* What priority will be given to each responsibility? A clear understanding of the different weights assigned to each area will help the employee prioritize well. Ideally, these priorities are reflected in the performance appraisal process as well. At the same time, it is important that the subordinate's scope of authority be clearly delineated.

3. *Mutually set goals for each priority area.* Priorities and goals are different. A priority involves how much attention to direct and where. A goal is a specific performance objective to be met. Each priority should have its own goal or set of goals.

4. *Pay attention to the basics of goal-setting theory* (Chapter 9). Research on goal-setting shows that those leaders who do it well improve quantity and quality of performance significantly and sometimes dramatically (Earley, Wojnaroski, and Prest 1987; Locke and Latham 1990).

5. *When providing instruction, be sure to pay attention to the basics of information and learning theory.* It is worthwhile to keep four elements in mind. First, people work better when they understand the rationale behind an instruction or direction. Second, clear language aids learning. Third, providing examples or demonstrations whenever possible is a characteristic of good instruction. Finally, good instruction involves checking for comprehension rather than assuming that comprehension occurred.

INFORMING

Informing provides business-related information to subordinates, superiors, peers, or people outside the organization. Three important functions are accomplished by informing activities. First, informing facilitates coordination of work. Second, informing shapes the mood about work and strategies that will be most effective. Third, informing serves a public relations or image function. Top management, especially in organizations where there are no personnel specifically designed to handle public relations, frequently hears the disheartening message that "you're doing so many good things, but nobody knows about them."

Informing occurs through oral communications (e.g., one-on-one discussions, telephone calls, speeches, and briefings) as well as written communications (e.g., email, memoranda and letters, postings, reports). The more technical aspects of informing simply provide the information that people need to do their jobs and to coordinate tasks. Informing also provides an opportunity for managers to shape mood and strategy by selecting information to relay and the manner of delivering it. Bad news may provide an opportunity for improvement; good news may be a cause for celebration. Finally, informing is an opportunity to promote individuals, the unit, or the organization.

GUIDELINES FOR INFORMING

1. *Determine what information others need and want.* People need information from leaders whose jobs make them linking pins in the organization (Likert 1967). Talk to people about the types of technical or routine needs they have related to production, coordination, and job assistance so that they can respond effectively in their various roles. People not only need information, but they want it in order to be involved and to have their concerns allayed.

2. *Determine the best way to relay information.* Good leaders are very careful about the means, quality, and number of sources that they provide. The more important the information, the more sources of information the leader may want to use. Frequently, leaders want to ensure that subordinates and others have direct access to technical information so that the leaders can focus on more strategic information.

3. *Manage information flow strategically.* First, it is important to guard against information overload. It may result in diminished productivity due to trivial information acquisition, the ignoring of all information, inappropriate interpretation of information, or failure to distinguish critical data. Therefore, good communicators restrict information to relevant issues, but provide expanded access on a special or as-needed basis. Second, information can shape the mood of the recipients. Information can stir people to action, caution them to be more careful, or arouse enthusiasm about a difficult project. On the other hand, information manipulation, excessive secretiveness, or distortion will eventually result in an unfavorable impression of a leader.

4. *Inform people about accomplishments and promote successes.* Potentially, one of the best aspects of a leader's job is the dissemination of information about what the unit or group has achieved. This encourages subordinates, raises the reputation of the unit or organization, and often results in preferred access to resources in the future.

DELEGATING

Delegating is a type of power sharing in which subordinates are given substantial responsibilities and/or authority. While it is related to other forms of participative leadership such as consultation and joint decision-making and is often arrayed with them as the most robust form, delegating is actually a distinct category.

Delegation has two major elements: the designation of responsibility and the allocation of authority. Designation of responsibility involves the assignment of duties, whereas authority is the right to control appropriate resources and to make formal decisions. Unfortunately, it is possible to be delegated many responsibilities and little formal authority with which to accomplish them; it is also possible for subordinates to be delegated few responsibilities with substantial authority. Delegation is considered to be effective when authority is commensurate with responsibility, meaning that the individual has sufficient formal authority to get the job done well. Imagine a gardener who is given the responsibility for an impeccable entrance to the building when it opens to the public in the morning, yet is not trusted by management to have access to the keys of the toolshed. Delegation in that case would not be effective because authority was not commensurate with responsibility. Or imagine a middle manager who is given responsibility for contributing to the corporate marketing plan from his own team, yet is not given access to the plan's introduction or overview or others' contributions. Again, delegation would be ineffective because authority and responsibility were not properly matched.

Level of authority ranges from minimal to complete authority. Authority is minimal when nonroutine decisions must be determined jointly with the next layer of management or when all decisions must receive prior approval and the process is not automatic. Authority is substantial when the approval process is largely perfunctory or when notification and action are simultaneous. Authority is full when decisions are not subject to immediate review except under extraordinary conditions. As a leader ascends in the organization, it is common to have an increasing level of both responsibility and authority. However, leaders who delegate with substantial authority must always retain their own authority in the hierarchy and not lose sight of the work being done at lower levels of the organization. Retention of one's own authority and having proper awareness of what is being done in the organization can be important in preventing unethical behavior, as in the case of Walt Pavlo (see Chapter 7). Note that maintaining awareness of responsibilities delegated is unrelated to what some inappropriately refer to as "micromanaging"; rather, it is part of the proper execution of one's leadership responsibilities.

The virtues of effective delegation are many. It can improve decisions when subordinates are competent in or closer to the issues to be handled. It can lead to greater job satisfaction and is a form of job enrichment. Delegation helps busy leaders free up their time for other responsibilities. Finally, it is a powerful form of personnel development.

The reasons for not delegating can be both legitimate and illegitimate. If subordinates are not competent because of lack of training, experience, or temperament, then it is unwise and unfair to delegate to them, at least in the short term. Some responsibilities and authority cannot be delegated because of issues of confidentiality. For example, a department manager may not be able to delegate either responsibility or authority involving personnel matters to the staff personnel coordinator because of legalities pertaining to confidentiality. Yet all too often, leaders fail to delegate for the wrong reasons. Some simply fail to consider other people's judgment as good as their own, perhaps because of ego or perhaps because of a general distrust of other people's ability. Other leaders may be too concerned that a mistake will be made "during their watch," and they feel they can prevent it only by closely guarding their decision-making authority.

GUIDELINES FOR DELEGATING

1. *Assess opportunities for delegation.* Delegation should be done with forethought. Delegation may mean an analysis of the leader's responsibilities and workload as well

as the subordinate's. Increasing levels of authority in terms of decision-making or independence is a good way to reward and develop subordinates. However, delegation is not an opportunity for abdication of one's own responsibilities.

2. *Emphasize personnel development and empowerment when possible.* Certain types of tasks or situations are more appropriate for delegation. When the subordinate is as qualified or more qualified to handle a responsibility because of time, experience, or closeness to the work, delegation should be strongly considered. It is also important to delegate not only tasks that are easily within the subordinate's range, but also some tasks that might require a moderate stretch in the subordinate's capabilities. Excessive delegation causes burnout and is a significant reason for turnover of high-quality employees.

3. *Balance responsibilities and authority.* Most managers feel far more comfortable delegating responsibilities than delegating the complementary authority. To employees, being handed responsibility without commensurate authority feels like additional workload without the tools to accomplish it; the result is frustration. However, **empowerment** means that employees are given the requisite authority. Of course, grants of empowerment should be accompanied by assignment of accountability, too.

4. *Specify conditions of delegation carefully.* To the degree possible, it is very helpful to specify the new responsibilities, scope of authority, and the rewards and punishments for not meeting standards or using authority well. In most cases, it is best done before delegation occurs. Clear reporting of responsibilities, so that the superior can monitor or be aware of progress, will generally forestall many problems.

PROBLEM-SOLVING

Problem-solving involves the identification, analysis, and handling of work-related problems. It is related to, but different from, other important competencies discussed in this book, such as operations planning, conflict management, and decision-making. Operations planning schedules work to prevent problems to the greatest degree possible; it has a proactive and long-term focus, whereas problem-solving is usually more reactive and short-term. Conflict management is a special type of challenge involving people who may be in an emotional situation, and therefore it often requires special skills. Decision-making is oriented toward direction-setting and policy; when carried out by executives, there is an eye to the organization at large. In contrast, problem-solving tends to be case-by-case and usually operationally focused.

Fixing problems, breakdowns, and interruptions are major responsibilities of management. Many managers go from problem to problem at a frenetic pace (Mintzberg 1973). Managers who are good at solving problems are likely to be successful; however, problem-solving can be addictive because of its adrenaline rush and hands-on nature and can choke out forward-thinking leadership behaviors. On the other hand, some managers find problems annoying, distracting, and/or overwhelming so they procrastinate in dealing with them, pass them off to others ("passing the buck"), or ignore problems altogether. Thus, managing problem-solving is as important as the skills that go into problem-solving itself.

Depending on the type of problem to be solved, different types of tools are used (Scholtes 1993). If it is a breakdown in operations planning, then the tools discussed in that section of this chapter, such as flowcharts and work mapping, might be used. If the nature of the problem is unclear, then different approaches might be useful, including identification tools such as check sheets or other simple means for collecting data; **Pareto charts**, which rank problem elements; cause-and-effect diagrams, which link related types of problems; and "is/is-not" analysis, which identifies when, where, and how the problem occurs. If the problem is a control issue or a deviation from standards, then more common tools are control charts, time plots, and scatter diagrams, all of which are methods of graphing trends in order to detect variations and problems. If new solutions are necessary, brainstorming and nominal group technique—a variant of brainstorming that enhances input from all group members— may be the best tools if time is available.

GUIDELINES FOR PROBLEM-SOLVING

1. *Classify the problem.* Managers at all levels are bombarded with real and potential problems. This results in the need for problem management. The leader must briefly assess the type of problem, its severity and criticality, and identify the most responsible party to solve it. This is a kind of triage effort.
   a. Which problems need to be handled *immediately* because they can be solved quickly, are critical, or are severe and are likely to be solved successfully?
   b. Which problems need to be deferred? Generally, there are two times when problems are deferred. During a crisis, all but the most critical problems are deferred. Second, problems that need more analysis are generally deferred in order to bring in other people, gather more data, use more robust problem-solving techniques, or implement more complex solutions.
   c. Some problems can be appropriately delegated, or passed on to others, temporarily shelved, or ignored altogether. Time management guidelines that have been popular for many years encourage leaders to classify problems as they are identified so that if they are delegated or temporarily shelved, it is done so immediately and the problems need not waste anybody's time by being revisited again and again.

2. *Identify the root problem.* A key aspect of problem-solving occurs after the general problem area has been classified and it has been determined that the problem is to be handled now. This step involves separating symptoms of the problem from the root of the problem. If this step does not take place adequately, the real problem is not likely to be solved. Take, for instance, an insurance company whose revenue is suffering because policy renewals are down. An immediate response management might take would be to advertise to current customers in order to bring up renewals. Managers might even target just those customers whose policies are within three months of expiration. However, a better response would be to identify the actual, underlying

problem: What has caused renewals to decline? Management might learn that renewals are down because the compensation structure encourages salespeople to develop new clientele rather than cultivate existing customers; sales staff get low financial reward for the renewal of even large policies. In other words, the root problem that needs to be addressed by leadership is a sagging compensation structure that rewards salespeople for abandoning their existing customers in favor of new customers, and mere advertising would have done nothing to target this issue. But if leadership addresses the root problem, renewals would increase. One powerful tool for carrying out this guideline is the "fishbone diagram" developed by Kaoru Ishikawa, referenced previously in this chapter.

3. *Analyze difficult problems.* A leader's true skill in fixing problems lies in handling the difficult ones, handling multiple problems with a single solution, finding innovative solutions for problems, or, best of all, turning problems into opportunities. This type of problem-solving invariably requires some genuine reflection or empirical analysis. Good problem-solvers cull reasons for the problem, look for connections, and allow their minds to mix and match problems together for broader solutions. Many problems are poorly understood and additional information is required in order to resolve them. Managers should not simply rely on gut impressions, because several problems may be occurring simultaneously, and fixing only one may solve only a small part of the overall problem. Some of the many strategies that can be used to approach problem-solving are illustrated in Exhibit 5.3.

4. *Generate alternatives.* Ambiguous and difficult problems invariably can be approached in multiple ways. Rarely is there a single way to attack a problem, and generating alternatives hones thinking and provides opportunities to graft portions of one solution onto another. Generating alternatives is often required by executives in order to include important stakeholders both internal and external to the organization.

5. *Choose an alternative.* Leaders must be prepared to make some decisions unilaterally, some with consultation or jointly, and to delegate other decisions entirely, even when they have identified the problem and conducted the analysis. Good problem-solvers understand that both narrow and broad participation have their strengths, and vary their inclusiveness according to the characteristics of the problem situation. Narrow participation is faster in times of crisis, more efficient for trivial or easy problems, more suitable when the decision-maker is well informed, more fitting when the goals of employees diverge substantially from those of the organization, and more appropriate when confidentiality is an issue. Broader participation enhances buy-in of multiple constituencies, encourages involvement and a sense of ownership, is more likely to provide a systems perspective because of multiple perspectives, tends to be very important when others have critical information, is more apt to arrive at an innovative solution, and is much better at providing development opportunities for others to learn about management or the issues affecting the organization (Vroom and Jago 1988).

6. *Take responsibility for fixing problems.* Just because a solution is decided upon does not ensure that action will occur. There must be a commitment to follow through.

Exhibit 5.3

Five Improvement Strategies

All problems share a similar decision-making protocol: identify and clarify the problem, identify the alternatives, choose an alternative, implement the decision, and evaluate the results. Because of the different types of problems, however, different strategies are employed to emphasize different aspects of the decision-making process. Some of the most common strategies for problem-solving in organizations are the following:

1. **Collect data or collect better data.** One of the most common situations when a problem arises is that the existing data do not provide the basis for an informed decision about the problem. When this happens, good problem-solvers must clarify data collection goals, develop procedures and operational procedures, work with people to collect quality data, and check for data reliability. This strategy sometimes leads to obvious solutions, and sometimes it simply provides the substance for a more rigorous analysis of the problem. Leaders might focus on the following tactics:
   - Study the needs and concerns of customers.
   - Conduct time-and-motion analysis.
   - Analyze exactly where problems are occurring.
   - Experiment with a process.
2. **Define the process more accurately.** Sometimes processes are not well defined or have been adjusted over time so that confusion exists. Just a clear map of the process may help substantially with obvious improvements as well as with training. Common elements of this strategy are flowcharts of the process and diagrams of the physical workflow.
3. **Standardize a practice.** When variations of practices exist, and the variations are not related to substantial and useful customization, then standardization may be important. Standardization helps with quality control, consistency (fairness), and quality improvement. The most important element of standardization is to identify best practices. Also important is testing these practices to ensure that they work well in all cases. Standardized processes are easier to measure, monitor, and fix. Important mass-production processes should be under statistical control; that is, they should be monitored continuously and the data should be charted regularly for process consistency.
4. **Error-proof the process.** What are the common mistakes that are made in a process? How can those mistakes be reduced or eliminated? Some of the common methods for simple problems are changing and improving forms, providing better-written directions, providing overlapping methods of information (such as both a written and graphical presentation of information), and providing a checklist for the user.
5. **Reengineer a process to streamline it.** Sometimes a process is too long and unwieldy. This occurs over time with the ad hoc addition of steps and with changes in technology and locations. Reengineering allows for rationalization of the process; that is, reengineering allows people to examine the entire process at a single time to reintroduce simplicity and efficiency. Noncritical steps are eliminated. Since many of these noncritical steps may be approvals, workers may need to be made aware of new accountability that may fall to them for process accuracy and timeliness.

Implementing a solution requires many of the leader characteristics discussed in earlier chapters: willingness to assume responsibility, energy, resilience, flexibility, continual learning, technical and analytic skills, communication skills, and, sometimes, courage.

MANAGING TECHNICAL INNOVATION AND CREATIVITY

Managing technical innovation and creativity involves establishing an environment that encourages and provides the tools for learning, flexibility, and change, and that also provides implementation support for new or cutting-edge programs or processes.

Exhibit 5.4

A Flamboyant Leader for Organizational Innovation

A corporate leader who is known for creativity, innovation, and flamboyance in his business empire as well as in his personal life is Richard Branson, founder of the Virgin label conglomerate. Richard started life as a middle-class boy whose family hoped he would become a lawyer, but he disappointed them by getting poor grades (he suffers from dyslexia) and dropping out of school. His first successful business venture, at age sixteen, was the publication of the magazine *Student*. He sold records out of the trunk of his car and used the money he saved to start a mail-order company. He used the money he earned from the mail-order company to buy a record store, and the proceeds of that to leverage it into a chain. Over the years, he added 360 acquisitions to Virgin Music Group—airlines, books, trains, comics, wines, health care, fitness clubs, finance, and space travel, among others. He sold off elements when they began to lose appeal, including the final sale of 125 stores throughout the United Kingdom and Ireland in 2007 as a final retreat from over thirty-five years in the music industry. Branson's net worth is pegged at $2.5 billion and he was knighted in 1999 for "services to entrepreneurship." His creativity and innovation are demonstrated in a number of ways:

- Many of the ideas generated have been his own: he started Virgin Airways as a result of being infuriated by a flight cancellation. Today on Virgin America passengers can enjoy mood lighting, plug in to 110v power at every seat, and order fresh food whenever they want it.
- He accepts numerous (small) failures as he searches out big successes.
- He has used extremely clever and sometimes controversial advertising that has given his product lines an edge.
- He has used his adventure-filled, glamorous life—he has set several world records in ballooning and speed boating—to promote his product lines.
- Many of his ventures have been aimed not at revenue generation, but at making the world a better place, such as his creation of The Elders, a group of distinguished former world leaders who promote peace, and his creation of a $25 million prize for removing greenhouse gases from the earth's atmosphere. He has a foundation called Virgin Unite to support entrepreneurial approaches to social and environmental issues by uniting business and the social sector to work together. He started his first charity at the age of seventeen by establishing the Student Advisory Centre.

It is useful, but not critical, for leaders themselves to have new insights into situations and be able to make organizational improvements from their own insights. It is *more* important today for leaders to be able to recognize and support the ideas of others than to be the source of those ideas themselves. To get a sense of the many roles that business leaders can have in managing technical innovation and creativity, read in Exhibit 5.4 the case study of the entrepreneur who founded Virgin Records.

Managing the technical aspects of innovation and creativity is highly related to managing personnel change and managing organizational change. However, they are separated here and elsewhere (see Yukl 2006) because (1) the concrete microbehaviors constituting each are quite often different, and (2) the change behavior domain is so large and important but also very difficult for contemporary managers. Managing organizational change focuses on wholesale shifts in the policies, directions, major processes, or culture of the organization (see Chapters 11 and 12). Although a part of the difference is the sheer scope of change, often there is a qualitative difference as well. Whereas an innovation might be the integration of a new geographic information system (GIS) for program analysts, an organizational change might be the *systematic* redistribution of resources based on the findings of that new GIS analysis. Yet just because new technology is available or a new policy is promulgated does not mean that people will like, accept, or implement it. Thus, managing personnel change—mental attitudes, physical readjustments, and the ability to cope—is quite separate from the other technical and structural aspects of change. Examples of brilliant technological breakthroughs that go unutilized for years because of resistance by personnel are not uncommon, as are examples of line workers and supervisors who ignore or even sabotage organizational change policies with which they do not agree.

Because *managing* innovation and creativity is really mostly about *increasing* it throughout the organization at a grass-roots level, it is highly related to the concept of the **learning organization**. Senge's definition of the learning organization is one "where people continually expand their capacity to create the results they truly desire, where new and expansive patterns of thinking are nurtured, where collective aspiration is set free, and where people are continually learning how to learn together" (Senge 1990, 3). Another popular definition is Garvin's: "an organization skilled in creating, acquiring, and transferring knowledge, and at modifying its behavior to reflect new knowledge and insights" (Garvin 1993, 79).

Despite widespread agreement about the enabling conditions for learning organizations (Kanter, Stein, and Jick 1992), they have not flourished as they might because of the exceptional challenges confronting them. First, by definition, the structure is less clear. Typically, learning organizations are flatter than others, have looser formal links, and look more like networks. While the links are looser in terms of rules and regulations, tight informal links are required in terms of cooperative synergies. Because of the need for constant reorganization to adapt to new problems, they tend to be self-organizing and "messy" (Wheatley 1992). Individuals have larger, but far less defined, roles. When these features are properly functioning, they give rise to learning organizations, but, improperly implemented, they lead to confusion, lower productivity, infighting, and lack of organizational focus, among other dysfunctionalities. Second, this type of amorphous structure gives rise to a high degree of stress for many individuals who prefer more "organized" environments, stable conditions and standards, sharper role clarity, and high job security. Those who do work in less structured environments expect higher incentives for staying in the organization. Because of the loose management structures, the types of people bred by a different form of organization are easily alienated and more likely to move elsewhere if conditions do not seem ideal. Third, learning organizations require highly trained individuals. This requires background education in the discipline, organizational knowledge about systems, processes, culture, and the like, and training in the skills necessary for the job. But it also requires advanced skills to make greater use of learning by sharing, comparing, systems thinking, competing, and suspending disbelief. Advanced learners not only learn about basic knowledge and skills that are organizationally based, but also become adept at learning how to learn in order to solve entirely new problems. However, the cost of hiring and training employees, including self-training, rises dramatically as better-educated individuals join the organization. Thus, recruiting and retention problems for learning organizations are particularly challenging.

Guidelines for Managing Technical Innovation and Creativity

1. *Create an environment that fosters learning, flexibility, and change.* In a fast-moving environment, learning and change are constant, requiring an attitude of flexibility.

Leaders need to be able to convey the importance not only of innovation and creativity through words but also through actions.

2. *Promote a mind-set that will encourage high-quality change and innovative learning.* An organization can support lower levels of learning—what Senge would call **personal mastery** or technical training and team learning—without really engaging in the types of learning that characterize learning organizations with their absorption of innovation and thirst for useful change. This requires special qualities. First, significant problems must be seen in the context of broader organizational patterns rather than as discrete events. Second, organizational members must systematically challenge assumptions and mental models (patterned ways of interpreting information based on past experience). Mental models are useful in assisting people to deal with large amounts of information, but they can frequently be based on outdated, situationally specific, or incorrect information.

3. *Provide the tools and opportunities for learning and innovation.* Leaders as managers can provide a number of tools for fostering a learning and change-friendly environment. Tools can help ensure that organizational members have the necessary resources. Leaders can encourage others to see the opportunity to learn from failures and surprises. Leaders can sponsor and support experimentation. Another popular practice is benchmarking. The best-known version of this is when an organization looks at the practices of a high-performing competitor or partner in an area of the organization's own strength. Through discussions, site visits, and creative discourse, a team adapts practices to its own organization. Benchmarking can be interpreted more broadly to mean any rigorous use of comparison. Therefore, it is also possible and quite useful to benchmark against other units in the organization and even one's own past performance. This aspect of benchmarking approaches trend analysis. Another useful tool is competition. It is particularly appropriate at the group level when products and services compete with others in or outside the public sector and when there is a sense of apathy. Friendly professional competition can be useful within a unit if it leads to stimulation and striving. Intercolleague competition must be carefully balanced with team goals, however, because, as David Sarnoff founder of National Broadcasting Company (NBC) quipped, "Competition brings out the best in products and the worst in people."

CONCLUSION

Task-oriented competencies include monitoring and assessing work, operations planning, clarifying roles and objectives, informing, delegating, problem-solving, and managing innovation and creativity. Exhibit 5.5 provides a review of task-oriented competencies. For many, task-oriented competencies lack the glamour of other leadership competencies. Some leadership experts prefer to think of them as management—a more technical aspect that is easier to teach and in greater supply (Zaleznik 1977). Yet many detailed studies over the past fifty years have indicated that task-oriented competencies are a cornerstone of leadership of successful organizations.

Exhibit 5.5 **Summary: Review of Task-Oriented Behaviors**

Task-oriented behavior	Subelements of behavior	Major recommendations
Monitoring and assessing Gather and critically evaluate data related to subordinates' performance, service or project qualities, and overall unit or organizational performance	• Define what is important to monitor and observe • Offer consistent and disciplined review of the information • Integrate qualitative sources	• Define and measure key indicators of progress and performance • Compare progress with plans • Maintain a variety of sources of information • Ask clarifying questions • Encourage open and honest reporting • Conduct review meetings
Operations planning Coordinate all tactical issues into a detailed blueprint	• Decide on a planning model • Determine what logistical elements are necessary to include • Coordinate the plan with others • Implement the plan	• Identify the type of action planning necessary • Determine the logistics that need to be planned • Consult and coordinate to ensure planning accuracy and buy-in • Implement plans and follow-through
Clarifying roles and objectives Work with subordinates to guide and direct behavior by communicating about plans, policies, and specific expectations	• Define job responsibilities • Set performance goals • Provide instruction	• Mutually define job responsibilities • Establish priorities among job responsibilities and establish a scope of authority • Mutually set goals for each priority area • Pay attention to the basics of goal-setting theory • When providing instruction, pay attention to the basics of information and learning theory
Informing Provide business-related information to subordinates, superiors, peers, or people outside the organization	• Facilitate coordination of work • Shape the mood about work and strategies that will function best • Serve a public relations or image function	• Determine what information others need and want • Determine the best way to relay information • Manage information flow strategically • Inform people about accomplishments and promote successes
Delegating Use a type of power sharing in which subordinates are given substantial responsibilities and/or authority	• Designate responsibility • Allocate authority	• Assess opportunities for delegation • Emphasize personnel development and empowerment when possible • Balance responsibilities and authority • Specify conditions of delegation carefully
Problem-solving Identify, analyze, and handle work-related problems	• Recognize problems • Investigate problems • Resolve problems	• Identify and classify problems • Analyze difficult problems • Generate alternatives • Choose an alternative • Take responsibility for fixing problems
Managing innovation and creativity Establish an environment that encourages and provides the tools for learning, flexibility, and change and that also provides implementation support for new or cutting-edge programs or processes	• Create, acquire, and transfer knowledge in an organizational context • Modify organizational behavior to reflect new knowledge and insights	• Create an environment that fosters learning, flexibility, and change • Encourage a mind-set that will encourage high-quality change and innovative learning • Provide the tools and opportunities for learning and innovation

Task-oriented behavioral competencies form a basic dynamic for leaders at all levels and in all positions. Leaders need to get things done correctly, fix problems, and stay up-to-date. However, as one would logically expect, the task focus is not consistent across levels and types of positions. Just as line workers tend to focus almost all their attention on concrete tasks, executives at the other end of the spectrum focus on broad organizational tasks.

Problem-solving comes out at the top of nearly everyone's list in terms of importance. It often requires both technical understanding and the ability to work with people, as well as good comprehension of the overall system within which problems occur. It takes time to build up the experience base to handle the variety of problems that occur, and good problem-solvers have an indefinable creative spark. Problem-solving has a dark side, too. It is especially easy for leaders to devote too much of their time to problems because they are rarely in short supply. Yet this means that problem prevention may not be adequate, people in the organization may be receiving less attention than they need and would like, and more robust elements of organizational direction-setting are being overlooked.

Some task-oriented competencies—monitoring and assessing, operations planning, clarifying roles and objectives, and informing—are critical but frequently underappreciated. When these competencies are performed well, they tend to prevent many problems from occurring downstream in the management process and to allow for more effective delegation. Some leaders learn to practice some of these competencies outside the office by reading reports and writing memoranda at home. Some leaders carefully discipline themselves to review roles and objectives frequently to ensure clarity of operational focus. Some effectively share these responsibilities with others, especially those from operations planning, ensuring that there is buy-in and quality assurance. Leaders who fail to keep up with these basic competencies are the very leaders who may be unlucky and find their careers derailed or their organizations lurching into crises because of "unforeseen" problems that better basic management might have identified and fixed.

KEY TERMS

assessment phase	monitoring and assessing work
causal mapping	operations planning
empowerment	Pareto charts
fishbone method	personal mastery
informing	project management
learning organizations	task domain

RESOURCES

Students or student teams may be assigned resources on the Internet, such as those that follow, that complement topics covered in the chapter. Greater richness and depth in class discussion should result.

The fishbone method or Ishikawa Diagram is explained at the following website in the context of Six Sigma. There is sufficient information on this site for student teams to apply the technique to what they may know about a university or community problem in order to find the root cause of the problem.

- iSixSigma, "Tools & Templates: Cause & Effect." www.isixsigma.com/index.php?option=com_k2&view=itemlist&task=category&id=68:cause-effect&Itemid=200.

The "Women in Cell Biology" posted an interesting article on whether gender makes a difference in perception of leaders. They conclude: "people may not recognize task-oriented leadership behaviors when they encounter a female leader." Although the bases for the findings purport to be from "a study," its methodology and specific findings are not shared.

- Kristyn A. Scott, "Female Behavior Is Often Unrecognized as Leader Behavior," *ASCB Newsletter*, June 2007. www.ascb.org/files/0706wicb.pdf.

Best practices of learning organizations are summarized by Albany Medical College.

- School of Public Health, University at Albany, and Albany Medical College, "What Is a 'Learning Organization'?" www.albany.edu/sph/Hoff_learning/hpm_tim_learnorg.htm.

DISCUSSION QUESTIONS

1. What do you consider your strongest task-oriented behavior (as defined by this chapter)? Why? Provide an example.
2. What do you consider your weakest task-oriented behavior (as defined by this chapter)? Why? Provide an example.
3. Select a work area in an organization to identify the quantitative and qualitative aspects that a leader would use to monitor and assess the task performance.
4. Provide an example of both underplanning and overplanning at the operations level. What are the types of symptoms (bureaupathologies) that occurred?
5. What does goal-setting theory teach us about clarifying roles and objectives?
6. Discuss how the competency "informing" is related to the competencies of "developing staff," "motivating," and "articulating mission and vision," but nonetheless different from them as well.
7. Why would an employee sometimes be upset by delegation? What are some recommendations that help leaders to delegate well?
8. What is the classic, five-step protocol for problem-solving?

CLASSROOM ACTIVITIES

Imagine that in a "360-degree" review, similar to the "360" review on skills presented in Chapter 4, you received the following information about your task competencies from subordinates, colleagues, and your boss, following your own self-evaluation:

Task competency	Leader's effectiveness at skill (5 = high; 1 = low)			
	Self	Subordinates	Colleagues	Superior
Monitoring and assessing work	3	2	3	2
Operations planning	4	2	3	3
Clarifying roles and objectives	4	2	3	3
Informing	5	2	2	4
Delegating	5	2	3	2
Problem-solving	5	4	3	3
Managing innovation and creativity	5	3	4	3

1. In groups, analyze implications of this feedback information. In particular, why do you think that the different categories of respondents might rate you differently in some cases?

2. Describe what actions you would take.

CASE ANALYSIS 1

Earl sat back with his feet on the desk, deep in thought on how to get his team back on track. Delivery deadlines for avocados were not being met for over 16 percent of all shipments to customers, and as customer service manager, he was responsible. The problem had been escalating because just three months ago when he last tackled the problem with his team, their "unmet rate" was 12 percent of all shipments. At that time, he met with his team and attempted to motivate them to a higher rate of accuracy and timeliness. He thought that a rewards program would be helpful, so he made it a point each month to show public appreciation and praise for individual customer service representatives who met the 5 percent maximum rate. He coupled the positive rewards with a verbal message to those who did not meet the 5 percent maximum rate to "work smarter." Earl had heard some complaints about dwindling team spirit, and he realized that the data were speaking for themselves. He knew that he had to try another method.

After talking to his supervisor, Earl decided to use modified causal mapping as a problem-solving technique to identify the root of the problem. Calling the team together for a Friday afternoon retreat, he said, "We are going to discuss all the possible reasons why we're not meeting delivery deadlines as we should. I know you've been trying since we last discussed this problem three months ago, but our numbers have gotten worse. I'll write 'delivery deadlines not met' here in the center of the board." The group then took over an hour to generate as many reasons as they could think of why the "unmet rate" was too high. The list boiled down to six likely general causes of the problem: poor communication down the chain to shipping; poor communication up the chain to accounting and marketing; planning; internal customer management; information technology; and internal teamwork. Earl then announced that they would tackle each of these six general causes and identify as many reasons as possible why each of the issues contributed to the high "unmet rate." Someone on the team suggested that they could save time by dividing into subgroups that would each work on one issue. Earl said, no, it was important that everyone contribute to the entire discussion as well as hear the entire discussion. When they turned their attention to the first issue, poor communication with shipping, they came up with several possibilities: lack of advance communication upon immediate receipt of orders; reliance on technology as opposed to personal communication; lack of individualized accountability in shipping for particular customers; absence of interdepartmental planning between shipping and customer service; lack of understanding of shipping's responsibility when delivery specifications are incomplete or inaccurate; and lack of data on common characteristics or circumstances of the 16 percent of shipments that did not meet delivery deadlines.

Next, the group focused on the second likely issue in having an "unmet rate" that is too high, and so on through the list. It was a long afternoon, and the group left with a lengthy list of about forty possible causes of the problem as a basis for action.

DISCUSSION QUESTIONS

1. To what extent were the guidelines given in this chapter met by the approach taken by Earl? Which guidelines have not yet been met?
2. What is a good approach for Earl in taking the next step of applying the guidelines from this chapter for problem-solving?
3. Is the problem-solving approach taken by Earl primarily task-oriented behavior? Explain.
4. Why did Earl's initial motivational approach fail to get desired results?
5. The members of the customer service team that reports to Earl would show variation in their approach to problem-solving. If that is the case, would Earl have to use different methods with different team members to motivate them to achieve minimum delivery deadlines? Why or why not?

CASE ANALYSIS 2

You are a new supervisor. You have been the best performer in the unit and were rewarded with this promotion. You like to ensure that the details of tasks are very well taken care of. The previous supervisor was not perceived as successful at any level. Operations were sloppy, people were not happy, and the unit was not well connected to the organization. You now are in charge of seven employees.

Four employees have been with the unit a long time. Lupe is very accurate but slow. John is very fast but somewhat inaccurate. Mary is inaccurate and slow but is the most cheerful and pleasant person in the unit. Barbara is accurate, fast, a bit sour in general, and currently upset that she did not get the promotion instead of you. Sandy has been with the unit only for a year. It is difficult to tell whether her accuracy and speed are going to continue to improve. Currently, she is both a bit slow and her accuracy a bit weak. Both Bob and Ron are new, young, and floundering. They frequently ask each other questions rather than asking the supervisors or lead workers. Neither seems very serious about the job.

DISCUSSION QUESTION

As you analyze the seven people in your unit, assess the task-oriented competencies that you will need to perform well. Discuss the competencies that apply (specifically for this case: monitoring and assessing, operations planning, clarifying, and delegating) and what you would do in the first two months on the job. Differentiate where necessary between the handling of the group versus the individuals.

6 | People-Oriented Leadership Behaviors

You can make more friends in two months by becoming really interested in other people than you can in two years by trying to get other people interested in you.
—Dale Carnegie, 1888–1955

The focus of Part II has been the managerial leadership behaviors that most contribute to leader effectiveness. The traits and skills related to those behaviors were introduced. Behavioral theories, such as the managerial grid, which integrates concerns for tasks and concerns for people along two axes, were presented. Task- and people-oriented factors were then separated in order to examine the two individually and at length. Task-oriented factors were studied in the previous chapter. Here, attention is focused on people-oriented factors. As was emphasized earlier, organizations need people-oriented behaviors, but not to the exclusion of task-oriented behaviors. A careful balance must be struck between task- and people-oriented behaviors so that leadership may be as efficient and effective as possible. Just as there is no "one best way" to lead in every situation, sole focus on the concerns of people is not always the best approach for a leader.

Nevertheless, because these people-oriented competencies are so central to organizational activity, management is often defined as "getting things done *through other people*" (refer back to a more sophisticated discussion of management in Chapter 1). In fact, some writers consider people-oriented competencies essentially synonymous with management (e.g., Mintzberg 1973). Overall, we consider these competencies an extremely important component of both management and leadership.

The Ohio State studies define "people-oriented behavior" or **consideration**—a behavioral competency cluster that evolved in the 1950s—as supportiveness, friendliness, concern, and inclusiveness (Hemphill and Coons 1957). The University of Michigan study also emphasizes "relations-oriented" behavior, which includes helpfulness, trust, thoughtfulness, delegation, and recognition.

In order for people-oriented competencies to be as central to leadership as suggested, leadership must move beyond the perception of "dominating" or "exerting authority." But even so, remember that "being dominant" in business is actually a result of effectively employing affiliative behaviors, rather than a result of having the most muscle. People-oriented competencies are quite different from dominating behavior, but also they are quite different, at the other extreme, from accepting low standards or avoiding difficult communications.

Jim Collins's book *Good to Great* (2001) points out that leaders who are egoistic and call attention to themselves are essentially misrepresenting the meaning of "people-oriented" behaviors. Calling attention to oneself for personal gratification is the virtual antithesis of being humble and exercising the will of leadership needed for corporate greatness, according to Collins. "In over two-thirds of the comparison cases [comparing leadership of companies in general to leadership of great companies], we noted the presence of a gargantuan personal ego that contributed to the demise or continued mediocrity of the company" (29). Collins points to twelve significant corporate cases that ring in the annals of America's business history. At first blush, these companies appear to have had charismatic CEOs, but actually, Collins says, they were all cases in which a charismatic CEO interfered with the long-term success of the organization. Clearly, being "people-oriented" does not mean turning the spotlight on oneself.

To reiterate, leadership behaviors in the *task domain* include monitoring and assessing work, operations planning, clarifying roles and objectives, informing, delegating, problem solving, and managing innovation and creativity. They were covered in Chapter 5. In this chapter, seven leadership competencies in the *people-oriented domain* are examined: consulting, planning and organizing personnel, developing staff, motivating, building and managing teams, managing conflict, and managing personnel change. Although they constitute the bulk of people-oriented behaviors, the list could ultimately be longer. Furthermore, the list of discrete considerate actions that help make those behaviors effective is infinite.

Intuitively, managers may feel that people-oriented leadership behaviors engender happy, motivated employees who perform well. But does that chain of reasoning necessarily hold? The people-oriented "soft" competencies have been somewhat more difficult to demonstrate quantitatively in the research than task-oriented competencies in terms of employee performance. They have been easier to correlate to employee satisfaction, but the correlation of satisfaction with performance is weaker. When development and motivation of a team are the desired long-term objectives, studies show that the "democratic leadership style" has a positive outcome. However, results are mixed in studies when performance objectives involve solution of a problem or are shorter-term.

It is important for you to master leadership competencies in the people-oriented domain because, when practiced effectively, they promote a healthy work environment. Yet we know that many work environments are unhealthy in the eyes of workers because of perceived dissatisfaction with the boss's people-oriented skills (CareerBuilder.com 2004). Consider this chapter a quest to define for yourself as a reader which people-oriented behaviors are already your strengths and which should be further developed in order to promote a healthy work environment in the organization you serve.

All seven people-oriented leadership competencies are examined separately. They are reinforced by obvious, but endless, expressions of understanding, interest, genuine concern for team welfare, and value in others and their ideas. Leaders may do things that make it pleasant to be a contributing member of the team, or they may simply explain their actions in a manner that enforces the value placed on understanding by team members. Actions that support active listening, coaching, and empowering, as well as genuine interest in the welfare of the team, make these behaviors even more effective. A discussion of each competency begins below.

CONSULTING

Consulting involves checking with people on work-related matters and involving people in decision-making processes. It can be done via one-on-one meetings, calls, email, or other communications media. Consulting can occur in small-group gatherings, staff meetings, all-organization meetings, or various types of group- and mass-written communications.

Consulting has two distinct elements. First, it refers to soliciting information such as suggestions, ideas, and advice. The information may be solicited with simple questions, such as "What do you think is the problem?" or "How do you think things are going?" The second element is an invitation to be involved in decision-making to some degree, whether highly indirect and informal or highly direct and structured. Finally, for purposes of definition, consultation refers to checking with and involving *all* organizational members. Although consultation with one's subordinates is a critical dimension, consultation with one's boss may be no less important.

Consulting is related to many competencies. Unlike informing, which emphasizes data dissemination, consulting requires an active feedback mechanism, emphasizing questions and data collection. Consulting is related to other assessment and evaluation competencies: task monitoring and assessing, which focus on internal technical data collection and analysis, and environmental scanning, which focuses on external technical data collection and analysis. While other assessment and evaluation competencies emphasize "hard" data, consulting emphasizes "soft" data.

Consulting is also related to decisiveness, delegating, and decision-making competencies. As a decision-making model, consulting falls between decisiveness and delegation, as will be discussed below. Broad-based and important decisions generally have extremely heavy data demands that can rarely be met without consultation. Consultation assists decision-making by enhancing buy-in, decision education, and legitimacy. Despite its relationship and overlap with other competencies, it is distinct enough so that when managers are asked about the quality of consultation, they have no problem understanding and responding to the question.

An example of the consulting process may involve something as routine as a job hire. A common, people-oriented process in academic settings, it also works to the benefit of private organizations. A manager may cobble together a departmental committee to attend a job fair, scouting for potential employees and holding preliminary informal discussions with prospective applicants. The committee reviews and discusses all applications for the position, and current departmental employees offer their suggestions and recommend the top candidates for interview. When the candidates are brought in, the manager of the department not only conducts an interview based on information gathered by the committee, but also has the candidates meet with employees of the organization in order to get further informal input. Ultimately, the final decision remains in the hands of the manager, yet a consultative process is extended to those with whom the new employee will work. The leader structures and controls the decision process, utilizes as much of the input as is appropriate, and is ready to step in at any point should unique situations arise such as confidential feedback on a recommended candidate or a violation of process.

The distinctions among subtypes and other competencies are most important with consulting, decisiveness, and delegation. In the simplest sense, they can be arrayed on a spectrum with authoritarian decision-making at one extreme, consultation as a decision-making model in the middle, and delegation at the other extreme where authority is given over to subordinates. Yet these scenarios tremendously understate the subtlety of decision processes, especially in the consultation range. Vroom and Yetton (1973) provide a lucid analysis, distinguishing two types of consultation in addition to two types of unilateral decision-making and delegation. Their models are helpful so that leaders do not confuse the styles as arrayed on the spectrum, thinking that every time they ask others for information about an issue, they have used a delegative or consultative model of decision-making. Essentially the decision participation range for this leader-subordinate model is as follows:

- Autocratic decision model 1: You make the decision yourself with the information available.
- Autocratic decision model 2: You make the decision yourself after getting information from others. You may or may not tell others why you need the information; however, the emphasis is on collecting data, not getting advice.
- Consultation decision model 1: You share the problem or decision issue with individuals and ask for input; however, you make the decision unilaterally, and your decision may or may not reflect others' preferences.
- Consultation decision model 2: You share the problem or decision issue with a group and ask for input; however, you make the decision unilaterally, and your decision may or may not reflect others' preferences.
- **Delegation decision model**: The leader structures the decision-making and facilitates the final decision by the individual or group. The leader does not try to influence the group except to ensure a process that facilitates decision quality and consensus. The leader implements the decision by the group or individual.

The main factors Vroom and Yetton point to in determining the correct approach in any given situation are the importance or nature of decision quality, subordinate information, problem structure, subordinate decision acceptance, subordinate alignment with organizational goals, and subordinate consensus.

We will distinguish only two types of consultative decision-making. In **participative decision-making**, subordinates and others are actively involved in providing ideas and suggestions in the decision-making process. Although the leader ultimately makes the decision, others have substantial opportunities to influence that decision. In quality participative decision-making environments, others know that while their ideas may not determine every decision, they do have influence over a significant proportion of decisions over time. **Joint decision-making** is similar to Vroom and Yetton's delegation model. That is, the leader manages the decision-making process, but does not make the actual decision. Leaders still have significant influence because of the narrowness of the decision parameters and the opportunity to control the process.

GUIDELINES FOR CONSULTING

1. *Evaluate the decision environment surrounding substantive decisions.* Although all decision environments have a unique blend of conditions, the parameters of those environments are relatively standard (Vroom and Yetton 1973). The following standard parameters should be considered: What information is needed and who has it or can get it? The more information that is already in the leader's domain, the more likely the leader is to take a primary role. However, even when leaders have all the technical information, certain types of interpersonal and judgmental information may not be available to them without consultation. How critical is time? The greater the time pressure, the more likely that the decision is made in an "executive mode." Sadly, some managers always seem to be in a crisis mode, overwhelmed by decisions that should have been delegated and shared. How important might the development and inclusiveness of others be? Some loss of decision quality may be well worth the inclusion and learning it brings. How likely are others to cooperate with the leader and/or group? Some issues are so divisive or personal that leaders are loath to bring them into a group discussion.

2. *Seek as much input as possible for substantive decisions.* Even if decisions are determined unilaterally, others like to know they have been consulted for relevant information. Not only does it make subordinates and others feel respected and useful, good information is critical for good discussions. It is the responsibility of the decision-maker to solicit information and not to assume that notification of a decision process will be sufficient to get all relevant data. Leaders must encourage others to provide information, develop listening skills, record ideas, and show that they are building on the ideas of others, as exemplified in Exhibit 6.1.

3. *Utilize the ideas, suggestions, and input of others for substantive decisions to the maximum degree feasible.* Leaders should seek to maximize decision inclusiveness to the degree that time, decision quality, and cooperation will allow; autocratic decisions should be limited in number. Good leaders let others know the guidelines so that decisions do not seem arbitrary or peremptory. In particular, maximum inclusion tends to ensure maximum information, buy-in, and development. Depending on the nature of the decision, maximizing decision inclusiveness means pushing it down the participation or delegation spectrum as far as feasible. Even when a decision-maker retains a great deal of authority in a participative process in which only information (not decision alternatives) was requested, other people greatly value public or private acknowledgment and appreciation of their contribution.

Exhibit 6.1

Dick and Jane: The Management Version

Dick and Jane grew up in the same neighborhood at the same time, went to the same state university, and earned MBAs. In fact, Dick got his graduate degree before Jane by several years, yet Jane was now the division head and Dick was only a frontline supervisor. It seemed to Dick that Jane was better liked and trusted than he, even though he was more outgoing and worked very hard to be fair. But their respective career progressions were not the issue today.

Today Dick was going to Jane because he was angry that he did not get an exemption from the statewide hiring freeze for the information technology specialist II that he wanted to hire. The freeze had come just as the job was posted and was effective for all those to whom an offer had not been made. While Dick had not yet offered the position at the time, he had felt sure that he would be granted an exemption until his immediate supervisor declined to make an exemption request. He was appealing to Jane.

For her part, Jane knew that Dick had an appointment and knew the broad facts of the case. She often thought that her undergraduate degree in counseling psychology was extremely useful for this part of the job. She still remembers the lectures on Rogerian psychology and active listening skills: *maintaining attention, expressing empathy for the person while listening neutrally to the facts, restating the person's points for accuracy and clarity, suspending preconceptions, avoiding premature judgments,* and so on. Indeed, to this day she keeps some aphorisms framed on her wall: "He listens well who takes notes" (Dante) and "Give every man thine ear but few thy voice" (Shakespeare).

When Dick came in, Jane greeted him at the door with a warm smile and asked about his family, whom she knew. After the pleasantries, she asked Dick to tell her the problem, allowing him to start at the beginning. Occasionally she interjected summaries of his points and once she asked a follow-up question. After he had fully expressed his case and was beginning to repeat himself, Jane asked for potential solutions. She explained that she was unlikely to get an exemption unless she offered to give up another position under the current fiscal constraints. Did he have suggestions of a slack area? If she were able to receive permission for a "term" employee (for a two-year term with full benefits), rather than a regular classified position, did he think the applicant would be agreeable? At the conclusion of their meeting, she said that she would talk to Dick's supervisor, who she knew was supportive of the request but simply realistic about the challenges involved in the exemption. If the supervisor had another unfilled position, she would suggest trading it for the information technology specialist until the hiring freeze was lifted. If not, she would make a strong request for a term appointment. If that failed, he would have to wait until the freeze was lifted.

Dick left the office knowing that the probability of filling the position immediately was still only 50–50. Despite the lack of guarantees, he knew that Jane had listened to his needs carefully and would do all she could within her scope of authority. Dick was no longer angry because Jane respected and appreciated him. Yes, he had always liked her. Jane listened.

Discussion

This section of the text deals with the people-oriented competency of consultation. Apply the principles presented in the text to Jane's reality as the division head. Do you think she should have handled the situation differently?

PLANNING AND ORGANIZING PERSONNEL

The planning function can be separated into several distinct competencies. Planning and organizing personnel involves coordinating people and operations and ensuring that the competencies necessary to do the work are, or will be, available. It also involves self-planning.

One element of planning and organizing personnel is fitting people to schedules and making the appropriate changes as work and personnel need change. For success, one must ensure that the critical competencies of the assigned jobs are understood and available. This aspect overlaps with the human resource management competency relative to performing general management functions such as authorizing positions, recruiting, and hiring.

Coordinating people and operations is facilitated by leaders adopting a people-oriented behavior that does not require a "yes" answer for everything, while still keeping an eye on the task to be accomplished as well as on overall employee satisfaction.

Consider Juanita, for example, who oversees departments of various sizes. Juanita saw the importance of consistency in the planning function. A few staff employees in office jobs applied to have a 4–40 workweek, which involves four ten-hour workdays rather than five eight-hour days. Although one department had three office staff and could conceivably place one or two employees on the 4–40 schedule, inequity would be introduced for others whose jobs simply did not have comparable flexibility. Whereas some might see the people-oriented solution as approving all staff requests, Juanita denied them in order to ensure that, first, there would be equity across comparable positions within the organization, and second, qualified office staff would be available when others needed their support. In the long run, her position for the planning and organizing of personnel was an appropriate people-oriented approach, with an eye on the work to be done.

Another element is *matching the talents, interests, and preferences of people to the work*. People are not interchangeable cogs in a machine; reflecting their interests and natural abilities in assembling jobs, projects, and teams makes an enormous difference. In identifying the core competencies of managers in working with people, Buckingham and Coffman (1999) pull out talent and job fit as the two most critical elements of selection and development. In recent years, leading self-directed work teams in different environments has become a leadership imperative in innovative organizations that seriously strive for full involvement of employees (Chapter 12 will have a comprehensive look at leader development and self-directed teams).

A third element is *personal time management skills*. The ability of leaders to manage staff is largely determined by their ability to self-manage. Good time management means that leaders analyze the use of their time and that they have a plan for goal achievement. They avoid wasteful activities and productively harness many "reactive" activities as strategic opportunities. Finally, they allot time for reflection and the planning process itself.

GUIDELINES FOR PLANNING AND ORGANIZING PERSONNEL

1. *Ensure that specific staff assignments and schedules are understood and accepted.* Three aspects of good scheduling are sufficient data, fairness of policies, and clarity of assignments (with a feedback loop if possible). Getting sufficient data about organizational needs and potential personnel demands is critical for a schedule to be coherent. The more organizational needs that can be mapped and demands that can be anticipated, the less chance that scheduling will be subject to excessive changes. Such data can be collected by analysis of organizational needs, group meetings, and group communications, and augmented by individual communications. Another

aspect of scheduling is the set of policies that is used and the perception of fairness. Employees are conscious of others' assignments and will tend to be highly critical of those assignments if they do not agree with or understand them. Therefore, while leaders want to retain flexibility, it is best to do so using broad principles. Finally, clarity of the group assignments is critical. This is less vital in ongoing operations, but crucial in new or changing operations in which roles are unclear and whole functions may be neglected.

2. *Match staff preferences and competencies to the work as much as possible.* The more the individual preferences, personalities, and experiences of employees can be accommodated, the better. Some people may be better interacting with others, some in producing detailed analysis, and still others at getting new projects done quickly. A major aspect of customization or specialization of scheduling involves building an appreciation of the different roles people play and the importance of playing to their strengths.

3. *Stay on top of scheduling changes.* Changes create major opportunities for operational glitches and even systems malfunctions. The oft-heard refrain is "I thought that So-and-So was going to do that." Feedback loops and confirmation of changes are the best ways to prevent problems.

4. *Review long-term organizational competency needs to ensure organizational capacity.* Good leaders are constantly assessing the overall competency needs of their organization or unit. Those planning and organizing personnel need to document gaps and weaknesses so that they can be addressed through formal training, staff rotation, one-on-one coaching, inspirational exhortation, selection criteria changes, and so on.

5. *Manage your personal schedule effectively.* Some leadership analysts place this among the chief qualities for effectiveness. It is hard to respect leaders who do not have the discipline to manage their own time well or address all their major responsibilities. This includes the daily and weekly scheduling of activities and the ability to reorganize priorities constantly, without losing sight of long-term goals. It also includes the ability to use the natural energy cycle to maximum effectiveness and an ability to make sure that the important matters get accomplished (Bhatta 2001). Your personal energy cycle involves a prime time of your day when your energy is alive, as well as the more down time of day when your focus is slower. To work with, rather than against, this natural cycle we should schedule challenging meetings and complex thought when the brain is in highest gear during peak performance times. There are many important jobs that can be done during "down time" that may actually help a person feel recharged. For example, leaders whose focus slows by late afternoon could schedule "management by walking around" or congratulatory calls to employees who have "been caught" doing things well in order to get that important time in the day without sacrificing a part of their energy cycle when they can deal well with rapid-fire complex issues more easily.

DEVELOPING STAFF

Developing staff involves improving subordinates' effectiveness in their current positions and preparing them for their next position or step. Clarifying establishes a baseline of information and direction. **Developing staff** focuses on assisting employees to be comfortable in their positions, reach higher levels of productivity over time, and prepare for future prospects. It builds on the baseline that clarifying had established. Clarifying and developing can be seen as two elements establishing a continuum from a short-term, technical focus to a long-term, career focus. Again, Chapter 12 covers staff development when it speaks of preparing others for leadership.

It has long been debated whether there is a measurable payoff in corporate performance for firms that invest significantly in developing staff. In response to this question, the American Society for Training and Development collected data on employee training expenditures at hundreds of publicly traded companies (Bassie et al. 2001). Portfolios of the companies were then developed, showing that companies in the top 20 percent in spending on staff development earned a five-year average of 16.2 percent, or 6.5 percentage points per year more than the Wilshire 5000 index. Companies offering the least investment in staff development had significantly lower returns.

Providing formal training is only part of the picture of developing staff. There are three major elements for the leader who wishes to develop staff: supporting, coaching, and mentoring. Supporting is the emotional component of development. Support helps employees identify with their job, focus energies on productive issues, and accept criticism or hardships. Employees who feel that they have friends at work are shown to be more productive and more likely to remain (Buckingham and Coffman 1999). A supportive relationship will generally facilitate the acceptance of criticism and even disciplinary actions and is especially important in times of special hardship.

Coaching helps employees do a task more effectively. After employees have received their initial instructions and training and have been made aware of the standards they are expected to meet, they are still not at peak performance. While the primary responsibility lies with the employee to improve performance, this responsibility is shared with the superior, whose job it is to provide intermittent on-the-job training and suggestions. It is important to note that training provided in the clarifying phase and coaching during the developing phase are both critical, and weakness or omission of one lessens the value of the other.

Mentoring refers to supporting a person's career and is actually a type of career counseling. (Sometimes on-the-job training is called mentoring, but this is really a misnomer.) Mentors act as performance or behavior models and provide advice on the culture of the organization and profession, the right job-related decisions to make, and the best way to interpret significant issues or concerns.

GUIDELINES FOR DEVELOPING STAFF

1. *Show courtesy to and interest in all staff, and demonstrate positive regard for others to the greatest degree possible.* Courtesy and good manners are the formal structure of consideration. Showing interest in others demonstrates an even higher level of support.

Good active listening skills assist greatly in showing interest. Positive regard does not mean that the weaknesses, errors, or "sins" of others are overlooked; it simply means a person's basic humanity is appreciated and valued.

2. *Promote a person's self-esteem and reputation.* A leader can support a subordinate's self-esteem by praising consistent work, accomplishments, and positive qualities. This can be enhanced by promoting a person's expertise and reputation to superiors and peers. Subordinates can be introduced to other significant or important people inside or outside the organization, and they can be given assignments with visibility.

3. *Listen to personal problems that affect work performance and take the time to counsel subordinates.* When subordinates have a problem in their personal lives, it often affects their professional performance. Supervisors must take time to show compassion about the basic problem so that they can determine how to help most appropriately. For most routine or temporary issues a friendly ear is enough, with some detached advice and appropriate encouragement. Although managers should not allow themselves to assume the role of therapist, "light" counseling, from listening to appropriate advice, is often part of the job.

4. *Analyze subordinates' overall performance and identify deficiencies.* Leaders must take the time to analyze how well subordinates are doing through observation, review of work products, and conversations with the subordinate. It is important for the manager to help the subordinate participate in the analysis or self-diagnosis.

5. *Monitor and correct errors.* Timely and precise error correction is a foundation for performance improvement and prevents many problem trends from occurring, such as unsatisfactory practices that become routine or fossilized. New employees are most open to correction and suggestions, but monitoring and correcting are needed even at senior levels in order for people to develop.

6. *Provide career advice and encouragement.* Leaders let subordinates know how to do well in their current position and can help employees discern and prepare for future careers. The leader as model is an important form of career advice; successful bosses are more likely to have successful employees (Graen et al. 1977). Part of the modeling that is useful to employees is to observe the superior's development activities. Just as important as providing information and modeling behavior is the encouragement of subordinates to think of both enrichment and advancement opportunities.

7. *Provide special opportunities for subordinates to prepare for a future position.* Because leaders have superior resources and authority, they can often provide special opportunities for individuals or whole groups. Leaders can allow people to take additional training, authorize reimbursement for educational classes, allow subordinates to represent the division in meetings, provide opportunities for them to attend conferences, and so on.

MOTIVATING

Motivating is a general term that refers to enhancing the inner drives and positive intentions of subordinates (or others) to perform well through incentives, disincentives, and inspiration.

Elements of motivating include positive incentives (e.g., recognition and rewards), **disincentives** (e.g., disciplining), and inspiring. Recognition involves intangible incentives such as showing appreciation and providing praise. It includes actions such as informal positive verbal comments, informal tributes or awards in public settings like staff or division meetings, written praise in notes or annual evaluations, and formal commendations ranging from letters of positive acknowledgment to plaques and trophies. Recognition generally costs nothing and is immensely motivating but underutilized, according to most researchers. Recognizing is often a neglected managerial practice, even though it can be one of the most effective to "strengthen desirable behavior and task commitment" (Yukl 2006, 74).

When there is a problem employee, a natural managerial reaction by some is to deliver a solution to the employee in question. In contrast, Toby, who owns and manages a chain of sporting goods stores, meets with problem employees and asks them to provide possible solutions. Lance, one such problem employee, often arrives late for work, is periodically found texting his friends, and does not utilize the correct sales approach. Toby actively works with him to establish achievable goals in order to motivate Lance to improve his performance. Together they address the obstacles that are perceived to stand in the way of Lance achieving the specific desired goals upon which they have settled. Toby follows up after one week and again after two weeks to see, in depth, how Lance is doing. On the third such contact, Lance acknowledges, "You could have just fired me, but you didn't. You were right when you believed in me, and I'll show you what I can do." Motivating employees can be a powerful tool.

Rewarding involves tangible incentives such as promotions, increases in pay, increased discretion, superior work assignments, perquisites, or "perks," and additional responsibilities or authority. Pay and promotion rewards can be highly constrained in various situations such as in challenging economic times, in a traditional union environment, or in public sector organizations. When rewards are possible, they need to be based on performance goals that are important to the organization and represent different types of contribution, using clearly explained guidelines. It is important to find out what individuals or groups find attractive, so incentives will be as motivating as possible.

Disincentives should be used more strategically and less often in most management situations. They include any sanctions that reduce perquisites, pay, work flexibility, status, honor, and pride, or even terminate employment and impose fines or imprisonment for actions that violate or defy administrative rules or laws. Disincentives can be mild, for example, a verbal rebuke for carelessness, or extremely harsh, for example, a charge of criminal misconduct. If positive incentives are too uncommon, disincentives are usually too common and too heavily relied upon. Taken together, positive incentives and negative disincentives work at the lower end of Maslow's (1954) hierarchy of needs, such as basic living needs (via income), security, and basic human interactions (e.g., positive work relations).

Exhibit 6.2 **Vroom's Expectancy Theory**

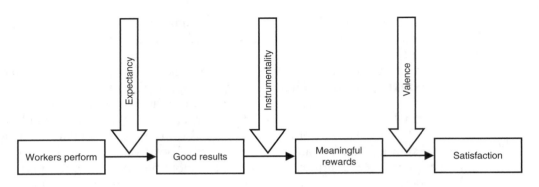

In stark contrast to use of disincentives is the motivational technique of inspiring, which works at the higher end of Maslow's hierarchy, providing achievement, self-actualization, and spiritual connectedness. Inspiring involves providing encouragement to work for group and organizational goals regardless of personal benefit. A classic example of inspiring is illustrated by volunteers who pour into hurricane-ridden areas, enduring in the midst of terrible conditions with inadequate equipment, food, and water, but nonetheless serving with pride and satisfaction. Whatever the situation, inspiring may emphasize that all fail if the organization fails (the rational appeal), "do it for the team" (the emotional appeal) or "do it as a favor for me" (the personal appeal). When the motivational appeal of inspiring is effective, short-term sacrifice is seen as a justified and virtuous contribution or badge of honor.

While the original work on motivation is based on behavioral conditioning, initially the work of Thorndike, Pavlov, and others, and later popularized through Skinner (1953, 1971, 1974), it was converted into management terms by Vroom (1964). **Expectancy theory** sets out the stimulus-response chain that must work effectively for high performance to occur through positive incentives. First, workers have to know their efforts can in fact lead to good performance (Vroom calls this linkage *expectancy*). Next, workers need to see the relationship between good performance and the delivery of work-related rewards (Vroom calls this linkage *instrumentality*). Just because good performance is achieved, will rewards occur? The final linkage, **valence**, is between the reward and the desirability of the reward in the eyes of the recipient. Additional compensation may be a weak motivator if the recipient is more desirous of time off, more support (less stress), or better working conditions. Leaders monitor all the stages, not only identifying problems for the group as a whole, but also examining the barriers to positive motivation for each individual. Exhibit 6.2 identifies the basic elements of expectancy theory.

A well-known leadership theory related to leadership style and motivation is path-goal (House 1971; House and Mitchell 1974), reviewed in Chapter 3, which holds that different leadership styles are effective in different conditions, using the logic of expectancy theory.

GUIDELINES FOR MOTIVATING

1. *Recognize as many people as possible and appropriate.* Because recognition is effective in motivating people, it should be an important practice for leaders. Leaders can recognize improvements in performance, maintenance of high standards and reliability, good organizational citizenship, commendable efforts that failed, and so on. It is important not just to reward a few good performers or those with high-visibility jobs. Frequent and timely recognition is more motivating than recognition long after the fact. Specificity in recognition is particularly important for a number of reasons. First, recognizing specific behaviors illustrates an understanding that makes the praise more believable. Second, it reinforces ideal practices whereas general recognition does not necessarily do so. Third, specificity reduces the risk that recognition is perceived as a popularity contest.

2. *Use an appropriate form of recognition.* There are many forms and levels of recognition, and it is important to use as many as possible for appropriateness and variety. While "managing by walking around" to stay in touch, the manager should be able to intersperse verbal praise and occasional suggestions for improvements without being critical. Staff meetings should have a recognition component in which the leader quickly reviews current or special accomplishments. Informal appreciation lunches can be as motivating as formal awards programs. "Nice try" discussions should quickly follow failures; such discussions can easily segue into analyses of what went wrong and how things might be done differently.

3. *Explain how rewards and significant commendations are distributed.* People must know the rules of the game in order to follow the rules and be motivated to seek high levels of performance. If a desirable internal position will be opening in the next year or so, it is useful to tell those eligible what qualifications will be sought so that they can groom themselves for the position if interested. If priorities have shifted, it is important to let people know as soon as possible so that they are not surprised later. Explaining how rewards and commendations are distributed will ensure that managers are clear about the elements and standards of performance they will later be identifying and tracking.

4. *Find out what rewards are attractive.* Money is always nice, but money may not be available, and it may not be the prime motivator in every case. A sense of what people value in rewards, as well as what type of recognition is meaningful, is critical in using recognition and rewards most effectively.

5. *Explain rules and procedures to ensure that subordinates understand the consequences of deviations.* When rules and procedures are not explained and documented, the liability generally flows up to the manager! It is important for managers to respond to infractions promptly and fairly, without showing favoritism to any individual or group. Additionally, it is important to note that not administering punitive action for noncompliance may result in lost credibility, encourage wayward behavior, and ultimately redound upon the leader.

6. *In order to avoid hasty and incorrect conclusions, always investigate the facts before using reprimands and punishment.* A savvy leader (or lawyer) knows that there are two or more sides to every story and that it is imprudent not to gather data from alternate perspectives before taking managerial action. When infractions are reported, leaders need to be trained to withhold judgmental or accusatory comments until additional information is gathered. Some additional suggestions are to remain calm and collected during the process, to express a sincere desire to help the subordinate, and to try to engage the target person in the resolution of the problem.

7. *Use punishments that are fair and commensurate with the seriousness of the violation.* This practice recommends that disciplinary actions be administered sequentially so that the target has the opportunity to understand problems and concerns and to take self-corrective actions. It is important to note that discipline is fact- and situation-specific: No set regimen can be determined in advance without knowing the specific facts and context. For example, some low-performing employees may start by getting oral reprimands, eventually require written reprimands, improve for extended periods, and later have deteriorating performance requiring starting over at the oral reprimand level. Occasionally an employee's violation is serious, requiring skipping steps in the chain.

8. *When attempting to inspire, use energetic or emotional language with symbols, metaphors, and inclusionary terms such as "we," "us," and "our."* Inspiring is both a technical and emotional undertaking. Inspiring is assisted by language that captures the imagination or strikes clear mental images. The leader should utilize not only rational logic (especially self-interest), but also emotional appeals (e.g., emphasizing group membership and pride) and personal appeals (based on the request of the leader). Effective appeals enable employees to appreciate the long-term benefits of hard work and sacrifice.

BUILDING AND MANAGING TEAMS

Managing teams involves creating and supporting "true" teams in addition to traditional work units, and team-building involves enhancing identification with the work, intramember cooperation, and esprit de corps of both work groups and teams. The general people-oriented behavior of managing teams is the focus of this chapter.

There are three important parameters that capture the differentiation of work groups in organizations. The first parameter is membership. Is the work group or team membership inclusive of all the members of a unit more or less automatically, or are members selectively recruited or assigned? Are members selected from within a work unit or from a variety of units? Second, what is the work function and scope of the group? Third, to what degree is the level of authority extended for independent decision-making of the group? Are most ideas proposed, monitored, and approved by a leader with formal authority in the area (as is common in traditional work groups), or does the team have some degree of independence in how their work is handled? Needless to say, these parameters give rise to a large number of group permutations.

Traditional groups are composed of all members of the unit who take care of ongoing operations and have a formal leader who makes most of the important decisions. Frequently called **work groups**, they are an indispensable element of organizational effectiveness. When the group has selective membership, a specialized objective, and some independence, but is still from the same unit or work area, it is called a project team. As group autonomy increases, the tendency is to move to language that identifies a "team" as opposed to a "group." When the membership is from a variety of functional areas, it is called a **cross-functional team**. Both cross-functional work teams and cross-functional project teams are common.

Some teams are informal. But the more well-known team-based organizations have formal team structures. Sun Microsystems was an example of an organization with formal teams that were employed for special projects, particularly those with business purposes such as squeezing development time. Anyone at Sun could start a special project team, for instance, but they were required to find a manager who would fund the project and approve a team charter.

Why do organizations have teams or work groups in the first place? Both traditional work groups and different types of teams have their benefits and liabilities. Some of the strengths of work groups are clear membership, clear lines of authority, efficiency of operations, and stability.

Potential liabilities of work groups can also be significant. They include the lack of creativity, stifling of individual initiative, excess of rule maintenance (as much by members for protection as by leaders for control), and aversion to change. Work groups are not well suited to handle the volume of problems, customization, and organizational modifications that typically occur in business operations—teams are.

The benefits of teams include the ability to select appropriate skills for a particular project, the creativity and synergy they engender (especially in handling nonroutine work), their flexibility of structure, and the fact that most teams can be easily disbanded at the end of an assignment or their usefulness to the company. When teams have a high degree of self-management, they have been shown to generally report a higher degree of satisfaction as well.

Among the potential liabilities of teams are lopsided representation, coordination problems, divided loyalty and role stress or confusion, time consumption, lack of commitment, and challenges in implementation. Exhibit 6.3 lists ten common problems with teams.

Efforts to increase the positive effects of diversity are normally considered a part of building and managing teams, just as handling the negative aspects of diversity are grouped with managing conflict (the next competency to be discussed). Diversity, as discussed in Chapter 10, has the potential to increase the creative power of teams, one of their most valuable features, as well as ensure adequate representation and fairness.

Leaders can substantially enhance the conditions for facilitating team effectiveness. Making sure that the task structure and team structure are a "fit" requires thinking through design issues in advance. Providing clearly defined objectives and scope of authority is critical. What is the team tasked with, in what time frame, and with what authority? Leaders need to make sure that the team membership mix is appropriate

Exhibit 6.3

Ten Common Problems That Teams Encounter

An excellent, common sense review of teams is provided by Peter Scholtes (1993). Chapter 6 of his classic book reviews the types of problems commonly encountered by teams.

1. **Floundering:** Teams commonly have problems starting, moving from one stage to the next, and even finishing up the project. They may be overwhelmed by the task in the beginning, lack the expertise to tackle the problem, have problems with consensus, or have problems letting go of the project.

2. **Overbearing participants:** Often when some members of the group have higher rank or status based on credentials or expertise, they insist on a disproportionate role in team decision processes. Although such members can contribute substantially, they also discourage discussion with which they do not agree and thus can both diminish creativity and the legitimate role of other participants. Overbearing participants generally do not talk a lot; they simply insist on holding sway when they do.

3. **Dominating participants:** When members of the group insist on airing their opinions and views at length, regardless of their level of expertise, they dominate by force of personality. This diminishes the role of others and is simply frustrating or boring for others.

4. **Reluctant participants:** Opposite of the dominating participants are the reluctant participants. While quiet participants are not necessarily a problem, they do represent special challenges in eliciting their ideas or when excessive introversion saps the energy of the group.

5. **Unquestioned acceptance of opinions as facts:** Teams often have to elicit a variety of types of information and data from participants. Often opinions are expressed authoritatively as facts, and other members of the group are reticent to express their skepticism. A phenomenon known as "groupthink" can occur when the team fails to question opinions that should be questioned; the failure may occur because the opinion is voiced by an esteemed member of the group that others do not wish to question, or because of momentum toward unanimity that members are reluctant to counter, or because of high group cohesion that interferes with critical evaluation of ideas.

6. **Rush to accomplishment:** When a member or members do not take the time to assess problems thoroughly or analyze their decision and action processes, they risk accomplishing the wrong thing or making important mistakes.

7. **Attribution:** Attribution is the normal process of assigning motives to actions that we observe. However, attribution can be problematic when it is not based on solid data and insight. When team members disagree as a part of the creative process, negative or largely unfair attributions become a likelihood. These negative attributions make all further interactions of the group very difficult.

8. **Discounts and plops:** When a team member makes a comment or suggestion, the idea may be discounted (contradicted or potentially even ridiculed) or it may "plop" (be completely ignored). In the creative process, many ideas must be vetted that are not ultimately acted upon, so the trick is to make sure that the feelings of participants are treated with respect even though all their ideas may not be used.

9. **Wanderlust:** This phenomenon happens when team members lose track of a meeting's purpose, either because of a lack of team discipline or in order to avoid a sensitive topic. Discussions wander off in many directions at once or stray off the purpose of the team for an extended period.

10. **Feuding team members:** While creative differences are helpful and healthy for teams, feuding team members are not. Often these feuds predate the team and may very well outlast it, too. The challenge for the team is to keep these feuds from dominating the discussion or tenor of the meetings.

in technical skills, interpersonal skills, number, and representation. Teams in which volunteers self-select can also have some members specifically invited for better balance or to fill skill gaps. A team should be given some authority, and generally substantial authority, which needs to be clarified upon its establishment. Just because teams have good members and well-defined purposes does not mean that the designated leader's responsibilities are over. Teams need strong outside champions to assist

Exhibit 6.4

Colman Mockler Jr.: Soft-Spoken But Firm Leadership

Colman M. Mockler Jr. was CEO of The Gillette Company from 1975 to January 1991, when he died of a heart attack at his office in Boston. After becoming Gillette's treasurer in 1965, he moved quickly up the hierarchy of the multinational corporation. In his first two years as CEO, he spent most of his time working with the top management team, trying to place the right people in the right positions. He successfully resisted two hostile takeover attempts, one by Revlon and another by an investment group that bought stock in order to initiate a proxy fight. In some of these battles, his personal financial gain would have been enormous, but he fought instead for the long-term greatness of the company and survival of innovative products that would likely have been lost had the takeovers succeeded. "His placid persona hid an inner intensity, a dedication to making anything he touched the best it could possibly be. . . . It wouldn't have been an option within Colman Mockler's value system to take the easy path and turn the company over to those who would milk it like a cow, destroying its potential to become great" (Collins 2001, 25).

In addition to resolute steadfastness, Mockler was known for balance in his life. His work as a leader was impacted by his values and faith. He believed in putting the right managers in place and trusting them to work within the authority of their position. This trust made it unnecessary for him to work most nights or weekends, so instead he devoted that time to his family and his alma mater, Harvard, where he served many years as a member of the university's governing body.

An example of his trust in others is seen in the story of the development of Sensor. Gillette was a deliberate company, introducing new products slowly in the 1980s world of disposability—metal blades on plastic handles. Sensor hit the market in 1990 with a splash, offering the mechanical advance of laser-welded twin blade cartridges, far beyond the usual chemical advance such as improvement in lubricating strips. It was a risky move for a market accustomed to disposable razors because it introduced a permanent handle; the risk was noted in 1989, when cheaper disposable razors accounted for more than half of all blade sales. But if Sensor was successful, it would bring Gillette even greater profit margins.

Mockler quietly pushed people to defend their points of view. He ultimately decided on a metal Sensor because of a personal appeal made by John Symons, the group general manager for European operations who had increased profits by focusing on metal razors. Symons claimed that people would pay more for a well-designed permanent handle, and he defended that position to Mockler. Seeing Symons's potential with the Sensor, within a few months Mockler delegated the Sensor project to him. The first year's sales goal of 20 million Sensors was reached in just eight months. Being soft-spoken did not interfere with Coleman Mockler's success as a leader. Similarly, keeping his life well balanced was a positive attribute to his success.

with resources and implementation issues; they also need adequate information and occasional guidance during the project to make sure that they are on track.

Long-term positive effects of people-oriented leadership behavior through motivational praise, appreciation, coordination of the right people to operations, and the building and managing of appropriate teams can be seen in legendary stories about leaders such as Colman Mockler of Gillette (Exhibit 6.4). Mockler excelled with a balance of task-oriented behaviors and resoluteness that contributed to Gillette's long-term success. Yet it was his complement of people-oriented competencies that emerged strongly in his general approach to interactions.

GUIDELINES FOR BUILDING AND MANAGING TEAMS

1. *Analyze the work in order to assess the best group structure to use.* Today leaders must be extremely sophisticated in using a variety of structures well. Since worker characteristics include substantial experience, specialized expertise, or forms of work

alienation, and/or since work context demands frequent customization, rapid change, solution of numerous problems, or implementation of entirely new challenges, traditional work group structures are likely to be suboptimal. Various forms of delegation can include either individuals or groups (delegation was discussed under both delegating in Chapter 5 and consulting in this chapter).

2. *When setting up new or special teams, be careful to think through the design elements carefully.* Typical issues include membership, mandate, authority, linkage, and group incentives. Membership varies by the type of work necessary. A mandate even for small groups is important to avoid confusion. At the same time, the grant of authority should be addressed. Does the group need approval prior to action? Another important question is how the team links to the management structure. Will there be an internal liaison? Is there an official executive champion outside the team? Finally, what types of incentives motivate the team as a whole and the members individually?

3. *Provide teams with special training.* Training for teams can include tips on getting started, analytic tools (e.g., the use of Pareto charts and nomination group technique), monitoring group progress (e.g., end-of-meeting reviews, alignment sessions), troubleshooting problems that teams commonly incur, and tips for disbanding, among others.

4. *When building a team, emphasize common interests and shared values.* Although heterogeneity and diversity add to creativity and comprehensiveness, it is the sharing of common interests that engenders group cohesion and enables high performance (Katzenbach and Smith 1993). Team leaders or facilitators should help the group establish common interests and strengthen the sense of collective fate. A well-known model of team development involves four phases: forming, storming, norming, and performing. Teams that have substantial missions but have not worked together in the past sometimes pay insufficient attention to forming, only to find the storming phase of group development that much more difficult to overcome, and the specter of distrust that much greater (Scholtes 1993).

5. *Enhance group identity and morale.* Groups that have a strong identity are likely to perform well. The trappings of group identity can make a significant difference. Social interactions, breaking bread together, and factors such as nonstandard work times can make a big difference. Recognizing group importance, progress, and successes is extremely important. Further, the success of resolving a problem, launching a new product, or meeting new standards of excellence should be recognized.

MANAGING CONFLICT

Conflict management is used to handle various types of interpersonal disagreements, to build cooperative interpersonal relationships, and to harness the positive effects of conflict. It is most highly connected with team-building because managing conflict is often a prerequisite. It is also related to clarifying roles and objectives, because much conflict arises out of unclear responsibilities and work linkages. It is related to problem-solving in two ways. Interpersonal conflict is a special type of problem that managers must handle carefully so that they do not become dysfunctional; substantive conflict, successfully managed and integrated, breeds a creative ferment that can contribute to innovative problem-solving.

Types of conflicts that occur are divided into two major categories, although in reality most problems are a blend of the two types. Some conflicts arise out of differences of opinion that are *substantive* in nature and are termed "problem-based." The second class of conflicts has *personality* as its basis. In an extreme case, colleagues fight over inconsequential issues because of a lack of trust or personal animosity. When **personality-based conflict** occurs in their work group, leaders often

- share concerns about the conflict and the well-being of the protagonists,
- try to retain neutrality,
- strongly discourage personality-based discussion and unprofessional behaviors,
- build on positive perceptions while exploring negative perceptions, and
- insist that protagonists try to find ways to change dysfunctional behaviors.

In **problem-based conflict**, leaders often

- first seek to identify shared values and objectives (normally wider in scope than the conflict),
- seek disclosure of perceptions of critical needs from each party,
- look at a variety of ways to address those critical needs, and
- persist until the protagonists agree on a solution or course of action, ensuring that the conflict remains substantive and does not morph into personality-based conflict.

Ralph, supervisor of a unit reporting to Joan, was unable to explain to his own subordinates why they received the amount of operating funds that was assigned. He reacted negatively toward Joan personally and was heard saying erroneous and negative things about her management of the budget. The fact was that Ralph, who had been in his position for three years, still failed to understand the nuances of the budget and rarely took advantage of supervisorial training available on the organization's financial software package. Joan could have come back at him in a personal way, challenging or disparaging his low level of understanding. She could have escalated her response to focus on his insubordination. Instead, she patiently continued to try to increase Ralph's knowledge of the budget. By attending to the underlying problem that caused the conflict, Joan refrained from creating a situation that would have likely led to his personal embarrassment and perhaps to his dismissal. She purposefully chose this approach to the conflict because she felt that, in other ways, Ralph had respectable skills as a supervisor.

A principle that is sometimes difficult to accept in the midst of a situation like the example with Joan above is that if *either* party defines the conflict as personality-based, it is personality-based, at least until *both* parties are willing to treat it as problem-based.

Three main elements of conflict management are identified in the previous definition (Fisher and Ury 1981; Rahim 1992; Thomas 1992). Essentially, conflict management involves reactive, proactive, and creative aspects. The *reactive* portion applies when the conflict has already occurred—either escalating out of past disagreements or arising suddenly. In these cases, the manager's job is to resolve conflict (the most common conception of conflict management).

When a series of related issues is present, conflict managers seek to resolve the issues jointly rather than separately, so that there is maximum ability to exchange and negotiate across issues. When issues have both a problem and personality basis, ideally facilitators work on personality problems first (to build trust and cooperation).

Good managers are *proactive* in creating environments in which the likelihood of dysfunctional conflicts is minimized. Such managers are skillful at highlighting the different types of contributions of various individuals and are aware that good teams need variety. They are also skillful at highlighting the importance of professionalism and what it means.

Yet conflict management can be more than reactive or proactive—it can be *creative*. Substantive conflict has positive aspects that, when properly cultivated, bring significant value to work groups and teams. For example, the complete absence of conflict may indicate an unhealthy level of "groupthink," where everyone thinks in a nearly identical fashion and relies excessively on "the way we've always done it," resulting in their being blind to emerging problems. Managers good at conflict management do not try to eradicate conflict, but rather channel it in productive ways to enhance friendly rivalry and group originality. Modest levels of competition among group members spur more demanding individual goals, while simultaneously improving group goals.

GUIDELINES FOR MANAGING CONFLICT

1. *In conflict resolution, set the stage for positive interactions and analysis.* Facilitators establish credibility and rapport by expressing both concern for each of the parties separately and the need for improving the situation. Maintaining impartiality is critical so that participants trust the process and both sides can be told without prejudice. Fundamental ground rules must be established. Instead of allowing negative feelings to be expressed, the facilitator should elicit recognition of mutual contributions and the benefits of joint cooperation, along with the reasons for the conflict and a disclosure of the needs people want met. The facilitator should not let these needs be defined too narrowly, so that the mix of solutions can be as broad as possible.

2. *In conflict resolution, seek common ground for genuine consensus.* When participants in a dispute trust the process, they are more likely to consider a range of acceptable solutions. Brainstorming a variety of ideas provides a range of acceptable solutions. Frequently, side benefits can be identified at the same time, so that the solution is not just the cessation of a negative situation, but also potentially a positive enhancement

of the process. It is important not to allow issues to be handled separately, because often the hardest issues are left to the end. Good conflict managers are able to keep the parties discussing the issues until they find a win-win proposition.

3. *Create an environment that reduces the likelihood of dysfunctional conflict.* Good managers are effective in preventing most conflict from arising in the first place. They create an environment in which the diverse contributions and talents of different players are appreciated. Managers who work with low performers need to make sure that their performance does not continue to be substandard. Additionally, good managers can instill an atmosphere that discourages unprofessional behavior. Finally, in a well-managed environment the manager can often place the responsibility back on the parties in conflict to work it out for themselves. Allowing participants to manage and discover their own mutual accommodation can lead to a greater sense of professionalism and shared mission.

4. *Utilize the positive aspects of conflict.* Some conflict is healthy, particularly when it is substantive in nature. In a high-performing environment, openness to different ideas and approaches is embraced. Members of such groups may argue vociferously in a committee meeting but go to lunch together immediately afterward without a hint of ill will, just as golfers or handball players may aggressively fight over a point, only to laugh together later. In many situations, friendly competition (a type of contained conflict) is considered not only appropriate but also necessary to keeping analytic and creative skills well honed.

MANAGING PERSONNEL CHANGE

When organizations are in trouble, some of them rally by making the changes necessary to survive. However, some organizations do not, so they consequently flounder financially or simply eke out an existence. Necessary change may not occur for various reasons: management and labor are locked in labor disputes, leaders lay blame for problems elsewhere, workers are concerned about their jobs and their futures, and so on. In these instances, leadership is weak and often brought down by an inability to manage personnel change.

Managing personnel change involves establishing an environment that provides the emotional support and motivation to change. It focuses on the people side of change. It is highly related to—and indeed is the other half of—either microlevel or macrolevel change: managing technical innovation and creativity, and managing organizational change. This competency is born of the reality that people must want to change and be assisted through what is often an uncomfortable or even painful process.

It is instructive to think about personal and emotional aspects of dramatic change in order to gain insights into the organizational setting. Examples from personal life might involve a divorce, the loss of a loved one, or an unexpected drop in income. Organization-wide or radical process change in a unit can cause similar reactions in people (Woodward and Bucholz 1987). The first stage in this well-known pattern is denial and disbelief. The second stage is anger. Who is responsible for the mishap?

The third stage is mourning and the final stage in a good situation is adaptation, where one picks up one's life and moves on. For major change, the trick is not to skip these phases, but to move through them, let go, and embrace the future.

There are many reasons why people may resist change. Some reasons are rational and some are emotional, but they must all be overcome if change is to be embraced. On the rational side, change may have some high costs in financial terms, for example, the purchase of new equipment, and in personal terms, for example, the replacement of familiar routines. One of the main reasons for resistance to change is a lack of trust in those proposing it. People also resent the intrusion and interference that accompany change programs. Often, people deny that change is even necessary. Because many change efforts are unsuccessful and because many people experience a series of mini-failures even during successful change, foreboding about personal failure can be great. Finally, many change efforts represent a change in values that people may resent and resist.

While it may be impossible to address all these concerns fully, successful change efforts must address most of them, or else apathy, lack of cooperation, and even defiance will doom the efforts. The following guidelines discuss the types of strategies that are generally necessary to minimize resistance to change.

GUIDELINES FOR MANAGING PERSONNEL CHANGE

1. *Generate a sense of importance or urgency about the need for change.* Whenever possible, change efforts should be initiated with data, examples, and anecdotal evidence of the need for change. Such evidence might be performance reports, discussions of legislative mandates, customer complaints, or economic trend data. People are naturally attached to the past and need assistance in the form of documentation or proof to separate from it. If the change is substantial, it is important to create a sense of urgency. For example, it may be necessary to outline the costs that will be incurred or the liabilities that will arise by not taking action.

2. *Involve and empower people in change processes.* When people are involved, their sense of self-determination and their ability to monitor their self-interests increases the likelihood of buy-in. In some cases subordinates may be put in charge of designing the overall change effort. Even when the overall effort is to be designed by those normally in charge, there should be ample opportunity to involve people in the details, progress, and suggestions for corrective actions.

3. *Be honest about the challenges of change.* Major change initiatives always entail setbacks, process failures, and course corrections. Even champions of change may have moments of frustration, fatigue, and discouragement. If there has not been a realistic preview of the challenges, people may balk at the first sign of difficulty. Identifying the need for perseverance and flexibility is important at an early stage. When changes are traumatic, it is better to identify the realistic threats to job security boldly, make the necessary cuts as soon as they are clearly identified and practical, and emphasize fairness and continued support to those who will be adversely affected.

4. *Ensure that people are well informed about the progress of change.* Lack of information breeds rumors, suspicion, and distrust. Further, lack of information may falsely signal a loss of support for change. Reports on the progress of change, even when there have been setbacks or a lack of forward movement, indicate interest and support for change initiatives.

5. *Exhibit ongoing support for the challenges of change.* This can be done in a number of ways. One of the most powerful is to participate in change activities personally, either continuously or from time to time as appropriate. Another form of support rejects easy solutions that do not fix underlying problems. Another type praises efforts toward progress, rather than waiting for completion. Yet another form of support is to explain the vision behind the change in different ways as the process continues, so that people have different insights into what they are trying to accomplish. Fresh explanations also motivate in that they remind people that the work is all the more important for its challenges.

CONCLUSION

People-oriented competencies are central to leadership and need to be developed in balance with task-oriented behaviors. The seven people-oriented competencies discussed in this chapter are consulting, planning and organizing personnel, developing staff, motivating, building and managing teams, managing conflict, and managing personnel change. Exhibit 6.5 is a summary of people-oriented competencies and major guidelines associated with each of the competencies. These "soft" competencies are related to employee satisfaction and, although less directly, to performance results. They do not reflect an acceptance of lower standards or an avoidance of difficult communications about substandard performance.

Managing innovation and creativity requires flexibility, an eye for fresh ideas, and the ability to create a learning organization culture. People-oriented behaviors are critical to effectively supporting the creative environment and a learning organization culture.

As a competency cluster, people-oriented behaviors add an important element to the business of leadership, not only for supervisors and executives, but also for lower-level managers, who have a slightly more streamlined emphasis in this area in terms of where they focus their attention.

To the degree that we define leadership primarily as influencing others, these competencies are core to the leadership endeavor. Indeed, one school of theorists defines leadership largely as the people- or relations-oriented competencies, although this text defines leadership more broadly. Even if the leadership definition one prefers does not identify people-oriented competencies as the highest priority, it is hard to conceive of them as not being vital and substantial because they are so instrumental in the dynamics of leading. These competencies may be no easier or harder to learn than other competency clusters, yet they certainly can be more subtle to master because they emanate from within the leader.

Exhibit 6.5 **Summary: Review of People-Oriented Behaviors**

People-oriented behavior	Subelements of behavior	Major guidelines
Consulting Check with people on work-related matters and involve people in decision-making processes	• Solicit information from employees on their work environment and how results could be improved • Invite employees to be involved in decision-making to appropriate degrees	• Evaluate the decision environment surrounding substantive decisions • Seek as much input for substantive decisions as possible • Utilize the ideas, suggestions, and input of others for substantive decisions to the maximum feasible degree
Planning and organizing personnel Coordinate people and operations, and ensure that the competencies necessary to do the work are, or will be, available; also involves self-planning	• Fit people to schedules and make the appropriate changes as work and personnel needs change • Match the talents, interests, and preferences of people to work • Use personal time management skills	• Ensure that specific staff assignments are understood and accepted • Match staff preferences and competencies to the work • Stay on top of scheduling changes • Review long-term organizational competency needs to ensure organizational capacity • Manage personal schedule effectively
Developing staff Improve subordinates' effectiveness in their current positions and prepare them for their next position or step	• Support is the emotional component of development • Coach to help employees do a task more effectively • Mentor to aid a person's career development, sometimes referred to as career counseling	• Show courtesy to and interest in all, and demonstrate positive regard to others to the greatest degree possible • Promote a person's self-esteem and reputation • Listen to personal problems that affect work performance and take the time to counsel subordinates • Analyze subordinates' overall performance and identify deficiencies • Monitor and correct errors • Provide career advice • Provide special opportunities for subordinates to prepare for a future position
Motivating Enhance the inner drives and positive intentions of subordinates (or others) to perform well through incentives, disincentives, and inspiration	• Provide positive incentives (e.g., recognition and rewards) • Provide the negative disincentives that are sometime necessary to set the acceptable bounds of behavior and to punish poor work and rule infractions • Provide inspiration to encourage working for group and organizational goals regardless of personal benefit	• Recognize as many people as possible and appropriate • Use an appropriate form of recognition • Explain how rewards and significant commendations are distributed • Find out what rewards are attractive • Explain rules and procedures to ensure that subordinates understand the consequences of deviations • In order to avoid hasty and wrong conclusions, always investigate the facts before using reprimands and punishment • Use punishments that are fair and commensurate with the seriousness of the violation • When attempting to inspire, use energetic or emotional language with symbols, metaphors, and inclusive terms such as "we," "us," and "our"

People-oriented behavior	Subelements of behavior	Major guidelines
Managing teams and team-building Create and support "true" teams in addition to traditional work units; team-building involves enhancing identification with the work, intramember cooperation, and esprit de corps of both work groups and teams	• Train employees about differences between traditional work groups and teams • Inform employees about how individuals benefit from outstanding team performance • Train teams in intramember cooperation and self-management for problem-solving and improving results • Structure rewards for outstanding team performance	• Analyze the work in order to assess the best group structure to use • When setting up new or special teams, think through the design elements carefully • Provide teams with special training • When team-building, use and emphasize common interests and shared values • When team-building, enhance group identity and morale
Managing conflict Use to handle various types of interpersonal disagreements, to build cooperative interpersonal relationships, and to harness the positive effects of conflict	• Manage conflict that has already occurred—either escalating out of past disagreements or arising suddenly out of a clash of opinions or personalities • Proactively create environments in which the likelihood of dysfunctional conflict is minimized by enhancing a sense of professionalism in which employees work through their differences maturely • Use the positive aspects of conflict for creativity, dynamism, and to avoid "groupthink"	• In conflict resolution, set the stage for positive interactions and analysis • In conflict resolution, seek common ground for genuine consensus • Create an environment that reduces the likelihood of dysfunctional conflict • Utilize the positive aspects of conflict

KEY TERMS

consideration

consulting

cross-functional team

delegation decision model

developing staff

disincentives

expectancy theory

joint decision-making

participative decision-making

problem-based conflict vs. personality-based conflict

valence

work group vs. team

RESOURCES

Students or teams of students may be assigned resources on the Internet that complement topics covered in the chapter in order to increase the richness and depth of class discussion. Although sites that tend to be enduring have been selected for this Resources section, the currency of webpages must be verified.

How does women's mastery of people-oriented competencies differ from that of managers in general or from men's mastery in this area? Several groups have contributed important research on this topic over the years, including this study done in collaboration with the Center for Research on Women at Wellesley College.

- Sumru Erkut, "Obstacles to Women's Leadership Lessened, Not Gone," Wellesley Centers for Women. www.imdiversity.com/villages/Woman/careers_workplace_employment/women_leadership_obstacles.asp.

Consider the career of leaders in the police force. Are their people-oriented competencies less important than the competencies exhibited by other managers because of the arena in which they work? Evaluate the position taken by the author of this article in *The Police Chief* magazine.

- Donald Grinder, "People-Oriented Leadership," *The Policy Chief*, 70 (October 2003). http://policechiefmagazine.org/magazine/index.cfm?fuseaction=display_arch&article_id=112&issue_id=102003.

A journal article by Blane Anderson discusses the use of humor as a management tool. After reading the article, describe the conclusions you draw about knowing how and when to use humor in a leadership situation where you are expected to promote teamwork and accomplish organizational goals.

- Blane Anderson, "Humor and Leadership," *Journal of Organizational Culture, Communications and Conflict*, January 2005. http://findarticles.com/p/articles/mi_m1TOT/is_1_9/ai_n25121986.

DISCUSSION QUESTIONS

1. What are the differences between supporting, coaching, and mentoring?
2. If a leader does not fundamentally appreciate or respect the people with whom he or she works, would that leader's people-oriented behaviors be different than they would be otherwise? Why or why not? Your answer should reflect your perspective on the extent to which one's people-oriented behaviors reflect the "leader within."
3. Good people skills seem to make people more satisfied at work, but not necessarily more productive in the short term. What might be some of the deleterious effects of an excessively directive style in the long term? How

would your answer differ if the question asked about deleterious effects of a heavily task-oriented style in the long term?

4. Operational managers rarely report developing as their top priority, but they do report that it is time-consuming and affects many management behaviors. They also report that it is difficult to do and often a problem. Speculate on some reasons why this might be so and whether those perspectives may be short-sighted.

5. What is the difference between work groups and "true" teams? What are some of their comparative strengths and weaknesses?

6. Team-building is generally a synonym for enhancing the cooperation of work groups or team members. What are some concrete strategies for doing so?

7. What are the differences between personality- and problem-based conflict? How do the methods for handling these different types of conflict vary?

8. Many leadership scholars consider people-oriented behaviors to be best judged by subordinates because these behaviors disproportionately affect them. That is, when receiving leadership survey feedback, they would say it is generally more important to pay attention to one's subordinates than to one's superior or colleagues in this area. Do you agree or disagree? Why?

9. Discuss the differences between consultation as a form of assessment and as a form of decision-making.

10. Personnel planning is both an art and a science. That is, it has some rather technical aspects but it also has some creative aspects. Explain.

11. What are the competencies of a people-oriented leadership that you feel would be most successful in getting the job done for the organization you serve?

CLASSROOM ACTIVITY

Imagine that in a "360-degree" review, you received the following information about your leadership skills from subordinates, colleagues, and your boss, following your own self-evaluation.

	Leader's effectiveness at competency (5 = high; 1 = low)			
Competencies	Self	Subordinates	Colleagues	Superior
Consulting	3	2	3	2
Planning and organizing personnel	4	2	3	3
Developing staff	4	2	3	3
Motivating	5	2	2	4
Building and managing teams	5	2	3	3
Managing conflict	5	4	3	3
Managing personnel change	5	3	4	4

1. In groups, analyze implications of this feedback. In particular, why do you think that the different categories of respondents might rate you differently in some cases?

2. Describe what actions you would take.

CASE ANALYSIS

Eleana was not a new manager but was new to the Boxwood unit. She had been assigned to "clean up the mess." Her last assignment was very successful. She had taken over an important evaluation project, analyzed the defects, gotten approval for major design changes, and implemented them in relatively short order. The small staff, which had been floundering without good leadership or a good design, was very grateful. In her new assignment at the Boxwood unit, Eleana quickly assessed the problems by personally analyzing the work. The cases flowing through the unit were being handled in the old production-line fashion, so three to five people handled each case. Unfortunately, the manual log-in system was time-consuming and out-of-date, no one took ownership over individual cases, and the physical flow of the cases was often inefficient.

Following successful models elsewhere in the agency, Eleana decided to institute an electronic monitoring system for the cases and to have them processed by a single case manager and reviewed by a single supervisor. This would mean installing a new monitoring system and extensive cross-training. The unit was slightly understaffed but was unlikely to get additional staffing. Therefore, efficiency changes would be difficult. Eleana brought the unit together and announced the changes. She described the changes clearly and set out detailed plans for implementing them.

Although initially stunned by the sweeping changes, most of the employees went along with them. Because Eleana made it clear that she would replace those unwilling or unable to adapt, there was a good deal of fear in the unit. At first, people seemed to throw themselves into accomplishing the changes. However, soon a number of problems occurred, despite Eleana's planning. The custom-designed case monitoring program ran into many glitches and was just as cumbersome to use as the old one. The cross-training in different programs was extremely time-consuming, so productivity fell and the error rate rose. Eleana knew that this was customary in this type of work redesign, but the employees in the unit were discouraged. Because of the backlog, Eleana got permission to order overtime. She thought the employees would be pleased with the opportunity for time-and-a-half pay, but instead they did a great deal of grumbling and resented having to work the extra hours. Several of the best workers transferred out or found other jobs despite Eleana's urging them to stay. It was unclear whether Eleana would eventually succeed in the long term, but in the middle term the workers in the unit were dissatisfied with her plan and found her distant and uninvolved.

DISCUSSION QUESTIONS

1. Critique Eleana's leadership in this case using principles from the chapter to evaluate why events unfolded as they did.
2. Make recommendations for any personnel changes Eleana should consider.

EXECUTIVE LEADERSHIP BEHAVIORS

Leaders carry out managerial functions at all levels of the organization, including the supervisorial and mid-management levels. When those mid-managers move into senior positions at the executive level of the organization, they have an opportunity by authority of their position to effect visionary and even transformational changes. Part III of the text helps leaders prepare for the kind of big-picture thinking that marks a successful executive. Both self- and group-enrichment come by way of understanding that what is in the best interest of the company as a whole is in one's own best interest. Traditional managerial roles are still embraced by the executive, but at this level of leadership they are typically supplemented by actions that are more strategically oriented for the long-term success of the organization in its competitive environment.

Not everyone aspires to move into an executive role. If this is a personal goal, the importance of understanding executive leadership behaviors is vital. If it is not a personal goal, as a student of business it is still of critical importance. Understanding executive leadership behaviors fosters a means by which to become a better employee or supervisor. In the presence of a charismatic or transformational leader, it allows for an appreciation of the dynamic itself and can assist in the decision to be part of change for the better of the organization as a whole. In working with a vision-oriented leader, it provides an understanding of how to be involved at all position levels and how to be a positive influence on business activities such as strategic planning, for instance. If the goal approach is used in the organization, a clear understanding of why it can be beneficial and how to participate in the process to support a healthy outcome for the organization as a whole becomes evident. These insights, and more, are all made possible through the examination of executive leadership behaviors.

7 Charismatic and Transformational Approaches

My strong point is not rhetoric, it isn't showmanship, it isn't big promises—those things that create the glamour and the excitement that people call charisma and warmth.
—Richard M. Nixon, 1972

What is the leadership fire that ignites a follower's torch, heightening his commitment and drive for results? What is the spark that ultimately leads to a huge and purposeful flash of change for an organization? Is it primarily sound management practices in action? Is it the words of a leader, promising to give people what they want? Is it an authoritative personality that seems to charge the environment with electricity and stimulate people into action? Or is it uncommon personalities to which people are drawn because of that individual's ability to communicate a sense of magnetism, persuasion, and power? This chapter will examine these questions in depth.

Following years of prosperity after World War II, the U.S. economy waned and lost much of its preeminence by the 1970s, suffering from "stagflation" characterized by sluggish, or *stag*nant, output growth, high in*flation* rates, and rising unemployment. It is not a surprise that the field of leadership theory responded with new directions. In the 1980s, the new theories of leadership that emerged diverged markedly from those that grew out of the Ohio State and University of Michigan studies discussed in the previous chapter. There was a swell of interest in strong leaders who could provide boldness, incisive strategies, wide appeal, and sweeping changes when necessary. It was widely felt that "the problem with many organizations, and especially the ones that are failing, is that they tend to be overmanaged and underled" (Bennis and Nanus 1985, 21).

The perspective of being **overmanaged and underled** was clearly articulated as early as 1977 in *Harvard Business Review* by Abraham Zaleznik, who taught the psychodynamics of leadership. At the time of his writing, the duty of management was seen as focusing on budgets and process, stability and control. In contrast, the business of leadership was seen as focusing on human aspects of inspiration and passion, vision and chaos. Management was a function with the ability to deal with complex systems and to keep the current system functioning. Leadership was about relationships that offered the ability to deal energetically with environmental change and to bring about purposeful transformation within the organization. Organizations were likened to individuals—when time was not spent on visionary growth and change, it tended to be used for routine day-to-day events or putting out immediate "fires."

In simple terms, overmanagement from the supervisor's perspective is spending too much energy making sure that things are done the way he or she wants them done. In a similar fashion, being underled, from the supervisor's perspective, results in spending too little time getting to the important matters at hand, such as inspiring positive change.

As true as Bennis and Nanus's observation is about being overmanaged and underled, another counterbalancing perspective is that an organization can be equally stifled by being overled and undermanaged. "In fact, there are far too many organizations today—both in government and the private sector—in which the person at the top *over*leads and *under*manages. All too often these organizations experience failure not because of a lack of ideas, goals and inspiration, but because they can't get their acts together and make it all happen. In the real world, leadership and management can't be split" (Kent 2001).

The point Kent makes is clear, that a careful balance of what we think of as management (e.g., organizing and controlling) and as leadership (e.g., planning with vision) is truly the ideal. Imagine, for instance, the medical director of Arrowhead Regional Medical Center, Dr. Dev GnanaDev, being without a well-rounded balance of management and leadership skills. As an MBA graduate, his leadership is strong, and he helped guide a visionary effort to build a solvent new San Bernardino County hospital in Colton, California. However, as an MD, he also kept sight of the fact that the medical leadership he provided had to present a clear-cut structure for hospital processes to control factors ranging from safety to disease management. In his endeavors to accomplish the task, Dr. GnanaDev was successful because he was trusted for his medical knowledge balanced with his good management background, and his strong, well-articulated vision as a leader (GnanaDev 2008).

Three major studies preceded and prepared for the theories that emerged in the mid-1980s. A classic and prominent approach was by Max Weber, the "father of bureaucracy," as discussed in Chapter 3. The brilliant German sociologist also provided insights into charismatic, or personality-based, leadership. He derived his interpretation of the concept from the Greek word *charisma*, meaning "the gift of God's grace," especially in religious contexts, to suggest divinely inspired talents. The person blessed with talents needed by a society or organization, particularly in crisis, would rise to the occasion, bringing radical solutions. Followers come along not only when they are attracted to an inspiring leader, but also when the leader's repeated success validates their transcendent powers. Initially, it may seem incongruous for the same theorist to talk on one hand about impersonal bureaucracy and on the other about personal charisma. Actually, the two notions are brought together by an understanding of Weber's perspective on the role of bureaucrats versus the role of the charismatics. Whereas bureaucrats administer to the day-to-day activity of an organization for its long-term stability, the charismatic leader emerges in the face of crisis to inspire major change. With new purpose and perhaps new principles established by the impact of the charismatic leader, the bureaucratic administration would then again emerge to guide the organization to an equilibrium of routine, predictable activity for the purpose of ensuring long-term stability. Of course, the two approaches to organizational life are not always followed in tandem, whereby one operates in lieu of the other as the engine that drives the organization. Charismatics are not only the top executive leaders, but also they can be found at the middle and even bottom levels of large bureaucracies. Charismatics can be invaluable at the divisional or unit level when they inspire significant change because of their personal power among peers.

Given the significance of the word "gift" in the meaning of charisma in business today, one could say that scholarly focus is shifting from *who is gifted* (i.e., leaders are born) to *the gifts that charismatic leaders employ* in order to bring change (i.e., leadership can be learned).

In 1977, Robert House published a book with a chapter titled "A 1976 Theory of Charismatic Leadership." Charismatic leaders were said to be those who, having extraordinary effects on followers, cause them to perform beyond conventional expectations. Organizations perform at higher levels as a result of cohesion, inspiration, and a strong sense of values, all of which can be imparted by a charismatic leader. House, Spangler and Woycke (1991) later wrote that charisma "refers to the ability of a leader to exercise diffuse and intense influence over the beliefs, values, behavior, and performance of others through his or her own behavior, beliefs, and personal example." As if from a divine source, charismatics emanate a sense of power that few can resist. People with great communication skills and/or great power often take on significant charismatic elements. However, the pervasive nature of television and the invasive nature of modern reporting may make the aura of charisma more difficult to sustain, since charisma has a tendency to be diminished by overexposure.

It was James McGregor Burns, however, who emphasized somewhat different aspects and popularized the term transformational leadership (1978). It is appropriate to group charismatic and transformational theories together because of their strong similarities, but they are so distinctive that a student of leadership should understand where they tend to diverge as well.

Charismatic approaches are leader-focused and tend to focus specifically on the personality and emotional communication of vision by the leader; they thus show strong interest in leaders' qualities and character. On the other hand, transformational theories are organization-focused and tend to center on leaders triggering tremendous change. Transformational leaders have extraordinary effects not only on their followers in meeting organizational or social needs, but also on organizations or social and political structures themselves. As the major theories from the two approaches have been revised and expanded, they tend to merge more and more into a single approach rather than the reverse, particularly when the leader is involved with orchestrating significant change, such as the type of change required by the U.S. economy in the 1970s or the 2010s (see Chapter 11).

A brief sketch of the charismatic Lee Iacocca, the former president of Chrysler whose leadership inspired a company turnaround in the 1980s, provides an example of the complexity of extracting a large personality out of a great change process, or vice versa. It comes as no surprise that in his 2007 book on leadership—*Where Have*

All the Leaders Gone?—Iacocca's description of the nine Cs of leadership included charisma (along with curiosity, creativity, communication, character, courage, conviction, competence, and common sense). The Biggest C, he wrote, is crisis because leaders are made in times of crisis.

CONGER AND KANUNGO'S CHARISMATIC LEADERSHIP THEORY

Based in part on House's early work on charismatic leadership, Conger and Kanungo proposed a theory of **charismatic leadership** in 1987, which they later refined in book-length treatments (1987, 1998). Their focus is on *how* charisma is attributed to leaders. What is it about the leader's context in conjunction with the leader's personality and behavior that produces the perception of charisma? The account of Lee Iacocca in Exhibit 7.1 illustrates many of the concepts of Conger and Kanungo's theory. For example, Iacocca accepted a symbolic salary of $1 a year as he worked to achieve the vision he championed. One factor in the theory of charismatic leadership is that people are more likely to attribute charisma to a leader when the leader self-sacrifices or takes personal risks while working to achieve a vision.

The context, according to Conger and Kanungo, has to be problematic in some way for the emergence of charismatic leadership. The stronger the sense of crisis or emergency, the more likely that charismatic leadership can emerge, and do so flamboyantly. "In some cases, contextual factors so overwhelmingly favor transformation that a leader can take advantage of them by advocating radical changes for the system. . . . [Yet] during periods of relative tranquility, charismatic leaders play a major role in fostering the need for change by creating the deficiencies or exaggerating existing minor ones" (Conger and Kanungo 1998, 52–53). Some "negative charismatics" may even create a sense of crisis or deficiencies for personal advancement, even when real crises do not exist. Thus, the situational demand for charismatic leadership is a moderating factor; long-term disappointments, outright failures, and debacles all substantially increase the chance for charismatic leadership but guarantee neither its emergence nor its success.

Even if the environment has major deficiencies or is in a state of crisis, followers are likely to attribute charismatic characteristics only to leaders who have certain traits and behave in certain ways. First, charismatic leaders are dissatisfied with the status quo and are interested in changing it, sometimes through unconventional means. Leaders with charisma frequently have vision, which in turn makes their leadership more compelling to followers. **Vision** is an image of what the organization can become and its effective position in its environment; vision points to an image of the desired future of the organization. *Vision* is future-oriented as opposed to *mission* which is oriented to the current organizational purpose.

Charismatic leaders may have an idealized vision of the future that is highly discrepant from the current and projected state of affairs, but they are able to communicate with confidence and enthusiasm about their vision or proposal. Charismatic leaders are willing to articulate their bold notions of how things could be, and they are interested in leading others to a better future. Generally, they tend to elicit inspirational effects by communicating emotionally as opposed to using a participative management

Exhibit 7.1

Charismatic or Transformer: Lee Iacocca

When great change occurs, there is inevitably a big personality (or two) involved. Often it is difficult to separate the personality from the change itself and to accurately assess the significance of force of personality—convictions and charisma—from the technical and political skills of a "change master." Some would say that the role of happenstance is difficult to separate out also, although happenstance of the overall situation generally does little more than push one leader into the spotlight more than another because of that individual's expertise relative to the environment. The 1979 case of Lee Iacocca is a timeless example of a transformational leader highly focused on bringing about tremendous change and being the "trigger" of that change. There is no doubt that he was also a "big personality," in the best sense of the words.

Lido Anthony Iacocca was born in 1924 and joined Ford Motor Company as a student engineer in 1946. He soon moved into sales and headed marketing by age thirty-three. In 1960 he became general manager of the Ford Division and by 1970, as president, he was second only to Henry Ford II. Within six years, the company showed a profit of $1.8 billion, but by 1978, the two men were embroiled in a battle of trying to outmaneuver each other, and Iacocca was fired.

As fate would have it, the tenth largest corporation in the United States, Chrysler, was headquartered in the same city. It was unprofitable, inefficient, losing market share, and heavily debt-ridden. In the middle of a fuel crisis, Chrysler found itself specializing in gas-guzzling cars. On the brink of bankruptcy, Chrysler aggressively went after Iacocca and hired him as its chair. At the helm of the failing company, Iacocca communicated his radical plans, closing plants and laying off workers. He approached Congress in 1979, asking for a loan guarantee, saying that the government had bailed out the airlines and the railroads, and now it must do the same for the automobile manufacturer. He was successful; both the House and the Senate approved $1.5 billion loan guarantees, and Iacocca used the infusion of money to release the company's first compact, fuel efficient, front-wheel-drive cars. Iacocca hired an engineer (who had also been fired by Ford) who then released Chrysler's first minivan. Adding further to the benefits of good product, Iacocca obtained discounts from suppliers and wage concessions from his workers.

By now Iacocca had gained the reputation of a can-do executive. He took an annual salary of $1 per year to make the point that everyone must sacrifice for the good of Chrysler in order for the company to survive. There was no question in Iacocca's mind that the No. 3 automaker must successfully pull through. Iacocca was heard saying in ads, "If you can find a better car, buy it!" Saving Chrysler became a personal battle for Iacocca and a patriotic battle for the nation. In turn, the company began to rebound. In turn, that began to reshape the corporation's culture. The loans Iacocca had secured were due in 1991, but under his leadership, Chrysler paid them back in 1984, less than four years after receiving them and fully seven years early! He appeared on television saying, "Chrysler borrows money the old-fashioned way. We pay it back." Iacocca and Chrysler were inseparable in the public's mind. From that time on, until his retirement in 1992, Iacocca was a celebrity, a national hero, and an American patriot. The country loved what Iacocca had accomplished through his fight for America, his hard work ethic, and gutsy independence.

After those celebratory years, the situation changed again, along with the times. The automotive industry and the economy were subjected to yet another round of influences. But that, as they say, is another story.

style. Because of their opposition to the status quo, charismatic leaders are willing to be perceived by many (initially) as unconventional or proposing values different from those that have prevailed. Indeed, their advocacy is so passionate that they are willing to take personal risks or make personal sacrifices. As Conger and Kanungo note, "because of their emphasis on deficiencies in the system and their high levels of intolerance for them, charismatic leaders are always seen as organizational reformers or entrepreneurs" (1998, 53).

Many leaders respond to situations that allow or encourage charismatic behaviors, and in fact exhibit those behaviors, but are still not successful because their execution of them is flawed. In opposing the status quo, charismatic leaders must propose an alternate vision. That vision should be based on external assessments, such as the needs of constituents or the market, rather than the internal needs of the leader. It should also include a realistic assessment of the resources available to achieve the vision. Frequently, the environment shifts even as a plan or vision is being crafted; leaders who are inflexible about adapting to changing needs may doom their enterprise. Because changing cultures and traditions calls for unconventional behaviors and new values, they invariably create some opposition; if charismatic leaders create too much opposition at any one time, however, they are likely to fail or lose power. Charismatic leadership is also based on the leader's passion, confidence, and exceptional ability to persuade and sway people. But these same abilities may also predispose the leader toward a variety of dysfunctional behaviors over time: excessive egoism, contempt for superiors who withhold agreement, a tendency to turn nonsupporters into a hostile out-group, a propensity to turn supporters into sycophants, dismissal of contravening information, and encouragement of overreliance on the leader rather than an emphasis on subordinate development. Because such leaders enjoy not only position and expert power but also enormous personal power, opportunities to use their power in self-serving ways are enormous, often leading to unconscious temptations. Conger and Kanungo also describe the leader who is charismatic but in a negative way:

> Charismatic leaders can be prone to extreme narcissism that leads them to promote highly self-serving and grandiose aims. As a result, the leader's behaviors can become exaggerated, lose touch with reality, or become vehicles for pure personal gain. In turn, they may harm the leader, the followers, and the organization. An overpowering sense of self-importance and strong need to be at the center of attention can cause charismatic leaders to ignore the viewpoints of others and the development of leadership ability in followers. (1998, 211–239)

The causal-chain implicit in charismatic leadership is outlined in Exhibit 7.2.

An enormous strength of charismatic leadership theory is that it is descriptive of the world around us. It acknowledges that some impactful leaders—such as Margaret Thatcher, Charles DeGaulle, Nelson Mandela, and George Patton—are charismatic, while other leaders equally effective in terms of impact—such as Bill Gates or Paul Volcker—are noncharismatic. A charismatic leader who is ethical uses power to develop and serve others. The spotlight is shared with others in a spirit of interdependence rather than usurped by one who may be dwelling in the light of narcissism.

Not all charismatic leaders are famous, like Lee Iacocca or John F. Kennedy. Some are renowned only in their town or region or industry sector. Take, for instance, the leadership of Tom Slide, president of his high school senior class in Topeka, Kansas, and star basketball player on his college team. After earning a marketing degree at a top business school in the East, Tom decided to go back to Topeka and start his own firm, Slide Marketing. The road to ownership and success was not easy. Employees were aware that he was willing to sacrifice for the business by mortgaging his home to provide sufficient capital to grow the business. Tom honed his public speaking skills, and in his personal relations he came across as humble, although he always claimed to offer a vision of organizational success through marketing that was radically dif-

Exhibit 7.2 **Charismatic Leadership Causal Chain**

Leadership styles
- Noncharismatic (lack of charismatic style)
- Good charismatic (ideal style)
  - Opposes the status quo and strives to change it
  - Has idealized vision that is highly discrepant from the status quo
  - Articulates strong and/or inspirational articulation of future vision and motivation to lead
  - Unconventional or counternormative
  - Exercises passionate advocacy
  - Is willing to incur great personal risk and cost
- Bad charismatic (misuse of charismatic style)

Ideal conditions
- Need for change and/or higher goals

Success of charismatic behaviors by leader
- Vision based on external assessments rather than projections of personal needs
- Realistic estimate of environment
- Realistic estimate of resource estimates and constraints
- Ability to see recognize shifts in the environment that call for a change in one's vision
- Ability to inspire trust and confidence and avoid excessive alienation
- Avoidance of the use of self-serving power, etc.

Performance goals
- Follower satisfaction with leader
- Follower trust in leader
- Group cohesion
- External alignment and organizational change

Source: Conger and Kanungo (1998).

ferent from any other approach. The company webpage cited how Tom's expertise was championed in business magazines and blogs. Employees were loyal to the man, and he became a local hero of sorts, frequently interviewed in the media on virtually any regional business issue. Though not famous outside his community, Tom Slide embodies the spirit of a charismatic business leader.

Whether famous or not, it is clear that charismatic leaders can be effective agents of change. Their method is more than flashing a winning personality or an appealing visualization of the future. Research suggests that charismatic leaders employ consistent communication strategies for bringing about change, recognizing that there is great power in language for shaping norms and attitudes One study, for example, empirically analyzed speeches of twentieth-century presidents and found that during the stages for change there are "consistent communication strategies for breaking down, moving, and re-aligning the norms of their followers" (Fiol, Harris, and House 1999, 450). Differences in speech patterns help to explain why charismatic leaders are effective during the stages for change. The use of "negation, inclusion, and abstraction [occurred] more frequently during the middle phase of their tenure as leaders than in the earlier and later phases" (470) and also occurred more frequently during the most critical stage of change: moving (472–473).

Charismatic leadership is not without its flaws. Researchers such as Rakesh Khurana (2002) have found that if struggling companies looking for a new CEO seek a charismatic executive, their troubles may become worse. When corporate performance sags, directors in search of new leadership who succumb to pressure, fire the CEO, and hire a "savior" may enjoy only a brief period of satisfaction. Executive charisma does not necessarily result in organizational performance. Charisma may inspire awe, but not necessarily on-time delivery or quality output.

Khurana reports that "charisma leads companies to overlook many promising candidates and to consider others who are unsuited for the job" (2002). He cites the 1993 example of Kodak's directors, who made much ado about firing CEO Kay Whitmore. Two months later, they appointed Motorola's CEO, George Fisher. They envisioned Fisher as the savior who would soar into the Kodak picture with a flourish and right everything in due course. The fact was, however, that the company had not adopted digital imaging when it should have, so it was behind the curve when compared to its competition. Even a charismatic CEO could not change that history. After six turbulent years of cutbacks, restructurings, and a free fall in operating profits following an initial appearance of market gain, Fisher stepped down as CEO.

Kodak's next CEO, Daniel Carp, worked five years on the serious adaptation to digital imaging. In 2007, Kodak experienced a profit—the year when the company completed the transition to digital technology and the new CEO, Antonio Perez, claimed a compensation package of over $11 million. This example illustrates how a corporate board, hailing a charismatic leader selected from the outside, misinterpreted the allure of charisma and expected it to be the antidote to the strategic errors of its past. The energizing leader who ignites followers to venture in new directions in a different setting may not always be the wise choice simply because of the ability to inspire awe.

Charismatic leadership theory recognizes that for every good charismatic, it is possible to have a negative charismatic as well. There have been Roosevelts and Hitlers, Gandhis and Saddam Husseins, Mother Teresas, and Jim Joneses. In the case of many **negative charismatics**, the leader's focus shifts from organization to self.

One example of a negative charismatic that illustrates the shift in focus from organization to self is collections manager Walter Pavlo. "By the time he was 40, Walter

A. Pavlo Jr. had graduated with a master's degree in business from Mercer University, worked as a manager at MCI, concocted a $6 million money laundering scheme, served a two-year sentence in federal prison, and was divorced, unemployed, and living again with his parents. It's a story that should scare any MBA straight" (Porter 2008). Pavlo, whose conservative upbringing belied his subsequent behavior, was a charismatic, energetic young collections manager who was under corporate pressure to show profits in the billing of $1 billion per month for MCI's carrier division. Without proper oversight, he began to cook the books and ultimately brought down with him others who were attracted to his charismatic style. At some point, Pavlo admitted that his focus shifted from the organization to himself. In fact, at a low point, he began to hate the organization as if to give himself psychological permission to use customers in his schemes (Pavlo and Weinberg 2007). After prison, he told his tragic tale at business schools so that future leaders would not make the unethical choices that he did. One of Pavlo's important messages was that leaders must supervise managers who are admired by others, have access to money, and are under pressure to produce "unfeasibly high" results. This does not mean that the charismatic manager is not to be trusted, but rather that no employee should be allowed free rein without oversight. Pavlo's message regarding proper supervision of charismatics is consistent with guidelines for effective delegation in any situation—supervisors at any level of the organization who delegate responsibility with commensurate authority must retain their own authority as well as knowledge of the work being done.

Other leaders with charm who are viewed as charismatic may be hollow when it comes to substance. According to ChangingMinds.org (1998), "A typical experience with them is that whilst you are talking with them, it is like being bathed in a warm and pleasant glow, in which they are very convincing. Yet afterwards, as the sunbeam of their attention is moved elsewhere, you may begin to question what they said (or even whether they said anything of significance at all)."

There can be flawed charismatics such as Bill Clinton, Oliver North, or Mao Zedong. Charismatic leadership theory has also significantly expanded our understanding of negative charismatics. It is important to understand the negative syndromes as well as the positive ones if one is to have a robust understanding of leadership.

Charisma, like other personality characteristics, is itself neither noble nor bad; it can be used for good or evil. Great generals and great heads of state often acquire charismatic qualities, even if they were not innate, such as Alexander the Great, Charlemagne, Joan of Arc, Elizabeth I, Napoleon, George Washington, Winston Churchill, and Mahatma Gandhi. Cult founders often espouse these charismatic qualities as well. A famous example of negative charisma is cult leader Jim Jones, who triggered mass suicide among his followers at Jonestown, Guyana, in 1978 (Exhibit 7.3). This case is a complete counterpoint to the earlier example of Lee Iacocca, except for the fact that others saw charisma in both of these leaders.

Charismatic leadership theory is not without its problems, of course. It is certainly not a comprehensive leadership theory inasmuch as it acknowledges but largely ignores noncharismatics and leadership situations that are not particularly built around crises or significant change. If anything, it is moderately dismissive of noncharismatic leaders even though they may be more numerous and extremely necessary in

Exhibit 7.3

Negative Charisma: The Case of James Warren Jones

The charisma of cult leader Jim Jones became evident when an investigation into his alleged cures for cancer and arthritis threatened his message to followers, causing them to leave Indiana en masse for Redwood Valley, California (which he selected when *Esquire* magazine listed Ukiah as one of nine cities in the United States that could survive a nuclear war). In 1977, when an investigation into Jones's church for tax evasion threatened its tax-exempt status, followers then left California for a so-called utopian community dubbed Jonestown (named for Jim Jones himself) in Guyana, South America. A mix of religious and social ideas, combined with the charisma of James Warren Jones, ultimately led to the planned mass suicide of 909 cult members of the People's Temple church in Guyana in 1978.

Jim Jones was born in 1931 and died in the mass suicide from a gunshot to his head. He was described by people who knew him when he was young as an isolated, withdrawn child who killed animals so he could preside over their funerals (Bates 2006). A neighbor took him to the Pentecostal Church as a child, where some thought that he might have found acceptance. Jones sold pet monkeys to raise the money needed to found a church in Indianapolis in 1955, a church that eventually became known as the People's Temple. By 1960, the People's Temple became affiliated with the Disciples of Christ and Jones was listed as its ordained pastor, even though he had no formal education in theology. He initially invoked the Bible but later wrote a booklet titled "The Letter Killeth," highlighting what he thought were absurdities and lies in the Bible. Jones soon began invoking his own texts, along with the Communist Party newspaper Pravda. Probably influenced by his mother, he promoted racial equality and social justice as central principles of the People's Temple, and about 70 percent of Jonestown residents were black and impoverished. Jones felt that when residents called him "Father" and, on demand, sent him notes and letters of support addressed "Dear Dad," it was proof of his acceptance.

Life in the jungle of Guyana was very difficult. On top of long workdays, residents had numerous meetings and even Russian language classes at night. Jones made it clear to his interracial residents that they were building the Promised Land in order to escape racial injustice in the United States. Perhaps because of the pressures, Jones began taking drugs, often to excess. Some days he had difficulty speaking coherently and would ramble on to his followers over the public address system, preventing them from sleeping well. When Jones's top assistant deserted the flock of followers, he claimed that Jones brainwashed the residents and held them there as if in a concentration camp. Some defectors who feared for their kin called themselves the Concerned Relatives and repeatedly appealed to congressional representatives for assistance.

In the 1970s, Jones's charisma continued on the path to corruption as he punished members who were not fully loyal to him. In the mid-1970s, loyalty tests were given at Jonestown: some members of the leadership were given a drink that they were first told was poison. As members one by one fell to the ground, faking affliction, the drink was given to others to test their loyalty before everyone was told it was only a check to make certain they were ready to die for the cause of the People's Temple.

Deeper investigation did not begin until November 18, 1978, when Representative Leo Ryan of California, along with media representatives and several Concerned Relatives, went to Jonestown to investigate charges of abusive behavior. Although loyal members of the flock greeted the investigators with a standard message of the wonderment of their life, over the course of a day, sixteen members asked to return to the United States with Congressman Ryan. As the departing party made its way to the airstrip several miles from the compound and were preparing to board their two airplanes, gunshots rang out, killing Representative Ryan and four others.

Later that same day, Jones gathered the remaining residents together, announcing that the outside world had forced them into "revolutionary suicide," a term borrowed (albeit not accurately) from Huey Newton of the Black Panther Party. Residents presumably understood Jones's call and lined up obediently. Parents and children alike drank from a vat of purple Flav-R-Aid, similar to Kool-Aid, which was laced with cyanide, sedatives, and tranquilizers. A heavy aura of pure, negative charisma ruled the scene, with very few followers taking the path of independent thinking. Almost one-third of the 909 who died at Jonestown were children. Another third were senior citizens, many of whom may have been injected with poison.

the daily operations of organizations. This may be because charismatic leaders are "called upon" to do greater things, and their force of personality—derived from superb communication skills, excellent talent for drawing vivid images, and ability to persuade others—is relatively uncommon. President Barack Obama became known during the 2008 Democratic campaign for the presidency for his stirring rhetoric for change as well as a contagious drive for hope. His charisma led many to believe that if "called upon" to do great things, he would be uniquely equipped to come through as a leader.

Finally, the emphasis of charismatic leadership theory is essentially on personality-based leadership, and when the focus is broadened to skills that charismatic leaders employ in order to bring change, the theoretical base shifts only slightly to interpersonal communication and influence. Useful and important though these perspectives are, the study of charisma does not give a full picture of leadership because of its emphasis on both heroic and despotic leadership types. We next examine transformational leadership theory, which frequently involves a charismatic leader, but is more organizationally based and less personality-based, although still considered change-oriented leadership.

TRANSFORMATIONAL LEADERSHIP THEORY

Transformational leadership theory may or may not involve an extraordinary charismatic leader at its center. But **transformational leadership** always results in follower commitment to organizational objectives along with increased follower skills and self-confidence, often resulting from empowerment. A variety of forms of transformational leadership have been put forward. We will review three—first Tichy and Devanna's model, then Kouzes and Posner's—and finally Bass's "full range theory."

TICHY AND DEVANNA'S TRANSFORMATIONAL LEADERSHIP MODEL

Researchers have found that charismatic leadership is not an essential ingredient for major organizational change. Instead, leaders of organizations achieving major change use transformational behaviors and may or may not be identified as charismatic individuals. A model by Tichy and Devanna (1990) emphasizes organizational needs first and examines the cascading behavioral needs second. They assert that "more than ever the key to global competitiveness will be widespread capability of institutions around the world to continuously transform." In addition, "increasingly excellence is the condition not just for dominance but for survival." Therefore, "transformational leadership is about change, innovation, and entrepreneurship" (1990, iv, xii). Their model also emphasizes the *temporal phases of change* reminiscent of Lewin, who proposed that change requires unfreezing, changing, and refreezing the organization (1951). However, they use a three-act play as their metaphor for the temporal phases, linking both organizational and individual needs to each of those acts.

Tichy and Devanna provide only two alternate styles: a managerial style and a transformational style. They assert that managers are relatively commonplace but that transformational leaders are rarer and increasingly critical to organizational success. Managers are "individuals who maintain the balance of operations in an organization, relate to others according to their role, are detached, impersonal, seek solutions acceptable as a compromise among conflicting values, and identify totally with the organization." Leaders—transformational leaders, that is—are "individuals out to create new approaches and imagine new areas to explore; they relate to people in more intuitive and empathetic ways, seek risk where opportunity and reward are high, and project ideas into images to excite people" (1990, xiii).

The transformational leader must change organizations and people in successive stages. The first stage is *recognizing the need for revitalization*. Because of the competitive environment and the speed of responsiveness required in that environment, the need for revitalization is nearly ubiquitous. The second stage is *creating a new vision*. New ways of doing business must be contemplated, refined, rehearsed, and widely articulated. The third stage is *institutionalizing change*. As the new vision is understood and accepted, new structures, mechanisms, and incentives must be put in place. This requires a creative destruction and reweaving of the social fabric of the organization. Keeping the motivation of individuals high remains key so that they continue their inner realignment and adaptation to new internal scripts.

The inclination of the leader to induce change is the intervening variable; the moderating variables are the "triggers" for change. Thus, like most transformational models, Tichy and Devanna are less interested in specifying the exact conditions under which the preferred style is useful than they are in articulating the general set of behaviors that has universal utility. The causal-chain model representing their theory is presented in Exhibit 7.4.

KOUZES AND POSNER'S LEADERSHIP PRACTICES THEORY

The leadership practices theory employed by Kouzes and Posner (1987) represents another approach in the transformational school. Rather than starting with a chronological approach, as did Tichy and Devanna, they started with an empirical approach. They asked: *According to leaders themselves, what leads to excellent leadership based on their personal experiences?* Kouzes and Posner originally surveyed 1,330 individuals using a critical incident methodology focusing exclusively on "personal best" experiences. They assert that the five major practices they identified, each composed of two "commitments," covered more than 70 percent of respondents' descriptions of personal best scenarios. Subsequently, they designed a leadership instrument called the Leadership Practices Inventory (LPI) (1993), which has been highly popular in the training sphere, as have their writings. Both the instrument and their framework are pragmatic but largely atheoretical. That is, they are based on survey research about actual trends, but the explanation of how the practices all fit together is weak, even though each of the practices they advocate is consistent with research findings. Like Tichy and Devanna, Kouzes and Posner focus exclusively on the transformational style. They omit laissez-faire, directive, and achievement styles, for the most part, while they emphasize supportive, participative, and inspirational styles. (See Chapter 2 for an in-depth discussion of styles.)

Like other transformational theorists, Kouzes and Posner (1987, 1993) use a uni-

Exhibit 7.4   **Transformational Leadership as Change Master Causal Chain**

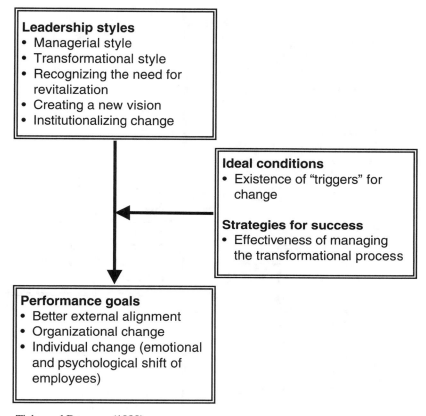

Leadership styles
- Managerial style
- Transformational style
- Recognizing the need for revitalization
- Creating a new vision
- Institutionalizing change

Ideal conditions
- Existence of "triggers" for change

Strategies for success
- Effectiveness of managing the transformational process

Performance goals
- Better external alignment
- Organizational change
- Individual change (emotional and psychological shift of employees)

Source: Tichy and Devanna (1990).

versal approach. Their critical-incident methodology does not discriminate based on level of leadership within the organizational hierarchy (supervisor, middle manager, or executive) or types of situations. The only moderating factors, then, are the quality of implementation of the five practices themselves.

As the first practice, they assert that successful leaders must "challenge the process," a type of leadership emphasizing quest and courage. In turn, the two supporting practices are, first, searching for opportunities, and second, experimenting and taking risks. The second practice involves "inspiring a shared vision" composed of the commitment to envision the future and to enlist others in a common vision by appealing to their values, interests, hopes, and dreams. This inclusion of other people's ideas and dreams flows into the third practice, "enabling others to act," which is a type of participative style. It consists of fostering collaboration and strengthening others. Kouzes and Posner assert that other researchers found this to be the most important practice, and one that leaders themselves mentioned in 91 percent of the cases they studied (1987, 10). The fourth practice involves "modeling the way," which is composed of setting the example and planning small wins. The final practice involves

Exhibit 7.5 **Causal-Chain Model Implicit in Leadership Practices Theory**

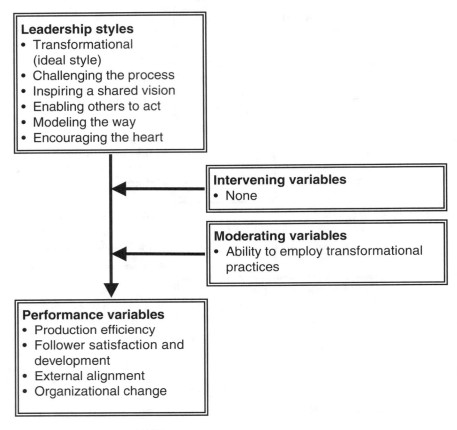

Source: Kouzes and Posner (1987).

"encouraging the heart." It is a supportive style composed of recognizing contributions and celebrating accomplishments. The causal-chain model based on their theory is shown in Exhibit 7.5.

Because it is based on real practices culled from more than 1,000 managers, Kouzes and Posner's Leadership Practices Inventory has pragmatic appeal. What do leaders need to do to be excellent? Indeed, it is clear that Kouzes and Posner have identified and loosely amalgamated the important inspirational, supportive, and participative styles. This has led to the popularity of the approach, which has been greatly enhanced by especially readable and dynamic books aimed largely at a nonscholarly audience. However, the weaknesses of the approach are also significant. Most importantly, although the approach tells a persuasive and rational story, the LPI has weak discriminant validity, making it ineffective for specifying verifiable transformational leader behaviors (Carless 2001). Moreover, the theory should not be mistaken for a comprehensive theory of leadership.

BASS'S FULL-RANGE THEORY

The next theory we review is the most comprehensive of the transformational approaches. If Tichy and Devanna excel at providing a good articulation of transformational leadership as a process over time, and Kouzes and Posner excel at providing pragmatic microcompetencies, Burns and Bass (1978 and 1985) excel at providing a solid theoretical framework that resulted in the "**full-range leadership**" theory. Bass credits Burns with being the first to provide a comprehensive theory explaining how transactional and transformational leaders differ; Bass cites Burns' description of the transactional leader as one who approaches followers for the purpose of exchanging one thing for another, such as jobs for votes (1990, 23). The idea of the "transforming leader" grew from Burns' description of the leader who lifted followers from petty preoccupations to common goals. Bass extended Burn's approach, developing a typology of leadership behaviors with the "full range" extending from transformational leaders who are charismatic and motivate through inspiration, to transactional leaders who motivate by exchanging rewards for achievement, to laissez-faire leaders whose approach is to avoid active involvement. Laissez-faire or nonleadership normally provides haphazard or unpredictable results; transactional leadership provides conventional results; and transformational leadership provides, as Bass' book title indicates, "performance beyond expectations." When Bass extended Burns' earlier research, he suggested that leadership can simultaneously display both transformational and transactional characteristics and that the approaches are not mutually exclusive; rather, transformational leadership augments transactional leadership. The additive nature of his theory is portrayed in Exhibit 7.6.

Understanding differences between transactional leadership and transformational leadership is an important distinction, because both can establish appropriate goals and coordinate goal achievement. However, the transactional leader works less to change the framework within which she leads than does the transformational leader. The transactional leader focuses on watchful guidance, or management, within a closed system, or organization, which as a result may become increasingly out of touch with the environment, while the transformational leader will work without those boundaries, attempting to turn the tide to link the organization externally for strategic opportunities to change in response to its environment. One of the world's most famous businessmen, Walt Disney, is attributed with saying that "there are three types of people in the world today. There are 'well poisoners,' who discourage you and stomp on your creativity and tell you what you cannot do. There are 'lawn mowers,' people who are well intentioned but self-absorbed; they tend to their own needs, mow their own lawns, and never leave their yards to help another person. Finally, there are 'life-enhancers,' people who reach out to enrich the lives of others, to lift them up and inspire them" (Maxwell 2008, 19). The transformational leader is the last, enriching others by raising expectations and inspiring them, thinking beyond the organization itself and perhaps even achieving revolutionary change. But meanwhile, it is transactional leadership that probably constitutes the bulk of most leader behavior and research on leadership.

In transactional leadership, rewards and benefits to followers are exchanged for

Exhibit 7.6 **Bass's Continuum of Leadership Styles** ("Full-Range Theory")

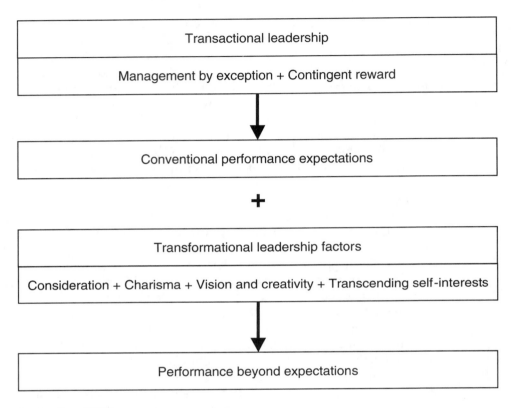

Source: Bass (1985).

their fulfillment of agreements with the leader. The more progressive and positive half of transactional leadership is contingent reward. Managers using contingent reward find out what employees value and vary the incentives that they offer accordingly. An employee willing to take on one assignment may be released from another. A high-performance employee may get a large raise or a promotion. Such leadership is at its best, generally, when the work and incentives are negotiated and mutually agreed upon in advance. While contingent reward is a fundamental part of most organizational systems and represents a practical reality—people expect rewards for hard work—it does have its weaknesses. First, by itself, contingent reward systems can easily lead to extensive tit-for-tat systems where only what is specifically rewarded gets done. Second, contingent rewards generally apply to individual workers and thus do not directly account for group achievements. Furthermore, an exclusive reliance on contingent rewards may leave many, perhaps most, managers and executives with few leadership options when resources are extremely scarce or diminishing and yet the organizational needs are critical or increasing.

Management-by-exception is one use of leadership as contingent reinforcement;

the approach calls for a leader to respond only to mistakes or deviations from standards, viewing them as corrective opportunities, which in turn emphasizes negative feedback. In the more lax or passive form of management-by-exception, the manager intervenes and takes corrective action only after a mistake has been made or a problem has become obvious. An active management-by-exception style indicates that the manager is monitoring more closely and intervening prior to problems going outside the unit. Neither of these approaches is necessarily bad in itself. However, Bass holds that it is generally an inferior style that should be used sparingly because the feedback given signals employees to maintain the status quo. Extensive use of this style may create intimidation and discourage initiative and creativity.

Transformational leadership was described in general earlier in this chapter. Bass asserts that transformational leadership is a widespread phenomenon across levels of management, types of organizations, and around the globe. It is therefore a universal theory without contingency factors for performance results, whereby followers are motivated to perform beyond even their own expectations as a by-product of trust and respect for the leader. As with other transformational theories, it assumes that both the quality of the transformational factors executed and the number of styles or factors used will have a moderating effect on the performance. That is, there is a substantial additive effect of the styles that invokes higher-level needs in followers.

Bass identified four elements of transformational behaviors based on his behavior description questionnaire called the Multifactor Leadership Questionnaire. The activation of these four elements—individualized consideration, idealized influence, inspirational motivation, and intellectual stimulation—engenders follower motivation.

The first behavioral element designated as transformational by Bass and others in the transformational school, called **individualized consideration**, refers to coaching, professional and personal support, individualized treatment based on specific needs, increased delegation as employees mature professionally, and so forth. In short, it boils down to respect and empathy. It is highly similar to the supportive roles proposed in **transactional theories** as discussed previously.

Bass's second element, **idealized influence**, is very similar to the concept of charisma. Those who exhibit idealized influence function as powerful role models for their followers. Followers identify with the leaders' goals and emulate their actions. This requires a perception by followers of a high level of integrity and wisdom.

The third behavioral element in Bass's taxonomy is **inspirational motivation**—in a sense, the most critical element of a transformational style. When leaders successfully use inspirational motivation, their followers are able to transcend their self-interests long enough to become passionate about organizational pride, group goals, and group achievements. Through enhanced team spirit, leaders are able to motivate followers to pursue higher standards or to make sacrifices without reliance on extrinsic incentives. Although the greater good is expected to redound to followers at some point in the future, there is generally not an exact commitment or transaction contract because of the uncertainty or abstractness of the goals.

The fourth element, **intellectual stimulation**, is the behavior of transformational leadership that encourages people to create new opportunities, to solve problems in new ways, and to envision a different ability to reexamine competing values. This style

Exhibit 7.7 **Transformational Leadership in "Full-Range Theory" Causal Chain**

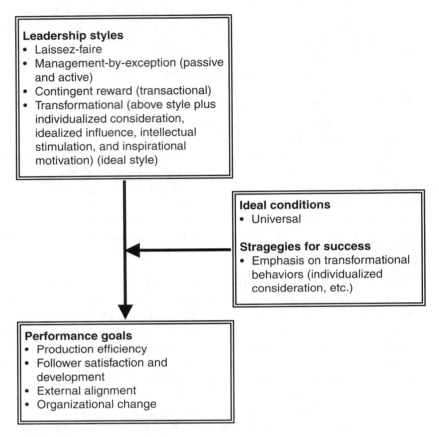

Source: Bass (1985).

emphasizes techniques such as information sharing, brainstorming, vision articulation, and employee development targeted at specific organizational improvements. Leaders who invoke intellectual stimulation to transform an organization are often thought of as idea people or visionaries.

Later versions of Bass's theory include laissez-faire leadership as a third category distinguished from transformational and transactional. Starting with an essentially nonleadership style, laissez-faire takes a hands-off approach to leadership, as we discussed in Chapter 2. Laissez-faire leaders in this approach are largely uninvolved in operations, often slipshod about details for the situation at hand, resistant to participation in problem-solving, lax in decision-making, negligent in providing feedback, and indifferent to their subordinates' needs. The theory does not account for those occasions when the style is used purposefully, as when competing demands necessitate overlooking a particular area of responsibility or when indifference is appropriate.

The causal chain implied in Bass's model is illustrated in Exhibit 7.7.

All four transformational elements are generally present in concert in successful change initiatives, but that is not to say that the leader must supply all of them. Colleagues may supply their own consideration; low-key trust may successfully substitute for brassier charisma; young, highly motivated professionals in the group may provide the intellectual stimulation; and inspirational motivation may be largely the result of a rich and proud tradition as well as a professional indoctrination instilling strong ethical values.

Of all the transformational theories, Bass's is the most highly researched and has a good deal of positive support. Further, one gets the sense that Bass's approach builds on earlier transactional theory, even though the earlier theory and concepts are somewhat downplayed. It has its weaknesses, however. One of the most obvious is its universality, which in turn implies that transformational leadership is superior to transactional or other approaches in all leadership levels and situations. This flies in the face of the day-to-day reality of many leaders, especially those working at operational levels where stability is critical. Second, the overlap of transformational concepts with other leadership topics is problematic. Part of the problem is structural, however, because higher-level human motivations that are associated with transformational leadership are abstract and complex. Additionally, the nomenclature of the concepts is not always easy to understand. Even though Bass's transformational factors have the mnemonic of all starting with the letter *i*, differences between concepts such as those between individualized consideration and idealized influence have to be explained and memorized.

Regardless of the particular transformational theory followed, the executive who is bringing momentous change to an organization is supported by informative writings on the specific steps to take in transforming an organization. When these steps are not followed, they become the errors that explain why the transformation effort failed. In the previous explanation of the stages of transformation, and the steps that undergird these stages, focus is on the vision for change along with sufficient communication of that vision to all involved. Without the vision being sufficiently known, transformational effort may seem to employees to be little more than a lot of projects without purpose or meaning.

John Kotter, recognized as one of the world's great authorities on leadership after having studied leadership up and down the hierarchy for over thirty years, advised that the following errors be avoided for transformational effort to be successful (2007).

1. Not establishing a great enough sense of urgency
2. Not creating a powerful enough guiding coalition
3. Lacking a vision
4. Undercommunicating the vision by a factor of ten
5. Not removing obstacles to the vision
6. Not systematically planning for and creating short-term wins
7. Declaring victory too soon
8. Not anchoring changes in the corporation's culture

COMPARING APPROACHES TO LEADERSHIP

Comparing the similarities and differences between the charismatic, transactional, and transformational approaches provides a good means of concluding this chapter. Coming later in time, transformational theories absorbed many aspects of both charismatic and transactional theories, thus creating some overlap.

At the beginning of this chapter, we mentioned that charismatic leaders are frequently dissatisfied with the status quo and may be willing to use unconventional means to bring about change. They have an idealized vision of the future and are able to communicate it with confidence and enthusiasm. They may be markedly similar to the transformational leader in their ability to elicit inspirational effects by communicating emotionally as opposed to using a style that emphasizes the status quo. Although charisma is not an essential ingredient of transformation, charisma is frequently considered a component of transformational leadership. Whereas the relationship between subordinates and a charismatic leader may inspire love or hate, they are rarely bland. If leader-subordinate relationships are excessively bland, the possibility of inspiring transformation of the organization is doubtful. Thus, charismatics are less frequently associated with transactional leadership.

The theoretical emphasis of transactional leadership focuses on supervisors in a closed system. Researchers are interested in keeping variables limited and testable. Transformational researchers are more interested in executives, political leaders, and social leaders in relatively open systems. Such leaders function as the nexus between the external economic and political environment and the internal organizational environment, and they have to adjust the latter to conform to the former. Because of the wider perspective that transformational researchers seek to explain, they either use a larger number of variables or must be more abstract in their explanations.

Transactional leaders rely heavily on certain types of power: legitimate (power from formal appointed authority), reward, and punishment. As formal managers, transactional leaders have the mantle of authority and the ability to administer and adjust incentives. Moreover, transactional researchers have frequently assumed expert power and tend to ignore referent power (power based on personality and likability). Transformational researchers, on the contrary, emphasize expert and referent power. To make a major impact, for good or ill, leaders have to be perceived as wise and brilliant, and they must have enough personal appeal to sell their ideas and be trusted. Such leaders can use their power indirectly through emotional appeal and at a distance through ideological appeal.

Transactional researchers were originally highly influenced by economic perspectives, such as social exchange and expectancy theory. The basic self-interests and immediate needs of followers are the focus, ranging from pay to clear instructions to adequate resources and working conditions. Follower motivation is considered largely a rational, calculative process. On the other hand, transformational researchers emphasize stimulating individuals' interest in group productivity and organizational success. Transformational researchers frequently examine followers' motivations to emulate or idolize leaders for personal or ideological reasons. Follower motivation is a more symbolic process based on ideology, inspiration, and the intellectual belief that past patterns are no longer functional.

In transactional settings, organizational conditions are assumed to be stable, or, at the very least, the leader is responding to the organizational condition as if it were stable. Problems in organizations involve adjustments, exceptions, or refinements in properly functioning systems. In transformational settings, the assumption is that change is inevitable, constant, and healthy. This is particularly true in the new economy in which the U.S. market must contend with vigorous global competition. Of particular interest to transformational researchers are the roles of crisis, organizational collapse, and other dramatic forms of system deterioration.

Performance expectations in transactional theories tend to emphasize "good" performance. To be reasonable, efficient, effective, sustainable, and consistent, performance should be engineered by management with the substantial input of employees. Good performance is the goal in systems that have already been well designed. Transformational theories tend to assume that standards or quality has stagnated or languished, or that adaptation to new processes, technologies, changing environments, or organizational structures is required. Exceptional performance is necessary for organizational success, whether that entails higher productivity levels, a greater contribution in adaptation and innovation, or effective organizational transformation.

Leader behaviors in transactional theories strongly emphasize the task- and people-oriented domains (see Chapters 5 and 6). In particular, they emphasize monitoring, operations planning, clarifying roles, informing, delegating, problem-solving, consulting, personnel planning, developing staff, and motivating. Leader behaviors in transformational theories strongly emphasize organizational-oriented behaviors (see Chapters 8 and 9) as well as people-oriented behaviors. They do not completely neglect, but certainly downplay, task-oriented behaviors. They emphasize environmental scanning, strategic planning, vision articulation, networking, decision-making, and managing organizational change, as well as informing, delegating (empowering), managing technical innovation, consulting, developing staff, motivating, building teams, and managing personnel change. A rough comparison of these differences between transactional and transformational theories is displayed in Exhibit 7.8.

CONCLUSION

Charismatic leaders have extraordinary effects on their followers. Under their leadership that brings inspiration and a strong sense of values, followers often perform at higher levels. Transformational leaders are triggers of extraordinary organizational change. Under their leadership, organizations or political and social entities may undergo significant structural change. Charismatic and transformational leadership frequently have agents in common, but actually the two notions are distinct. The former involves a magnetic quality of the leader and the latter involves a type of change that can be brought about by various types of leader, whether charismatic or not.

Conger and Kanungo focus on how charisma is attributed to leaders. They contend that for charismatic leadership to emerge, the context has to be sufficiently problematic to allow for dissatisfaction with the status quo and for radical change to be acceptable. Charismatic leaders may be known locally or throughout a nation. Charisma can lead to positive or negative outcomes. Charismatic leadership is not for every

Exhibit 7.8   **A Rough Comparison of Transactional Theories and Transformational or Charismatic Theories**

	Transactional	Transformational
Theoretical emphasis	Supervisors	Executives
	Closed system	Open system
	Narrow range of variables	Broad range of variables
Leader's type of power	Legitimate, reward, punishment	Expert, referent
	Direct influence at close range	Indirect influence, including influence at a distance
Follower motivation	Self-interests such as pay; immediate needs such as resources, group compatibility	Group interests such as organizational success; psychic satisfaction such as emulation of leader
	Rational processes (calculative)	Symbolic processes based on ideology or breaking with the past
Facilitating conditions	Stable; refinement of functioning systems	Unstable; need for change; crisis
Performance expectations	Good performance	Exceptional performance either in terms of quantity or adaptation
Leader behaviors emphasized	Monitoring, operations planning, clarifying roles, informing, delegating, problem-solving, consulting, personnel planning, developing staff, and motivating	Environmental scanning, strategic planning, vision articulation, networking, decision-making, managing organizational change as well as informing, delegating (empowering), managing innovation, consulting, developing staff, motivating, building teams, and managing personnel change

Note: Because of the tremendous variety of transactional and transformational theories, there are some exceptions to these general trends.

situation. For example, charisma is not a substitute for solid management that brings continuous improvement.

Tichy and Devanna focus on transformational leadership, with the belief that charismatic leadership is not required in order to bring about major organizational change. They examine leadership over time; before institutionalizing change, transformational leaders first recognize the need for revitalization and then create a new vision. The leadership practices theory by Kouzes and Posner is another mechanism for examining transformational leadership and recommending competencies or practices. By interviewing individuals on their "personal best" experiences, they advocate practices consistent with their findings—challenging the process and searching for opportunities, inspiring a shared vision, enabling others to act by fostering collaboration in a participative style, modeling the way, and, finally, "encouraging the heart" with a supportive style.

The full-range leadership theory by Bass provides a good visualization on a continuum from laissez-faire nonleadership to transactional leadership to transformational leadership. The approaches are not thought of as mutually exclusive, but as one approach augmenting another. Transactional leadership, constituting most leadership behavior, is not revolutionary, but brings incremental improvements by offering incentives to employees for achieving desired results. Transformational leadership involves behaviors or elements Bass calls individualized consideration, or coaching and personal support; idealized influence, which is similar to charisma; inspirational motivation, which allows followers to transcend self-interest in favor or organizational achievement; and intellectual stimulation, which supports people creating new opportunities and solving old problems in new ways.

KEY TERMS

charismatic leadership
full-range leadership
idealized influence
individualized consideration
inspirational motivation
intellectual stimulation

management-by-exception
negative charismatics
overmanaged and underled
transactional theories
transformational leadership
vision

RESOURCES

Bernard Bass has heard his detractors question the morality of transformational leadership. He and coauthor Steidlmeier make it clear in this paper that real transformational leadership must be grounded in a moral and ethical foundation.

- Bernard M. Bass and Paul Steidlmeier, "Ethics, Character, and Authentic Transformational Leadership," September 24, 1998. www.vanguard.edu/uploadedFiles/Faculty/RHeuser/ETHICS,%20MORAL%20CHARACTER%20AND%20AUTHENTIC%20TRANSFORMATIONAL%20LEADERSHIP.pdf.

Bill Gates was cited in this chapter as a "noncharismatic" individual. Draw your own conclusions about this icon's charisma by reading an in-depth article on Gates, such as the following one. You will read about a man known for an aggressive and confrontational style, shown by actions such as firing Microsoft's first president after he had been on the job for less than a year. Yet Gates and his wife have used their wealth to establish a foundation to benefit primarily minority students' education and global health issues.

- "Bill Gates," Answers.com. www.answers.com/topic/bill-gates?cat=biz-fin.

Walt Pavlo was discussed in this chapter as a charismatic, successful manager who gave in to pressures for personal gain. Until recently, he lectured at many universities to tell business students that there are—and should be—dire consequences for surrendering personal ethics. Hear him speak in several short videos by searching YouTube.com for his name; be sure to include the NightLine broadcast that is posted at www.youtube.com/watch?v=sPUuHn5_L1g ("CON Walter Pavlo Corporate Manager Steals $6 Million," October 9, 2007).

DISCUSSION QUESTIONS

1. Describe the differences and similarities between charismatic and transformational leadership.
2. What were the precursors to charismatic and transformational theories?
3. Discuss Conger and Kanungo's theory of charismatic leadership.
4. Many business, political, and religious leaders who are cultural icons have been "good" charismatics. Discuss the appropriateness of "good" charismatic leadership in business. What type of charismatic leader is best for an organization? Should charismatic leaders be in lower-level supervisory roles as well as at the top of the organization? Do you think that all leaders must be somewhat charismatic to be effective? Do you think you are or can be a charismatic leader?
5. Explain Bass's additive model of high-performance leadership. Which factor does he claim for the transformational arena that was formerly subsumed under transactional approaches?

    Assuming for a moment that Bass's theory of leadership is correct, why is there so little successful transformational leadership anywhere, including in the public and nonprofit sectors? Why is it so difficult to be a high-performing transformational leader in today's organizational environment?

    Compare and contrast the differences between transactional and transformational approaches.
8. Kotter used this quip to highlight differences between leadership and management: "No one has yet figured out how to manage people effectively into battle—they must be led." Have you encountered a leader who could, figuratively speaking, lead people effectively into battle? What effect did that person have on you?
9. Would Kotter's eight mistakes to avoid come naturally to a charismatic leader who is attempting to bring transformation? Defend your position by referring to the central meaning of Kotter's points and to the description of a charismatic leader.
10. Which single leadership theory do you feel you can use to best explain organizational change? (Refer to this chapter and prior chapters.)

CLASSROOM ACTIVITY

This classroom activity is based on Exhibit 7.3. In groups of about five students, prepare to answer the following questions and discuss with the class as a whole. Before the discussion, students are encouraged to read some of the excellent analyses available of the events in Jonestown and to use those readings in their responses. In the context of this chapter's focus on negative charismatics, discussions should downplay the many conspiracy theories that abound and emphasize instead the phenomenon of ultimate commitment to a cause and to its leader. For example, the Department of Religious Studies at San Diego State University hosts a site with summaries, transcripts, and audiotapes of hundreds of survivors of the People's Temple as well as those who later committed suicide. The government documents section of the university library holds transcripts of the 1979 hearing held by the U.S. House of Representatives Committee on Foreign Affairs. There are also many books on the topic, including some with extensive commentary on Jones's personality and charisma.

1. Why did Jim Jones have power over his followers? Is that power the same thing as "charisma"?
2. Why was Jim Jones's influence over 900 people in Jonestown so strong even though he was so clearly negative in his influence?
3. The visit of Congressman Ryan was a precipitating event in the mass suicide. If he had not visited Jonestown, what does your group hypothesize would have been the future of the People's Temple? Why?

CASE ANALYSIS 1

Devon sat there and thought about the next phase of his marketing plan. It had been a whirlwind experience so far, and he knew it was not going to get easier. Nonetheless, he had high hopes for himself and was ready to take appropriate risks to bring the marketing department's staff in alignment with ambitious goals. He did not have the same flair as his predecessor, but he thought he had what it takes to make a big difference through hard work and competence.

His predecessor, Randy, quit within five months on the job. As a department head within the marketing division, Randy had been an outsider, hired to test market a new product line for the company, a sleek electric car called Green and Gorgeous. He had interviewed brilliantly. He was highly articulate; he knew an enormous amount about doing customer surveys and how to leverage that information in order to secure additional resources to "get product to market," as he called it; he exuded confidence and enthusiasm. Initially he was popular and operations went very well. He encouraged people to work harder for the common good, successfully got the funds for a major customer survey, and was seen everywhere. The problems started when Randy presented the results of the customer survey to senior management staff at their request. He did not provide a preview of his remarks to the marketing division VP, who assumed that the initial overview would reveal findings relative to the one new product line of Green and Gorgeous, not recommendations on various lines for which Randy was not responsible. Because of the extensiveness of the data (a forty-page booklet filled with statistics, graphs, and pie charts on multiple product lines), Randy concentrated on only a few highlights and his recommendations. The data clearly indicated to Randy that there was great interest in Green and Gorgeous, at the expense of other current priorities. Randy had recommended a phase-out of funding on test marketing other lines in order to increase funding for a new marketing campaign in his own area.

The reactions were varied. The marketing division VP was shocked and chagrined. How dare Randy make product recommendations outside of his own product area without reviewing them with her first and getting her approval! Of the six other members of the senior management staff, three were very taken with Randy and his ideas. Two members had no major reactions except that they wanted to study the data before taking any stand. One member was angry because he had received the study only two days before and had not had any opportunity to shape the recommendations before they were presented. He was, after all, directly involved with product lines that had been negatively evaluated by Randy through the survey, although what he said was that he liked Randy's ideas but was steadfast in fiscal constraint for building up unproven lines at this point. Also, when Randy's recommendations leaked outside of the senior management team, one marketer involved with a different product line said that he wanted equal time to do a competing study.

Despite a great beginning, things disintegrated rapidly after that. The VP reprimanded Randy, and because Randy was not aware of the impending trouble that he had stirred up, he was unapologetic. Unconcerned with the political patchwork and financial limitations of the company, he wanted to proceed with alacrity and continued to push hard. Meanwhile, Randy's aggressive and bold style had started to polarize the department. When he failed to act on an egregious sexual harassment allegation against a line employee, he was put on administrative leave and quit shortly thereafter.

Devon, as Randy's successor, had stabilized the situation. He had investigated the sexual harassment allegation as required by law and likely avoided a lawsuit against the company. He had also spent time with everyone in the department so that employees were not demoralized. However, he could tell that the luster and excitement that the division experienced briefly with Randy was gone. Also, when Devon took a tough look at the other lines' marketing plans, he realized that they were mediocre. Ideas and initiative did not seem to percolate up anywhere, and the overall mentality was "what a lot of work," and "that's good enough." Yet Devon did not want a mediocre division. Although he did not want to make the same mistakes that Randy had made, he did want to take advantage of some of his ideas and recreate some of the excitement.

DISCUSSION QUESTIONS

1. Use charismatic theory to describe what happened to Randy.
2. Use transformational theory to describe steps that Devon needs to take to be more than mediocre.
3. How effective would transactional leadership be in helping Devon move the division forward? Why?

CASE ANALYSIS 2: A CASE OF TRANSFORMATIONAL LEADERSHIP

In 2010, Stater Bros. was a chain of 167 supermarkets, with annual sales of $3.77 billion, 19,000 employees, a new 2.1 million square foot office and distribution center, and the largest privately owned supermarket chain in Southern California. But it was not always that big. How did that growth come about? A significant part of the vision was achieved in 1999 when chair and CEO Jack Brown acquired forty-three former Albertsons and Lucky stores to add to Stater's existing 112 supermarkets.

On August 9, 1999, an amazing communication went out from the office of Jack

Brown: "Stater Bros. Markets, the largest locally owned supermarket chain in Southern California, has announced that the former Albertsons supermarket in Temecula will reopen at 9:00 A.M. on Tuesday, August 10, as a Stater Bros. supermarket." The store closed Friday night as Albertsons and, remarkably, opened Tuesday morning as Stater Bros.

The Temecula store was the trial run for Jack Brown and his executive team. Jack had a thirty-five-year veteran in Donald Baker (2009), who headed operations as executive VP and senior VP of store operations. Don had strong relationships within the food industry and was dedicated to helping bring Jack's shared vision to reality. Following Jack's leadership, Don assembled the operations team that would oversee key aspects of the planning and implementation.

Jack, Don, and the team assessed strategy, scanned the organizational environment, and mapped out transformations. They strategized, deciding to tackle the new stores by area utilizing what they learned in their trial run. They met with future employees and explained what they were doing and why it was worthwhile. Jack told them, "I'm going to adopt you—your same pay, same hours, same store, same benefits, same seniority. There is a place at the table for everyone to join our Stater family." It would have been easy for employees to find the transformation overwhelming, but under Jack's influence, the organizations being acquired were ready to buy in, face any problems, and identify new opportunities.

In successful acquisitions, leaders must deal with many detailed operational issues while planning the execution of change. Transformation mandates that leaders seek to benchmark and learn from others' successes and failures. To that end, the top management team turned to an industry peer and long-time personal friends. Stater Bros. leased two jets to take fifteen employees to meet with their counterparts at a Missouri-based grocer, Schnucks. The Schnucks employees shared invaluable experiences. They warned in particular about the challenges of integrating front-end (checkout) systems. At the outset Schnucks had not bought new cashiering and inventory equipment for its stores and later had to perform a costly installation, interrupting operations. Buying and installing new equipment before each store reopening would save Stater Bros. thousands of dollars.

In order to spur his employees to perform beyond conventional expectations, Jack expressed his vision clearly in an emotional appeal to his employees so that the talent needed would rise to the occasion. Over 800 employees and suppliers became enthusiastically involved. For twenty-five days, two stores a day were tackled in thirty-six-hour transformations until all forty-three were completed. While one crew worked on new checkout systems, another trained front-end staff. Cranes hoisted new banners. Entire stores were cleaned top to bottom. An attorney who oversaw legal issues of the merger described the timing of the accomplishment as nothing short of amazing given the legal risk and legal protections involved in connection with corporate merger or acquisition transactions.

Jack led the process throughout, as changes in the organizational culture and environment of the stores being acquired were addressed. The leadership team figured out how all 36,000 items in each store would be remerchandised within a twenty-four-hour window. Prices were lowered by 10 percent. Where work ethics differed, clarifications were spelled out. All Stater employees—new and old—would dress the same and thus appear cohesive to the public. Employees in parking lots would don bright safety vests. Customers were to be greeted.

Job duties were altered overnight. The three employee unions involved were supportive and helpful. Two former managers were chosen to join the new team. Hundreds of employees from multiple stores at one time were given essential training in the few hours before each store reopened under the Stater name.

Jack says that in this case study, some people would see only a case of acquisitions done right, without realizing that "if there is a story here, it is about the people. I think companies make a mistake. They think they're just acquiring assets, but they're really acquiring the responsibility for people and their futures" (Brown 2010).

DISCUSSION QUESTIONS

1. What evidence do you see in this case as to why Jack Brown is described in the region served by Stater as a "charismatic leader?" What attributes prescribed by Conger and Kanungo would apply?
2. In your judgment, did the charisma of the leader contribute to a successful transformation of the organization?
3. Apply the characteristics of transformational leadership as described in this chapter to the case. What was transformed beyond the forty-three stores that were purchased?
4. We noted in this chapter that transformational leadership results in follower commitment to organizational objectives along with increased follower skills and self-confidence. What was done by the leadership in this case to illustrate how follower commitment to Stater's organizational objectives was achieved?

8 Vision-Oriented Leadership Behaviors

In every economy, there is one crucial and definitive conflict . . . the struggle
between the past and the future, between the existing configuration
of industries and the industries that will someday replace them.
—George Gilder, "The Kinetic Economy," *Wealth and Poverty*

Development of an organization that *thinks* and *envisions* is not an easy task. The Western culture tends to focus on action. Superman! John Wayne! Spiderman! It is common to criticize a manager for "not acting as a leader" because he does not take John Wayne–style action quickly. Yet a fundamental responsibility of management, particularly at the executive level, is to create an organization that is capable of envisioning the future environment and developing alternatives now for tomorrow's organizational success in that environment. The executive who creates this thinking organization may not look and act like John Wayne, the enduring icon of rugged individualized action. He or she is more likely to be reflective and to value the insights of other thinking individuals.

According to a John Wayne notion of vision, a leader is the person who has the vision and shakes up other people to come alongside his view of the world. That would be an erroneous assumption. A leader is more often akin to an orchestra leader who listens well and can effectively unite the music from individual contributions. Even though the orchestra leader does not write the music alone, he expresses it and interprets it in such ways that others may hear it. Likewise, the business executive is not the sole creator of a vision, but rather is one who listens well to others and pulls together from others the components that create a bigger picture that she interprets, integrates, and communicates. It is incumbent upon those leaders throughout the business to understand how to participate effectively in such processes.

As noted in the previous chapter, **vision** is an image of the desired future of the organization. It reveals what the organization can become and a future-oriented understanding of the organization's effective position in its environment. One hallmark of effective leadership is the ability to see the big picture of an organization in its environment and to communicate vision for that organization to its stakeholders.

In this chapter, we first meet several vision-oriented leaders and then explore seven competencies that help them and others become thoughtful executives within thinking organizations. As entry-level workers think about making their way up the corporate ladder to supervisor, manager, and maybe executive roles, they need to develop organizational skills such as creating vision and inspiring others toward that vision. Finding good role models is one way for employees to learn how to master the competencies involved in organization-level leadership.

A UPS president and thirty-three-year veteran of its management team, Noel Massie (2008) tells student groups that they should read at least one or two business-related books per month after commencement. Otherwise, these new graduates have a tendency to start acting like egoists over time, thinking they alone have all the answers, when in fact they are not refreshing and broadening their insights for visionary leading! The point is not the exact number of books to read, but rather to remain in touch with ideas about an ever-changing tomorrow. The function of leadership is to influence by virtue of the vantage point from which one can observe and garner a broad understanding of the business context. Massie tells students that a leader has to possess enough humility to recognize that constant learning is the key to achieving the ability to remain in touch with ideas for crafting a better future.

Every year in workshops directed to his 400-plus executive leaders, Massie presents and leads discussion on a particular management book that had been assigned to all present. He then uses the book as a foundation for ongoing references throughout the year. The benefits of this exercise allow for new ways of looking at issues, alignment toward goals, and consistent messaging throughout the organization. Furthermore, the top executive himself is shown to be a leader who is pushing for constant learning.

The book Massie used one year, for example, was *Monday Morning Leadership* by David Cottrell (2002). The following year he chose *12 Choices*, also written by Cottrell (2005). The books aligned the team around the principle that groups work best when all members understand what the "main things" are, or their purpose. Cottrell makes it clear, in Massie's words, that organizations can fail simply because people interpret objectives differently. The first book highlights how to avoid that pitfall by telling the leader to always keep the "main thing" the main thing. The second book focuses on the power of choice that, Massie points out, we all have daily. This book starts with the first choice of avoiding being (or acting like) a victim.

Massie emphasizes that it is the leader's investment in creating a healthy, thinking atmosphere that is extraordinarily valuable. When leaders show that they are willing to invest in the group's intellectual growth, the group becomes interconnected with its members and its external environment. This also satisfies the first duty of leadership, which is to accept responsibility for the welfare of the group and its actions.

Vision-oriented behaviors are directed more toward positioning the organization in its environment and less toward managing employees with people or task behaviors. That is, they are more macro- than micro-oriented. They emphasize scanning the environment and planning strategically. They explain what the organization does and why that is worthwhile. They influence the organization to face its problems and to identify its opportunities. Facing organizational problems does not make everyone happy, and identifying needed shifts in order to reposition the organization for opportunities is work that does not necessarily engender wholehearted enthusiasm. But such is the business of leadership.

This section of the text emphasizes the behaviors common to leaders in senior positions of corporations, including executive-level positions. But these behaviors are also essential for those in all levels of management, as well as informal leaders and entrepreneurs in small companies or start-up enterprises. In the last chapter we studied how leaders can bring about transformational change, sometimes by virtue of their charisma, and sometimes by virtue of strategic planning. Whether change is transformational or incremental, it can be strategically oriented for the long-term success of the organization as an outgrowth of vision-oriented leadership behaviors.

Successful entrepreneurs are frequently vision-oriented innovators who wish to bring scientific innovations to the marketplace. When they can favorably marry their product dreams on the scientific side with their organizational skills on the business side, they can be successful in achieving the vision of technology transfer. The entrepreneur's vision-oriented behavior can focus on directing the organization toward positioning itself well in its environment. The emphasis of these vision-oriented competencies forces attention on the external perspective and a systems approach (i.e., the "big picture"). More attention is paid to the big-picture organizational issues of culture and change. Mobilizing people to tackle the tough challenges of adapting organizational culture and implementing change is the job of the leader.

In addition to those executives formally charged with the strategic visioning of the organization, workers, supervisors, and managers who are leaders can impact organization-level activity by utilizing vision-oriented behaviors. It should be noted that leaders' vision-oriented behaviors are not limited to the organizational activity they oversee, as community-minded leaders, for instance, apply those same competencies to advance the region served by their organization.

Some visionary leaders have a highly measurable impact in their region as they seek to make a difference rather than seek fame. They devote personal time to service as board members of economic development entities, business schools, and trade organizations. They volunteer service as "executives-in-residence" to help guide and mentor college students. They often lead philanthropic efforts in the communities where they work. Some continue to pay employee salaries "on company time" when they volunteer designated hours for community concerns such as education, health and arts. A university advancement vice president and former CEO said:

> Managerial and executive positions give one a platform for leadership to help guide both the region and one's industry—two different sets of focus, each with unique complexities. Students of business, accept the leadership challenge to cast your vision wide, going beyond positioning your own organization for success in its business environment, to helping guide and improve the environment in which you live. A leader's responsibility is great, but the joy and meaning from fulfilling that responsibility is greater. True leaders illuminate the path to success, believing the best way to predict the future is to create it. (Sharp 2009)

Some visionary leaders head companies whose names are familiar nationally. For example, Walt Freese, CEO or "chief euphoria officer" of Ben & Jerry's (2006), began one of his annual Social and Environmental Assessments with this statement:

> It's clear to me that in the hyper-paced world we live in we don't allow ourselves enough time for reflection. That's why I believe it's so important that, for 18 years now, Ben & Jerry's has written an annual report on our social and environmental performance. This process creates time and space to look back at the path we've traveled each year and determine how to stay on course as a values-led business.

The sense of vision for this ice cream company is unique in its industry, and the CEO's stated emphasis on reflection is an important component of that approach. It is worth noting that by establishing itself as a company with a social mission and environmental sensibilities, Ben & Jerry's accomplishes its marketing not by traditional advertising but rather by means of integrated marketing campaigns.

An examination of the components attributed to vision-oriented behavior will assist in a greater comprehension of exactly how thoughtful leaders and thinking organizations develop over time. The competencies presented one by one in each of the following sections are *scanning the environment, strategic planning, articulating the mission and vision, networking and partnering, performing general management functions, decision-making*, and *managing organizational change*. These seven competencies are at the organization level of activity. In Exhibit 1.3, we compared the types of actions that a leader engages in at each *behavioral* domain—task, people, and organizational—in order to be well rounded. We now turn to the actions that were cited relative to the *organizational* domain.

SCANNING THE ENVIRONMENT

Scanning the environment is often thought to be the initial competency of vision-oriented leadership behavior. It involves gathering and critically evaluating data related to external trends, opportunities, and threats on an ongoing basis. It is similar to both monitoring and consulting in that it can be informal, ongoing, and not necessarily systematic, except that the focus is on external rather than internal affairs. It is related to strategic planning in its external perspective, but the data-gathering phase in strategic planning is generally conducted on a more formal, short-term, and systematic basis. It provides the base for most organization-oriented competencies, especially networking, partnering, and decision-making.

Environmental scanning provides leaders at all levels with fresh ideas, enhances credibility, and ensures vigilance with regard to unexpected events. For example, a manager in the emergency room of a hospital may learn about a new medical practice that saves money, or an IT manager may be better prepared for a "copycat" scandal by monitoring events internationally. The importance of environmental scanning increases in times of rapid change, resource constraints, or paradigm shifts. The prudent manager who foresees a midyear economic slump from growing inventories will start pruning expenses and postpone noncritical financial commitments.

Three elements of this competency can be identified. First, **environmental scanning** involves broad and informal *monitoring and consulting* outside the organization, including political, demographic, technological, economic, local market, and industry arenas. Data are gathered by talking with people, attending conferences, reading, and doing research in targeted areas. This element emphasizes breadth.

The second element involves *identifying external opportunities and threats*. In the enormous flow of information that is provided by the environment, what are the critical issues to monitor and potentially act upon? Among many other less important issues, for instance, a manager in the airlines industry may be simultaneously monitoring escalating oil prices, decreasing competition, and a greater demand for subsidization or governmental support because of increasing regulation. Organizations that use formal strategic planning processes (see the next section) will scan annually for external opportunities and threats as part of a formal SWOT (internal strengths and weaknesses, and external opportunities and threats) analysis. Regular formal SWOT analysis is important because if there are significant changes, they should immediately trigger all variety of reexamination of the organization's strategic plan. A strategic plan cannot be considered static when there are changes shown in general environmental scanning or specifically in a formal SWOT analysis. Environmental scanning of this type is more than a formal annual activity for the vision-oriented leader; the competency is part of the leader's everyday activity. Because the senior management team is externally focused and because they network with other top-level managers, they are uniquely positioned to incorporate environmental scanning into everyday communication.

The third element involves *investigating external trends* of significance. When critical trends are observed, the savvy leader puts out feelers and gathers strategic data. For example, the election of new council members who have been openly critical of changes in zoning ordinances may spur developers to launch educational campaigns and promotional efforts and to become politically active. Exhibit 8.1 illustrates historical examples of the importance of good environmental scanning.

GUIDELINES FOR SCANNING THE ENVIRONMENT

1. *Identify multiple relevant sources of external information.* All sources of information are incomplete and biased to some degree; multiple sources provide a balanced perspective. For example, client complaints are a valuable but highly skewed source of information. Complaints identify weaknesses or system breakdowns. Client data supplied by random surveys provide a much broader, balanced scope, but do not provide the level of insight that can be obtained from complaint data. Surveys help identify aberrations and patterns. Together, complaint and survey data can provide a leader with a client profile that is both broad and deep.

2. *Reflect on the significance of external trends.* Today senior managers are bombarded with enormous amounts of information. Lurking in those data may be clear signs of an economic downturn, a tight job market, or a deteriorating public relations image. It is a leader's responsibility to read continuously for external perspectives and to review and reflect on data to distill trends that may not be immediately apparent.

3. *Follow up on the significant external trends.* External monitoring should lead to internal adjustments. Sometimes those adjustments are relatively rapid and ad hoc. For example, many organizations found themselves woefully behind the technology curve in the 1990s. Environmental scanning indicated that the problem was not simply

Exhibit 8.1

The Importance of Environmental Scanning

The quality of environmental scanning is related not only to the breadth and quality of information gathering, but also to good data analysis and follow-up. For example, the September 11, 2001, terrorist attacks on the World Trade Center and the Pentagon suffered from insufficient information, poor analysis of the information that was available, and an absence of follow-up despite previous threats of terrorist attacks on the World Trade Center. Environmental scanning is important for all organizations; however, the importance of good environmental scanning is more obvious when misjudgments of huge proportion are committed. A prime example has been in the U.S. automobile industry.

In the 1973 oil embargo, Arab nations withheld oil shipments to nations that supported Israel in its conflict with Syria and Egypt. Gasoline prices jumped from 25 cents per gallon to over one dollar per gallon. Some gas stations briefly had no fuel or sold limited amounts of gasoline per customer. People waited in lines for gasoline. Drivers on interstate highways were subject to a new speed limit of fifty-five miles per hour in order to conserve fuel.

All the while this embargo was in the making, most American cars had been designed larger and heavier and more powerful each year. Many V8 cars produced by the Big Three got fifteen miles per gallon or less. Had the carmakers not noticed that the Japanese were exporting four-cylinder subcompacts during the same period? After the oil embargo in 1973 and again in 1979, there were futile attempts by the domestic auto manufacturers to react to the new age of limited energy resources and unpredictable prices. There was not much they could do, however, since for decades the entire industry had invested in big, inefficient engines and large cars to put them in. Very few research programs aimed at more fuel-efficient drivetrains, alternative fuels, and other ways to meet the new demands, so manufacturers responded with hastily designed smaller cars and even more hastily designed diesel engines. Detroit's two main responses proved to be an industry nightmare (Jackson 2008).

When gasoline again was readily available and perceived as relatively inexpensive in the eyes of U.S. buyers, the Big Three car manufacturers once more returned to their comfortable ways of old. SUVs and trucks guzzled gas or diesel and again positioned the Big Three in the market unready to meet another oil crisis.

The Big Three could have focused efforts on fuel-efficient cars, but they did not. By 1979, there was a second oil crisis in the United States. Again, the major automobile manufacturers were completely unprepared. Unfortunately, their misjudgment, due to poor environmental scanning, coincided with a Japanese penetration of the U.S. market. The Japanese offered a product that better met the needs of American consumers during the oil crisis.

In 2008, a third oil crisis raised the price of regular fuel at the pump to over $4 per gallon for the first time in U.S. history. Had the environmental scanning efforts of the American automotive industry improved enough so that manufacturers were ready? In this third crisis, it was not only the Big Three that were saddled with excess capacity and fleets of unsold trucks; Toyota Motor Corporation joined them as well (Shirouzu and Linebaugh 2008). By 2008, Toyota had become the largest carmaker in the world and had many successful fuel-efficient lines, but it had also invested substantially in the manufacturing of heavy trucks and SUVs. With knee-jerk reaction, Toyota modified truck plants and the Highlander SUV plants in Mississippi to adjust the output and produce high-demand hybrids. As the leading producer of hybrids in the United States, Toyota predicted that the adjustment in manufacturing would allow the company to adapt readily to the change in demand. Simultaneously, Toyota gave incentives to reduce inventory of its Tundra trucks. The trucks, designed to be competitive with Ford's F-series, had not positioned Toyota as strategically as it had been in earlier oil crises when its environmental scans had seemed remarkably on target. In 2008, Toyota reported its first loss in seventy years.

poor recruitment, bad timing, or other technical problems, but rather systemic issues. Therefore, to deal quickly with the problem, special compensation schedules were often instituted for information technology (IT) staff who were elevated several pay grades from where they would normally be classified.

4. *Link scanning and strategic planning.* Good environmental scanning by leaders is a prelude to the data-gathering that occurs in strategic planning. It should inform

and guide the strategic planning exercise and provide an intuitive check on the more systematic and formalized data gathered. To extend the previous example, the IT industry bubble burst after the new millennium upgrades. Technology costs dropped and IT workers became relatively abundant as the industry laid off thousands. The short-term strategic planning issue for leaders in IT was whether or not to reinstate the former salaries for incoming IT workers.

STRATEGIC PLANNING

Planning is a blueprint for action. Strategic planning is a systematic process and management tool for making decisions about desired organizational outcomes and how those future outcomes are accomplished in order to shape and guide the organization.

It emphasizes the future, astute analysis, wise option selection, and coherence among decisions. Without planning, lasting organizational change is unlikely. It provides a common frame of reference for the organization and defines the feedback loops so critical for contemporary high-performing organizations (Halachmi 2003).

Strategic planning is related to but can be distinguished from operations planning, personnel planning, environmental scanning, and decision-making. Strategic planning is broader, combines an external and internal focus, and is longer in time frame than operations planning. While personnel planning emphasizes the development of people, strategic planning emphasizes internal "fit" with the environment. The data-collection phase in strategic planning is less frequent but more formal and disciplined than ongoing environmental scanning. The process used in decision-making and strategic planning is similar; however, here, strategic planning refers to the comprehensiveness of the decisions and the systematic alignment of current and future decisions in a broad organizational context. These distinctions are not insignificant. For example, good supervisors may engage in operations and personnel planning without ever being involved in strategic planning.

Similarly, some executives are very well connected and informed about what is going on both in the environment and in their organizations, but are incapable of leading effective strategic planning. A strategic plan cannot be the brainchild of one individual—intelligent as he or she may be. It must emanate from processes with broad organizational input in order to achieve broad organizational understanding with readiness for implementation. Leaders at all levels of organizational activity must be well equipped to participate effectively in giving such input.

Strategic planning is part of the strategic management complex in contemporary organizations: strategic planning, performance measurement, program evaluation, and performance budgeting (Haas 2003, 899). Performance indicators provide the measure of success. Program evaluation provides the in-depth analysis of efficiency, effectiveness, appropriateness, impact, and so on. Performance budgeting provides the linkage of strategy and indicators with funding (Khan 1998).

Four elemental building blocks of strategic planning are discussed here. The first element of strategic planning involves *defining the mission* of overall organizational purposes and the vision of the preferred future of the organization. Good strategic planning clarifies this big-picture perspective, as well as adjusts or changes it. Formerly, many small and even some large businesses assumed their missions and visions once defined were good evermore, but the importance of reexamining mission and vision in a dynamic environment has become universal. Thoroughly reexamining mission need not be done annually, but some organizations report that they automatically reexamine mission every two years and immediately whenever there is an unexpected change made apparent from their annual SWOT analysis.

The second element of strategic planning involves *defining objectives* or organizational purposes at the departmental or unit level. Different operational units contribute different aspects to the overall purpose. For example, a marketing research firm will have different objectives for operational units carrying out routine advertising projects; general marketing consultation by customer, special research for development of organizational branding of its customers, media production, including streaming video; field services; international marketing; telephone surveys; administration of its own firm, including public relations and human resources; and so forth, depending on how they are organized and how it envisions its own primary purpose. Strategic issues include the amount of resources allocated to each unit and the units' coordination.

The third element involves *defining alternatives and selecting the best ones* to accomplish objectives. In strategic planning, the selected alternatives are generally called strategies. Frequently, organizations generate many alternatives that could be desirable, but in the aggregate, not all are practical. For example, if a firm such as W.L. Gore and Associates focuses its product development efforts into already-diverse areas of electronics, fabrics, industrial products, and medical products, it might make strategic decisions to go "deeper" with new product lines in the same areas rather than "wider" into new industries that would call for different expertise, different distribution systems, and so on. Such strategic decisions would guide many operational decisions that follow, including the qualifications of any product specialists that would be hired.

The fourth element or level is related to *goals and their concrete measures*. What are the specific targets for accomplishment and what are the indicators of success? Goals and measures should have an array of outputs and outcomes. In hospital administration, for example, the goals of an accounts receivable department may include "days service outstanding" (DSO) as a measure of accounts receivable. In order to have meaning, the measure must then be compared to a predetermined standard and then compared to the department itself over time. When the standard is met, this might then translate into an output measure such as improved financial performance of the hospital or increased cash flow.

GUIDELINES FOR STRATEGIC PLANNING

Note that the following process is not as linear as depicted; in particular, the second through fourth steps are largely concurrent, as are the fifth and sixth steps. Furthermore, each organization customizes strategic planning to suit its needs and will define its nomenclature differently.

1. *Define the strategic planning process itself.* Because organizational strategic planning must be broad and comprehensive, decisions need to be made about time, resources, and the type of process to use. The traditional corporate-style strategic plan usually designs carefully cascading objectives, strategies, and goals with supervisory and managerial input and executive approval. In another model, only the broadest mission and objectives are set by executives, and divisions or units are encouraged to behave as relatively independent strategic business units. An approach such as this might be more useful in limited types of organizations, such as those with members educated to the strategic possibilities of the company (perhaps a structural engineering firm or a CPA firm).

The latter approach above is **logical incrementalism**, a term coined in about 1980 (Mintzberg and Quinn 1991) to suggest that the strategic planning is a nonlinear process that cannot be accomplished at a company retreat or achieved any way except through constant integration. This approach is defended as viable recognition of the complexities faced by organizations. If goals are announced too soon, the claim is that the organization can become rigid when it should still be taking in data and responding to what is learned. Every organization will likely want some elements of logical incrementalism, short of giving employees a feeling of strategic drift.

2. *Collect systematic and comprehensive data.* Three types of data need to be collected. First, the organization should have a great deal of *performance data* that can be summarized for comparison over time. Second, it is likely that a number of special *program evaluations* (Newcomer 1996) or specialized organizational assessments (Van Wart 1995) have occurred in the intervening period between the current and previous strategic planning process, which also provide data. Third, *environmental data* can be included from generalized scanning as well as from more formalized scanning.

3. *Review the mission and capabilities of the organization.* During strategic planning is a good time to review the basics and make sure the organization is well aligned with its environment and its own competencies. At the macro level, the organization reviews its mission and overarching vision. Most of the time this is largely pro forma; however, major changes (such as technology breakthroughs or collapse of a product line) or new leaders may cause a more robust review. Another perspective for corporations with a variety of missions competing for resources is portfolio analysis (Wind and Mahajan 1981), which provides a chance to analyze and realign different services and product lines. Good strategic planning processes always engage a rigorous analysis of objectives and their related strategies. Well-known techniques are the SWOT analysis already described (analysis of strengths, weaknesses, opportunities, and threats), and the review of core competencies.

4. *Identify major issues and alternatives.* The scope of change that the organization will attempt must be defined. Rarely do organizations make a radical shift in their mission and overarching vision. When they do, it is important to be highly conscious of the major shift in purpose and direction. Also, good strategic planning processes

generate numerous possible alternative strategies. Such strategic analysis encourages creativity and insight and is the heart of the entire process. When this aspect is superficial or deemphasized, the entire process tends to be a formalistic exercise with little strategic utility or broad buy-in (Mintzberg 1994).

5. *Select alternative strategies.* Choices must be made. When they are not, resources tend to be squandered, or the strategic process breaks down.

6. *Develop a step-by-step plan.* Planning mechanisms include traditional documents (e.g., "strategic plans," annual reports, or business reports) as well as budgeting documents. Plans may include a definition of the work products, components of the process (the mission, objectives, strategies, goals, and measures), a system of feedback and evaluation, and a system of accountability. In the strategic planning analysis approach, this perspective emphasizes the formal aspects of the system (Lorange 1980).

7. *Implement the plan.* One of the greatest of all complaints about strategic plans is that they sit on the shelf unused. Typical reasons for nonuse include superficial strategic analysis, lack of integration, and lack of commitment. Good plan implementation includes attention to data collection, use of strategic targets for rewards and "fire bells" (organizational indicators that performance is inadequate and needs immediate action), and a commitment to updating. Further, sometimes an intermediate strategic process substitutes for a more comprehensive approach called "**strategic issues management**." Such an approach emphasizes immediate identification of critical or timely issues (Ansoff 1980).

ARTICULATING THE MISSION AND VISION

Articulating the **mission** means defining and expressing an organization's purpose, aspirations, and values. Mission is oriented to the current organizational purpose, in contrast to vision, discussed earlier in this chapter, which is more future-oriented. Formulating or expressing the mission provides the context for strategic planning, organizational change, informing, and motivating. Although it is often a highly visible part of strategic planning, Mission articulation also occurs outside the strategic planning process and serves nonstrategic purposes as well. It relates strongly to managing organizational change, for which it is particularly critical. To the degree that it relays basic information, mission articulation is related to the skill of informing; in terms of inspiring greater productivity and sacrifice, it is related to motivating.

Articulating the mission has both explicit and implicit aspects (Johnston 1998). The explicit elements are the various types of mission statements that are used as a part of strategic planning, public relations, budget documents, and internal communications. The creation of these documents became more prevalent in the 1990s when major economic and technological changes caused large shifts in the organizational universe. In common parlance, mission statements refer to brief descriptions of a company's present purpose for both external and internal use, answering the question, "Why do we exist?" An inexperienced businessperson might say that the company exists for the purpose of making profit. But such a remark begs the question of the company's fundamental purpose, of which one important by-product is profit.

An example of mission statement formulation at cosmetics firm Mary Kay, founded in 1963 by Mary Kay Ash, illustrates the concise but purposeful word choice involved in thinking through the fundamental corporate purpose for the written mission. No word used was by accident. Richard Bartlett, the former president of Mary Kay, specifically put aside financial goals as part of the corporate mission statement in favor of a philosophically oriented statement that was more inclusive. When Bartlett was named president and chief operating officer of Mary Kay in 1987, he noted that the organization was almost a reversal of the traditional structure in that the executive team was nearly exclusively focused on celebrating and supporting success of its independent sales teams, literally considered to be uppermost in the organizational hierarchy. Bartlett signed off personally on the following mission statement: "*To achieve preeminence in the manufacturing and marketing of personal care products by providing personalized service, value and convenience to Mary Kay customers through our independent sales force.*" The mission gave manufacturing a preeminent status in order to emphasize competitive quality products. "I wanted, frankly," indicated the president, "to draw the manufacturing group into this mission so that they are not feeling separate from it—they are a part of it" (Camerius 1989, 12).

Another purposeful choice was the use of the broad term "personal care products" in the new mission, which replaced wording that had previously identified Mary Kay as the leading but narrowly defined "teaching oriented skin care cosmetic company." "Personalized service" was a phrase intentionally continued, to reflect how the firm was known for twenty-five years. The word "convenience" was used to emphasize the centrality of the consultant saleswoman on the Mary Kay independent sales force who brought the quality of suitable comfort to the customer.

The implicit aspects of mission articulation are as important as explicit word choice. Imagine, for example, if transformational leaders, described in the previous chapter, brought change without purpose. Change would be undirected confusion. But with mission and vision, there is a sense of direction even in the face of change. Leaders must have a deep understanding of the mission of the organization in order to convey its meaning both inside and outside the organization and, most important, to facilitate its evolution and implementation. Edgar Schein (1985) asserts that managing the culture of an organization is the most important responsibility of a leader. This is more difficult than it sounds, however, because missions (1) tend to be much "messier" and more complex than is supposed, (2) tend to be somewhat contentious because of the different views of stakeholders, and (3) are not easy to make dynamic, much less exciting, after many compromises have been made to achieve a consensus. Exhibit 8.2 considers a leader who has done an exceptional job of articulating a compelling vision in the "messy" and complex food conglomerate world.

Missions should be challenging yet attainable because they are grounded in the present. They should not be unattainable, wild-eyed, or whimsical products of the imagination. The most common elements of mission articulation are the mission per se; the vision, which tends to be more future-oriented; and the values, which provide the undergirding belief system. The mission is the commonly understood "purpose of

Exhibit 8.2

A Compelling Vision and Strategic Transformation

Of all the competencies, many people think that articulating the mission and vision best separates great leaders from good leaders. The story of the Swiss company Nestlé, the largest food group in the world, founded in 1905 with the merging of two nineteenth century organizations, is a good example of clarity of vision. During the eleven years through 2008 that Peter Brabeck served as CEO, sales grew by 50 percent and profit margins increased. For example, in 2006 he learned that of the company's 130,000 variations of its brands, 30 percent were not profitable (Ball 2007). Before moving out of the CEO role to become chair of the board, he eliminated thousands of items and weak brands, enhancing efficiency enormously. At the same time, however, he closely tracked the most hopeful innovations, bought new companies, and invested in emerging markets. These corrective measures may have been related to the accusations that the company had an unfocused vision. In a *Fortune* interview (Gumbel 2008), Brabeck discussed how he shed the 1990s exemplar that "focus," meaning concentrating solely on core areas of expertise and excellence, was the appropriate vision in order to achieve operating efficiency. That, he said, would have meant not investing in new markets and ridding the company of lower-margin businesses simply to make earnings ratios look good. For some companies a narrow focus might be good, but for a far-flung food conglomerate such a simplistic vision was not smart, he asserted. Instead, for long-term growth and long-term margin improvement, Brabeck searched for ways to combine organizational complexity with operating efficiency. Part of the complexity lay in dealing with increasing intolerance for quality problems and sourcing controversies in third-world countries. Thus, he said, Nestlé moved "from being a process-technology led agro-industry company into one that is a research-led nutrition and wellness company. That's a strategic transformation."

the organization in terms of the type of activities to be performed for customers" (Yukl 2006, 296). The organization's purpose includes the services or products that it is to provide, its customers or clients, its geographical context, and its market niche.

The vision includes the aspirations of the organization, the goals it wants to achieve, the strategies it intends to use, and the special niche or competencies in which it expects to excel. While mission statements focus on the "what now," vision statements focus on "where tomorrow."

Values statements focus on "how." Values incorporate an ethical dimension from the perspective of all stakeholders, as discussed in Chapter 11. Values deal with the beliefs about the standards and principles that organizational members should use to actualize the mission and vision. Values are probably the most important aspect of organizational culture, which describes the norms for attitudes and beliefs of an organization.

Statements of mission, vision, and values are presented in innumerable formats. The format seems to matter less than that they are widely understood and have a real presence in the organization.

GUIDELINES FOR ARTICULATING THE MISSION AND VISION

1. *Clarify the mission and vision, what is working, and key competencies.* Leaders must know the organization in order to express its purpose with conviction and passion. They must be able to positively assert the accomplishments of the organization, as well as those things that are working well. Leaders must know the inherent strengths of the organization so that they can capitalize on them.

2. *Identify areas of opportunity and growth through key stakeholders.* Key stakeholders include employees, customers, strategic vendors, corporate partners, and interest groups.

3. *Arouse commitment to the mission and vision and instill optimism for the future.* Yukl (2006, 298) summarizes the transformational literature, which has extensively studied arousing commitment and instilling optimism. Here are his steps for formulating a vision:

- Involve key stakeholders.
- Identify strategic objectives with wide appeal.
- Identify relevant elements in the old ideology.
- Link the vision to core competencies.
- Evaluate the credibility of the vision.
- Continually assess and refine the vision.

4. *Refine the mission and vision.* Mission articulation is an evolving process though which people learn from both successes and failures and find new ways to improve. Good leaders constantly ask two questions: What type of progress is being made? How successfully is the organization living up to its values? When mission articulation is stagnant, goals tend to be too easy, failures too readily accepted, and organizational dynamism too low.

NETWORKING AND PARTNERING

Networking means developing useful contacts outside the leader's direct hierarchy. Networking occurs through scheduled and unscheduled meetings, telephone calls, observational tours, and written messages. **Partnering** entails developing working relationships that are voluntary but substantive outside the organization or within the organization but outside the normal chain of command. These competencies are important at every level and become even more important at senior levels, in which more external adjustment is necessary and more environmental scanning is expected. They are also more important in organizations or divisions where processes or products change rapidly, a constant flow of information about the environment is necessary, processes or responsibilities are structurally shared with other divisions, or resource constraints require close cooperation with other groups. For example, an audit division might represent a relatively rare case in which networking and partnering would be low because of the confidential nature of the work, while a sales division might engage in an enormous amount of networking and partnering through customers and vendors. Strong networking and partnering competence in many jobs lends to one's perception of referent and expert power.

Networking and partnering are related, in particular, to environmental scanning, delegating, consulting, and motivating. Networking is related to environmental scanning because both seek external information; however, networking is more focused on building relationships over time and the public relations function of the contacts.

Consulting and networking both involve "checking with people"; however, the former is primarily an internal function and the latter is an external function. Similarly, while both consulting and networking-partnering seek to heighten productivity by encouraging people at both the mutual exchange and the achievement levels, the focus is internal to the unit or organization in one case, and external in the other. Partnering and delegating are related as they both concern the legitimate and effective sharing of responsibility; delegating does this with subordinates, while partnering does this outside the unit or agency.

Three elements comprise this competency. The first is *information sharing*, which correlates strongly with successful networking. Through networking, both routine and strategic information is shared. Routine information might be related to general levels of productivity or normal personnel changes. Strategic information might be related to special opportunities due to new technology, a new program, or an economic shift. Information sharing is common and extremely valuable in solving problems. A human resource manager may call a colleague in another organization when rewriting disciplinary procedures. A department store buyer may pick up valuable tips while at the monthly professional lunch for purchasing personnel.

The second element is providing *mutual support* or professional "favors." The adage "you scratch my back, I'll scratch yours" may be applicable. An executive active on the board of the humane society may expect peers from other organizations to support the building campaign of the charity. The support must not come with an expectation for preferential treatment in the regular business relationship, but simply because of mutual interest in community causes. This level of interaction is similar to moving from acquaintance to friendship. The primary "favor" here is the contribution of time, a valuable resource for all leaders. Attending an event sponsored by the other, sitting on an advisory board, or critiquing a plan prior to public distribution are all examples of mutual support. Favors may also include the donation of appropriate resources.

The third element is *sharing of responsibility and benefits*, which correlates strongly with successful partnering. The sharing can be a joint venture, major resources, or a team approach to a task that might otherwise be performed on a contractual basis. An example of beneficially shared responsibility, or incentive partnering in this case, is when a transportation agency (the principal) and the engineering firm that has contracted to build a major structure (the agent) agree to incentives for early completion or quality upgrades and to mutually work toward achieving those higher standards. Several things happen to the relationship. The principal is more engaged in the process and in suggesting alternatives when problems arise. Regular review and progress meetings have a robust brainstorming and creative element to them. Finally, both parties try to keep the relationship cooperative and mutually beneficial, rather than legalistic.

Higher levels of partnering generally require a substantial degree of reciprocal influence, one important type of which is called cooptation. **Cooptation** engages potential opponents by bringing them into the planning process. A discussion of this concept involving the Tennessee Valley Authority and its business prospects is given in Exhibit 8.3.

Exhibit 8.3

Partnering for Mutual Advantage

A historical example of public–private partnering is seen in the case of the Tennessee Valley Authority (TVA), both because of its long-term political controversy and a famous administrative study by Phillip Selznick, *TVA and the Grass Roots* (1949). During World War I the federal government built two nitrate plants and a dam in Tennessee. For years there was debate about what to do with these resources, with bids going out to sell them to the private sector at one point. However, in 1933 Congress created (at President Franklin Roosevelt's request) the TVA as a model regional planning authority (despite its success, the model was not duplicated). It was set up as a federal government corporation. The agency's primary functions were electricity generation, flood control, agricultural and industrial development, and improved river navigation. From a small operation in 1933, sixty years later it served seven states and had 160 power distribution centers, twenty-nine dams, three nuclear plants, and eleven coal-fired plants (Schultz 1998).

Successful though it became in later decades, the TVA initially faced strong opposition from local interests even after it was created. Despite its mandate to help the region, there were many concerns about unfair competition (especially in electric generation, concerning which the TVA's constitutionality was challenged), outside meddling, and economic disruption. Conscious of its need to get the support of local interests, the TVA developed a strategy of cooptation.

Cooptation referred to the strategy employed by the TVA board of directors in gaining the acceptance, and ultimately the strong support, of initially hostile local interests by granting their representatives membership on the board. The board developed the Consumer Connection as an economic development program linking the TVA to valley communities to cultivate business opportunities that develop and retain existing business for increase in the tax base as well as for expansion of job growth. TVA partnered with local chambers of commerce and economic development organizations to provide market analysis. Economic development was eventually listed along with energy production as a purpose of TVA.

Partnering must be carefully managed. Sufficient funds frequently bring with them hospitality expenses, introducing a different dimension to "partnerships." After the utility entertained various industrial prospects at NASCAR events, spending more than $360,000 from 2000 to 2003, congressional pressure was brought to bear for control of non-essential expense (Flessner 2008). Despite internal policies to limit such activity, there is a touch of irony that, in 2006, TVA staff bought cigars for Tennessee legislators when ethics reform was the topic being debated.

What remains clear is that without the positive and aggressive community partnering that the TVA engaged in, it could have never sustained itself as the highly successful, mega-government corporation that it is.

GUIDELINES FOR NETWORKING AND PARTNERING

1. *Look for occasions to make linkages and to stay in touch with outside contacts.* There are innumerable opportunities to make and build contacts: professional meetings, community functions, ceremonial occasions, and others. Those leaders who cut themselves off from these types of networking opportunities may find that they are perceived as distant or professionally narrow in scope (Kaplan 1984). Of course, there are a few rare individuals who spend so much time networking that they neglect operational functions; this is perhaps unconsciously true when people are looking for a new position or playing a major role in a national professional organization.

2. *Provide assistance (favors) for others.* Bonds are often built up through the exchange of favors. Taking time to help others with their problems builds up tremendous goodwill. Favors must be within the bounds of proper discretionary authority and must not involve misuse of corporate resources for personal gain.

3. *Choose strategic alliances for joint collaboration.* It is rare that a unit or division of a business does not have to collaborate extensively with other constituencies. Perhaps the collaboration involves a jointly sponsored conference, shared facilities or personnel, or a cooperatively run project. These relationships are created and maintained by leaders with good networking and partnering skills. But not all alliances are strategic, and those leaders who do not effectively discern the nonstrategic alliances may either squander resources or even engender ill will. Among the questions that need to be asked are these: Does the partnership really add to the capacity of the organization? Is the partner reliable and willing to follow through on the understanding?

PERFORMING GENERAL MANAGEMENT FUNCTIONS

Performing general management functions means carrying out structural responsibilities related to the organization—human resource management, budgetary and financial management, and technology management are key among them. Major aspects of human resource management include personnel policy, staffing (recruiting and selection), classification, compensation, performance appraisal, and labor relations. Financial management includes the elements related to budgets and financial control, such as monitoring and resource allocation. Technology management includes office system communications, data processing systems, management information systems, and geographic information systems. This competency is essentially the ability to build and maintain the management infrastructure and to coordinate the various subsystems of the organization. If general management functions are carried out in a manner that is consistent with and supportive of the organizational vision, the vision is more easily attained.

These functions are included as a leadership competency because of their necessity as important cost centers of the organization. Sloppy selection practices can easily lead to negligent-hiring or discrimination lawsuits, weak or inflated budget requests leave divisions or units starved for resources, and ineffective IT does not allow organizations to attain productivity increases demanded by a competitive environment.

Performing general management functions is most closely related to operations and strategic planning. General management functions focus on the technical expertise needed to administer human resources, finance, and information technology. Indeed, some leaders become specialized managers of these areas, some leaders focus on creating major changes (such as a new compensation and classification system), and still other leaders are only indirectly responsible for these areas.

GUIDELINES FOR PERFORMING GENERAL MANAGEMENT FUNCTIONS

1. *Acquire a basic management education.* All the general management functions are covered in the management curricula of good academic business programs. Classes include accounting, finance, marketing, strategic management, and information technology, as well as courses that supply knowledge and skills useful for performing these functions, such as organizational behavior, business law, supply chain management, and systems analysis. For proper oversight of organizational processes, senior execu-

tive leaders need these overarching backgrounds as they move through the ranks, even if they are able to delegate many of the tasks requiring them. Budget skills actually become more important at the most senior levels because of the discretion bestowed upon them for resource allocation.

2. *Learn the specifics of organizational management functions.* Although commonality among personnel, financial, and technology systems is vast, the differences between organizations are critical. Leaders who personally do not know the rules are less respected and more prone to employee and legal challenges. Some leaders hold monthly workshops for new supervisors as opposed to the common one-time orientation workshop. The purpose is to mentor the new supervisors—even if they are experienced in another firm—so they can quickly learn the specifics of management functions in their new organization.

3. *Integrate general management functions into an annual cycle and regular routines.* Good managers have regular management routines to scan financial, personnel, and performance data in order to prepare for major management events and to identify trends that need attention. Leaders who lose track of these regular routines may fail to give sufficient notice to employees for data that must be supplied or fail to identify early warning signs when things are not performing as they should.

DECISION-MAKING

Decision-making denotes a substantial thought process with the generation of alternatives and the selection of the most favorable one affecting the organization or its stakeholders. Here, we reserve the term "decision-making" to mean making major organizational choices by understanding the fundamental issues and factors involved and by structuring an appropriate decision framework.

Just as **problem-solving** supports operations planning and enhances technical innovation and creativity, **decision-making** supports strategic planning and enhances organizational change. Conflict management, another specialized type of decision-making discussed in Chapter 6, is essentially problem-solving that involves people; that is, it is limited in scale and uses a specialized decision framework. Decision-making is also related to decisiveness and delegation, presented in Chapter 5.

Decisiveness is the specialized characteristic of leaders to act quickly depending on circumstances without damaging decision quality. Important though decisiveness may be, most leaders need to exercise it only occasionally. Delegation also affects decision-making in terms of the level of participation of subordinates. In decision-making, delegation is only one of many options. Effective leaders do not constrain themselves to the use of a single decision framework. Some situations, such as the security problems evoked by September 11, 2001, or the shift in strategies brought on by changes in the business model, require radical systems changes; in other situations, leaders realize they have to adapt their own strategy because of another company's shift in strategy that changes their own environment (Exhibit 8.4). Some require a legal framework, some invite "democratic" modes of choice selection, and other

Exhibit 8.4

One Strategy—But Not Just One

Strategy is a plan to use one's strengths to greatest advantage while minimizing one's weaknesses. Strategic planning is weaving together many strategies to achieve overall success in a field of endeavor. Strategic planning can be complex for many reasons. First, the success of an initial action does not guarantee the success of a strategic plan. Intervening activity can derail the ultimate outcome of even the best-laid plans. As the saying goes, it is possible "to win the battle, but lose the war." Second, strategic plans must evolve with time.

An example of how strategic planning is affected by another company's strategy comes from the story of a California company called Care Level Management LLC, founded in 2001. Leaders realized they had to adapt their own strategy because of another company's strategic shifts that changed their own environment. Care Level Management's purpose involved providing new and better options in health care for the chronically ill and elderly. In 2006, with national media fanfare, the company launched a new approach to medical care with Blue Cross of California. A physician house call system was designed to give elderly and chronically ill patients twenty-four-hour access to in-home care. The strategic goal was to fill a new (or very old) niche, and the compelling marketing message was to reduce health care costs by cutting unnecessary hospitalizations and visits to emergency rooms.

But by mid-2008, the company filed a petition for reorganization under Chapter 11 in U.S. Bankruptcy Court, reportedly because of unexpected loss of the large Centers for Medicare and Medicaid Services demonstration project that was central to the strategic plan.

Just one month later, INSPIRIS, a Brentwood, Tennessee, company that specializes in care management services for elderly and chronically ill patients, made the decision to acquire what remained of Care Level Management in order to expand its service line for in-home care (Hurter 2008). During the transition phase, members of both executive teams worked closely together to ensure smooth and uninterrupted operations. It was also during the acquisition and transferal of leadership that changes to the original strategic plan for Care Level Management were adopted in order to better reflect the strategic plan and core business focus of the new company, INSPIRIS, under whose banner Care Level Management now operates.

The initial strategic plan of Care Level Management did not include a path of action identical to INSPIRIS. Nevertheless, in the business of leadership, being available for acquisition in order to keep the business concept alive may gain overriding importance. Enough commonality existed between the two organizations for one to essentially adopt the strategic direction of the other, thus ensuring continued options in health care management for the chronically ill and elderly.

decisions may be better structured around, and with the cooperation of, the special interests of those directly involved. Some decisions, such as those dealing with historical landmarks and cultural icons, should pay homage to the traditional values of the community, while other decisions need to be made in the chaos that exists.

David Rosenbloom (1998, 354–355) identifies the following common problems that occur in decision-making:

- lack of clear goals;
- excessively rigid adherence to rules or past practice;
- oversimplifying problems because of the specialization of the experts handling them;
- excessive use of "quantification" and underappreciation of qualitative factors; and
- underutilization of program and policy evaluation.

The elements of decision-making include: (1) understanding the factors in the decision environment and (2) understanding and being able to utilize the appropriate decision framework. These elements of decision-making are discussed next.

Numerous factors affect the way that decision-makers handle problems. Sorenson (1963) calls these factors the upper limits of decision-making. Simplifying, these factors help us determine whether decisions (or problems) are relatively obvious and easy, or complex and wicked (i.e., issues that are largely unresolvable and in which the goal is merely mitigation and the means unclear). One factor is clarity, which can include issues that are (1) instinctive, (2) simple, (3) well defined but without a clear solution, or (4) poorly defined. Some decisions can be handled instinctively because both the means and ends are clear, and others are simple after contemplation. Problem-solving occurs most when the solution is unclear, but the problem can be relatively well structured and defined in rational terms. The type of issue to be resolved affects the way decision-makers proceed; usually matters that are predictable or recurring require problem-solving, but visionary matters are rarely predictable.

Decision-making occurs most when problems are imperfectly or poorly defined and nonrational elements are involved, such as when customers demand expensive additional services in times of financial austerity. When the matters are novel or unique, they typically require decision-making.

An important factor affecting problem-solving and decision-making is the restraint not only from information, but also from the time available to resolve a problem. Herbert Simon (1947) concludes that the best we can hope for is **bounded rationality**: a finite and practical amount of information in a reasonable amount of time to handle the numerous problems that confront a manager at any one time.

In understanding the factors in the decision environment, another factor to be considered is the number of decision-makers to be included. Some problems and decisions can be settled unilaterally by one decision-maker. More complex ones require the involvement of a variety of constituents.

As stated above, the second key element in decision-making is the use of decision frameworks. Models of decision frameworks typically include the reasoned-choice model, the incremental model, the mixed-scanning model, and the garbage can model.

The **reasoned-choice model** is the most amenable to problem-solving when the problem is relatively well structured—i.e., problem identification, analysis, alternatives generation, choice, implementation, and assessment. It is a combination of an economic approach ("rational man") and pragmatic approach ("administrative man").

The **incremental model** describes pragmatically how we "muddle through" decision-making as we adjust over time to changing factors around us (Lindblom 1959). This model acknowledges that there are many decisions to make and they require too much information to explore fully, particularly given the changing organizational environment and context. The incremental model advises a course of action of making an adjustment that will require the fewest resources to make an improvement and then see what happens. These small "incremental" adjustments are possible when the best information is on hand and they take the least time to investigate. With these "successive limited comparisons" come the benefits of building on past experience, reducing the risk of a major failure, and building in the opportunity to learn from small successes and failures.

The incremental model has an appeal for vision-oriented broad decision-making in a highly uncertain environment. But it would hardly allow for the kind of transformational change described in Chapter 7. Also, leaders must use caution not to have it be a model of default when a more forthright approach seems difficult or risky.

Mixed scanning (Etzioni 1967) recommends that the decision-maker first scan the external environment for radical economic, technological, or competitive shifts and, simultaneously, examine the organization for major systems malfunctions. The decision-maker can then deploy time and energy to investigate the problem and is prepared to make or recommend a major change in the organization, if necessary. Generally, however, the internal and external scanning will not reveal a major problem, at which time the decision-maker reverts to an incremental mode.

The most descriptive process used by default with many complex matters is glibly called the **garbage can model** (Cohen, March, and Olsen 1972). Under this model, problems and solutions are not necessarily directly connected. It is as possible that an important solution will find an appropriate problem to answer, and vice versa, although they were not designed as problem—solution. The garbage can holds problems and solutions that are dumped into the can randomly and become associated with each other randomly; decision making is thus unintentional and occurs by chance. Ultimately, the selection of problems to handle, solutions to use, and players who will decide are determined as much by luck, timing, and ideological appeal as by "rational" (i.e., efficiency and effectiveness) considerations. The garbage can metaphor simply alludes to the messiness of the decision-making process and the fact that although almost all of the elements are present, only certain problems and solutions are plucked out for serious deliberation.

To understand the garbage can concept in organizational decision-making, an analogy can be made to personal decision-making. We frequently experience major life decisions being made personally in a manner illustrated by the garbage can model. Think about an important life decision such as *where will you reside for the next ten years of your life after graduation.* Undoubtedly a few students scan the external environment, map strengths and weaknesses of different organizations in different places, and apply for job openings methodically. Others, however, may bump into someone like a faculty advisor who volunteers that she heard about a great opening at X company in Y city and that she would be happy to recommend the student; the student applies, gets the job, and moves to Y city and lives there for the next ten years. Major decisions were made in this situation by a series of chance events, and we can describe many important life decisions—and organizational decisions—that are made according to the garbage can model. Bear in mind that we do not *recommend* the garbage can model, but we know that it accurately *describes* some decision-making.

It is not suggested that a decision-maker *consciously* select the model of decision framework in every situation, but rather that the decision-maker be aware of those models in order to understand and shape the decision-making dynamic. Sometimes it would be appropriate to extract the more structured problems from a garbage can and move the process toward a reasoned-choice model. Sometimes it would be appropriate to move the process of decision-making in an important and changing environment toward an incremental model to minimize possible loss.

GUIDELINES FOR DECISION-MAKING

1. *Analyze factors in the decision environment.* Leaders need to decide efficiently the nature of the decision environment. What type of problem is it? How important is the problem? Who should be included in the decision mix and at what level? Leaders need to be careful not to handle all problems in the same way. Leaders who always insist on the widest inclusion of others in the decision process may find that very little gets accomplished, while leaders who rarely use inclusive practices may get much more done but have little buy-in from the affected groups. Good analysis of decision factors allows for parsimonious use of precious time, resources, energy, and focus.

2. *Determine the issues implicit in the decision environment and different decision-making approaches.* Because the real issues can be subtle, they may not be immediately apparent. The problem of a high error rate in a service agency may seem to be a simple efficiency or effectiveness issue related to defective training. However, many other values may be involved. Very low pay may lead to a lack of satisfaction. A strict management culture may maximize alienation. Values only become that much more complex, and often ideologically conflicted, in the policy environment.

3. *Remain aware of the appropriate decision framework.* Leaders need to be able to use either an incremental approach to fine-tune procedures or a reasoned-choice approach for select problems that deserve more substantial analysis. In the longer term, the ideal is a mixed-scanning approach: the leader scans for shifts in the environment or problems in the organization requiring rare but major changes and a thorough analysis, and also uses an incremental model for commonplace changes. Finally, senior leaders are frequently called on to become involved in complex and radically changing issues where an eclectic and messy garbage can framework prevails. Those leaders must feel comfortable and even be proficient in the organized anarchy of the environment, whether technology-driven, economic, or competitive.

4. *Implement the decision framework.* Because different frameworks require different skills to execute well, leaders need to be careful in working within those frameworks. In addition to ensuring that the decision process is accomplished, decision implementation should include an evaluative element. An example showing the negative consequences of not following these guidelines is given in Exhibit 8.5.

MANAGING ORGANIZATIONAL CHANGE

Because change involves such an extensive set of activities, it has been divided into three competencies in this taxonomy. Already reviewed in the task and people domains were managing innovation and creativity, and managing personnel change. Organizational change is the broadest level of change. It involves large-scale change in the direction, structure, major processes, or culture of the organization.

The *direction* of an organization can be fundamentally redefined. As such it changes the backgrounds sought in people who are hired, the skills that are needed, and sometimes even the products or services offered. Xerox once saw itself as a copier

Exhibit 8.5

Critique of a Decision-Making Fiasco: Toyota

One well-known example of a decision-making fiasco came to a head on about January 28, 2010, when Toyota had recalled 9 million vehicles worldwide to fix a possible problem of unintended acceleration—more cars than it sold the previous year.

Akio Toyoda, grandson of the company's founder, came forward after the controversy was well publicized and said at a news conference, "I apologize from the bottom of my heart for all the concern that we have given to so many customers." However, for the news conference, the decision had been made not to address some serious questions. For example, it was known that the company changed Prius software and braking hardware in January 2010 for cars in production, but what about cars bought before the software change? Current owners were left confused (Schmitt 2010). Questions such as "were the problems electrical or mechanical?" surfaced because of executive communications that were considered too sparse. Jim Lentz, President and COO, Toyota Motor Sales USA, placed a video on the corporate website saying, "I know that we've let you down. I apologize."

Concerns were voiced from every corner, not just from consumers. The vehicle with a quality brand was suddenly being investigated by the national Highway Traffic Safety Administration for loss of braking capability. Kelley Blue Book said that Toyota would be devalued depending on the response time of the company. Toyota's stock fell in value.

Values of quality that had been implicit in making Toyota the benchmark of the auto industry had seemingly become secondary to the rapid development of new products. The decision-making steps that undergirded this public relations disaster began several years prior to 2010 when achieving 15 percent of share of global sales became the top priority (Spear 2010). When the leadership made the decision to stop production because of unintended acceleration of its vehicles, they had taken the step that was the hardest for the company to take—at least temporarily interrupting achievement of its global sales goals.

Discussion Questions

1. If the decision-making guidelines in this chapter had been followed, what factors would have been discussed by the leadership early on that might have averted the crisis?
2. Initially, when there were accidents and complaints reported about the gas pedal and braking systems, what decision-making approaches would have helped the company respond to the situation more quickly?
3. In your opinion, if Toyota had responded more quickly, would sales still have declined and the company stock dropped in value?

company. But its vision and self-definition radically changed when it began seeing itself as a leader in document technologies, products, and services that improve customers' work processes. That fundamental change in vision brought a radical change in the company's goals and plans. Change marked virtually every decision that would follow. Xerox still produced copiers, but the door was open to a new world beyond.

Organizational change may occur through a change in *structure* as reflected in the organization chart. An example of this process is highlighted in Denny's 2008 structural transformation in order to achieve better support of its franchise focus. Structural change was engineered when the mix of franchised restaurants in the Denny's system reached over 75 percent following a franchise growth initiative that allowed some franchisees to purchase company stores and have exclusive development agreements in those markets. In the new arrangement, three executive officers dealing with sales, brand, and franchise and four regional VPs dealing with franchise restaurants in a region report to the CEO. Through its new structure, a franchise focus will follow naturally (Denny's Corporation 2008).

Another type of organizational change occurs with *process or technology shifts*. Radical changes in the package delivery services industry, for example, occurred with development of equipment that allows for clear tracking of a package anywhere in the delivery chain.

Finally, there are wholesale attitudinal changes, better known as *culture* changes, which lead to dramatic differences when successfully implemented. Organizations ranging from major corporations and universities to city governments and small independent chains are known to have implemented culture change. One classic example is IBM, which was willing to accept fundamental culture change in order to survive because it was losing billions of dollars in the early 1990s.

As the recruited CEO for a drifting IBM, Lou Gerstner writes of his well-documented instance of culture change while at its helm (2003). Facing unique challenges in 1992, Gerstner focused first on making the New York–based company solvent and stopping the proposed breakup of its parts. Then he turned his attentions to changing the way divisions worked so that IBM employees no longer felt in competition with each other. He tied employee compensation to the company as a whole in order to maximize employee buy-in. Gerstner began a system of rewarding teamwork and fast production, further emphasizing the mind-set that all competition lay outside the walls of IBM, not within. The culture change that was instituted at IBM was an evolutionary success, not only because of good leadership, but also because of the broad base of support for change, ranging from the board to the management and the employees.

Organizational change is highly related to managing innovation and creativity and personnel change. It is also related to, and builds on, other organization-level activities. Environmental scanning and networking are important for most changes in order to achieve good alignment, which is almost always a factor in change at this level. Strategic planning is necessary to institute the change over time. Decision-making skills are integral to organizational change. Perhaps most noted is the necessity of articulating the reformulated mission and vision. Managing organizational change involves utilizing all these competencies in ways that keep the organization adapting and evolving in the most effective manner possible.

Many consider organizational change to be the supreme leadership competency, not only because of its fundamental importance for the long-term health and survival of the organization (Schein 1985), but also because of its difficulty. Kanter, Stein, and Jick (1992, 5–9) point out five challenges for those trying to institute organizational change:

- It is hard to make changes stick. The originators of innovations are generally not the same people as those who need to take advantage of them.
- There are clear limitations to the use of managerial authority in making change.
- Attempts to carry out programmatic change through a single effort are likely to fail because of the resistance of systems to change.
- The need for change may make it harder. The demand for change is generally greatest when the ability to change is least because of diminished resources.
- Some of those employees best at new practices in one realm may show severe limitations in another, which undermines the overall effort.

The elements of managing organizational change include first providing a rationale, then a plan, and finally implementing the change. Providing a rationale for change simply means getting information and making sense of it. The information should come from a variety of sources, including environmental scanning, the top management team, organizational surveys, performance data, supervisory personnel who are in touch with customers, program evaluations, legislative mandates, financial analyses, networking, benchmarking, and visioning.

The plan provided for change must be practical, challenging but realistic, and widely understood. Ideally, the plan is understood in a context that explains why the status quo is not tolerable. It must consider not only the technical aspects, but the social aspects of the change process as well. Planning processes can occur in three ways, depending on the circumstances and skills of those involved. Sometimes the plan is created primarily by the top management team and chief executive officer. The leader is often called upon to personally provide the plan when the circumstances are dire and high visibility is needed to boost morale. The virtue of this approach is that it fulfills a leader's more heroic role; the weakness is that without the general plan being followed by more detailed plans throughout the hierarchy, the general plan will not have support for detailed implementation. Organizational change is sometimes achieved through a strategic planning process. The virtue of this approach is that it is already structured to identify goals and performance measures; the weakness is that the cycle may not coincide with external events and opportunities for change. Finally, sometimes a special structure is created to initiate and later monitor change. This is known as a parallel learning structure. It might be a quality council or a special task force. It commonly uses one or more special organizational planning conferences wherein teams or standing committees take charge of various aspects of the change. It has the virtue of being organic and integrated; it has the weakness of being difficult to get started and being resource-intensive to carry out. This is a common approach for smaller-scale organizational changes.

Implementing the change involves the who, what, when, and where. Laying out the responsibilities provides the capability for technical monitoring. Executives and leaders throughout the management team need to know if the plan is meeting its objectives in a timely way. Units, teams, and individuals also need direct feedback on their conformance with goals. Because large-scale organizational change efforts cannot be fully planned the way an engineering project can, the implementation must allow for learning and adaptation. Generally, whoever promotes the plan is responsible for the adaptation process as well. In recent years, however, there has been much more receptivity to the use of various types of cross-functional improvement teams that are empowered to identify problems and recommend solutions to keep major change efforts on track (discussed in Chapter 12).

GUIDELINES FOR MANAGING ORGANIZATIONAL CHANGE

1. *Analyze the organization and its need for change.* Leaders should use their strategic position to gather data and be prepared to make a compelling case for change.

2. *Create a shared vision and common direction for change.* It does little good for everyone to agree that there needs to be change if they disagree about the causes and the direction that the change should take. Creating a shared vision is often enhanced by making some dramatic, symbolic changes, using vibrant and evocative language, and involving many people in the process. Why the status quo is inadequate must be clearly understood.

3. *Leaders must also realistically determine the politics of change.* Who is going to oppose the change? What is the best way to line up support? How can some key positions be filled with supporters? Who can act as competent change agents?

4. *Design an implementation plan for major changes.* Decide who will construct the plan. It might be the leader, enabling structures, or task forces. Make sure the plan includes the who, what, where, and when elements.

5. *Institutionalize and evaluate major changes.* Change the relevant aspects of the organizational structure. Monitor the change for lack of progress as well as for the need to make adjustments. Be sure to support people in the change process.

CONCLUSION

This chapter reviewed organization-level competencies—scanning the environment, strategic planning, articulating the mission or vision, networking and partnering, general management functions, decision-making, and managing organizational change. Exhibit 8.6 offers a review of the competency definitions, elements, and guidelines. Executives with an eye on macro change give this category special attention and assign it importance. Although macro change is less of a focus for supervisors, lower-level managers and supervisors have been affected by the flattening of organizational structures and the empowerment that was emphasized beginning in the early 1990s.

KEY TERMS

bounded rationality	mission
cooptation	mixed scanning
decision-making vs. problem-solving	partnering
environmental scanning	reasoned-choice model
garbage can model	strategic issues management
incremental model	vision
logical incrementalism	

RESOURCES

Students or teams of students may be assigned Internet resources that complement topics covered in the chapter in order to increase the richness and depth of class discussion. Although sites that tend to be enduring have been selected for this Resources section, the currency of webpages must be verified.

Exhibit 8.6 **Summary of Chapter 8**

Organization-oriented behavior	Elements of behavior	Major recommendations
Scanning the environment Gathering and critically evaluating data related to external trends, opportunities, and threats on an ongoing and relatively informal basis	• Involves broad, informal monitoring and consulting outside the organization • Identifying external trends, opportunities, and threats • Investigating external trends of significance in detail	• Identify multiple relevant sources of external information • Reflect on the significance of external trends • Follow-up on the significant external trends • Link scanning and strategic planning
Strategic planning Disciplined efforts to produce fundamental decisions and actions that shape and guide an organization	• Defining the mission of the overall organizational purposes and the overall vision of preferred future for the organization • Defining objectives of organizational purposes at the departmental or unit level • Defining alternatives and selecting the best ones to accomplish objectives • Selecting detailed goals and their concrete measures	• Define the strategic planning process itself • Collect systematic and comprehensive data • Review the mission and capabilities of the organization • Identify major issues and alternatives • Select alternatives (strategies) • Develop a step-by-step plan • Implement the plan
Articulating the mission Defining and expressing an organization's purpose, aspirations, and values	• Interpretation of the organization's legal mandate or central dominant theme • Defining and expressing the aspirations, overarching goals, broad strategies, and special niche or competencies that the organization expects to excel in • Expressing values through the various operating philosophies of the organization having to do with governance systems, organizational structures, and systems of accountability	• Clarify the mission/vision, what is working, and key competencies • Identify areas of opportunity and growth through key stakeholders • Arouse commitment to the mission and optimism for the future • Continually assess and refine the mission and vision
Networking and partnering Developing useful contacts outside the leader's direct subordinate-superiors chain of command. Developing working relationships that are voluntary but substantive outside the normal chain of command	• Sharing information • Providing mutual support or "favors" • Sharing responsibility and benefits (partnering)	• Look for occasions to make linkages and to stay in touch with outside contacts • Provide assistance ("favors") for others • Choose strategic alliances for joint collaboration

Organization-oriented behavior	Elements of behavior	Major recommendations
Performing general management functions Carrying out general structural responsibilities related to the organization	• Using human resource management knowledge and skills • Using budgetary and financial management knowledge and skills • Using technology management knowledge and skills	• Acquire a basic management education • Learn the specifics of organizational management functions • Integrate general management functions into an annual cycle and regular routines
Decision-making Making major organizational choices by understanding the fundamental values and factors involved and by structuring an appropriate decision framework	• Understanding the factors in the decision environment—complexity, information availability, type of decision, involvement of others • Understanding the values involved—e.g., efficiency, effectiveness, legality, and the values implicit in the types of change or consensus supported • Understanding and being able to utilize the appropriate decision framework, including the reasoned choice, incremental, mix scanning, and garbage can models	• Analyze factors in the decision environment • Determine the values implicit in the decision environment and different decision-making approaches • Select or design the appropriate decision framework • Implement the decision framework
Managing organizational change Involves large-scale change to the direction, structure, major processes, or culture of the organization	• Providing a rationale for change—getting information and making sense of it • Providing a plan for change—practical, challenging but realistic, and widely understood • Implementing the change involves the who, what, when, and where issues	• Analyze the organization and its need for change • Create a shared vision and common direction for change • Leaders must realistically determine the politics of change • Design an implementation plan for major changes • Institutionalize and evaluate major changes

The Institute for Management Excellence publishes an online newsletter. Its August 2006 newsletter covers a reevaluation method as one aspect of leadership vision. "Stepping back and reevaluating is a skill that many leaders in the U.S. have forgotten in the short-term drive to constantly improve profitability, compete successfully and create new products or services."

- "Leadership Vision," *The Institute for Management Excellence Newsletter*, August 2006. www.itstime.com/aug2006.htm.

Read the following story about Xerox's Frank Pacetta. The website opens on page 19 of the book *Choosing to Lead*. Click to page 20 for Pacetta's top ten tips. Would you as a leader subscribe to similar tips?

- "To One Xerox Man, Selling Photocopiers is a Gamblers Game," in Kenneth E. Clark and Miriam B. Clark, *Choosing to Lead*, 2nd ed. (Greensboro, NC: Center for Creative Leadership, 1996). http://books.google.com/books?id=025JkXIK10 YC&pg=PA7&lpg=PA7&dq=VISION-ORIENTED+LEADERS&source=web& ots=2DAfroPqV8&sig=G0p-EYVCHNWDrakOmEM76v1CTRI&hl=en&sa=X &oi=book_result&resnum=8&ct=result#PPA19,M1.

In-depth analysis of the topic presented in Exhibit 8.1 and below is interesting in that it was written mid-crisis.

- "The Automotive Future: Three Scenarios and Their Implications," in National Academy of Engineering, *The Competitive Status of the U.S. Auto Industry: A Study of the Influences of Technology in Determining International Industrial Competitive Advantage* (Washington, DC: National Academy Press, 1982). http:// books.nap.edu/openbook.php?record_id=291&page=150.

Discussion Questions

1. Do you agree with the conventional wisdom that executives focus on organization-level competencies almost exclusively, while supervisors rarely do?
2. What do you consider your strongest organization-oriented behavior? Why? Provide an example.
3. What do you consider your weakest organization-oriented behavior? Why? Provide an example.
4. What are the differences among environmental scanning, monitoring and assessing, and consulting?
5. What are the primary foci of strategic management?
6. What is the difference between mission and vision statements? Provide an example of a value that might be primary in one organization but not in another.
7. Partnering is the most robust form of networking. What are some of its advantages? Why might it sometimes be difficult in some organizations?
8. Do you consider performing general management functions a true leadership competency? Why?
9. What are different frameworks used in decision-making? When are these frameworks most commonly used?
10. Managing successful organizational change is generally considered the most difficult of all competencies. Managing organizational change encompasses and coordinates numerous competencies. What competencies does it build upon and how?
11. Go back to "A Case of Transformational Leadership" at the end of Chapter 7. What vision-oriented behaviors do you see? What aspects of networking and partnering were important to Stater Bros. achieving its vision?

CLASSROOM ACTIVITY

You just got back information about your leadership skills. Discuss results with a small group in your class. The information indicates that you got the following scores from your subordinates, peers, and superior:

Leadership skill area	Self	Subordinates	Colleagues	Superior
		Leader's effectiveness at skill (5 = high; 1 = low)		
Environmental scanning	5	3	3	3
Strategic planning	3	2	3	3
Networking and partnering	4	3	2	2
Articulating mission and vision	4	2	2	2
Performing general management functions	5	5	5	5
Decision-making	4	2	3	3
Managing organizational change	3	2	2	2

1. Analyze what the hypothetical results mean. In particular, why do you think that the different categories of respondents might disagree?
2. Describe what actions you would take and a time frame.

CASE ANALYSIS: EXECUTIVE TRADE-OFFS

Kevin Wang was hired as the public affairs manager of a moderately sized bank with assets of $150 million, after having been a successful economic development director for a very large neighboring city. In his economic development position, he was highly focused on providing the right conditions for big projects, securing the funds and business partners, and personally monitoring the biggest projects to ensure completion and quality. He was very attentive to the city council that he worked for and the deal-making and follow-up that are characteristically common for directors in economic development agencies. Now, however, as the public affairs manager, his responsibilities are much broader in that he must work with the bank executive team and fifteen branches. In addition, he must work closely with an aging CEO in order to represent him personally in the community. When Kevin applied for the position, he felt that he could apply his skills related to partnering with the city for mutual advantage. The bank was experiencing growth, so there were funds to make changes, some of which he felt were long overdue. The executives who hired him had listened to his ideas during the interview process and were eager for his involvement in the community as a representative of the bank, since they had been without a public affairs director for a number of years. Thus, when he came into the job, he knew what his task was: contributing to economic development of the area and creating some flagship projects that would get regional attention.

Kevin decided to focus on personally putting together the strategic plan for these changes because of his expertise and the need to sell the ideas to the CEO and executive team. He solicited some input from the fifteen branch managers, but was astounded at their lack of insight into improvement of the bank's image. When he saw them at a quarterly meeting, he kidded them that their ideas for public affairs were proof that his job had been empty too long. "It's a good thing I ignored them," Kevin thought to himself when he received feedback from the executive team that his strategic plan appeared to be excellent. He was concerned that the branches did not understand the plan sufficiently to help execute it. After all, he could not be a one-man show for changing the economy of the area.

Along with the two key tasks, he took on branding the public image of the bank, which he felt was left to happenstance. The brand he developed was "Strength in Your Neighborhood." The CEO felt that the new brand was insightful. All advertisements contained that slogan, but bank employees were unclear on what was meant by "strength." Did it mean that they had more money to loan? Or did it just refer to the financial strength that the presence of a branch offers?

Kevin knew that many of the managers thought he was inaccessible, but he asserted that his role was primarily strategic and change-oriented. Besides, Kevin anticipated moving on to a larger bank in a few years anyway.

DISCUSSION QUESTIONS

Discuss the trade-offs Kevin Wang made in his organization-oriented behaviors versus his people-oriented behaviors.

1. What are the trade-offs that Kevin is making?
2. What—if anything—would you do differently, given either your understanding of the case or your personal style of management?

9 The Goals Approach and Assessment of Results

In Part III of this text, we have been dealing with organizational leadership behaviors, which are those that help to position the organization in its environment. The focus is more macro than micro. Planning and implementation activities are frequently carried out by teams involving all levels of the organization, led by those in the top management team and by executives. We have discussed charismatic and vision-oriented behaviors (Chapters 7 and 8), and now we turn to goal-oriented behaviors and techniques for assessing effectiveness by utilizing goal achievement measures. Development of goals is ideally a natural outgrowth of vision and mission (Chapter 8) and leads directly to formulation of a strategic plan. To round out the third category of *organization-related behaviors*, we examine the goals approach and assessment results.

Assessment of results is an essential ingredient for effectiveness and can be accomplished in many ways. Assessment of goal achievement is an important measure of organizational and managerial accomplishment.

This chapter focuses on how leaders decide what is most important to accomplish with their scarce time and resources. First they must assess their organizations, themselves, and their priorities and only then can they decide what to achieve. Global assessments help leaders set agendas, balance time, and focus on special efforts. At the heart of assessment is asking the right questions. As Oakley and Krug opine: "The single most valuable tool within any renewing organization is skillfully asked effective questions" (1991, 166). Furthermore, nothing is more fundamental to leading—showing or clarifying the way—than selecting and prioritizing goals.

Yet this seemingly straightforward task is difficult because leaders have extremely high demands on their time and the process of formulating good goals with appropriate priorities is simply not as easy as it looks.

Behavioral issues are important for executives in supporting organization-level goals. By virtue of his position, for instance, a vice president for marketing may sit on the executive team of an organization and be aware of a critical strategic goal from the supply chain area that may hinder marketing's plans. The executive must be able to pledge his loyalty to what is truly best for the organization, not just his part of it. Members of the top management team should share accountability for organizational goals with priorities given to the results of the whole. If the marketing executive focused only on defeating the critical supply chain goal, his behavior could ultimately interfere with organizational results. If the marketing executive continued calling attention to how the supply chain needs interfered with his own performance, not only would he appear to be complaining, but also his behavior would interfere with the possibility of achieving shared accountability for organizational results.

What does an effective statement of goals look like? There is no one best way to present a statement of goals, except that most useful goals are challenging but attainable, and measurable. They become more specific and less broad as they move from organization-wide to unit-level goals or as they move from high to low complexity. Similarly, goals typically establish deadlines as they move toward unit-level goals. Goals look different in different organizations. Goals written by dissimilar executives, managers, or committees typically look different. Contrast the two sets of goals shown below, the first from an insurance company with a regional focus—Angeles Insurance Company (2009)—and the second from the National Center for Atmospheric Research (NCAR 2009) with these goals as part of a five-year strategic plan.

Angeles Insurance Company will strive to

- improve market penetration to 12 percent by the beginning of FY 2015 through participation in more bid opportunities;
- establish closer, more responsive relationships with the independent agents, bringing their satisfaction scores to 90 percent on the agent satisfaction instrument; and
- match or beat competitors' bid response time at least 75 percent of the time by the end of FY 2015.

Contrast the measurable goals above with the ambitious but more indeterminate goals cited below.

Constructing and beginning operation by 2012 of a new supercomputing facility capable of housing Track-2–scale systems is NCAR's top priority. Over the next three to five years, NCAR will

- construct, with our Wyoming partners, the NCAR/University of Wyoming Supercomputing Center in Cheyenne, Wyoming;
- acquire and begin operating a suite of Track-2–scale supercomputers, networks, and data storage systems that are customized to support the requirements of the atmospheric and related sciences community;
- develop and support the software infrastructure specific to the simulation, analysis, and forecasting needs of the atmospheric and related sciences community;
- curate and develop research data sets, enable information extraction, and make the data and information openly and easily available to users;

- develop, maintain, and provide numerical analysis, visualization, archive, and access tools; and
- develop, maintain, and provide robust and portable observational cyberinfrastructure to support field campaign operations, acquisition of data from instruments and observing platforms, and near-real-time analysis.

Although these sets of goals are radically different from each other, neither is right or wrong as long as they effectively guide their organizations' future achievement. However, chances are good that if NCAR-style goals were written for the insurance company in the first example, there would be such a mismatch as to render the goals virtually useless.

SOURCES OF INFORMATION FOR GOAL-SETTING

There are five sources of information that leaders can use in setting goals on organizational effectiveness.

1. The first includes *performance data* on what the organization produces. What are the production numbers (loans processed, roads constructed, checks cut, etc.)? How do these relate to personnel and budget (efficiency)? What measures of effectiveness and quality exist (complaint logs, grievances, quality control)? Performance data can be extensive and highly detailed, and efficiency and effectiveness data are equally valuable.
2. A second source of data includes any documents that provide *information about the mission, vision, and values* of the organization.
3. Another source of information is the *employees* themselves. Because employees form a critical component of work processes, they are uniquely able to discuss perceptions linked to their positions.
4. A related source is the *stakeholders* served, including clients, customers, citizens, or other key shareholders such as a board of directors. Information can be gleaned through means such as conversations, surveys, or focus groups.
5. The final source involves using *benchmarks* with other units or divisions within the organization and with other organizations. Is it a learning organization? How does the company's unit compare to others? Does it study best practices and implement them? Is the organization itself a source of best practices?

Some additional tips on assessments are useful to keep in mind. Assessments should occur early in a leader's tenure. New leaders often declare an assessment period during which they gather and analyze data, as illustrated in Exhibit 9.1. Secondly, assessments ought to occur routinely. Such assessments are a common part of budget and performance appraisal processes or strategic planning. Third, information must be gathered broadly. All organizations need to look at performance, customer, client, *and* document data on a regular basis (Kaplan and Norton 1996). Benchmark data are useful to those who aspire to be above average in a particular market or industry. *Benchmarking* is a structured approach for identifying data appropriate for

Exhibit 9.1

A New Manager Discovers the Issues

Linder Investments is a real estate investment firm with a mission of acquiring multifamily properties in select markets throughout the United States. Linder is aggressively building its portfolio under the executive leadership of two founders with sixty years of combined experience in the industry. Because they have just made the decision to expand their mission to include new retail and office properties, they have hired two new product line vice presidents.

Jane Tyra is the new VP for retail properties. She has arranged with the founders for a period of up to six months before she actually begins to acquire retail properties during which she will study the markets and assess the geographical areas into which Linder should expand. She has also made arrangements to delay for a couple of months the hiring of her leadership team until goals have been clearly set and product decisions made. Jane feels confident that she will then know what strengths she would like to seek in the team she assembles.

Jane begins by networking in the profession to get to know her counterparts in other companies. As they become friends, she learns about their budgets and the means by which they hold their team accountable for profitable results. She interviews not just the founders, but also the top managers at Linder to learn their short-term and long-term vision for performance goals and expected results; she learns about performance on goals related to the multifamily properties owned by Linder. She establishes relationships with both public officials and public sector influencers who could impact the development of Linder's potential retail properties.

By the end of the first month, Jane is assembling the pieces of what will become the strategic plan she will propose to the founders. In it she includes how many leads will be generated each week, details about the responsibilities, qualifications, and accountabilities for the team of two that she wishes to hire, and the flow of purchases and profitabilities that she envisions. She sets a target date for market expansion, including when the first international deal will be closed.

In an internal analysis of strengths and weaknesses, Jane candidly points out the strength of Linder Investments' corporate reputation along with the weakness that corporate expectations are set higher than what is realistically deliverable in the first year.

comparison to a particular organization; through such comparisons, operations and results can be assessed, and improved processes or best practices can be identified. Often the first major initiative of a new leader is a substantial upgrade in the breadth and depth of data collection.

ASSESSMENT OF THE ORGANIZATION AND ITS ENVIRONMENT

We have discussed how an environmental scan is an important competency of vision-oriented leadership behavior. Whereas environmental scanning involves gathering and critically evaluating data related to external trends, opportunities, and threats, goal-setting requires a general understanding of organizational perspectives including the organization's environment. This discussion splits important organizational perspectives into eight elements, starting with task skills, which are the basic building blocks of any organization. It then moves on to role clarity, innovation and creativity, resources and support services, subordinate effort, cooperation and cohesiveness, organization of work and performance strategies. The discussion concludes with the nebulous but critical nexus between the organization and its external coordination and adaptability. Each section asks three basic questions: How do you know if there is a problem? How do you study the problem? Finally, what are the major areas for goals and strategies used to address a deficiency?

TASK SKILLS

Task skills, the finite microcompetencies necessary to accomplish work, include knowledge, physical dexterity, interpersonal capacity, and intellectual abilities (Fleishman et al. 1991).

If task skills appear to be a problem, three identification strategies may be used. One way to understand skill levels is to study the practices of those who excel. This strategy enhances "depth perception." A second strategy is to make individual comparisons based on observation, performance data, and/or work samples or document review. This strategy enhances error detection. A third strategy is group comparison based on data review or benchmarking. This strategy is especially useful for those experiencing suboptimal performance.

Analysis of both task and subordinate characteristics can identify areas of likely problems and point to more effective strategies. Task characteristics include the degree of structure and routine in the work versus its unstructured, episodic aspects, feedback provided by the work itself, and the intrinsic satisfaction provided by the work. There are also the aspects of pressure and hardship and, finally, there are reward structures. Analyzing subordinate characteristics is no less important. What is the level of experience, ability, or education? To what degree does a professional orientation exist and to what degree is it appropriate? How interested are the workers in incentives? Common problems include random, repetitive, procedural, or quality errors, and slow or plateaued production.

A number of goals and strategies can address deficiencies in task skills. Starting with worker characteristics, experience and ability can be improved through a better recruitment and hiring process. Additional testing can be required, standards raised, and training expanded. Some strategies address task skills and focus on the nature of the work. The scope of work can be shifted for either greater variety or specificity. Another strategy utilizes feedback systems as powerful teachers. A final strategy is to improve the linkage between work and rewards (e.g., increasing performance-based rewards) or to vary rewards to better fit employee interests and needs.

ROLE CLARITY

Role clarity is the accurate and precise knowledge that workers, groups, and managers have about what they are to master and how it integrates with the work of others. Role clarity is easiest when jobs are simple, routines are stable, individual roles do not overlap, and elaborate rules set worker protocols. Yet the contemporary world of work is constantly changing and role clarity is likely to become an increasingly difficult challenge for contemporary leaders. Role clarity is difficult to observe or measure directly. Nonetheless, its absence is not difficult to identify. When clarity is lacking, there may be certain types of work that are not done or confusion about who is supposed to take care of existing problems within the organization. Qualitative measures will quickly point out problems in this area. Employees often experience conflict or annoyance when role clarity is weak.

For individual role clarity to be high, then, workers must know the task skills that they "own" and must achieve the needed level of cooperation. Role ambiguity and role conflict also occur at a group level. For example, it is not uncommon for workers to disagree about whose job it is to answer customer complaints or to respond to special requests.

When deficiencies are discovered, what strategies can be used? Fundamentally, role clarity is a manager's responsibility because the division and coordination of work is the manager's job. One strategy is to improve job descriptions. Better role modeling assists new workers in seeing how different work connections are accomplished. Better job assignments and goal-setting at the individual or group level are further strategies. Finally, training may be a solution, especially if employees are unsure of their responsibilities.

Ideally, the overall structure of roles is determined by managerial work design while the details of role integration are worked out by worker self-determination, interactive goal-setting with the supervisor, and mutual accommodation among workers. When role clarity breaks down, leaders must step in and be more directive. For example, standard protocol for many fire scenes is that the first senior commander at a fire becomes the "incident commander" and clearly delegates roles to avoid ambiguity, overlap, and conflict. Even as other more senior commanders arrive on the scene, the incident commander retains this responsibility to preserve the critical work dimension. In the corporate world, project managers and account executives often have the same unifying leadership responsibilities.

INNOVATION AND CREATIVITY

Creativity is the ability to think in nonroutine ways, while **innovation** is the adaptation of old ideas or new ways to a new setting. Managers need to recognize the creative ideas of their subordinates and other organizations and be willing to consider and implement them. Innovation and creativity require change. As DePree (1989, 33) reminds us, however, "if there is one thing a well-run bureaucracy or institution finds difficult to handle, it is change." By studying various awards programs, Sanford Borins was able to predict the most common (perceived) causes of change (in order): internal problems, political pressures, a crisis, a new leader, and, lastly, a new opportunity (2000, 502–503).

Like role clarity, lack of innovation and creativity are primarily perceived in their absence through qualitative means. One signal of such problems is a "firefighting" or reactive management style where problems are constant and solutions are temporary, of poor quality, or after the fact. Another signal is when the environment has been ignored, as in the case of Motorola, which creatively worked to improve analog cellular phones after the market had shifted to digital technology. Another is a lack of "ownership" of problems by workers or management. The disincentives for change are strong (e.g., failure is punished, those making suggestions must do all the work) and incentives are simply nonexistent.

Sources of creativity can be understood from both individual and organizational viewpoints. *Individual creativity* emphasizes lateral thinking (de Bono 1985), which, unlike vertical thinking, is generative, provocative, nonsequential, positive, and strongly biased toward new possibilities. From the organizational viewpoint, lateral thinkers implicitly allow opportunities that generate alternatives, challenge assumptions, look at problems in reverse, focus on one element at a time, and play at and reorganize standard patterns to move past inflexibility. Suspending disbelief is critical to the success of lateral thinking. The best-known method in organizational settings is brainstorming, a family of methods that allows noncritical generation of ideas prior to analysis and selection.

Organizational culture and attitudes have a major effect on the use of creativity and the amount of innovation that occurs. Common features that encourage innovation are a positive attitude toward problems, a willingness to make changes, the acknowledgement of mistakes and failures, the questioning of current practice, and the discipline to occasionally look at how things fit together. These attitudes create a learning organization that is proactive in anticipating future problems and opportunities. Senge (1990, 3)—whose work is identified as among the seminal books in management in the past century—defined **learning organizations** as "organizations where people continually expand their capacity to create the results they truly desire, where new and expansive patterns of thinking are nurtured, where collective aspiration is set free, and where people are continually learning to see the whole together."

A key to creating this environment is an acknowledgment that all ideas cannot come from the top of the hierarchy (Kanter 1983). A brief history of corporate innovation is covered in Exhibit 9.2, illustrating the key role of the executive in establishing a culture of creativity.

Prior to devising specific strategies, it is important to remove disincentives and add incentives. Because two of the most important disincentives are skepticism about new ideas and punishment for failure, a strong message must be given that failure is acceptable and that generation of new ideas is mandatory. Incentives can include time on the job for experimentation, resources to implement experiments, pilot projects, public recognition, and even rewards. A variety of training, practices, and strategies may increase creativity and innovation, such as heightened entrepreneurialism, competition, benchmarking, experimenting, team synergy, and problem-solving.

RESOURCES AND SUPPORT SERVICES

Resource allocation encompasses the degree to which the workers or units have the equipment, personnel, facilities, and funds to accomplish work or to acquire the necessary information or help from other work groups (Yukl 2006, 31). "Resource allocator" is one of only ten managerial roles that Mintzberg (1973) identified by observing what managers do. It becomes an increasingly larger responsibility as leaders gain more senior positions. Frequently, resource allocation is not simply an issue of more; just as critically, the astute leader will consider less (allowing for reallocation) and fungibility (conversion of one type of resource into another or choices among resource needs).

Leaders learn about resource needs through observation, benchmarking, and discussions with subordinates, staff, and clients or customers. While weak performance data may not specifically indicate a resource need, they will indicate areas of consideration.

Exhibit 9.2

A Classic Case Study of Innovation

3M's "15 Percent Rule" is famous. It allows employees to spend 15 percent of their time "blue-skying" on independent projects.

3M was known as an organization comfortable in its own creative skin. If a manager was not entirely keen on your particular idea, you could move your work on that idea into your discretionary time on the job and not have to be accountable for results. Except for a worker's own, intrinsic motivation, pressure for quick success was not stressed because it was understood within the company that risk and even failure can at times spawn desired innovation.

Until 2000, when a more efficiency-driven CEO took the helm, at least one-third of 3M sales came from products released within the previous five years. 3M was synonymous with leading innovations such as masking tape, Thinsulate, Post-it notes, and the film that coats LCDs. The new CEO put systems in place that called for employees who spent a couple of months on a project to analyze, with charts and tables, everything from manufacturing to market issues. With the intent of speeding innovations to market, a new system, derived from the traditional Six Sigma methods (discussed in Chapter 5), was employed for the purpose of improving an existing business process. Known by the acronym DMAIC, it calls for

- *D*efining process improvement goals,
- *M*easuring current processes,
- *A*nalyzing data,
- *I*mproving the process through data analysis, and
- *C*ontrolling to correct deviations immediately.

In many organizations, DMAIC would bring an appropriate emphasis to systematic approaches, but at 3M many employees felt it placed a restrictive harness on the innovative processes with which the company had had such successes. By 2006 the efficiency-driven CEO had moved on to Boeing. Sales from new products released in the past five years fell from one-third to one-quarter of total sales. 3M's reputation as an innovative company had begun to wane, as reflected in the Boston Consulting Group/ *Business Week* annual listing of the world's fifty most innovative companies, in which 3M's ranking moved from third in 2006 to seventh in 2007 to twenty-second in 2008.

Discussions ensued on the real relationship between the new efficiencies and innovation.

Discussions of this thought-provoking dichotomy with wide applicability are found by returning to 2007 for articles such as *Business Week*'s "At 3M, A Struggle Between Efficiency And Creativity" that is online at www.businessweek.com/magazine/content/07_24/b4038406.htm (Hindo 2007).

Resource needs should be based on work needs, which are in turn based on the service and product standards desired by customers, employee needs, and the law.

Strategies used to address resource deficiencies vary greatly. Resolution may be as simple as requisitioning the necessary supplies or filling a position. Problems may require linking units in order to better partner personnel or equipment. Sometimes strategies include finding—or fighting for—altogether new resources. Finally, leaders today must be increasingly aware of and able to reduce or eliminate resources that are no longer efficiently or effectively used.

SUBORDINATE EFFORT

Subordinate effort is the extent to which subordinates strive to achieve objectives and the level of commitment they exhibit in their jobs. It is useful to differentiate among three types of subordinate effort. *Constant* effort results in the long-range production of basic services or products and tends to be exhibited through sustained

Exhibit 9.3 **Defining the Different Aspects of Subordinate Effort**

Level of motivation	Types of effort
Worker commitment	• Constant effort is consistently put forth without supervision
	• In times of special demand or crisis, peak effort is exerted without prodding
	• Workers engage in problem-solving on their own
Worker compliance	• Effort is generally consistent but some monitoring is necessary
	• Some special effort may be put forth in times of high demand, but extra incentives such as additional salary or time off are normally expected
	• Workers will assist with problem-solving when asked, but do not initiate problem-solving on their own
Worker resistance	• Effort is rarely constant; constant monitoring is necessary; disincentives are important in maintaining work production; workers feel that inadequate pay or poor work conditions do not merit constant effort
	• Workers refuse to exert peak effort because it is not in the job description, unfair, or simply burdensome; instead of increased productivity in high demand times, work slowdowns may occur
	• Workers are unwilling to assist in problem-solving because of the extra energy required or suspicion that management will use innovations "to squeeze more work out of them"

effort and work discipline. *Peak* effort results in short-term project completion, which tends to be exhibited through spurts of effort in times of high demand, crisis, or system change. *Problem-solving* taps the creative component of effort needed to come up with new solutions or to prevent future problems. Different jobs emphasize different types of effort; workers generally have innate preferences that may or may not suit work demands at a particular time. Exhibit 9.3 defines the different levels of subordinate effort.

As leaders try to assess the level of effort in their organizations, they may first turn to performance data. Such data, when reliable, provide good assessment. While information may be provided by interviews and discussions, it must often be discounted because of various types of bias. Organizational climate surveys are surprisingly accurate in this regard, largely because of the anonymity that they provide. Such instruments survey satisfaction with training, supervision, senior management, communications, pay, nonmonetary rewards, innate pleasure with the incumbent's job, colleagues' level of effort, and other aspects that affect motivation. Surveys are better at assessing peak and problem-solving efforts, which are necessary for high levels of productivity and high performance.

Motivation affects the level of effort. For ideal motivation, workers must have the appropriate ability, training, and resources to effectively accomplish work. Roles must be clear, and rewards should relate to worker preferences. Work itself provides motivation when varied and is enhanced when workers have involvement. Accountability can be enhanced when direct feedback mechanisms are built into the process. The quality of attention workers receive from supervisors also makes a substantial difference in motivation over the long term.

To improve workers' motivation, several strategies may be necessary and may require time to take effect. Motivation can be stimulated either by upgrading recruitment or training or by enhancing or customizing rewards. For example, many employees would prefer a job redesign to a small salary increase. Disincentives are important, though not as effective as positive reinforcements. But without disincentives there is ultimately no accountability for poor or delinquent performance. In the final analysis, an enormous aspect of motivation is the quality of supervision, whether it involves directing frontline employees or department heads. Buckingham and Coffman (1999) discovered that the single most important factor in the retention of employees (at the transactional level) was the quality of supervision.

COOPERATION AND COHESIVENESS

Cooperation and **cohesiveness** describe the degree to which individuals work effectively and contentedly in groups or teams in order to share work, information, and resources, as well as the degree to which they establish strong identifications with the group and the overall organization. Subordinate effort focuses on individual motivation, while cooperation and cohesiveness focus on motivation at the group and organizational level.

Cooperation and cohesiveness are organizational aspects that must be qualitatively identified through interviews, group discussions, and surveys. Good leaders look for signs of conflict, absence of cooperation and cohesiveness, and lack of group identification. Cooperation and cohesiveness are most conspicuously absent when conflict is present. In a more limited and strategic sense, however, organizations should allow and encourage constructive conflict in which individuals disagree with each other, have robust debates, and yet remain amicable because they value the necessity of examining different perspectives.

The most obvious source of cooperation and cohesiveness is the work structure itself, encouraged by manageable unit sizes, a balance of responsibilities and authority, the presence of group rewards, and the absence of excessive internal competition. Other sources include group stability, shared goals, and pride in traditions and mission. Leadership affects motivation by directly enhancing group cohesion, organizational prestige, and organizational vision. The quality of leadership itself—which, when effective, resolves conflict quickly and creatively—encourages group consensus and inspires members to relinquish their self-interests for the benefit of the group.

THE ORGANIZATION OF WORK AND PERFORMANCE STRATEGIES

The organization of work and performance strategies refers first to the way work is arranged and structured to maximize efficient and effective use of personnel, equipment, and other resources, as well as to the plans and measures used to ensure quantity and quality of production.

There are two important dimensions to the organization of work. The first dimension is to what degree work is structured, planned, and measured. Is it too much? Too little? A second dimension is the type of structure, plans, or measures that are used. In this dimension it is not a matter of too little or too much, but how the work is organized or measured. Exhibit 9.4 exemplifies an organization that has had to reinvent its structure and supply chain performance strategies in order to deliver on its goals.

Knowing when an organization has the right work and performance strategies is no easy task. Ultimately, it is difficult to know for sure how much organizational inefficiency and dysfunctionality are caused by fundamental patterns of the organization and how much are caused by other factors. However, strong indications of problems occur from three sources. First, does the organizational structure seem to reflect contemporary practices and needs or is it an inherited pattern? That is, do people consider the organizational structure helpful or do they consider it cumbersome? A second indicator is the presence or absence of plans. Is the quality of the operations planning high and strategic? A third indicator is whether workers and managers know production goals, how production matches those goals, and how individuals are contributing. Are there data of sufficient quality to let employees and managers know how they are performing in all respects, particularly in areas being measured?

Sources of good organization are based on appropriate designs, planning processes, and measures. Organizational design today leans toward competition-based hierarchies, team-based organizations, adhocracies, and other complex hybrids. Features include more use of external competition and internal benchmarking, flatter structures, more decentralization, fewer and broader rules allowing more discretion, consultation, and more readily changed structures. Planning processes include (1) operations planning with more input and flexibility, (2) personnel planning that holds employees accountable for personal skill development, and (3) strategic planning that allows for greater learning during implementation. Finally, performance measurement has become more sophisticated and requires that better data be available to both decision-makers and line workers through more selective criteria and technology. With excellent performance measurement comes the potential to connect performance and compensation in ways that are more precise than ever before.

EXTERNAL COORDINATION AND ADAPTABILITY

External coordination and adaptability describe the degree to which the organization is aligned with its stakeholders—customers, vendors, suppliers, and so forth—and adapts to changing circumstances. There are competing needs for stable external coordination versus adaptation to a changing environment. For example, some of the dramatic changes caused by the subprime mortgage and financial crisis of 2008 that leaders in various industries have had to deal with are explored in Exhibit 9.5.

One source of external coordination is to have full-time positions that act as liaisons with external entities, ranging from an ombudsperson with limited responsibility relative to public affairs, to all managerial positions responsible for interfacing with their external counterparts and stakeholders. Another source of external coordination occurs when employees work jointly with or invite input from external entities through task forces, advisory boards, partnering, and so forth. Any means of increasing communication aids coordination. Adaptation to the environment is largely affected by attitudes, but aided by a strong strategic planning process, an inclination to take

Exhibit 9.4

**A Quest for Higher Performance Through Changing Strategies:
The Whirlpool Corporation**

Whirlpool, No. 133 in the Fortune 500, is a Michigan-based company with manufacturing plants in more than a dozen countries worldwide. It is the world's largest appliance manufacturer, including thirteen different brands and such familiar names as KitchenAid, Maytag, Roper, and, under a partnership with Sear's, the Kenmore brand. From its humble beginnings in 1911 as the Upton Machine Company selling electric wringer washers, Whirlpool has continued on its 100-year quest for higher performance through strategic acquisitions, buyouts of whole companies, and, more recently, serious rounds of restructuring.

In about 2005 Whirlpool management realized that the worldwide marketplace was changing. First, whereas customers traditionally would think about appliance purchases for a long period of time, the majority began to make purchase decisions quickly when their old appliance being replaced broke down. This environmental change presented a problem for Whirlpool because it often took a week or more for retailers to receive appliances. Its supply chain was not structured so that the company could reach its new goal of getting appliances to customers within forty-eight hours (MacMillan 2008). Second, along with expansion in product offerings, there was significant growth in its "contract" business—sales to builders or companies that sell to builders. Third, Whirlpool acquired Maytag in 2005, which triggered entirely new needs for efficiency in distribution. The company set a goal for a distribution model that would allow it to consolidate shipments of slower-moving stock-keeping units while providing a free flow of high-volume stock-keeping units (Cooke 2008). In response to these challenges, the company began to reinvent its antiquated supply chain system for the first time in twenty years.

Distribution represents enormous cost to Whirlpool because of its bulky product line that needs to be transported to retailers worldwide. A new VP of the supply chain, Brian Hancock, found a "hodgepodge of warehouses, transport depots and factory distribution centers" when he took over in 2005 (Barrett 2009). The VP launched a four-year, $600 million program that would reinvent Whirlpool's supply chain and distribution structure in twenty North American plants, eleven in Europe, three in Latin America, six in Asia, and the network of factory, regional, and local distribution centers (Environmental Leader 2009). His effort resulted in inventory reduction of $250 million per year, efficiencies of $100 million per year, and the ability of the system to deliver product in forty-eight to seventy-two hours. How did Hancock accomplish such a feat?

Whirlpool, structured by region, previously had its ordering and delivery functions in separate divisions. Coordination was challenging when manufacturing was ahead of orders because excess inventory would be sent to temporary buildings and then had to be moved again to where demand was located. Many things were done to bring coordination to the system in order to meet goal. First, ten high-tech regional distributions centers replaced forty-one outdated warehouses. The new centers are large and well designed (for example, one center near Columbus, Ohio, extends more than half a mile, has 1.56 million square feet of space, and has 172 trucking docks). Also, new vehicles were developed to handle product variety in delivery (Barrett 2009). Warehouse internal-combustion trucks were replaced with electric forklifts, thus saving money and reducing greenhouse gas emissions at the same time. In addition, the clamps on electric trucks caused less damage to product (like refrigerators) that might be stacked five high. Another key strategic move was to restructure IT services in order to "bring global standardization of processes, enhanced speed of delivery and flexibility and scalability" (Savvas 2009). Improved IT systems allow carriers to triangulate shipments, meaning that when a delivery is scheduled to a Whirlpool customer, the trucking company picks up a load from another shipper and then moves yet another load back to the city of origin in order to avoid empty trucks moving wastefully down the highway.

Over the years, remaining competitive required the huge corporation to reinvent its structure and performance strategies related to the supply chain in order to deliver on its goals. While the supply chain was being overhauled, other major strategic changes were occurring simultaneously in other areas of corporate activity. This entrepreneurial mind-set and willingness to change strategies has kept a 100-year-old company fresh and in touch with its customers.

Exhibit 9.5

Leaders' Assessment of the Need to Reorganize and Reprioritize in the Economic Crisis Beginning in 2008

Leaders must take the time to assess the strengths and weaknesses of their organizations in a changing environment so they can enhance capabilities and mitigate weaknesses. They also carefully assess their leadership constraints given limitations imposed by the environment. Pre- and postcrisis responses were quite different in most major industries during the economic crisis that began in 2008.

Industry	Precrisis mode	Postcrisis response
Banks specializing in investment (aka bulge banks: Goldman Sachs, Merrill Lynch, Morgan Stanley, Lehman Brothers, and Bear Stearns)	High risk-taking and high leverage activities	Go out of business, become holding companies, or merge with a stronger, more conservative bank
Mortgage and loan government enterprises (e.g., Fannie Mae, Freddie Mac, and Ginnie Mae)	Promote home ownership aggressively (recklessly?)	Promote home ownership sensibly
Airlines	Restrict flight schedules due to the soaring costs of fuel	Restrict flight schedules due to the decrease in travel demand (ironically, no change)
Merchandizing	Emphasize luxury	Emphasize value
Insurance giants	Emphasize investment and noninsurance divisions	Back to insurance basics
Home builders	Build as fast as possible; emphasize high-end market with emphasis on suburban developments	Sell off devalued completed assets to reduce overhead; hold land; reduce operations 80 to 90 percent until market returns; seek dense housing developments in urban areas
Automobile makers (U.S.)	Emphasize high-end vehicles with high return (e.g., SUVs, Hummers); resist change	Emphasize value and environmentally focused vehicles; make radical changes to survive

advantage of conferences and learning opportunities, and a general openness toward doing things differently.

If there are deficiencies in external coordination and adaptability, then the organization may shift responsibility or add mechanisms for more direct accountability. When there are deficiencies, there is nearly always weak communication. Adaptability is best enhanced by creating a learning organization. Learning organizations are education-focused, highly collaborative, and open to change and innovation.

A list of the practical strategies used when deficiencies exist in the eight areas discussed is provided in Exhibit 9.6.

Knowing the status of an organization and its alignment with stakeholders is not enough. Effective leaders must also know their constraints. While constraints are not immutable, they are long-term structural conditions that can be influenced by leaders only over a substantial period of time. Legal-contractual constraints include laws,

Exhibit 9.6

Possible Strategies When Deficiencies Exist in an Organization

When task skills are lacking, weak, or outdated, consider:
- Improving recruitment and hiring processes (e.g., increasing testing and/or standards)
- Improving training systems
- Publishing model practices
- Enhancing workers' sense of professionalism
- Decreasing (or increasing) task variety
- Improving concrete, ongoing worker feedback systems
- Improving the linkage between work and rewards

When role clarity is ambiguous or lacking, consider:
- Providing better job descriptions
- Improving role modeling
- Clarifying job assignments through interactive goal-setting with individuals
- Clarifying group goals through interactive sessions
- Improving the training system
- Devoting more management attention to the area on an ongoing basis

When there is a lack of innovation and creativity, consider:
- Evaluating and reducing the subtle disincentives
- Enhancing rewards for innovation and learning
- Rewarding entrepreneurialism
- Stimulating friendly competition
- Increasing the use of external benchmarking exercises
- Encouraging more experimentation
- Enhancing team synergy in problem-solving
- Encouraging outside training and education opportunities

When resources or support services are deficient or lacking, consider:
- Improving utilization of the resource or service
- Ordering new supplies, equipment, etc.
- Borrowing, sharing, or partnering
- Rationing until a crisis or financial pinch is over
- Devoting time and effort to lobby for more resources
- Cutting service levels to reduce resource needs

When the effort of subordinates is lackluster or inadequate, consider:
- Improving recruitment if employees are not well suited to positions
- Enhancing training if basic worker skill levels are inadequate
- Improving and customizing rewards
- Establishing better worker accountability for performance and clear disincentives for nonperformance
- Improving supervisors' skills in managing people

When cohesiveness and cooperation are weak or altogether lacking, consider:
- Adjusting group size to create work teams on a human scale
- Improving group rewards
- Decreasing unhealthy competition that leads to squabbles over resources
- Finding ways to mitigate excessive turnover
- Encouraging the identification of shared interests and stressing group accomplishments
- Using more metaphors, symbols, and other emotive elements to encourage the spirit and enhance visualization of group goals
- Providing structured alignment sessions
- Holding leaders more accountable for handling conflicts and inspiring group cohesion

When the organization of work or performance strategies is suboptimal, consider:
- Devising an alternative structure by flattening, expanding, reengineering, restructuring, etc.
- Enhancing planning structures at operational or strategic levels
- Improving performance measurement systems

When external coordination is poor, or adaptability based on a changing environment is weak, consider:
- Shifting responsibilities of some workers to hold them directly accountable for better integration
- Creating or enhancing the role of an advisory board or similar structures
- Holding leaders accountable for better communications
- Enhancing responsiveness by creating a learning organization
- Inducing a sense of urgency to prevent future challenges and crises

regulations, organizational rules, and legislative-executive oversight. Limitations of position power include formal sources such as organizational structures and informal sources such as the culture of the organization. The availability of resources, or lack thereof, includes the scarcity of leaders' time, sufficiency of employees and pertinent subordinates, and any deficiency in amounts of budget allowance, equipment, and facilities. Finally, the leader's own abilities constitute a constraint inasmuch as the array of traits, skills, and behavioral competencies is so extensive and demanding. As overwhelming as constraints are at times, the ability to cope with them is in fact the mark of good leadership, as is the capability of pushing them back to manageable levels over time. Indeed, leadership could be defined in this perspective as the act of mitigating constraints and enhancing opportunities to perform strategically and decisively.

THE SCIENCE AND ART OF GOAL-SETTING

There is no better example of how leadership is both a science and an art than in the formulation of goals and their prioritization.

Scientific methods define and classify concepts, construct useful theories, and predict the future based on those theories. Accurate, concrete data about the organization must be gathered using methods that can be routinized in function (replicable).

Some managers are dedicated in practice to "**management by the numbers**," one way of approaching goal setting scientifically. A classic example is Harold Geneen, former president and CEO of International Telephone and Telegraph Corporation (ITT), who wrote extensively on the importance of managing with full knowledge of the numbers. He moved ITT from $800,000 in revenue in 1959 to being the eleventh largest U.S. industrial company and an international conglomerate, with $16.7 billion in revenue by 1977. He is said to have quipped that "when you have mastered numbers, you will in fact no longer be reading numbers, any more than you read words when reading books; you will be reading meanings." His 1997 obituary (Gilpin) stated that during the month before he retired, his managers sent him a typical 146 reports totaling 2,537 pages: "He read them all."

A process called **analytics** promotes all types of business decisions to be statistically data-driven, including the setting of goals and strategy in every area of business activity. Analytics is the science of analysis, or rather, how a business arrives at a particular decision based on the existing data available. Companies that have used this type of analysis for over twenty years include Proctor & Gamble, which sets goals related to its supply chain with analytics; Marriott, which sets its revenue management goals with analytics, and more recently Netflix, with its movie preference algorithms.

Still, goal-setting as a science is only half the picture. At every level of management where analytics is employed, it is key to have a feel for when to depart from the concrete and weigh the intuitive, the instinctive—the **art of goal-setting**. Goal-setting can be considered an art in that action is based on past experience and beliefs, uses customized methods to handle unique circumstances, and encourages passion and commitment. Leaders seek to understand what is significant and what works, use their understanding in practice, and intuit likely outcomes or futures based on different perspectives. Leaders must have an instinctive understanding based on eclectic or inconsistent experience (but informed by as much hard data as is in their backgrounds), must put understanding into action (anchored in explicable reasoning), and approximate likely outcomes based on different factual data sets (scientific), perceptual realities (quasi-scientific), and normative perspectives (philosophical).

Compare the approaches of two managers, both of whom have a reasonable hunch that their subordinates' effort is suboptimal.

One of the two takes a scientific approach. Manager A "knows" that his employees are not performing to their full potential. He is eager to work on this problem and is confident that it is motivational in nature. A pay difference exists between good and weak performers, and some workers are simply lazy. To correct this problem, the manager puts all salary increases into a bonus pool. Employees remain at their current rate and top performers receive a one-time bonus. The top performers (about one-third of the employees) start doing better and more work than ever—nearly 50 percent of all productivity. But Manager A is disappointed to learn that over half of the workforce is doing poorly, turnover is up, and filling new positions has become difficult. He has become even more convinced that lazy workers constitute a large and growing portion of the workforce and that he needs to hang on to his top performers all the more vigorously and simply recruit better workers.

Manager B also knows that her employees are not performing up to their full potential. She has informally assessed worker performance and has visited several high-performing units for comparison. She is unsure of the exact reasons for suboptimal performance. Having studied motivation theory, she knows that major reasons for poor performance are (1) poor selection processes, (2) lack of understanding of expectations or poor training, (3) lack of or poor equipment and supplies, (4) rewards that are insufficient or wrong, and (5) absence of belief that the job can be done well. This knowledge provides her with hunches. What does she do?

First she interviews all the supervisors and asks them to evaluate the performance of each employee and assess the reasons for poor performance, sorting the responses using her five categories. She conducts a survey of the employees, asking about their perceptions using those categories. Although the two sets of data do not match perfectly, she feels that she is able to define the problems accurately by combining the data. The data reveal that the work is not complex, so few seem to have capacity problems; better recruitment screening may reduce this problem, but the improvement would be negligible. Training is sound, but provides insufficient practice opportunities and lacks a mentoring program. This explains approximately 20 percent of the problem and can be remedied without difficulty. Only a few people (less than 10 percent) have significant equipment resource problems, and these problems are also easily remedied. The bulk of the problem is with extrinsic rewards. Insufficient monetary rewards are a problem for about 30 percent of the employees, and wrong rewards (consideration) are problems for another 30 percent. As in Manager A's unit, the pool of money is limited so she must be creative with distribution. To increase the salaries and give slightly larger adjustments to high-performing employees, she sacrifices a position but makes sure the division understands that productivity must increase to make up for the loss. She implements a supervisory training program. It takes her three years to fully analyze the problem, implement targeted solutions, and see results. Productivity rises significantly, and although the performance of her star employees is not as high as Manager A's, the performance of the bottom half of her employees more than makes up for this differential. Turnover has become a negligible problem and the reputation of the unit has improved dramatically.

In this example, Manager B used a scientific methodology to deduce that motivation was only one of the productivity problems. She used surveys for a variety of perspectives and studied individual cases. She interpreted data in light of her own experience and then acted. She did this by prioritizing and customizing a series of strategies. Finally, her zeal and commitment assisted her in working out a long-term solution and motivated others to follow her example.

From this example we can identify some of the skills of good generic goal-setting. Leaders must have a *deeply informed awareness of organizational needs* and the *discipline to expand knowledge or experience where it is insufficient*. Robert Terry observed that "leadership depends on an ability to frame issues correctly" (1993, xvii). Good leaders have and use hunches, but they should test and change them regularly.

Second, goal-setting must be based on beliefs as well as facts, leading to a *balance of competing values*. Though facts are needed, it is through beliefs that interpretations of the proper short- versus long-term or internal and external balances are achieved (Van Wart 1998).

Third, leaders must possess considerable *cognitive complexity* to master detail and order at the same time they master the wholeness and disorder in the organizational universe (Wheatley 1992). As Bennis and Nanus note, leaders assist organizations through "complexities that cannot be solved by unguided evolution" (1985, 18).

Fourth, leaders must be able to integrate their individual understanding with group understanding. This final goal-setting skill is *inclusiveness* (Denhardt 1992). Leaders must be stimulated by their unique vision of organizational needs leading to goal formation, but must nonetheless be informed by group needs and contributions.

Many situational factors determine the parameters of and motivations behind goal-setting. Chief among them are organizational environment, life cycle of the organization, level of responsibility, type of responsibility, leader personality, and leader tenure. These factors range from the externally determined to those closely linked to the preferences of leaders themselves.

SELECTING MAJOR GOALS

Goals are important because they drive people to seek efficiency and effectiveness through higher standards and concrete measures. Without goals, performance and standards are lacking, ambiguous, or unquestioned. Because goal-setting is essentially a meta- or overarching skill, it is related to specific behavioral competences (examined in future chapters) such as operations planning, personnel planning, strategic planning, and decision-making. Below are overviews of four requirements critical for all goal-setting activities: setting goals that are explicit, specific, and have timelines; setting goals that are challenging but realistic; consulting with stakeholders and communicate with them afterward; setting goals that are balanced and related to all important aspects of performance.

SETTING GOALS THAT ARE EXPLICIT, SPECIFIC, AND HAVE TIMELINES

At the beginning of this chapter, we described the goals of Angeles Insurance Company, whose focus was regional and whose goals were explicit, specific, and had deadlines. Implicit goals, like meeting deadlines, are built into many standardized production functions. However, explicit goals are critical for leaders because they set conscious standards and seek accomplishments that would be unlikely to occur without conscious effort. Those goals may be higher standards, resolution of special or nonroutine problems, or progress toward long-range projects. Goals should be amenable to change, spur creativity, and measure outcomes or results. For example, a decrease in the complaint rate is a better goal than deciding how many training sessions are held to address the problem. Finally, goals should have timelines so expectations of progress are demanded (even of oneself) and progress can be monitored. Unless they are targeted toward the big picture and offer specificity and timelines, goals are in danger of being as useful as New Year's resolutions on New Year's Day.

SETTING GOALS THAT ARE CHALLENGING BUT REALISTIC

One of the most concrete findings of social science research on goal-setting is that people respond best to goals that are challenging but realistic (Earley, Wojnaroski, and Prest 1987; Locke and Latham 1990). If all goals are easy, people frequently become complacent. Both folk wisdom and history point to the value of challenge as a necessary ingredient for great achievements. Yet if goals are too difficult, followers will become frustrated and annoyed or they simply will fail. To balance goals, leaders must consider the degree of difficulty. In addition, good goal development is based on good data about organizational functions and past performance.

CONSULTING WITH STAKEHOLDERS AND COMMUNICATING WITH THEM AFTERWARD

Although leaders must make the final determination of the goals that they will personally seek to accomplish, they are unwise to do so without abundant input. Consultative practices allow leaders to test goal appropriateness, glean new data to refine the goals, communicate prospective goals to others, and rehearse the strategies for themselves and others. It is not enough merely to have goals; they must be communicated and understood.

SETTING GOALS THAT ARE BALANCED AND RELATED TO ALL IMPORTANT ASPECTS OF PERFORMANCE

The coherence of goals is as important as their form. One important aspect of goal-setting is the balance of goals across organizational or leadership functions. This notion is built into the **balanced scorecard** approach (Kaplan and Norton 1996) and the integrated Baldrige (2008) approach that addresses all, or categories of the most important, factors that define the organization, its operations, and its results. All major areas of organizational performance should receive attention in order to ensure monitoring and improvement. A particular challenge to consider in goal-setting is the need to make sure that the goals are truly significant to those who must carry them out.

There are three metacategories for goals and each should be well represented by a competent leader.

First, technical performance goals are emphasized when a leader is new to the job and functionally specialized areas of responsibility, environments, and operational production and performance are under scrutiny.

Second, follower development goals are pronounced at the junior and middle levels of organizational management, in broad supervisory positions, in noncrisis situations, and when personnel shortages exist.

Finally, organizational alignment goals are used when leaders have special responsibility for organizational change and a need to ensure that they are in sync with the external environment—customers, legislative bodies, advisory boards, and the like.

A service and ethical focus is represented in all three of these metacategories. At its heart, ethical service means to consider others before oneself or one's own interests. It has a bewildering number of perspectives, including concern for the public at large; concern for clients, for the disenfranchised, for the organization and/or employees as a public good; and concern for the law as the authoritative will of the people. Ethical considerations must be built into the decision-making process itself. It is up to the dynamic leader to integrate this perspective into production, interpersonal, and organizational goals. Exhibit 9.7 illustrates the importance of balanced goals.

CONCLUSION

Good, and certainly great, leaders must have a clear sense of the goals they want to accomplish, and they must base these judgments on good data and analysis, or assessment.

There are eight major organizational issues that leaders must assess. Task skills are the microcompetencies that a worker at any level needs in order to work successfully.

Exhibit 9.7

Bhopal: The Need for Balanced Goals

Union Carbide (UC), a chemical and polymer company, is one of the oldest businesses of its kind in the United States, with a history extending back to the 1920s. Now a subsidiary of Dow Chemical, its goals included diversification by developing products from ethylene and propylene for the manufacture of a wide range of consumer goods, including antifreeze, polyethylene, pharmaceuticals, paints, and agricultural pesticides.

In 1969, the company came to agreement with the government of India to build a plant just outside Bhopal. To keep its license, UC built a second plant in 1977. In 1979, the plant began making its own methyl isocynate (MIC), used in the pesticide Sevin. MIC is a dangerous chemical; lighter than water, heavier than air, it hangs close to the ground when uncontained, potentially causing great harm. The plant was important to Bhopal since it employed 98,000 workers; to UC, the plant represented less than 2 percent of the corporation's net income.

Indian laws restricted overseas management of private firms: "The laws forbade Americans from working at or directly managing operations at the Bhopal plant. Instead, it operated under the direction of an Indian affiliate in which Carbide held a 50.9 percent interest" (Steiner 1991, 31). Under Indian rules, the last American manager licensed by India to be at the plant left in 1982.

On December 3, 1984, an epic tragedy occurred at the plant. There is still debate about what exactly transpired, but several facts are known. The plant was partially shut for maintenance. That night, workers complained that their eyes were stinging. A small leak was found but resolution was delayed because small leaks were common and it was employee break time. Meanwhile, water found its way into an MIC storage tank. The pressure forced a valve open, leading to the escape of forty tons of MIC, which blanketed the area. Almost 4,000 people died, and thousands more were injured in the largest industrial accident ever (Kurzman 1987). What went wrong?

In 1989, a strategic audit examined internal strengths and weaknesses and external opportunities and threats. Internal strengths included the fact that UC was known for adherence to safety standards "on a worldwide level and maintenance of an accident record substantially below the industry average." An internal weakness, however, was poor management of the Bhopal plant. Management took cost-cutting measures resulting in "the substantial reduction in qualified workers." The strategic audit noted that the operation manual says to KEEP WATER AWAY FROM MIC, but this was not enforced on the night of the tragedy (Trotter, Day, and Love 1989, 442). Management allowed deteriorating equipment, attrition among qualified workers, and lowered hiring standards. In 1982, ten safety deficiencies were discovered. By June 1984, UC headquarters was told that "most" of the problems had been rectified (440). UC downplayed the different rules between the two nations and focused on company goals such as profit margins and an attractive labor market.

External opportunities for UC included the fact that India was a poor nation eager for employment and the influx of cash. The chosen site was centrally situated near a rail spur and large water source, with sufficient energy. The plant quickly became surrounded by an endless supply of workers who moved to Bhopal in hopes of a job. One external threat was that there were few land use control measures preventing citizens from locating in shanties too close to the production plant and its emissions; another threat was the government ruling that no U.S. technicians or engineers could work at the plant from license renewal in 1982 through the plant closure date in 1984.

A full range of goals must include social goals. Ultimately, UC did not set goals at the Bhopal plant that were balanced in terms of safety, environment, community and long-term sustainability: "Central management should strike a balance between the competing demands of stakeholders and the firm's profit-seeking goals" (Trotter, Day, and Love 1989, 446). The Indian public was not educated for proper response in the event of leakage, although "safety standards of transnational corporations should be the same abroad as well as at home" (Ramanan 1992).

Role clarity is the accurate and precise knowledge that workers, groups, and managers have about which activities, functions, and roles they are to accomplish and how their work integrates with that of others. Creativity is the ability to think about and do things in nonroutine ways, while innovation is the adaptation of new ideas or ways of doing things (from any source) to a new setting. Resources and support services encompass the degree to which the workers or units have the tools, equipment, personnel, facilities, and funds to accomplish work or to acquire necessary information or help from other work groups. Subordinate effort is the extent to which subordinates strive to achieve work-related objectives and the level of commitment they have to their jobs. Cooperation and cohesiveness are the degree to which individuals effectively and contentedly interact in order to share work, information, and resources, as well as the degree to which they establish strong identifications with the group and the overall organization. The organization of the work refers to the way that work is arranged and structured to maximize efficient and effective use of resources, as well as to plans and measures used to ensure quantity and quality of production. External coordination and adaptability are the degree to which the organization is aligned with its external constituents—customers, competitors, and the like—and adapts to changing circumstances.

The overall competency of assessment can be seen in more specific behavioral competencies, such as monitoring and assessing work, consulting, and environmental scanning, which will be reviewed in upcoming chapters.

Like other major dynamics of leadership, effective goal-setting and prioritization—along with the self-discipline to fulfill one's aspirations—seem to be simple common sense, and they are. However, in practice they are all too often "more honored in the breach than in the observance."

Goal-setting is an art that requires personal judgments, customized responses, and intuitively based actions. Good goal-setting is also a science anchored in the discipline of data collection and analysis, implicit hypothesis, theory testing, and prediction.

There are four ideals to strive for in goal-setting. Goals should be explicit, specific, and have concrete timelines; they should be challenging but realistic; they should be related to all important aspects of the organization's performance; and leaders should be sure to consult widely in setting goals and to communicate them afterward. Particular attention should focus on goal balance. All leaders need to be able to integrate the ethical framework of goal-setting and decision-making that will create buy-in and trust.

Oversimplifying for clarity, effective leaders must set goals and do so consciously. John F. Kennedy stated that effort and courage are not enough without purpose and direction. Leaders must make sure that their goals are informed and balanced. Obvious though it may sound, leaders must act on their goals or revise them. Indeed, it is questionable whether a person can even be considered a leader if he or she does not conscientiously set, balance, and achieve goals.

KEY TERMS

analytics	learning organization
art of goal-setting	management by the numbers
balanced scorecard	resource allocation
cohesiveness	role clarity
innovation vs. creativity	

RESOURCES

Because Peter Senge's work is highly regarded for its contribution to the understanding of the learning organization, students of leadership should be familiar with creating and sustaining a learning organization. Different team members should be assigned to one portion of the topics, ranging from a biography of Senge to the five disciplines that are central to the learning organization, covered in this article from Infed.org, the encyclopedia of information education.

- Mark K. Smith, "Peter Senge and the Learning Organization," *The Encyclopedia of Informational Education.* www.infed.org/thinkers/senge.htm.

Is there a particular organizational structure that is best for innovation?

- Rolf-Christian Wentz, "The Organizational Structure of Innovation," *The Innovation Machine.* www.the-innovation-machine.com/?p=83.

Babson Executive Education released a publication titled "Competing on Analytics." Many noteworthy cases are discussed, including one about Harrah's famous pricing system and another regarding Amazon.com's investigation of whether to advertise on television.

- Thomas H. Davenport, Don Cohen, and Al Jacobson, "Competing on Analytics," *Working Knowledge Research Report*, May 2005. www.babsonknowledge.org/analytics.pdf.

DISCUSSION QUESTIONS

1. What general sources can leaders use for getting information about the organization in its environment? That is, where do leaders get the information to analyze how their organization is doing?
2. Goal-setting requires a general understanding of organizational perspectives including the organization' environment. What organizational perspectives should be taken into consideration?
3. Give an example of a well-stated organizational goal. Defend why it is a good example according to the criteria.
4. Why is it claimed that goal-setting is both a science and an art?
5. What are some tips for leaders about gathering global assessments?
6. What types of constraints do leaders need to assess?
7. Discuss two systems for ensuring balanced goals within an organization.
8. Although constraints are normally discussed in terms of their negative elements, how can constraints be viewed more positively when understood and mastered? That is, how can challenges be turned into advantages or opportunities? For example, how can legal and contractual constraints actually become a source of administrative power when detailed knowledge is achieved?
9. What is a learning organization?

CLASSROOM ACTIVITIES

For these first two questions, interview managers or executives in the community as indicated. Report results to the class.

1. Interview one or more people in executive or senior management positions. Ask what goals they have set for themselves and how they came to do so.
2. Interview a manager or executive about assessing his or her agency in terms of the eight organizational domains.

For the remaining questions, one half of the class should take one position, and the other half a different position.

3. Agree or disagree with the following statement: "Leaders have a job to do and whining about constraints is not part of it. Leaders need to do their best with the resources available, reduce constraints over time, and advocate for their agency or unit without becoming angry. Leaders who are chronically unable to meet challenges or chronically angry about the constraints that they face (real or exaggerated) should probably move on to another position."
4. Do you think that leadership (in general) is more an art or a science? Why? Is goal-setting as a specific leadership activity related to, say, assessment, leader actions and behaviors, and evaluation of leaders?
5. There is some controversy in the leadership literature about whether technical goals should be a part of the leader's personal repertoire. One school of thought holds that "we have too many managers and not enough leaders!" On the other hand, many leaders are directly responsible for technical matters. What is your opinion?
6. There is little disagreement that follower development is important but many leaders seem to neglect it. Speculate about why this is. What examples can you think of regarding successful follower development by organizational leaders?
7. There is little disagreement that organizational alignment is important but many leaders seem to neglect it, at least the more difficult aspects related to change. Speculate about the benefits, risks, and difficulties associated with organizational alignment.

CASE ANALYSIS 1: A MEDIOCRE UNIT

A new supervisor, Tom, takes over a unit that provides vehicle maintenance services. He has been promoted from a line position, having completed his bachelor's degree and a management training program. He has a good reputation in the unit and is accepted as a good choice for the position. In his new role, Tom has talked with his new subordinates recently as well as visited with a number of customers, all of whom are internal to the organization because of the unit's function. He has also visited several other similar units in the region. His general assessment is that the unit is about average as such vehicle maintenance operations go. However, he would like it to be above average for two reasons. First, nationally there has been a wave of outsourcing of all vehicle services and he wants to discourage this through exceptional performance. Second, he wants to have a reputation as an excellent manager.

Some areas seem acceptable at this point. The unit gets adequate resources and support, there is no significant internal conflict, and the unit is providing the general services required by the organization. However, Tom has noted that the turnaround time for repairs is slow, errors are a bit high, and unusual or special problems tend to be rejected by mechanics who treat them as "not my job" (by labeling them as unfixable or requiring expensive full-systems replacement for small malfunctions). The current system assumes a next-job-available system of assignment.

The strengths of this system are job enrichment, cross-functionality, and organizational simplicity (requiring less supervisory time). The weaknesses are less specialization and slower performance per job. The work in the unit is hard and the workers are not lazy; however, they tend to plod through their jobs. The system is based largely on seniority, so there is little financial incentive to be exceptional, and Tom is unlikely to be able to change this. Although average job completion time statistics are available for the industry, they are not used in the unit because workers view them as oppressive.

DISCUSSION QUESTIONS

1. How can Tom identify whether task skills are an area that needs to be addressed in a significant way? What types of task skill problems might be identified?
2. Other likely culprits of low productivity in Tom's unit are creativity and innovation and also role clarity. What are the symptoms? How could Tom handle this problem?
3. If Tom's unit is to improve, subordinate and group effort will also have to improve. How do we know this? What challenges does Tom face? Discuss how Tom might improve subordinate and group effort in his unit.

CASE ANALYSIS 2: A DEPARTMENT MUST PREPARE FOR A PARADIGM SHIFT

Mary has been the director of a human resources department at Columbia Cabinets for five years and has been in the business for twenty. Since starting at Columbia Cabinets, she has focused on consistency of employee effort, including in her own department, through task skills, role clarity, and motivation, and also on group effort through cohesiveness and cooperation. She has also worked to make sure that adequate resources are available for her department. However, major changes are occurring in the field, and Mary realizes that she needs to reexamine her department as well as how human resources is assisting managers.

New demands for accountability affect employees at Columbia Cabinets in several ways. First, prices obtained for standardized cabinets have been reduced because of increased foreclosures and a downturn in housing sales. Second, higher accountability standards are expected from suppliers to the industry in terms of timeliness of delivery and product quality. Third, higher productivity standards for savings in personnel cost to offset gains in materials cost are expected throughout the industry.

DISCUSSION QUESTIONS

1. Some sources of possible information are more valuable than others in this scenario. How should Mary collect information to help her assess what the goals and priorities should be? Which sources of information are more important and why?
2. Why are task skills and role clarity, normally the building blocks of performance, relatively unimportant *initially* in this case?
3. Discuss the ramifications of the major changes in the field on resources and performance strategies. Even as Mary collects information about how to address the fundamental changes that are likely, how can she be sure that employees are involved in the process as well and beginning to appreciate the scope of change that may be needed?

LEADING AND MANAGING HUMAN CAPITAL

IV

The notion of human capital goes back to pioneer economist Adam Smith and his *Wealth of Nations* (1776). Smith identified four kinds of fixed capital: machines, buildings, improvements of land, and human capital. Human capital was considered a means for production. Smith affirmed that the talents of human labor could be improved through education or training, which represented a cost that could be returned through an increased profit resulting from that improved labor. Theodore Schultz (1963), who earned the 1979 Nobel Prize for Economics, established the role of human capital in economic development, referring to education, talent, energy, and will. From an initial research focus on farming in developing countries, he drove the point home that investments in education can affect the economy as a whole because development of *people* is the root of economic growth.

A leader's effectiveness depends, in part, on the ability to employ principles of human capital theory well. A basic idea of the theory today is that worthy investments in human capital can lead to an improved talent base that in turn may lead to advances in the organization and improved societal results. It is therefore considered incumbent upon a leader at any level of the organization to strive to use the qualified talents of all to improve the overall human condition.

Personnel costs, including benefits, constitute 70 percent to 90 percent of budgets in almost every form of business. Further, it is estimated that over 80 percent of market value is allocated to intangible assets, with the bulk of those assets being human talent in its various forms, such as strategic knowledge and the ability to respond creatively to problems. It is said that an organization's only hope for competitive advantage is in having the right employees. What constitutes the "right employee" is not a simple equation of ability to carry out a task, but also includes a variety of intangibles such as thinking beyond the current job, behaving ethically, and developing oneself for leadership.

Attention to this essential business topic called human capital has come a long way in the 100 years since the emphasis on scientific management (finding the one best way to do a task in order to increase labor productivity). For example, there is human capital management software on virtually every enterprise resource planning (ERP) system, whether in Oracle or SAP. There is a human capital management journal and organization. Federal agencies can even follow a human capital balanced scorecard released by the Office of Personnel Management or a model of strategic human capital management released by the Government Accounting Office to help federal agency leaders better manage their most important asset.

Reliance on human capital is America's hope for successfully competing in the global marketplace. William Brock, former U.S. labor secretary under President Reagan, pronounced that if companies in every country in the world can buy "idiot-proof machinery" to compensate for workers with terribly deficient skills, and "if there are people in other parts of the world who will work for $5 per day and they have the same equipment as Americans who want $15 per hour, either we have to change the way people work here (not only work harder, but smarter, more effectively) or we have to compete on the basis of wages" (Hershberg 1996). If we are to change the way people work, we must constantly analyze the kinds of skills that employees need in organizations such as those where middle management has been cut in an effort to make the organization "lean." If the nation's human capital development system, both in education and in organizations, is not producing persons for the job market who are quick learners and problem-solvers, then it is imperative that the system be continuously improved. This section of the textbook sparks a discussion to that end.

10 Gender, Ethnicity, and Culture

> *In Iroquois society, leaders are encouraged to remember*
> *seven generations in the past and consider seven generations*
> *in the future when making decisions that affect the people.*
> —Wilma Mankiller, first female chief of the Cherokee Nation (1945–2010)

Leaders today are immersed in every perspective of diversity. Successful leaders understand the need to engage everyone, regardless of gender, ethnicity, culture, national origin, age, socioeconomic group, sexual orientation, religion, familial status, veteran status, or disability. There are complexities involved in working across differences. We know that the opportunity for success is enhanced when a leader has thought through these complexities in advance.

Part IV, the final portion of this text, introduces leadership issues associated directly with human capital. Rather than examining leadership theory to explain or prescribe behavior, we look at significant demographics of human capital as they relate to leaders. More than 2,500 years ago, Confucius said that all people are basically the same—just their habits differ (Steers and Sanchez-Runde 2002). Given the commonalities of the human condition, indeed we all have more in common than that which is different. We need clean water, food, and sleep; we crave love; we want a social existence with friendship (see the movie *March of the Penguins* if you think this phenomenon is limited to the human condition). We seek achievement and respect from others; we enjoy music; we want to understand why we exist on earth; and virtually every faith has a "Golden Rule" in its teachings. To focus on both our common humanness and our differences is healthy, but to ignore one at the expense of the other limits our efforts to be sensitive as well as to harness diversity.

Consider *chanoyu*, the Japanese tea ceremony. The ritual brings together the principles of respect, harmony, purity, and tranquility. It is filled with complexity and is taught by masters who have studied tea throughout their lives. Students of tea learn to bow properly as they receive the cup (*chawan*) with the right hand, and they slurp the last sip to communicate to the host how much they enjoyed the bitter, powdered tea. The chawan is then wiped using the right hand, turned counterclockwise, and returned respectfully. The custom and motions of chanoyu are unique, but the common humanness—a desire for respect, harmony, purity, and tranquility—is universal.

In the same vein of thought, the cofounder of Honda Motor Company, Takeo Fujisawa, spoke with authenticity about the common human condition when he said that Japanese and American managers are 95 percent the same, but differ in all important respects (Steers and Sanchez-Runde 2002). That quote resonates with a truth that speaks to the many factors of demographic diversity. Although we share far more in common than we differ, it is that 5 percent difference that can make diversity a tremendous asset or lead to infighting, intolerance, and dysfunctionality. Leaders play a key role in ensuring that diversity is a strength rather than a weakness.

A wide variety of demographic variables could have been mentioned in the first paragraph of this chapter on human capital because of the many important differences within the workforce that leaders must recognize. The bottom line in every case, regardless of the variable, is for the leader to always exercise caution not to label employees in demographic groups according to any perceived *negative* characteristics of their particular group. Variety in human capital, and an accompanying awareness of that variety, serves to inspire all to achieve a level of performance that brings about the best possible organizational results.

An example of one demographic is age. The older worker, whether termed the baby boomer or silver hair, is an important demographic for young leaders to understand. Similarly, the young workers of Generation Y, born into an age of instant communication technologies, are important for older leaders to understand. Whatever the variable, a leader must resist all temptation to sort employees by socioeconomic class or education or any other grouping and then label them according to their "stereotypical faults" (Ryan 2007). Better understanding of leadership issues for certain demographics brings macrolevel insight into groupings and opens the door for appreciating complexities. However, it does not follow that all *individuals* are best described by the general characteristics of their grouping. There are too many dimensions to an individual's psyche, and individuals are too complex for any single, simple approach to explain their attitudes and behaviors.

In Chapter 10, we focus specifically on the important considerations of gender, ethnicity, and culture. These demographics must be understood by the leader who desires to maintain a diverse and nondiscriminatory work environment, not merely to meet needed or specified legal requirements, but in order to be an effective leader. It is perhaps one of the purest cases wherein a leader seeks not to do things right, but to do the right thing. Whether the issue is customer and employee diversity or global business and the need to appreciate cultural diversity across nations, leadership is key to the wholesome integration of differences.

A powerful, contemporary example of diversity advancement occurred in 2008, a year that made American political history. It was the first year that either a woman would be elected vice president (Governor Sarah Palin on the Republican ticket) or a black man would be elected president (Senator Barack Obama on the Democratic ticket). So, on one hand, it was a great moment for American multiculturalism. Sadly, on the other hand, many felt that the media's treatment of these and other leaders differed depending on stereotypical assumptions relative to their demographic group of race, gender, or religion (e.g., spreading false rumors that Obama was Muslim, singling out presidential candidate Mitt Romney earlier in the race with stereotypes about his Mormon faith, and minimizing the legitimacy of Palin because of her role as a mother).

Diversity in business leadership has elements in common with political leadership, wherein ethical leaders help the public transcend differences for the common good, but also it stands as a special and unique consideration that we shall explore.

GENDER AS A FACTOR IN LEADERSHIP

If the point-of-purchase marketplace were the standard of measure for business leadership, then women would certainly dominate. Eighty-three percent of all consumer purchases are made by women (Wolfman 2007), including those purchases that may be perceived as more male-oriented—such as electronics, home computers, automobiles, and insurance. Again, although women are less likely than men to become self-employed, if the increasing numbers of women-owned firms were the measure of leadership in business, then women would appear to be advancing rapidly. Unfortunately, this kind of information does not accurately illuminate the real issues at play when discussing gender in relation to leadership.

The term "**gender**" as used in this book refers to sexual identity and the characteristics with which it is associated. "Gender" refers not only to the biological differences between the sexes, but additionally to the cultural understandings about such differences. In this text, it is the American culture that is used as a reference point relative to gender, but the reader should be aware that different international audiences, research, and practices could lead to some different observations and conclusions on this same issue.

Research on gender as a factor in the study of leadership usually focuses on the experiences of women in corporations, and it is not uncommon for the research to contrast women versus men. Two bodies of investigation then follow from two different perspectives: women *as leaders*, and leadership *of women* in the workplace. This section will cover both perspectives in terms of opportunity and equity.

If you are a female, like over half of the business student population in the United States, this section may strike a personal note. If you are a male working with women or leading an organization alongside women leaders, this section may pique your curiosity. Intuitively, gender seems as if it would be an important variable in business leadership, and research confirms this to be the case. However, when male-female differences are trivial, the findings should not be exaggerated because "the differences among women themselves (and among men themselves) are much greater than the mean difference between women and men" (Yukl 2006, 429)—leading us back to the statement by Takeo Fujisawa in the introduction to this chapter!

Exhibit 10.1 reviews two different research perspectives on gender and leadership, tied together with the causal chain approach to leadership. One line of research examines the lower percentage of women leaders and the reasons for it. Another important line of research explores the advantages of characteristics that women more clearly exhibit (e.g., listening and inclusiveness) and how the addition of these characteristics to the leadership process would enhance organizations. These and other issues related to gender and leadership are discussed below.

Exhibit 10.1 **Gender Approach and the Causal Chain**

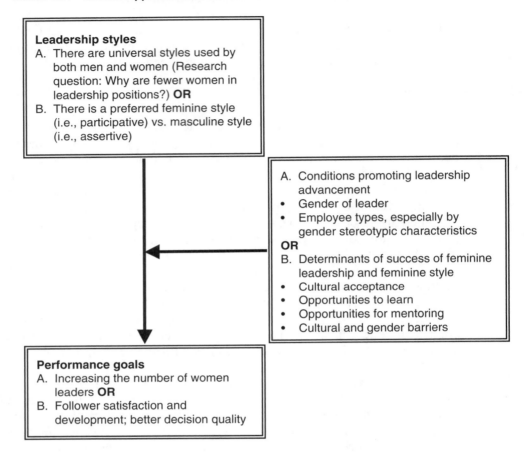

An important contribution of studying gender as a factor in leadership is that it closely examines the contemporary problem of gender imbalance at the executive level in almost all fields.

GENDER-BASED OPPORTUNITY AND EQUITY

The study of women in the workplace has long led to queries on gender-based opportunity and equity. Historically, women workers were clustered in certain positions and certain occupations more than in others, and they tended to be lower-paid in comparison to men. Indeed, it can appear difficult to shake the sands of time. According to the U.S. Bureau of Labor Statistics (2008), the five most prevalent occupations for women who work full-time in the workforce today are secretaries and administrative assistants, registered nurses, elementary and middle school teachers, cashiers, and retail salespersons. Though studies in this area continue, some researchers have argued that *because* women are clustered in those occupations, the occupations remain lower-paid than others.

Gender-based **occupational segregation** is the terminology used in research to describe this phenomenon. Some researchers claim that this historical reality reflects the fact that the labor force was comprised of a disproportionately high number of male executives; that is the simplistic perspective. Historically, both the number of women executives and the number of women workers in the workforce have been affected by a range of political, economic, and social factors.

When women are underrepresented in executive positions, the phenomenon is called the **glass ceiling**, a term coined in a 1986 *Wall Street Journal* article. The glass ceiling is what is described as an invisible barrier that prevents qualified women from advancing into the executive suite according to their ability and merit. Why has this barrier been regarded as glass, as something nearly invisible? The allusion refers to those obstructive, covert factors preventing upward mobility that are not easily noticed or detected, such as attitudes about women or discrimination that is subtle. These blockades are distinguished from the formal barriers to advancement to which everyone is subjected, such as one's education or experience requirements. Senator Robert Dole, who introduced the Glass Ceiling Act in 1991, said in the introduction to a commission report (Glass Ceiling Commission 1995, iii), "For this Senator, the issue boils down to ensuring equal access and equal opportunity."

Evidence abounds that the glass ceiling was imposed historically by the overt limitations that were placed on women's entry into high-level positions. An anecdotal example comes from the nation's first female U.S. Supreme Court justice, Sandra Day O'Connor (2007), who graduated from law school at a time when women were less than 3 percent of the legal profession. She was in the top of her class, but the only job offer she received from a law firm was to be a legal secretary. Even today, with women accounting for about half the enrollment of all law students, less than one-fifth of law firm partners are women.

The Federal Glass Ceiling Commission was established under President George H.W. Bush by order of Title II of the Civil Rights Act of 1991. René Redwood (1996), executive director for the commission, describes a fact-finding report (Glass Ceiling Commission 1995) that highlighted important survey data. In the top Fortune 1000 industrial and 500 service companies, men constituted 95 percent of senior-level management positions; 97 percent of them were white. These percentages meant that about 2,100 women were senior executives in these organizations when there were nearly 60 million working women.

Explaining the significantly low numbers of women in high leadership roles has long been a matter of controversy. Betty Friedan, arguably the most influential feminist in the 1960s, asserted that gender bias and inequity in social policies restrict women in the workforce, thereby trapping them into making beds and dinner in an effort to "keep the home fires burning" and, in the end, wondering "if that's all there is." In 1966, Friedan became the primary founder of the National Organization for Women, an organization that strives to bring women into equal partnership with men.

Some people have argued that the glass ceiling is a result of women's self-imposed limitations in the workforce. This perspective has been perpetuated for fifty years, since the days when Betty Friedan talked about the absence of women leaders, and was rebutted by a *New York Times* reviewer who wrote: "To paraphrase the famous line, the fault, dear Mrs. Friedan, is not in culture but in ourselves" (L. Freeman 1963). That perspective, in today's words, is that the trapped and imprisoned feeling that many women were expressing was the result of their rejection of established doctrine rather than from any negative limitations imposed on them by society.

More recently, some analysts believe that the glass ceiling is no longer a meaningful metaphor because it implies a specific barrier within the executive level of an organization. Instead, they say the metaphor should reflect the complexity and variety of challenges that women face at all levels of the organization and should acknowledge the disappearance of those challenges along the way, from entry-level to executive-level. Eagly and Carli (2007, 64) put forth the image of a *labyrinth* that confronts women: "Passage through a labyrinth is not simple or direct, but requires . . . careful analysis of the puzzles that lie ahead. . . . Because all labyrinths have a viable route to the center, it is understood that goals are attainable." There are scores of obstacles that women face in that labyrinth, ranging from the seemingly primeval remnants of discrimination and often subtle resistance of women's leadership to an underinvestment in social capital by women, perhaps due in part to the difficulties of today's work/family balance, and a basic social identity as wives and mothers.

Some research supports the notion that women's limitations to advancement are indeed frequently self-imposed. In fact, it is not uncommon to read that women are underrepresented in leadership positions today because they have not chosen to live their lives in a manner that is required of high-level and executive leadership. For example, upward mobility and earnings are known to relate to personal choices, such as the hours one works per week and the continuity of one's career. Although marriage and parenting are linked with higher salaries for men, the opposite is true for women. Women MBAs with children were found to work fewer hours per week and to interrupt their career progression more frequently than men, according to a study tracking careers of Chicago Business School MBA graduates between 1990 and 2006. Although male and female MBAs had similar incomes at the outset of their careers, their earnings soon diverged after they had children, particularly when the husband provided a substantial portion of the household income (Bertrand and Katz 2008).

When life choices remove women temporarily from the workforce, it is important for them to remain involved in their profession by appropriate means if they wish to return to the same point from which they departed their career track.

Not only do women in corporations frequently choose to work fewer hours per week, but also self-employed women work ten hours less per week than do their male counterparts (Gurley-Calvez, Harper, and Biehl 2009). On average, self-employed women spend three and a half more hours per week in household care than do women employed by others, and six hours per week more than do their male counterparts. Self-employed women also spend more time than employed men in providing childcare. This is especially true when it comes to "secondary" childcare, in which they are at the same location with the child but are multitasking, such as doing work for their company or managing the home, in addition to the functions of childcare.

It can be argued that society itself is at least partially responsible for the limitations women experience in their efforts to achieve organizational upward mobility. After World War II, which brought a significant and much needed influx of women into the workforce, the Women's Pay Act of 1945 was introduced to require equal pay. However, it was not until 1963 before an equal pay bill was actually signed and passed into law as an amendment to the Fair Labor Standards Act of 1938. The Equal Pay Act of 1963 was an attempt to prohibit sex-based wage discrimination between men and women in the same organization who perform jobs that require substantially equal skill, effort, and responsibility under similar working conditions. "Equal pay for equal work" is the general notion, allowing for wages to become unequal only because of unbiased systems such as a seniority system, a merit system or a system of wages responding to quantity or quality of production—but not unequal because of gender. Enforcement of the law remains an issue, and because wages are frequently considered confidential, inequities that do exist are often unknown by nonmanagerial employees themselves. According to the U.S. Census Bureau, in 2007 women of all races and educational levels earned 77.8 percent of what men earned. This is a significant move in the direction toward equal pay; however, it does illustrate that wages are still out of balance. The gains are somewhat diminished when compared to forty-seven years earlier, when in 1960 women earned 60.7 percent of what men earned.

In January 2009, with equal pay issues often addressed through litigation, President Obama signed into law the **Lilly Ledbetter Fair Pay Act**, thereby amending the **Civil Rights Act of 1964**. The legislation was named for Ledbetter, an Alabama woman who, at the end of a nineteen-year career as a supervisor in a Goodyear tire factory, had received lower pay than her male counterparts. Because of a statute of limitations, Ledbetter had lost the right to sue. The Supreme Court affirmed that she should have filed her suit within 180 days of the initial date that Goodyear first paid her less than her male peers—nineteen years previously! The new Fair Pay Act restarts the 180-day clock every time the worker receives a paycheck (Stolberg 2009).

GENDER AS A DEMOGRAPHIC

Today, women constitute almost half of the working population, including about half of all management and professional occupations. (However, occupational clustering does impact averages; for example, women comprise only 14 percent of architects and engineers, versus 86 percent of paralegals and legal assistants and 89 percent of dieticians and nutritionists, raising the overall percentage for employment in professional occupations). The movement of women into higher-paying positions is, in part, a reflection of the change in **educational attainment**, normally attributed to changes in college-level attainment. According to the U.S Census Bureau (1994):

> In 1940, the percentages of men and women 25 to 29 years old completing 4 or more years of college were close to equal, but at a very low level (6.9 percent compared with 4.9 percent). Between 1940 and 1970, both sexes increased their college attainment, but men's gains were significantly greater. The college completion rates for men and women 25 to 29 years old in 1970 were 20.0 and 12.9 percent, respectively. Since 1970, however, the college gains of young adult women have outstripped those of young adult men, until by 1993, there was no statistical difference in the proportions of men and women 25 to 29 years old with 4 or more years of college—23.4 and 23.9 percent, respectively.

Simultaneous with these educational gains, participation in the labor force rose from 4 out of every 10 women aged 16 and over in 1970 to 6 out of every 10 women in 2008, compared with 7 out of 10 men (U.S. Bureau of Labor Statistics 2008). Ironically, although women participate in the labor force in lower numbers than men, for those women who do want to work, the unemployment rate is typically lower than their male counterparts. At a recent height of unemployment in the United States in July 2009, adult women had a 7.5 percent unemployment rate compared to 9.8 percent for adult men (U.S. Bureau of Labor Statistics 2009).

The impact of education on gender-based opportunity is not just felt in the corporate world. The numbers of women who own their own businesses continues to rise. Between 1997 and 2002, the increase in the number of women-owned businesses grew to 6.5 million or 20 percent—more than twice the national average increase for all businesses. Again, this is likely to be a corollary of the fact that women are increasingly well educated and that women with advanced degrees are more likely than women with lower levels of education to become self-employed (Gurley-Calvez, Harper, and Biehl 2009).

Whereas advice to women (and men) that encourages them to obtain higher education is good, some well-intended self-help books for women focus exclusively on how to improve *themselves* (e.g., work hard, but be balanced) as opposed to how to improve *organizations* for women in the workforce (e.g., promote work-life balance). For example, if discrimination or harassment is rampant in an organization, improving oneself may have little bearing on the potential for advancement. If top management values only employees who work sixty-hour weeks, striving for work-life balance is nothing more than a dream. Some improvement for women clearly comes from the advancement of individual women leaders who by virtue of their exceptional performance squeeze through the cracks in that glass ceiling, but true lasting improvement comes from organizational development toward the advancement of women leaders in general.

When the U.S. Small Business Administration contracted for a 2009 study regarding factors involved in women's business ownership, authors reached a conclusion that the "development of policies that enhance work-life balance . . . and increase[d] human capital through the accumulation of education would serve to encourage women to enter into self-employment" (Gurley-Calvez, Harper, and Biehl 2009, 5). Again, the endpoint is not simply to offer self-help to women, but to *structurally* improve opportunities by creating and supporting fair-minded policies that are favorable to their entry in the workplace.

WOMEN AS EXECUTIVE LEADERS AND TOP MANAGERS

Women in top managerial roles have received attention in the literature, particularly since 1964 when Congress passed the Civil Rights Act. The act was intended to forbid racial discrimination in hiring, promoting, and firing, but the word "sex" was added at the last moment in a controversial move. Although the law has been in existence for almost fifty years and clearly delineates that there shall be no discrimination based on sex, just 15.4 percent of Fortune 500 officers (Pellet 2008) and, as of May 2009, twenty-eight CEOs in the Fortune 1000 (fifteen in the Fortune 500) were women.

The growing numbers of women serving on corporate boards are frequently cited as one measure of their acceptance into executive leadership. Since the first major tally of women board directors in 1995, the average annual increase in twelve years has been 0.4 percent, moving slowly from 9.6 to 14.8 percent; this rate, if continued, could bring parity in more than seventy years (Catalyst Inc. 2007).

The increasing numbers of females in executive positions are frequently cited as yet another measure of the movement of women into corporate leadership roles. The first large-scale, national study of women executives at the vice president level and above in Fortune 1000 companies was published in January 1996; the study focused on their perceptions as compared to those of CEOs (Catalyst Inc. 1996). The study was conducted because it was known that business organizations were experiencing a catch-22. On one hand organizations were struggling to keep top women for needed productivity, but on the other hand, they were doing nothing to eliminate the root factors that impede the promotion of women. It was found that in order to support the movement of women into executive roles in greater numbers, organizational strategies needed to include both structural and attitudinal changes, such as removal of the negative assumption of "risk" in hiring high-potential women, greater consideration of work balance with regard to personal responsibilities, and the necessity for stronger top-level commitment in promoting women into executive roles.

Research now deals also with more abstract questions such as striving to identify what makes some individuals give high energy to a leadership role in organizations, or what drives leadership engagement, and to compare the extent to which the drivers toward leadership differ between men and women. For example, both values and gender are studied together as determinants of leader engagement.

A study that is part of an ongoing series of research sponsored by the Families and Work Institute and Catalyst reveals that the common assumption of men and women leaders having very different work values does not hold true. The survey found, in fact, that men and women have almost identical work values. Further, the top three work values are rank ordered almost the same: they are "having a supportive work environment," "having a challenging job," and "having a good fit between life on and off the job," respectively (Galinsky, Carter, and Bond 2008). The noticeable difference that was observed between men and women was the intensity with which women identified with their top values. Overall, gender was not in play as a significant variable; however, region (North America, Asia, etc.) and whether leaders were "pipeline" or senior did weigh in as important variables.

Research sometimes demonstrates that there are differences in the performance of women and men executives. There is much research from which to cite, and some of it appears to be counterintuitive. For example, Boris Groysberg found that among male "star" stock analysts who switched companies, both personal performance and market value of the new company fell. However, the women who switched companies, comprising 18 percent of the sample bank, performed as well as those who did not switch companies (Groysberg 2008). It was noted that female analysts had built external relationships that were much more portable than men's and that women analyzed their prospective employers more cautiously and used a wider range of factors when doing so. Groysberg concluded that the coping strategies women used in their male-dominated organizations resulted in a skill set from which all leaders could learn. All students should take note that the difference between star and nonstar women was in whether or not a supportive mentor was actively involved in helping to shape their career.

Gender stereotypes typically identify the leadership characteristics that are traditionally attributed to men, such as assertiveness, decisiveness, independence, self-confidence, and competitiveness. When a woman adopts such attributes, perceptions of her may be more akin to shrill domination than to resolute leadership. Considerable research has concluded that individuals with stereotypical male leadership qualities are more likely to emerge as leaders, but that women are rated lower as leaders when they adopt those masculine styles (Cleveland, Stockdale, and Murphy 2000, 106–107). Rhode and Kellerman (2007, 7) concluded that in some situations when leadership requires a person who is both respected and liked, women more frequently risk facing a trade-off that men do not—being respected but not liked, or liked but not respected.

People do not necessarily translate perceived good performance into perceived leadership potential; it has long been thought that this is most true for women leaders. Women may adopt gender-neutral or traditional male leadership styles in order to appear as qualified and to compete with comparably performing men for leadership roles. Although women at the very top of their game may be sought after and may receive strong leadership ratings, the bulk of women who are high performers, but not superstars, receive disproportionately lower evaluations for leadership.

Other research focuses on *perceived* performance rather than performance itself, demonstrating differences in perceptions for male and female executives. Ibarra and Obodaru (2009), compiling data from thousands of 360-degree evaluations gathered in 149 countries, found that women outscored men in nine of ten different leadership dimensions, ranking lower only in *envisioning*. In other words, it was the *selling of their vision* to various stakeholders that was the area of greatest perceptual difference when contrasting the performance of both sexes as leaders. Selling one's ideas calls for a different set of skills than those required for actually achieving measurable objectives. When examining the remaining nine dimensions in the study, gender stereotypes did not lower the ratings of female leaders. Male respondents scored female leaders higher than male leaders (except for envisioning), and female respondents scored themselves higher on all dimensions (except for empowering and global mind-set, where men and women were perceived as equally competent). The authors concluded that women leaders who concentrate on communicating organizational vision for actual skill improvement will greatly improve how they are perceived as leaders.

ETHNICITY AND CULTURE AS FACTORS IN LEADERSHIP

This text adopts the *Oxford English Dictionary* (2008) definition of **ethnicity** as "pertaining to race; peculiar to a race or nation; also, pertaining to or having common racial, cultural, religious, or linguistic characteristics, esp. designating a racial or other group within a larger system." The study of ethnicity covers topics from racial and ethnic differences in leadership attitudes and behavior to leadership in the multicultural or multinational organization. In this section, we first focus on ethnicity as a demographic and then move on to examine ethnicity and perceptions of leadership within the walls of an organization that is culturally diverse.

In this chapter we do not use "culture" to center on differences between countries,[1] despite the fact that cultural differences between nations were the topic of the first such comprehensive research. We do not focus on the cultural differences U.S. leaders may face when working overseas or choosing to expatriate. Nor do we use the word "culture" as an abbreviation for either "corporate culture" or "organizational culture,"[2] which would lead to interesting but entirely different bodies of inquiry. **Culture**, as used in this text, refers to the range of behavior patterns, thoughts, and beliefs held by a particular group within the confines of the United States.

Research on ethnicity and culture as factors in the study of leadership focuses on the experiences of leaders of color and of international origin in the United States. Cultural values shape the attitudes of leaders in ways both conscious and subconscious. Most leaders also exhibit behavioral responses to their internalized values. There is some doubt, however, whether cultural differences will remain strong over time because of the likelihood that market convergence—both global and domestic—tends to cause the blending of style differences. Travel, technology, and the removal of physical borders all contribute to the blend. Leaders, too, who develop cultural competencies to promote their organizations' success internationally and in diverse markets may well be contributing to the mitigation of cultural differences.

In the early 1900s, it was assumed that American business leaders were rarely people of color. A leadership database compiled by the *Harvard Business Review* (2009) illustrates this demographic. The data chronicle the lives of 1,000 twentieth-century "men and women whose business leadership shaped the ways that people live, work, and interact." Among the 1,000 leaders were 3 Asians, 36 blacks, 2 Hispanics, and 959 whites. Thirty-nine of the 1,000 business leaders were women.

By the 1970s, research on ethnicity tended to focus on racial differences in leadership behavior and in multiracial work groups. Terminology was somewhat blurred, so in 1977 the Office of Management and Budget issued a new directive for federal statistics on race and ethnicity, establishing four racial categories (American Indian or Alaskan Native, Asian or Pacific Islander, black, and white) as well as two ethnic categories (Hispanic origin and Not of Hispanic origin). Initial research on culture focused almost exclusively on the differences in values and behaviors between leaders from different nations.

ETHNICITY AS A DEMOGRAPHIC

Ethnicity as a demographic provides a visual clarification of the inequality between racial and cultural groups in the workforce across all occupations. Data about the high unemployment rate of July 2009 (U.S. Bureau of Labor Statistics) shows that unemployment among white workers was calculated at 8.6 percent, compared to that of black workers at 14.5 percent and Hispanic workers at 12.3 percent. During good economic times of the past, ethnic differences had a proportionately greater negative economic impact. Many factors collectively help to explain those differences and

Exhibit 10.2 **Employment Status of the Civilian Population Twenty-five Years Old and Over, by Educational Attainment** (numbers in thousands and seasonally adjusted)

	July 2008	July 2009
Less than a high school diploma		
Civilian labor force	12,174	12,461
Unemployed	1,050	1,925
Unemployment rate as percent	8.6	15.4
High school graduate, no college		
Civilian labor force	38,819	38,362
Unemployed	2,062	3,602
Unemployment rate as percent	5.3	9.4
Some college or associate degree		
Civilian labor force	36,534	36,564
Unemployed	1,679	2,885
Unemployment rate as percent	4.6	7.9
Bachelor's degree and higher		
Civilian labor force	45,050	45,691
Unemployed	1,114	2,145
Unemployment rate as percent	2.5	4.7

Source: U.S. Bureau of Labor Statistics (2009).

impacts. Occupations where minority workers were traditionally clustered were quite often hit the hardest. Another contributing factor is education.

Omitting ethnicity from the equation, education alone accounts for significant differences between employment and unemployment rates, as shown in Exhibit 10.2. Shown are the seasonally adjusted rates from a period prior to economic decline to a period one year later during a peak in unemployment in July 2009, when economic hardship was rampant. Typically, those with high school diplomas have unemployment rates more than double those with bachelor's degrees, and those with less than a high school diploma have unemployment rates that are more than triple. Data were not different when the economy faltered. In the one-year period ending July 2009, those population groups that showed a successively lower level of educational attainment demonstrated a successively higher percentage of unemployment.

In the last twenty-five years, educational degree attainment by African-Americans has increased at all levels from the bachelor's degree to doctoral degree. Great changes were seen in the period from 1985 to 2000, when the number earning an undergraduate four-year degree more than doubled. For a period, black women received two-thirds of the bachelor's degrees awarded to blacks, but by 2009 black men earned 40 percent of the bachelor's degrees awarded to blacks, and black women earned 60 percent (U.S. Census Bureau 2010). Over one-fourth of all bachelor's degrees awarded to African-Americans are earned in business management (*Journal of Blacks in Higher Education* 2006). Despite this forward progress, 2009 online census statistics show that advances in education differ significantly across ethnic groups. Exhibit 10.3 illustrates educational attainment of the population eighteen years and older, by ethnicity.

Nonresident aliens constitute a group with an inordinately large percentage of individuals at the doctorate level, 28.49 percent of all groups earning the doctorate; in fact, the doctorate is the most commonly earned degree for nonresident aliens

Exhibit 10.3   **Educational Attainment of the U.S. Population Eighteen Years Old and Over by Ethnicity, 2009** (in percent)

	High School graduate	Associate's degree, academic	Bachelor's degree	Master's degree	Professional degree	Doctoral degree
All races	30.9	4.6	17.7	6.7	1.4	1.2
Asian alone	19.0	4.15	29.8	12.5	2.8	3.4
Black alone	35.2	4.5	11.6	4.5	0.6	0.4
Hispanic (of any race)	29.7	3.2	8.8	2.2	0.6	0.3
White alone	30.95	4.6	18.1	6.8	1.5	1.1

Source: Adapted from U.S. Census Bureau (2010).

in the United States. These data contrast to data showing that only 5.57 percent of doctorates granted are earned by the African-American population and 3.36 percent of doctorates granted are earned by the Hispanic population. The same story is told when you look at the data in terms of educational attainment by ethnicity. Whereas about 1.2 of the U.S. population as a whole held the doctoral degree, only .4 percent of the African American population and .3 percent of the Hispanic population held the doctoral degree (shown in Exhibit 10.3). Over the six-year period from 2000 to 2006, of master's degrees awarded, the percentage of white Americans who earned master's degrees declined by 4 percent; that percentage was picked up by other racial groups, particularly African-Americans (+2 percent) and Hispanic-Americans (+1 percent). If you examine the data in terms of educational attainment by ethnicity, you find that 12.5 percent of the Asian population earned master's degrees, compared to African-Americans at about one-third that rate, and Hispanics at about one-sixth that rate (shown in Exhibit 10.3).

Black and Hispanic populations were awarded a lower percentage of professional degrees earned than Asian-Americans. Similarly, when data are examined by educational attainment, almost 3 percent of Asians earned professional degrees whereas African-Americans and Hispanics earned professional degrees at about one-fifth that rate (Exhibit 10.3).

The payoff for increasingly greater educational attainment is reflected favorably in workforce data that include unemployment rates. The occupation with the lowest unemployment rate historically (at its peak in July 2009) is the category "management, professional, and related occupations." For this typically highly educated aggregate, the jobless rate as a whole was only 2.9 percent in July 2008 and 5.5 percent in July 2009. Other occupations ranged from a low of 8.6 percent in sales and office occupations to a high in construction of 18.5 percent in July 2009, expectedly reflecting the levels of education achieved.

The category "management, professional, and related occupations" comprised 37 percent of all employment of whites in 2008, according to the Bureau of Labor Statistics (36 percent in 2004). Among Asian-Americans, that category of work reflected 48.2 percent of employment (versus 46.5 percent in 2004). Among African-Americans, "management, professional, and related occupations" comprised 27.4 percent of all

2008 employment (25.4 percent in 2004) and among Hispanics, the percentage was 18.3 percent (up from 17.5 percent in 2004). These statistics reaffirm that ethnic groups with higher levels of education tend to work in occupations that have the lowest unemployment rates and, it follows, higher pay on average.

Despite the partial explanation offered by educational attainment, it must be noted that other variables are also involved when it comes to numbers of management and professional workers by ethnicity. A 1980 study (Jennings) of black American corporate executives with levels of education comparable to their white American counterparts found that 45 percent of the minority ethnic group identified *racial prejudice* as their greatest impediment to career advancement. The advancement of a few African-Americans into highly visible leadership positions in business, politics, and other fields has made some people assume that African-American executive numbers are no longer disproportionately low, or that the group is not underrepresented in top management. Actually, the advancement of a few into visible positions brought only a *perceived* transition from underrepresentation of African-Americans. Famous examples of those who made African-American leaders visible to all include the first African-American Olympian, Jesse Owens, to win four gold medals in track and field in 1936; the first African-American man promoted to brigadier general at the start of World War II, Benjamin O. Davis; the first black Texas state senator since 1883 and the first black woman to serve in that body, Barbara Jordan; and the first black American woman to head a Fortune 500 firm, Ursula Burns of Xerox in 2009.

Companies are discovering that even after they fulfill their minority recruiting and hiring goals, ascension within the ranks remains problematic. Statistics show that the pipeline allowing minorities to move into top corporate management positions in a way that would indicate a meaningful shift in the system is slim. According to Management Leadership for Tomorrow (Stodghill 2007), "while 15 percent of college graduates are African-American and Hispanic, they represent 8 percent of MBA students at the top 25 business schools, only 3 percent of senior management positions and 1.6 percent of Fortune 1000 chief executives."

The aforementioned aside, minorities are moving into entrepreneurial roles in relatively high proportion, which may explain in part why there is a lack of minorities to be found in the corporate pipeline. Over the last twenty-five years, there has been a 37 percent growth in self-employment among blacks and a 15 percent growth among Hispanics, both outpacing a 10 percent rate among whites.

Service on U.S. corporate boards is yet another indication of the advances made by minority groups into leadership positions. In 2000, 60 percent of U.S. corporate boards had ethnic minority directors, including African-Americans on 39 percent of all boards, with Hispanics making up 12 percent, and 9 percent of boards reporting an Asian-American member. As shown in Exhibit 10.4 (Korn-Ferry Institute 2008), the number of corporate boards with one minority member has increased substantially over time. It would seem to follow that increasing the ethnic diversity of a board, especially by having more than a single minority representative, would offer the strategic benefit of enhancing the board's level of understanding and appeal to diverse stakeholders.

Exhibit 10.4 **Percentage of Companies in North America With at Least One Director From an Ethnic Minority**

1973	1981	1988	1995	2001	2005	2007
9	18	31	47	68	76	78

Source: Korn-Ferry Institute (2008).

ORGANIZATIONAL COMMITMENT TO PROMOTION OF CANDIDATES OF COLOR

What factors help to explain an organization's commitment to promotion of candidates of color? Diversity practices in organizations vary with the strategic commitment of the CEOs, as moderated by their own demographic characteristics and psychological attributes (Ng 2008). The number and intensity of diversity practices actively endorsed by the CEO—including policy statements, active recruitment, training and development, compensation, accountability for diversity results in employment throughout the hierarchy, and community support—can solidly predict the employment outcomes for women and minorities. Whereas equal employment opportunity (EEO) law may force employers into patterns of nondiscrimination, successful employment outcomes for people of color results from the commitment and subsequent choices of top leaders, starting with the CEO.

The following case of BMO Financial Group is an example of an organization with a strong commitment to the diversity of its employees. Exhibit 10.5 describes a "**culturally competent organization**," generally thought of as an organization whose employees continually strive toward the ability to work effectively across cultures.

ETHNICITY AND PERCEPTIONS OF LEADERSHIP

The effect of ethnicity upon leadership is a complex and emerging area of study. The foundation for scrutinizing the various aspects of ethnicity and culture was laid over thirty years ago with a series of international studies on culture. Hofstede (1980) found trends in *international dimensions*, or aspects, while looking at the ethnicity and cultures of Hispanic countries such as Mexico, Spain, Brazil, and Chile, concluding that they are generally higher in power distance (a societal acceptance from below of greater power above one's own level), higher in uncertainty avoidance (a discomfort with ambiguity), and higher in collectivism (the value placed on groups) when compared to the United States. The dimension of femininity/masculinity did not have a common pattern in the Hispanic cultures; femininity (an emphasis on modest or caring behavior as opposed to the masculine attribute of assertiveness) tended to be higher in Spain, Brazil and Chile; conversely, the dimension of masculinity was higher in Mexico and the United States.

As previously stated, characteristics of cultures between different nations, are not necessarily helpful in understanding cultural characteristics of different cultures within a single nation. For example, **Hofstede's international dimensions** do not reliably uncover pertinent differences today relative to perceptions of leadership for

Exhibit 10.5

BMO: A Culturally Competent Organization

April Taggart (2007), BMO Financial Group senior VP for talent management and diversity, wrote that her firm struggled for many years to make its workforce more representative of increasingly diverse Canadian demographics in a bid to retain its best talent for building quality relationships with all customers. The Canadian workforce is surprisingly diverse, according to Taggart. For example, by 2017, 7.6 million Canadians will speak neither French nor English as their first language, and already one in five new entrants into the workforce are aboriginal people.

By better understanding the many facets of diversity, BMO made a concerted effort to enter into every relationship without any preconceived cultural or racial assumptions. But BMO soon discovered that it was not enough to guard against cultural bias. The company also needed to take advantage of the varied perspectives that stem from organizational diversity, respect them, and use them constructively.

"Simply stated, cultural competence at BMO is about fostering effective and productive working relationships in cross-cultural situations" (Taggart 2007, 1). The notion of cultural competence means that employees forget all cultural biases and make informed decisions based on their keen understanding of diversity.

In the late 1980s, the Employment Equity Act was passed to provide access for four disadvantaged groups in particular: women, visible minorities, aboriginal people, and people with disabilities. Along with that legislative push, executive leadership at BMO provided a strong pull to the rest of the organization. The company designated task forces relative to each protected group to recommend BMO policy, resulting in more than 100 changes to human resources practices. As a consequence, BMO has successfully tapped into the culturally diverse markets represented by each of the task forces. To that end, classes in diversity training are now offered at BMO throughout all levels of the organization. The company is adamant that continuous learning will allow for the survival of a more flexible corporation in a changing business world. At the same time, simple moves were enacted as well, like the use of an online calendar that lets employees avoid scheduling mishaps due to culturally different holidays or events of cultural significance.

Former BMO president Tony Comper was an enthusiastic supporter of an equitable workplace. He said: "We will create a diverse workforce that reflects, at all levels and in all groups, the communities that BMO serves. We will create a supportive work environment in which equity and diversity inform and influence all our business goals" (Taggart 2007, 3).

Discussion Questions

1. Would Canadian law alone, or BMO executive leadership alone, have been likely to achieve the same result at BMO as the company did under their circumstances? Why or why not?
2. What is "cultural competence" as BMO defined it? Is that a realistic definition for U.S. firms and for employees in U.S. firms? Explain.
3. Do you believe that there is a business benefit to an organization's commitment to ethnic equity? Defend your position.

the Hispanic culture *within* the United States. This holds particularly true for regions that have a large Hispanic population. For example, in a preliminary study examining the relationship between Hispanic leaders and perceived satisfaction with supervision and perceived effectiveness of supervision, Romero (2005) assigned students at one university to read leadership prototypes and scenarios describing a Hispanic or Euro-American leader and a leader with a directive or participative leadership style. Students, with their ethnicity and leadership style known, are equated to "followers" in the author's analysis of this study. The students (i.e., followers) indicated their preferred leader, and which leader was more likely to be effective and to have satisfied followers; both ethnicity matches and mismatches, and leadership prototype matches and mismatches were studied. There was general support for the idea that *perceived effectiveness* is higher when leader style matches follower style. However, Romero found no effect of Hispanic ethnicity on leadership in terms of *perceived satisfaction* with supervision when leaders' and followers' styles matched. In fact, there was no significant effect at all in regard to Hispanic ethnicity affecting leader behavior perceptions. In addition, there was no statistically significant difference between leader perceptions of Hispanic and Euro-American leaders. Both ethnic groups selected the participative leader as being more effective and as having more satisfied followers.

Some researchers hypothesize that ethnic-based perceptions of leadership are becoming more singular in the United States because of the blending of cultures in business when common organizational goals become the focus. Needless to say, generalizations cannot be based on one study, but it will be interesting to see if this hypothesis is supported by future research.

A different aspect of ethnicity as related to perceptions of leadership is in the extent to which the minority person is expected to adopt perceived mannerisms of the predominant culture in order to "fit." The extent to which ethnic minority women are expected to adopt the appearance of the dominant culture as measured by hairstyle, attire, cosmetics, jewelry, and mannerisms has been studied (Kamenou and Fearfull 2006) in the case of women of non-U.S. origin whose communities differ from white American culture. It was found that minority women felt the requirement to "fit" in order to become part of influential networks and experience greater career advancement. Clearly, leaders should avoid requiring a monoculture approach if they are to truly embrace diversity.

The cultural characteristics of people native to other nations are not necessarily transferred and mimicked by cultures within the United States, However, there is some claim that eventually theories may forecast that ethnic dimensions of leadership in particular groups, especially groups in densely populated areas, have a tendency to revert to the dominant characteristics of their indigenous cultures. For example, the deeply rooted family and group orientation of many Asian cultures may help to explain Asian-American leaders' appreciation for a style of cooperative and shared decision-making. Different leader views about what is ethical in business may emerge from varying cultural backgrounds through the conduit of ethnicity or religion. Leadership theory in this area does not yet have sufficient grounding in research for the development of constructs that have reliable application in the United States.

ETHNICITY AND PERCEPTIONS OF ORGANIZATIONAL SUCCESS

The perception of organizational success is an important consideration for top management, and ethnicity can affect that perception. For example, when Fox News talk-show host Glenn Beck commented on-air in August 2009 that President Obama has "a deep-seated hatred for white people," thirty-three advertisers withdrew their commercials from airing during his show within about a week (Bauder 2009). Leaders of organizations typically do not risk viewers abandoning their products because of dubious comments made by a talk-show host, even when they know that their ads are simply interspersed by the network throughout the day for good coverage and even though Beck's audience continued to grow in size. Once again, we return to the statement that echoes throughout this text. The business of leadership is about doing the right thing.

Managers from different walks of life frequently jump to dissimilar conclusions about the impact that diversity can have on organizational performance. Some perceive that greater racial and ethnic diversity tends to bring creative ways of thinking to the forefront, which in turn leads to positive and innovative organizational results. Others feel that increased racial and ethnic diversity adds an increased tension that detracts from the main organizational goals; Tsui and O'Reilly (1989) found that the greater the demographic differences between leaders and their followers, the more that supervisors report effectiveness, and the more that subordinates report role ambiguity.

Where the truth lies concerning the correlation between organizational results and diversity has been the subject of numerous studies that address the issue from different perspectives. A focus on organizational results related to racial diversity in general showed a positive correlation. From data based on the 1996 to 1997 National Organizations Survey, a national sample of business organizations, it was found that racial diversity is correlated with increased sales revenue, more customers, greater market share, and greater relative profits (Herring 2009).

Roberson and Park (2007) studied the same relationship relative to the amount of diversity within the top echelon of corporate management. In 100 organizations listed as *Fortune*'s best companies for minorities, the degree of diversity in the twenty-five top positions was tracked over a five-year period, following financial performance. The bottom line revealed that when a *significant* percentage (over 25 percent) of an organization's leadership came from underrepresented races—blacks, Hispanics, Asians, and Native Americans—there was a measurable improvement in financial performance. However, when under 25 percent of the organization's top managers were from underrepresented racial groups, the opposite was true: net income of those organizations was substantially lower. Although Roberson and Park hypothesize that low levels of racial diversity may weaken organizational results, they conclude that "as the **proportional representation** of racial minorities rises, barriers to social interaction among leaders may decrease."

Managers with alternate perspectives suggest other conclusions about how ethnicity can impact individual pay and performance in an organization; some managers assume that the ethnicity of the leader makes a difference, and some believe that it is the ethnicity of the employee whose performance is being measured that determines the difference. Studies, yet inconclusive in aggregate, are emerging in an attempt to explain the pay differences between white employees and those of color who are working in the same job capacity with leaders of different ethnicity. A study of 437 teams in forty-six units of a single sales organization reached a number of conclusions, including that "ethnicity-based *earnings were smaller* in teams with proportionately more people of color, and gender- and ethnicity-based *inequalities were smaller* in units with proportionately more women and people of color as managers" (Joshi, Liao, and Jackson 2006, 459). These conclusions stemmed from findings on pay measured as annual base salary:

- The proportion of people of color on work teams was not significantly related to performance, but it was *pay* and *not performance* that was predicted by the interaction of individual ethnicity and team ethnic composition.
- Both Caucasians and people of color earned higher salaries when they worked in units with more in-group managers. Higher proportions of *minority managers* in sales units led to annual salary increases for employees of color and to slight decreases in annual salary for white employees, and vice versa.

In both the Joshi and Roberson studies, dollars rather than performance per se were measured relative to ethnicity. Good studies raise additional questions: what conclusions could be drawn on salary results of sales teams with *proportional representation* of minorities in team composition and in management, and what if the sample were a wide range of businesses from different industries instead of just one?

Organizational success may be compromised by a leader's inability to mobilize employees unless issues of cultural diversity are effectively addressed whenever there is any psychological departure away from shared goals (Ospina and Su 2009). For example, when leaders and their followers are from different cultures, ethnicity may become an important dynamic that could help or hinder success. In such situations, the leader may avoid any negative impacts by identifying common ground with employees through methods that reemphasize common goals and the equal desire for a favorable organizational climate in which to operate. In actuality, such leader methods are appropriate all of the time with all employees, but may be particularly helpful when perceptual differences among ethnicities are probable.

There are cases where environments are purposefully not diverse. When leaders are not in a culturally diverse setting, but rather in a closely knit residential neighborhood, a leader's handling of issues related to ethnicity may be different from those described above. If businesses in a particular ethnic neighborhood are united by in-group cooperation, they may act in a parochial manner by generally excluding other groups throughout the supply chain and even in marketing. Asian neighborhood groceries, for example, might be "mom and pop stores" operated by Asian immigrant entrepreneurs and their families, or chains operated in Chinatowns by investors of conglomerates headquartered in Asia. With affinity for the in-group, cooperative bases for interaction dominate. A study by Bowles and Gintis (2004) on the economics of ethnic networks leads to the demarcation of this special type of business setting in the United States. Bear in mind, however, that these few ethnic businesses do not represent the multicultural and multiethnic organizations that grow and prosper outside of ethnic neighborhoods.

CULTURAL DIFFERENCES WITHIN THE UNITED STATES

As established earlier in this chapter, "culture," as we use the term, refers to the range of behavior patterns, thoughts, and beliefs held by a particular group within the confines of the United States. Behavior patterns and beliefs can vary because of region, social grouping, country of origin, religion, professional group, ethnicity, or race, and in those situations we say that there is a unique culture. *Leadership* behavior patterns and beliefs vary because of unique culture, as well. In the United States, we generally advise leaders to be respectful of cultures other than their own, not because it is a legal requirement, but because it is the right thing to do.

Examples of culture differences are endless. Language typically identifies a cultural group, such as those that speak Italian. Dress may indicate a cultural difference. If you interviewed for a staff position in a law firm, you would know to dress differently than if you interviewed for a staff position at the auto speedway; the professional culture of the law firm would make a candidate in a polo shirt feel out of place. Cultural differences go beyond attire. Leaders in these two kinds of organizations have a particular culture that would cause them to analyze problems differently as a reflection, in part, of the effect of years of training and experience in the two very different environments.

As shown in the 2010 mortality data tables reported in many statistical abstracts from the U.S. Census Bureau, there are cities in the United States whose residents have a comparatively low life expectancy, such as Washington, DC. This may be due in part because of the high African-American population as well as the high-stress professional population. Conversely, there are cities in the United States that have comparatively high longevity rates because of the lifestyle of their citizens; for example, Loma Linda, California, ranks with Sardinia, Italy, and Okinawa, Japan, in having a high percentage of residents who reach 100 years of age. In Loma Linda, about half of the population is Seventh-Day Adventist, a group known to lead particularly healthy lifestyles, thus establishing its distinctive culture. This culture is defined not only by the abstinence from alcohol, tobacco, and drugs, but in myriad other ways as well. Since 1935, for example, the U.S. mail has been delivered on Sunday in Loma Linda because the Sabbath is recognized on Saturday rather than Sunday.

There are also cultures within cultures. An American of Mexican heritage, for example, is a member of a **subculture**, sharing an identity, a cuisine, and other traits that come from a common background or experience (Mexican), which exists within another culture (American). The phenomenon of cultures that exist within a single organization is important for a leader to understand. Sometimes organizations can develop *subcultures* that are part of the dominant culture but have some values that separate members from the larger organizational culture as a whole. Subcultures typically mirror and reinforce values of the larger culture of the organization but have additional values that are unique to the group. Alternatively, if subcultures develop values that contradict the core values of the larger organizational culture, they are called **countercultures**. People in both types of subcultures can engage in activities that develop important personal norms and values. "These activities can result in the emergence of coalitions sustained by specific sets of values, a form of *counterculture*" (Jones et al. 2004) that opposes or is deliberately opposed to the organizational values espoused by the formal management team or the dominant culture. An example might be a counterculture created by *non*family members hired into a strong family business, bringing with them a different set of personal and business values and a lack of in-depth knowledge of the family stories.

Like gender and ethnicity, culture differs in different situations and is an aspect of leadership that leaders should understand and respect.

CONCLUSION

Leadership theory relative to gender and culture does not yet have a sufficient grounding in research for the development of constructs that would have reliable application in the United States. Indeed, we know that there are significant philosophical differences among researchers about what is most important to emphasize, such as inclusion in a leadership world dominated by white males or the attempt to change that world to better reflect feminine and ethnic values and characteristics. Even with the lack of a comprehensive theory, we know that gender, ethnicity, and culture are important factors in the business of leadership. Without doubt, the matrix of gender, ethnicity, and culture needs to remain at the forefront of study in order to aid in the progression toward a greater sense of equity among leaders.

"What remains to be seen is whether the proponents of leadership diversity are able to build *strategic coalitions* that can catalyze these forces and make sure that the transformation process will be measured in years rather than decades" (Wolfman 2007). Although this statement was made in reference to gender, it is equally applicable to ethnicity. Strategic coalitions can be forged between organizations or individuals; women leaders of color, for example, who are mentored by white men can receive not only the support needed to help diversify the organization, but also an understanding of the leadership process that can assist in their personal success.

The building of strategic coalitions by definition implies that those who are diverse, and others who stand with them, work with the manifest purpose of bringing greater diversity into corporate leadership. A different means of achieving more suitable diversity is often brought on by external regulation. Consider, for example, the impact of the **Sarbanes-Oxley Act** of 2002, which was passed in reaction to major corporate and accounting scandals such as those at Enron and WorldCom. The act has mandated sweeping restrictions on board membership for ethical reasons, thereby establishing a need for new directors. Although ethical norms such as integrity are universally accepted, organizational pressures and structural problems can lead to different definitions of what "integrity" means between different organizations. Sarbanes-Oxley dealt with structural issues, and now a majority of *independent* directors is required; compensation decisions must be made by independent directors in public company boards, management, and public accounting firms. Restriction of **interlocking directorships** (with CEOs essentially sitting on each other's boards and setting each other's compensation, an arrangement that is potentially rather self-serving) has also led to the need for more independent directors. When new directors are needed, companies can look to new, independent names, including women and ethnic minorities.

Quality research can positively or negatively influence the impact of gender on leadership. The topics of gender and ethnicity relative to leadership raise the issues of what data can effectively explain actual differences between leaders and whether diversity brings special—and desirable—attributes, such as enhanced understanding of diverse markets or greater collaborative and supportive skills, to the table.

KEY TERMS

Civil Rights Act of 1964
counterculture
culturally competent
culture
educational attainment
ethnicity
gender
glass ceiling

Hofstede's international dimensions
interlocking directorships
Lilly Ledbetter Fair Pay Act
occupational segregation
proportional representation
Sarbanes-Oxley Act
subculture

RESOURCES

This chapter cites some of the interesting work that has been done on women in the workforce by the Bureau of Labor Statistics. Using the source document cited below, prepare a three-minute oral report for the class on another aspect of the topic that strikes you for its importance to managers. Be sure to use data from the *Databook* to support your case.

- U.S. Department of Labor, "Women in the Labor Force: A Databook," Report 985, May 2005. www.bls.gov/cps/wlf-databook-2005.pdf.

Read the text and declaration of purpose of the Equal Pay Act of 1963. Given what you have read about equal pay in the United States, discuss in class the reasons why women do not yet earn "equal pay" for "equal work." Do you note limitations of the act itself?

- U.S. Equal Employment Opportunity Commission, "Laws & Guidance." www.eeoc.gov/policy/epa.html.

The Equal Employment Opportunity Commission (EEOC) has written on "Glass Ceilings: The Status of Women as Officials and Managers in the Private Sector." What do you think are the most important data reported by the EEOC on the following site? From the multiple perspectives of your classmates, it is to be expected that different factors will emerge from the class discussion.

- U.S. Equal Employment Opportunity Commission, "Glass Ceilings: The Status of Women as Officials and Managers in the Private Sector." www.eeoc.gov/eeoc/statistics/reports/glassceiling/index.html.

The concept of "cultural competency" has application in most organizations. The following brief was part of a grant project for the Lucile Packard Foundation for Children's Health. After studying the site, discuss not only what cultural competency is, but also why cultural competency can be important to organizations as diverse as a financial services firm (see Exhibit 10.5 and a children's health organization).

• Laurie Olsen, Jhumpa Bhattacharya, and Amy Scharf, "Cultural Competency: What It Is and Why It Matters," California Tomorrow Brief prepared for the Lucile Packard Foundation for Children's Health, December 7, 2006. www.lpfch. org/informed/culturalcompetency.pdf.

DISCUSSION QUESTIONS

1. Gender, ethnicity, and culture were selected as variables for studying the influence of demographic differences on leadership. From your experience, do you believe that other demographic variables are as important or perhaps more important? Explain.
2. There is not yet a clear "theory of leadership" as related to gender or ethnicity. Do you think that will *ever* be possible? Discuss your perspective and what changes would have to occur in order to make this possible.
3. Based on the data cited in this chapter, which do you believe is further ahead as far as equity is concerned: gender-based leadership or ethnic-based leadership? Defend your position.
4. Occupational segregation has several possible causes. What do you see as the primary contributing factors? Why?
5. Enumerate at least three factors that are most important in achieving a culturally diverse organization. What is their priority order, and why?
6. Do you believe that a CEO should go beyond what the law requires in order to create a culturally diverse organization? Explain.
7. What fundamentals should leaders apply from this chapter? How would you use the information in this chapter as a leader?
8. What is the best way to describe the relationship between educational attainment and aggregate employment data?
9. This chapter cites the Korn-Ferry Institute regarding ethnic diversity on corporate boards. Explain and evaluate the significant strides that have been made over the years.

CLASSROOM ACTIVITIES

After carrying out the following interview, be prepared to report results back to the class.

1. Interview a woman in a senior management position. Ask what her experience reveals about (1) differences in the performance of men and women as leaders and (2) differences in the perception of men and women as leaders.

For the following questions, half the class should take one position, and the other half should take a different position. Ultimately, both sides should put subjectivity behind them and use objective material from the chapter in their analyses.

2. Agree or disagree with the following statement: "Leaders have a job to do

and whining about constraints is not part of it. Leaders need to do their best with the situation they face and advocate for their company. Leaders who are chronically angry about gender or cultural limitations (real or exaggerated) at their company should move on to another position."

3. Agree or disagree with the following statement: "By emphasizing organizational goals that every individual in an organization has in common, leaders should make every effort to eliminate ethnic differences in business. Leadership that differs based on ethnicity can only lead to misunderstanding with employees."

CASE ANALYSIS: EXAMINING GENDER AND ETHNICITY IN PERSONNEL DECISIONS

Walt Stuart has headed the IT department for twelve years, and in that time he has survived many issues that would have become heated were it not for his easygoing, very likable, and somewhat laid-back approach. He has fulfilled an important leadership role by helping to forge common ground, particularly when his department head colleagues have trouble coming to consensus. The time has come for him to retire. He has been asked to interview candidates so that he can make a recommendation for a replacement to his boss. The vice president to whom Walt reports has been pleased with his performance in moving the department of twelve employees in the needed direction over time.

Up until three or four years ago, IT was a closely knit and "traditional" department: it was primarily white, male, and functioned as a "good ol' boys network." This demographic and cultural makeup has been under long-term pressure to change. Walt knows that the department still needs to be stirred up because its in-house satisfaction rates have dropped; some in the department have been allowed to double-dip (holding two jobs at once), and that has taken its toll on performance.

Walt now has four candidates—although he is giving heavy consideration only to the top two. He has a tough decision to make because both have the technical skills necessary for the job. One candidate is Bob Lopez, a marketing information systems intern who has been with the company for two years and who happened to be selected in his first year as the company model for promotional materials. He is known for his ability as a smooth communicator and a reputable representative of the company because of his "good guy" image. He is easygoing and popular and has no enemies in the marketing department. He is Hispanic and takes pride in his heritage. He traced his ancestry in Mexico and on weekends he occasionally dons his boots, sombrero, short jacket and ornamental belt to play trumpet in a mariachi band. As an intern, he has never been faced with tough situations or serious personnel problems that had to be finessed. Walt's concern is that Bob has had little contact with an IT department per se, has not yet gone through the ranks, is not particularly hardworking, has only a bachelor's degree, and has no "vision" for the IT department.

The second candidate Walt is considering is Marilyn Beeman. Marilyn started as an IT specialist five years ago in another company within the industry. She is a white woman who was initially almost ignored in a cold and indifferent manner by her peers until her competence and dedication overcame their resistance; two years ago she was promoted to supervisor in her department over four other IT specialists. Marilyn has an MBA and has been through considerable IT and supervisorial training over the years. She is now admired by members of her department because she is business-like and task-oriented. In relations with her subordinates she is considered low-key but tough. She successfully disciplined a "rogue" IT veteran, although the encounter was contentious and gained her a few enemies. She consults with colleagues frequently, but only when there is an issue that needs broad input. Despite the nearly universal respect she garners as a competent IT supervisor, a large percentage of Walt's department would be unhappy with a female department manager, still a nontraditional area for women. Walt also knows that Marilyn will have an extremely difficult time with personnel issues that come before her initially or if she is perceived to make a mistake. She might also stir up a revolt if she is perceived to take an intransigent position such as tampering with work expectations.

DISCUSSION QUESTIONS

1. What leadership differences would you anticipate seeing between Marilyn and Bob in the department head role? Are those differences gender-based? Ethnic-based?
2. What do you see as the benefits or costs to the organization of bringing in a woman or a man of color?
3. If you were Walt, which of these two candidates would you be inclined to recommend to the vice president, and why?
4. How has Walt's leadership of the department affected the demands placed on his successor? What should he do to help in the transition for his successor? Are there differences you would recommend in that regard whether his successor is Bob or Marilyn?

NOTES

1. The student interested in reading about cross-cultural leadership would enjoy the GLOBE project (House et al. 2004) that involved 180 researchers in 62 different cultures to develop a theory that draws the relationship between leadership, culture, and organizational process.

2. "Corporate culture" refers to the general character of an organization and its values. The values of the founders are frequently long-lasting in corporate culture. For example, Southwest Airline's charismatic cofounder Herbert Kelleher resigned from the board of directors in 2008, but his legend continues to set a tone for employees to take their jobs seriously but to enjoy the work and have fun. "Organizational culture" is the values and norms that people in an organization share in order to get things done. Both these terms are important in leadership studies, but their meanings are different from "culture" as used in this chapter.

11 Leadership Imperatives for Inspiring Change

If you are not prepared to resign or be fired for what you believe in, then you are not a worker, let alone a professional. You are a slave.
—Howard Gardner, "The Ethical Mind"

Four leadership imperatives are introduced for consideration in this chapter because of their particular significance for inspiring positive organizational change in the twenty-first century.

Whereas our physical universe and its laws almost never change, our social universe is in constant motion. Leadership is in this social universe of continuous change. Profound changes are restructuring the essence of business (Drucker 1999), and leadership imperatives have emerged with new importance for the twenty-first century. Many such imperatives can be identified, but the four we chose for this chapter are so important that we believe they should become integral to your lifelong learning as a student of business management. The four imperatives are to lead ethically, to lead wisely, to lead with global awareness, and to lead with creativity.

Looking inward, executive and managers must (1) *lead ethically* by scrutinizing their plans, actions, and results in order to strive for high moral standards. In reality, there is no singular professional code for all business leaders to follow to ensure an ethical standard in the same way as required of medical doctors or engineers in order to practice and be licensed, but the imperative is there sure enough. As the winning commander in the 1991 blitzkrieg Desert Storm, General Norman Schwarzkopf, noted, more leaders are likely to fail because of lack of character than lack of competence (Mason 1992). Investments in human capital must include education about ethics so that leaders bringing change have guiding principles and clearly understand their application.

Virtually no single topic has captured headlines—usually with a negative spin—as did the lack of ethics in business in the first decade of the twenty-first century. Enron, Haliburton, Boeing, Countrywide Financial, Madoff Investment Securities, and Stanford Financial Group are a few examples of businesses that have run into ethical problems in recent years. Of course, although egregious ethical lapses can clearly ruin careers and damage companies, even ethical "oversights" (e.g., failing to inform appropriate stakeholders) and callous indifference to ethical concerns (e.g., the environment or employee development) can lead not only to a moral malaise, but to a downright loss of performance as well.

In order to inspire change, leaders must (2) *lead wisely* even though they face a barrage of challenges in fluctuating environments. Leading wisely during upward spirals in the economy seems easier than during downward spirals. Resources are plentiful, opportunities abound, and there is a euphoric sense of exceptional capability, entitlement, and even infallibility. Wise leaders do not sow the seeds of their own, and their organization's, decline by failing to employ sustainable strategies or think proactively. During a declining economy wise leadership becomes an even more critical imperative so that as tough choices are made, essential human capital and other core assets are protected. Wise leaders must provide short-term change but ensure that the resources for long-term successful organizational recovery are not destroyed in the process.

Also critical is to (3) *lead with global awareness*, regardless of the organization's location and current market. Thinking globally is essential for leaders so that they may understand their industry and the business environment to the greatest possible degree. A mandate for "thinking globally" is not to say that every organization must literally "go global." All organizations touch global activity in one way or another, whether it is importing parts, exporting across borders, outsourcing offshore, hiring employees from other nations, dealing with the fluctuating value of the dollar, or simply receiving multinational competition relative to their product or service.

A final leadership imperative today is to (4) *lead with creativity*, which should infuse everything from routine problem-solving to complex organizational change. Creative leaders question assumptions, reframe problems, and look at old problems in new ways (Bass 2008). They make decisions about whether to adapt or try radical solutions. They provide intellectual stimulation in open and empowering environments that allow outlandish ideas to be tamed into pragmatic realities. At their best, creative leaders use different strategies to infuse creativity into management and change, from the use of logic and hard work, to the intellectual blending of ideas, to the use of classical experimentation and the willingness to "just try things."

Although creativity can be demonstrated in manifold ways, from using new technology to creating process improvements, as our example we examine an area of opportunity for businesses in establishing public-private partnerships. Thus linked, private organizations can have significant impact and achieve results that neither they nor the public sector could accomplish alone. Creative businesses engaging in public-private partnerships can expand their market, decrease their liabilities, make handsome returns-on-investment, and promote the common good all at the same time. For their part, public agencies can contract to provide competencies and specialties that they lack, reduce costs and liabilities, and mold targeted areas of the corporate arena to emphasize the common good. Well-executed, public-private partnerships can be the classic win-win situation.

LEADING ETHICALLY

After the excesses of the market through the year 2008 and the enormous series of scandals revealing individuals and corporations exhibiting greed and graft of staggering proportions since 2000, virtually putting our national economic system in jeopardy, the nation is no longer willing to accept anything but *ethical behavior* in its business leaders (Trevino, Weaver, and Reynolds 2006). Following the **corporate social responsibility model** (Carroll 1979) for business and individuals, we have always demanded that business fulfill its basic corporate responsibility by providing value so that the organization could survive. Similarly, we demand that companies follow the law because that in turn safeguards the integrity of our contract-oriented economy. We also expect our business leaders to exhibit ethical basics such as honesty and integrity in their dealings. Finally, we hope that business leaders will strive to integrate social goals, especially as their success increases. For example, today we expect business exemplars not only to follow environmental regulations, but also to find ways to lead in reducing their carbon footprint. We also hope that those who have amassed fortunes will consider giving back to the community, as Andrew Carnegie, the steel magnate, did by creating thousands of libraries in small towns across rural America in the early 1900s, or as Bill Gates, the software magnate, has done by investing billions in educational pilot projects through the Bill and Melissa Gates Foundation.

In Chapter 7, we discussed how some people who were thought to be charismatic business and financial leaders turned to unethical behavior because they gave in to personal pressures and personal gain; think back to the unethical behavior of Walt Pavlo. In this chapter, we examine the need for *all* leaders to have an ethical imperative.

Fundamentally, an ethics-based approach assumes that the leader respects all stakeholders, including followers, customers, investors, and the public. It also assumes that a leader gives importance to the stakeholders'—as well as his or her own—standards and principles. A leader without trust cannot effectively inspire change among employees and stakeholders, yet in the wake of financial scandals, a Roper poll in 2005 showed that only 2 percent of the public believed that leaders of large firms were "very trustworthy" (H. Gardner 2007). Leaders who are financiers are particularly under scrutiny by the public because of negative influences; Bernard Madoff, for example, received a 150-year sentence in July 2009 for his $65 billion Ponzi scheme that harmed thousands of investors.

The individual leader's behavior is critical in the ethics-based approach. This approach stresses that leaders deemphasize their personal interests for potential gain whether or not they would "get caught." At the same time, the ethics-based approach requires individuals to practice ethical standards and principles consistently even if their organization does not enforce or reward ethical choices. The American public and the business environment have endured too many examples of accounting fraud for personal gain since the turn of the century, explaining the added importance given to this leadership expectation. The ethical imperative also requires introspection based on the acceptance and incorporation of honest feedback that promotes the goals of all stakeholders and thereby helps leaders abide by the highest standards.

An ethics-based approach to leadership is based on the level of social consciousness, self-discipline, and courage of the leader. In contrast, the most common symptoms of leaders with *unethical styles* are the lack of social awareness and the abandonment of their principles of right conduct, allowing them to use their positions for the benefit of themselves or a special group, often at the expense of others. Norman Schmidt, who worked at an investment group that went by various names, such as the Reserve Foundation Trust and Monarch Capital Holdings, is an example of someone who was temporarily regarded as a leader, but later exposed for having acted without social consciousness and having put personal gain above all else in a scheme promising huge investment returns. Schmidt took tens of millions of dollars from hundreds of investors and used their money to buy racing properties and cars for himself; for that he received a 330-year sentence.

Less egregious but still unethical are those leaders who simply use their positions as platforms for **ego-boosting** rather than accomplishing good. Ego-boosting could be said to be a human trait in general. Participants in one study rated themselves as above average on thirty-eight of forty traits (e.g., dependability, intelligence, maturity). People also rate themselves as more ethical than the average person. Leary (2004) concludes that people are nearly blind when it comes to the illusions they have about themselves. Given these normal human tendencies, leaders must become especially self-aware so as not to misuse their position and power. Truly ethical leaders do not fool themselves into thinking that they are ethical or that they act "sufficiently ethically" merely by virtue of proclamation.

Many managers are **ethically neutral** in their style because of their lack of introspection. They may be unaware of subtle ethical issues or fail to take the time to reflect on them. A senior manager, for example, may not know, because he is not amenable to receiving information about his supervisors, that one of them frequently uses a demeaning style with employees. Or the senior manager may know about the problem but chooses to ignore it. Managers who operate in this mode generally try to emphasize the basic procedural nature of work, rules, and technical fairness. Ethics, apart from rule breaking, is not a part of their job. Ethically neutral leaders range from those who are unresponsive or unaware to those who attempt to structure and conceive of their work as procedural and value-free. As individuals, they may be ethically neutral for a variety of reasons, ranging from their upbringing to a lack of courage to take a stand. Ethically neutral leaders do not actively encourage an ethical climate.

People of good character—*ethical leaders*—engage in three primary practices (Aristotle 1953). First, people of good character recognize ethical issues. They understand that many values invariably compete in social settings and that leaders are often the arbiters of who gets what in terms of values. Second, they take the time to reflect on issues that often pit one important value against another. Third, ethical leaders find ways to integrate the collective good into appropriate decisions. They do this in part by being clear on their ethical compass and how it applies to their business, and then by linking rewards and sanctions for appropriate behaviors to organizational processes.

A number of theorists have been interested in identifying not only ethical leaders but also highly ethical, or *exemplary*, leaders (Cooper and Wright 1992; Hart 1992). What characterizes the person of high character? Two elements are generally articulated: contribution and courage.

Making a substantial contribution to an organization, community, or system takes sustained hard work, perseverance, and involvement, which in turn require trust, empathy, and nurturance. Types of substantial contribution might include the accomplishment of a specific project of some magnitude with moral consequences or raising the moral consciousness of followers or the community. Heifetz (1994) proposes a facilitative role for leaders in the process of moral consciousness-raising. He believes that such leaders articulate the value conflicts of workers, organizations, and communities in rapidly changing environments. Exemplary leaders enable groups to sustain dialogues until coherent decisions can be reached that benefit all in win-win solutions. This means that the leaders must bring attention to the critical issues, foster honest and candid discussion, manage competing perspectives, and facilitate the decision-making process in a timely way.

The final or highest level of exemplary leadership is often perceived as the willingness to make sacrifices for the common good and/or to show uncommon courage. David Hart (1992) discusses such leaders as they confront moral episodes. Leaders who sacrifice may give extraordinary time, accept lesser pay, pass up career advancement, or forsake prestige in order to serve others. The best leaders may be those who make sacrifices but nonetheless feel joy at the opportunity to help (Block 1993; DePree 1989). Greenleaf (1977) calls these **servant leaders**. Servant leaders are highly concerned about empathy, openness, equality, listening, and unconditional acceptance of others. Indeed, they assert that the hierarchical model of leadership is often damaging to leaders. "Strong" leaders face many challenges:

> To be a lone chief atop a pyramid is abnormal and corrupting.
>
> A self-protective image of omniscience often evolves from warped and filtered communication.
>
> [I]n too many cases the demands of the office destroy these [leaders'] creativity long before they leave office.
>
> Being in the top position prevents leadership by persuasion because the single chief holds too much power. (Greenleaf 1977, 63–64)

However, some leaders are willing to make exceptional and painful sacrifices or decisions that require great courage. When they do, opportunities for greatness or, conversely, conspicuous mediocrity and/or failure emerge. Yet sometimes a decision is not so much dangerous to one's career as it is so enormous and controversial that it would be far less trouble simply to ignore it. The courage of such decisions can result in ethical greatness if the leader's integrity is mature. For example, Thomas Jefferson despised executive privilege but nonetheless doubled the size of the country with a unilateral executive order when he made the Louisiana Purchase in 1803. Exhibit 11.1 presents a general model of ethical leadership that differentiates good and exemplary characteristics.

Models of ethical leadership are generally proposed as universal theories. The one exception may be the highest level of exemplary leadership, which requires acts of extraordinary courage or sacrifice.

The quality of ethical leadership is determined by three cumulative factors. First,

Exhibit 11.1 **A Model of Ethical and Exemplary Leadership**

The Person of GOOD Character Will:
1. Recognize ethical issues

2. Reflect on ethical issues

3. Ingrate the collective good into appropriate decisions

The Person of HIGH Character Will Also:
4. Make a substantial contribution
   a. Carry out a project or good work, and/or
   b. Increase the moral awareness of the community
   OR
5. Exhibit sacrifices or courage for the common moral good
   a. Deny oneself for the common good
   b. Suffer abuse for the common good

how conscious are leaders of ethical issues? This cognitive element must be joined with a caring ethic that motivates leaders to integrate competing organizational values in wholesome ways. Second, ethical leaders are constant in practicing ethical reflection. This self-discipline is even more important for persons aspiring to be of high character. Third, the degree of courage that leaders have will affect their ability to make substantial personal sacrifices and, sometimes, achieve managerial martyrdom.

Whistleblowers frequently make decisions that require courage and substantial personal sacrifice along the way to reporting the inappropriate or illegal activity of executives. They do so not from a mind-set of "getting back" at any individual, but rather from their personal imperative to behave ethically and help make things right. They operate with conviction from the standpoint of ethics-based thinking, unlike others who may observe the same inappropriate activity of executives, but accept it for fear of losing their jobs. As a psychologist wrote: "A whistleblower steps back from those concerns and considers the nature of work and the community in a larger way. . . . He acts ethically even though it may cost him his respectful relation to his supervisor and ultimately, his job and relation to his colleagues. He is able to do this because his own momentary well-being is less important than the broader mission he has endorsed" (Gardner 2007, 53).

The performance goals for ethical leadership are dissimilar to other approaches that generally emphasize efficiency of production or follower satisfaction. *Increasing the common good* and the *empowerment of followers* are the most frequent goals proposed. These goals contrast especially with the power-based approach to leadership. Furthermore, ethics-based approaches implicitly emphasize the quality of decision-making as demonstrated by the more thoughtful, comprehensive methods they recommend (Cooper 1990). Exhibit 11.2 illustrates the implicit causal chain for ethics-based approaches.

Exhibit 11.2 **Ethics-Based Approach Causal Chain**

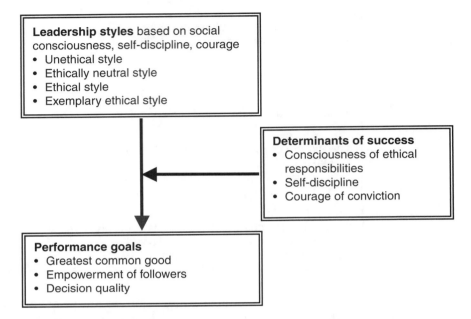

Ethics-based leadership has a number of strengths. It raises the question: For whom is leadership exercised? In this context, *enhancing the good for all stakeholders* must be its first consideration. Other approaches may emphasize productivity, success, or influence or add an ethical component, but they generally seem to be a footnote to the theory. Ethics-based leadership is also inspiring because of its examples and the challenges it lays out. Theoretically, ethics-based leadership provides valuable insights and recommendations with respect to the courage needed and the nature of leader character. One major weakness is that it offers little insight into the more pragmatic aspects of leadership. Ethical conundrums are, hopefully, relatively rare in a manager's routine. Moreover, ethics-based leadership frequently has an abstract, philosophical quality. This is partly a result of its intellectual heritage and partly due to the highly generalized normative base that it advocates. Yet despite the inevitable challenges, there is no imperative both more timely and timeless than leading ethically.

LEADING WISELY

Because we entrust so much of our fate to our leaders, we want them to be wise, to be able to integrate their knowledge, experience, and analytic skills in order to make decisions that will be prudent over time. This is the second leadership imperative. According to McKenna, Rooney, and Boal (2009), there are five elements to leadership wisdom. First, wise leaders use reason and careful observation. Second, they are not "numbers only" individuals; they use nonrational and subjective elements in making quality decisions. Third, wise leaders value virtuous and humane behaviors because they know that, in the long haul, it is not only ethical but also strategic to do so (Porter and Kramer 2002). Fourth, they ensure that their decisions are practical and oriented to everyday life to the highest degree possible. Finally, they are articulate in expressing the reasons for decisions in order to enhance transparency and understanding. This is easy to say, but in the rough-and-tumble of fluctuating times, this is a challenge.

When business is growing and the environment is supporting that growth, there is a tendency for managers to become complacent. Costs may gradually increase—or spiral—because the organization can absorb them. Complacency may lead to false confidence, causing blindness to a proper understanding of how the organization is really performing. In the face of managerial complacency, many decisions may be made that seem acceptable, but that ultimately prove to be unwise in the long term.

Suddenly the economic environment can land a punch with huge impact! Imagine the domino effect during the Great Depression with 9,096 bank failures from 1930 to 1933, or the S&L crisis with 1,617 bank failures and 1,295 savings and loan failures from 1980 to 1994, or 109 (and climbing) bank closures in 2008 and the first few months of 2009. Jobs are gone. Purchasing power dips. Retail sales decline and there are losses on home mortgages.

Even though many of the strategies that leaders use may vary, wise leadership is as important in economic downturns as it is in times of economic boom. In fact, if leadership was unwise during good times in terms of complacency, excessive profit-taking, overleveraging, and the like, it is likely that wise leadership will be critical for corporate survival itself in difficult times.

In the United States, we are accustomed to equating leadership with managing for growth; yet "the more growth the better" is not necessarily the wisest approach, particularly in a fluctuating economy. Aggressive but thoughtful growth works well for most businesses in a robust economy, but in an economy that is tenuously rising and falling, bringing stability over the long term may well be the most outstanding leadership contribution. Most business courses are geared to preparing future leaders as thoroughly as possible for expanding markets so that they may best take advantage of an ever-increasing economy. Though matching the business to any environment is important, it can prove difficult at times as businesses periodically run up against such variables as decreased consumer spending, bank insolvencies, or rising unemployment. To maintain loyalty and organizational momentum, employees need to see their leaders as adaptable, resourceful, communicative, and forward-thinking in a turbulent financial environment. And their leaders must be able to deliver.

Wise leadership is especially essential during downturns. Although somewhat masked from public scrutiny, wise leadership is essential *before* a downturn in *anticipation of environmental change*. Think about it . . . when did Noah build his proverbial ark? It was *before* the rain (McKinney 2010). Leadership can provide the glue that keeps organizations stable and can prepare them for those inevitable times when the environment becomes chaotic.

Organizational decline is a condition in which a substantial decrease in an organization's resource base occurs (Bowerman 1995). Decline may be caused by various factors, including the **organizational atrophy** that occurs when the organization

Exhibit 11.3 **Stages of Organizational Decline**

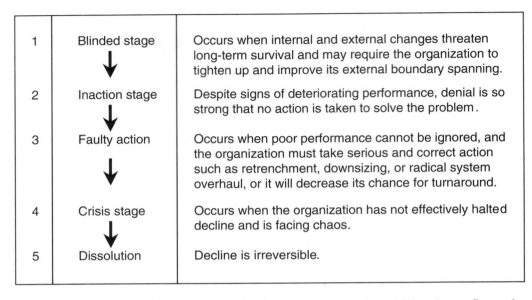

1	Blinded stage ↓	Occurs when internal and external changes threaten long-term survival and may require the organization to tighten up and improve its external boundary spanning.
2	Inaction stage ↓	Despite signs of deteriorating performance, denial is so strong that no action is taken to solve the problem.
3	Faulty action ↓	Occurs when poor performance cannot be ignored, and the organization must take serious and correct action such as retrenchment, downsizing, or radical system overhaul, or it will decrease its chance for turnaround.
4	Crisis stage ↓	Occurs when the organization has not effectively halted decline and is facing chaos.
5	Dissolution	Decline is irreversible.

becomes inefficient and inappropriately bureaucratic; vulnerability that reflects the organization's inability to prosper in its environment; and **environmental decline** when reduced resources are used to support an organization contained within a "shrinking pie." Exhibit 11.3 shows a model of decline stages. If those stages are not properly led, an organization in decline can move into dissolution.

Leadership should vary at every stage shown above. With true and practiced leadership from the beginning of a crisis in the business environment, considerable internal chaos may be averted, perhaps to the extent of preventing the drift from one stage to another more serious stage. At *stage 1*, leadership should actively refine its external communication at every level of the organization so that outside changes can be discussed and dealt with proactively. "**Boundary spanning**" means that employees develop cooperative working relationships with external groups, including customers, and then relay that information gathered back to the company; in other words, it is essential to complete a thorough exchange of information between the company and its environment. If managers do not aggressively adopt this approach, they are likely to be blind for lack of knowledge of organizational impacts that are forthcoming. Leaders will continually ask every stakeholder group what they need to do on an ongoing basis in order to remain competitive, and will proactively respond to information coming from others. If managers are blind to the environment and therefore slide into *stage 2* of decline, listening to information and advice must occur in order for them to be shaken from this state of denial. If they unwisely fail to acknowledge a problem at this point in the game, they will by default fail to take the needed action that could avert further decline.

Ford president and CEO Alan Mulally avoided blindness toward the recent economic shift impacting the automotive industry, and unlike the other two major U.S.

carmakers, Ford was able to turn down federal bailout money in 2009. Mulally describes himself as an officer with a conscious leadership approach who can both build and shrink companies as needed. When the U.S. auto industry was shrinking in 2009, Mulally was heard summing up the status of the industry with a familiar analogy coined by the father of hockey player Wayne Gretzky: "The industry needs to anticipate a permanent shift towards fuel efficiency. You don't skate to where the puck is. You skate to where it's going to be." Beginning in 2005, Ford wisely started its downsizing by cutting 50,000 jobs and seventeen plants. According to Mulally:

> I know how inter-dependent the world is. If [the economy] was going to slow down in the United States, I knew it was going to slow down around the world, which is exactly what has happened. You have to look at the world the way it really is and then deal with it. I've done that a number of times, both at Boeing and here. Where you really get in trouble is if the market is dropping and the economy's slowing down and you don't take action. (Clark 2009)

If the organization moves into *stage 3* of decline, organizational performance cannot be ignored, as the chances for turnaround greatly diminish at this level (Bowerman 1995). A leader must tap into various approaches that carefully examine alternatives for both generating revenue and controlling costs. In other words, thinking that "the first and only alternative is to lay off" does not contribute sufficiently to a well-rounded approach that deals with the reality the organization is facing. The leader must be cognizant of planning all action within the confines of any collective bargaining agreements, which typically restrain the types of personnel action that are considered in stage 3 decline.

If it is decided that downsizing is necessary in stage 3 or before, several actions can smooth the downsizing process:

1. "Overcommunicate" by giving transparency to the budget and seeking extensive input from others on both revenue and costs specifically and on regaining a position in the marketplace generally.
2. Provide advance notice of layoffs with as much detail and realistic information as possible, including the possibility of callbacks.
3. Arrange for employees to leave with dignity.
4. Provide assistance to displaced workers.
5. Use planned formal events to reduce confusion both for employees who are leaving and for those who will be remaining and likely picking up a heavier workload, perhaps for less pay.

If organizational atrophy is experienced, it is normally because, as the organization has matured, managers have failed to address chronic inefficiencies to such an extent that the proper time for revitalization may well have passed. In other words, those in executive positions are not a casualty of their environment in this case, but of their own inattentiveness to the need for innovation. The sooner leadership emerges to accept reality, the better positioned it will be to glean every idea possible on how to regain competitiveness and ultimately revitalize the organization.

Organizational atrophy can come about because of changes in industry structure to which individual companies are blind. Take, for instance, the newspaper and print media industry. There were two technologies working at odds with each other that were perceived as two separate things by business owners in the industry. Because of that misperception, attention was not paid to them in a simultaneous and timely fashion. Managers did not recognize new online customers who were getting their newspapers free as the same readers who would leave traditional print newspapers in droves. That major misjudgment has caused a meltdown in traditional journalism. Whereas the old business model brought revenue from advertising, newspaper sales, and subscriptions, the new model—for those who care to participate—brings revenue only from advertising, and Internet advertising at that. Revenue has continued to drop, including advertising revenue, in an industry that has become cash poor, especially in regions hit by serious declines in the housing market (and advertising for housing) and in the retail market (and advertising for retail) where unemployment was particularly high. *Time* cited a Pew study that in 2008 for the first time, "more people in the U.S. got their news online for free than paid for it by buying newspapers and magazines" (Isaacson 2009). In 2009 it was estimated that eight of the nation's fifty largest daily newspapers would be out of business by the end of 2010 (*Time* 2009). For those newspapers that should survive, even the basis of the new model is being questioned, in that traditional journalists now doubt the long-term integrity of an industry that relies on the advertising dollar for survival, as opposed to an industry that relies on readers who pay to read quality content.

Another type of organizational atrophy, sometimes called a **revenue stall**, frequently comes on the heels of dramatic growth. Levi Strauss & Company experienced a revenue stall in 1996, following a doubling of revenue within the previous decade. Several new product lines had been introduced that were very successful. But by 2000, revenue abruptly dropped 35 percent from four years previously, and the company's 31 percent market share in 1990 dove to 14 percent ten years later. When a company experiences revenue stall, it is suddenly as if nothing about the corporate strategy is successful, despite the fact that performance metrics did not forewarn of trouble ahead.

A study of major companies showed that the majority of them have experienced a revenue stall at some point in their growth. Further, the cause of the revenue stall was shown to be within management's control 87 percent of the time (Olson, van Bever, and Verry 2008). Normally the top management team is replaced in cases of stall, and unless the new team can take appropriate and corrective action, the company is generally unlikely to return to its former growth pattern. Although several possible strategic factors can explain the cause of a revenue stall, the most common is a leader's inability to respond effectively to new and competitive challenges. A red flag is raised whenever leadership is blinded by its own long history of success and fails to correctly read something such as a shift in customer valuation for particular product features. There are as many as fifty red flags that can help leaders diagnose whether or not their organizational high may soon come to a screeching halt. Levi Strauss's chief marketing officer admitted, "We didn't read the signs that all was not well. Or we were in denial" (Olson, vanBever, and Verry 2008, 54). As Exhibit 11.3

shows, the second stage of decline is inaction. Inaction is typically characterized by denial so strong that leaders fail to realize that the *opposite* is essential.

Organizational vulnerability can affect start-up businesses that are subject to excessively inadequate management systems while becoming established. A new produce-brokering firm, for example, may find survival particularly difficult if it cannot maintain a steady import supply because of changes in the value of the dollar. If the company were more fully established, with more supply sources, it would be better equipped to prosper, despite the cutoff of some suppliers. In these cases, leaders can benefit from professional affiliations that allow them to network and gain insight into dealing with the vulnerabilities to which they might be exposed.

When an organization is faced with an environmental decline, such as that of 2008 and beyond, leaders will find that a revenue stall may be outside of their control. At this point, they must determine where they are in the model of decline stages and respond accordingly. For example, if they are no further than the blinded stage (1), a serious wake-up call combined with increased communications with all stakeholder groups in a realistic manner may be sufficient to avoid movement into the second stage. When an organization is exiting the blinded stage, leaders should plan for a longer transitional term in order to avoid future negative effects of a knee-jerk, faulty action stage.

Leading an organization during environmental decline has challenges, but also it has opportunities if leaders are proactive before the decline stages take over. Through wise leadership, employees can be inspired to help avert later crises. For a leader to state the obvious is not particularly welcome ("we need to do more with less" or "we need to work smarter"), but inspiring followers to find creative approaches is needed. Positioning the company so that it is ready after a downturn is important, and it may represent long-term opportunity. For companies with cash, there is great potential for acquisitions during such times. A psychological opportunity may present itself, wherein there is the chance to cut waste where it has accumulated; during good times there is sometimes awkwardness or resistance to cutting back where there have been excesses. Keeping operating revenue in balance with operating expenses is of critical importance when the economic environment poses challenges.

Finding the best approach with employees is also important. Communication is different during downturns than it is in good times, when difficult personnel issues are typically restricted to those who exhibit poor performance. Robert Sutton (2009) offers advice to corporate leaders on being a good boss during difficult economic times:

- Keep employees informed on what will happen.
- Give employees an understanding of what changes are being implemented and why.
- Give employees the opportunity to influence how changes will take place.
- Show compassion by expressing empathy and sorrow when appropriate.

Keeping employees motivated is a significant challenge during periods of environmental decline. As leaders address the areas of predictability, understanding, control, and passion, taking the right approach is also necessary. Followers respond to a positive

Exhibit 11.4   **Attributes That Impact Leadership Effectiveness or Vary With Culture**

Universal facilitators	Being trustworthy, just, and honest (integrity)
	Having foresight and planning ahead (charismatic–visionary)
	Being positive, dynamic, encouraging, and motivating and building confidence (charismatic–inspirational)
	Being communicative, informed, a coordinator, and a team integrator (team builder)
Universal impediments	Being a loner and asocial (self-protective)
	Being noncooperative and irritable (malevolent)
	Being dictatorial (autocratic)
Culturally contingent	Being individualistic (autonomous)
	Being status-conscious
	Being a risk-taker (charismatic–self-sacrificial)

Source: Adapted from Javidan et al. (2006).

outlook on the organization's future, but not to phony optimism. Kenneth Freeman (2009), who served as chairman and CEO of Quest Diagnostics, and prior to that at Corning Glass Works, believes that leaders during a recession must be decisive in shrinking operations, while at the same time they must ensure that all stakeholder groups are treated with consideration. Freeman recommends a **"soft hands" approach**, one that treats employees with dignity by "overcommunicating," being visible, and delivering messages that are grounded in reality. Such an approach treats everyone ethically and equitably yet still honors company commitments. All these principles are certainly consistent with the approaches recommended in Exhibit 11.4.

In the environmental decline that shook the nation in 2008, articles emerged on how workers could protect both their own job and their company in a recession. Consultants advised workers to "develop contingency plans," "expect the unexpected," and "give your leaders hope" so that they would come across as duly positive and confident. Much of the advice for protecting a company and its environment would serve leaders well in good economic times also. For example, selling to business customers by traditional means is challenging in environmental decline, and alternate means of achieving results in the marketplace should be continually explored. One variant to the standard approach may be "**provocation-based selling**," which involves up-front time to ready the sales and marketing teams for thought-provoking presentations. This method identifies a critical strategic issue of the customer and a provocative point of view on that issue that would capture the attention of executive decision-makers (Lay, Hewlin, and Moore 2009).

Another example of advice that would serve wise companies well in both good and bad economic times is to innovate, even when resources are constrained. Results such as those that Apple achieved from innovation when it created iTunes and the iPhone can be achieved by others. Perhaps their innovations will not reform the market as did iTunes, but innovation strives to keep the company robust, much like the shoe manufacturer who maintains a steady stream of "what's new" in shoe fashion. Partnerships that combine left-brain logical analysis with right-brain intuitive creativity can be helpful, whether in the boardroom or in vendor relations. "Uncreative people have an annoying tendency to kill good ideas, encourage bad ones, and demand multiple rounds of 'improvements'" (Rigby, Gruver, and Allen 2009). Sometimes logical left-brain thinkers cannot recognize a good innovation, and outstanding right-brain innovators would not understand how to bring new ideas successfully to market. With mutual respect for their different skills and abilities, partnerships between the two can help a company innovate successfully in any economy, including during environmental decline.

In the 2008–2010 decline, it was clear that the **value-for-money strategy** was a successful one, given the rise of such businesses as Wal-Mart when compared to premium retailers. With whatever means they can, successful firms offer consumers the opportunity to economize. Value shoppers are the norm in times of environmental decline (Williamson and Zeng 2009).

Many economic effects can combine to raise significant challenges for marketers in the immediate downturn and in the recovery that follows. These challenges may create new segments of consumers, and value can be a factor they add to the equation. Among these new segments of consumers there may be a slam-on-the-brakes group that feels hard hit financially; the pained-but-patient consumers who economize less aggressively than the first group; a comfortably well-off set of consumers who feel secure; and the live-for-today consumers who respond to the recession by extending their timetable for major purchases but still continue to spend. The first two groups will settle for lower-cost products, whereas the latter two groups will continue to buy their favorite brands at prerecession levels, although the comfortably well-off will be more selective than the live-for-today group in purchasing luxuries (Quelch and Jocz 2009).

Faced with environmental decline, many companies will exhibit the need for cash, having been careless with working capital and credit in good times. Receivables and inventory very likely house a source of potential cash. Kaiser and Young (2009) give six principles for managing working capital and looking inside your own company to find it, including not rewarding the sales force for growth alone, not overemphasizing production quality, not tying receivables to payables, not managing by current and quick ratios, not **benchmarking** competitors to become complacent when metrics are in line with industry norms, and not managing to the income statement. The argument here is that receivables and payables are separate sets of relationships and should be managed differently. Again, the wisdom of these principles is universal, but they are particularly important for leaders during times of environmental decline that can make organizational survival a special challenge.

In sum, wise leaders are almost countercyclical in their decision-making. While taking advantage of the good times, they understand that good leadership also requires long-term preparation for the market dips, economic downturns, and corporate disasters that will occur from time to time. Wise leaders work against complacency and excessive short-term profit-taking by all stakeholders. Similarly, in tough times, wise leaders help their organizations to cut proactively but prudently in alignment with the environment and organizational miscalculations, to figure out where their organization is in terms of organizational decline and what it needs to do to return to prosperity, and to articulate a reasoned, practical, humane approach that will instill confidence in all stakeholders.

LEADING WITH GLOBAL AWARENESS

Thinking globally is a leadership imperative in today's business not because every organization is a multinational, but because *all* businesses are increasingly touched or dependent upon global activities and functions, no matter whether it is importing parts, exporting merchandise, outsourcing offshore, hiring employees from other nations, dealing with consequences of the value of the dollar, or simply facing multinational competition relative to their product or service. But as omnipresent as the need for global awareness has become, it is frequently a confusing concept because different aspects of global awareness are discussed in an unorganized way. Actually, global awareness is a composite of five different elements, an understanding of global cultures, global market intrusion, global market opportunities, global business organizations, and global organizational networks.

First, global awareness is *an understanding of global cultures*. We have already talked about the impact of world cultures in the United States in Chapter 10, but being sensitive to the different world cultures is also frequently an enormous business advantage today as never before. For example, House and his colleagues divide the planet into ten distinct world cultures (House et al. 2004); awareness of these cultures is especially critical to those such as multinationals who will have employees and offices on the ground. But most leaders cannot and do not need to master the intricacies of ten different cultures; nonetheless, they do need to master the understanding of *global business culture*, which depends on building and maintaining trust across national boundaries despite cultural differences.

Vipin Gupta, a pioneer in the field of leading with global awareness, is coprincipal investigator of the Global Leadership and Organizational Behavior Effectiveness (GLOBE) research program, involving more than 170 investigators from 62 countries for the study of culture and leadership. He does *not* conclude that to be an effective global leader one must know everything about those sixty-two countries. Instead, Gupta says, "A global executive needs to have a culturally sensitive approach that would allow culturally responsive engagement in any part of the world. The new global business culture is to navigate the cross-cultural diversity of the global business world with the same level of confidence and sensitivity as one is now challenged to do in multiethnic and diverse local communities at home base" (2010).

Multinational firms require leaders who are culturally sensitive and strong global leaders. In fact, a survey of Fortune 500 executives reported that having competent global leaders was the most important factor in business success. Despite that level of importance, 85 percent of the executives said they did not think they had an adequate number of competent global leaders (Javidan and House 2001).

Jean Stephens is a prime illustration of a strong global leader with global awareness and cultural sensitivity. Stephens, CEO of the U.S. firm RSM International, based in London, is the first woman to lead a Top Ten accounting network. (For the fourth consecutive year, RSM McGladrey/McGladrey & Pullen is ranked number five by *Accounting Today* among accounting firms, ranked according to revenue from U.S. operations [Carlino 2010]). During her leadership roles with RSM, first as COO and now CEO, she has been responsible for implementing the organization's worldwide strategy and increasing its presence by 75 percent through addition and growth of member firms. Working with the board of directors and managing partners from member firms such as those in China, India, Egypt, Russia, Ukraine, Saudi Arabia, Chile, and Peru, she adapted to a wide variety of cultures and business practices and earned respect worldwide, including in cultures where women's contributions are not always valued equally. RSM members now include over 30,000 people worldwide, including seventy-two managing partners in eighty-five countries. Stephens's approach for building international trust is to be up-front and transparent, with no hidden agendas. "Yes, there are different styles in different cultures, and leaders have to be sensitive to this. But people are people around the world. Informal relationships and good camaraderie help to maintain trusting partnerships. But there are also tough issues, and as long as I'm true to myself and honest, we can get through even the toughest of them" (Stephens 2009).

Leading thinkers who look to the global executives of the future echo the sentiments of Stephens regarding trust. O'Toole and Bennis (2009, 56) note that in the past, the tool for evaluating leaders was to measure the wealth they created for investors. But in a fast-paced global economy, the new means for evaluating leaders is "the extent to which executives create organizations that are economically, ethically, and socially sustainable." But how does a leader accomplish the task in the new global business culture? With transparency, honesty, and candor. It is the leader's responsibility to create a *culture of candor* by establishing appropriate systems and norms and through personal modeling that fosters and builds trusting partnerships. A culture of candor, as Stephens describes, is being true to oneself and honest to others.

A manager like Jean Stephens is called an **expatriate** because she is a professional sent abroad by her company to live in a different country from where she was born. As midmarket[1] companies plan to increase their global presence, even despite turbulent worldwide economies, more people from small and medium-sized firms will find themselves working overseas. An international company usually has staff to coach and assist expatriates and their families, sometimes in learning a new language rapidly or finding a school for family members. Success as an expatriate, however, is not based only on external support. Success is most likely when prospective expatriates are given free choice regarding acceptance of an international assignment (Cerdin and LePargneux 2009). They should not be led to believe that accepting a particular international assignment is required for career advancement, and they should not be required to accept an assignment that they feel is not a good fit for their personal or professional life. They should know in advance the length of the assignment if a minimum or maximum stay is to be imposed. Because their assignments may be ambiguous and because uncertain international environments may bring lack of clarity, they should develop and obtain approval on appropriate assessable goals; they should also have the confidence that when they repatriate, accomplishment of those goals will be positive for their overall career development.

A complete global business model of leadership does not yet exist, although strides are being made toward that end. Categorizing how leadership adapts to a national culture is a preliminary step in that direction. But as important, we need to reinforce those overarching traits that are critical to building trust, such as honesty and integrity. We find especially useful the listing of attributes that affect leadership for better or worse as shown in Exhibit 11.4.

We stated earlier in this chapter that global awareness is a composite of five different elements. An understanding of global cultures was the first element discussed. Second, global awareness is *an understanding of the new trend toward global market intrusion*. Fewer and fewer companies can "hide" from competition that is being heightened and affected by global influences. Manufacturing, commodities, finance, and retail are common fields in which international competition frequently becomes intense, sometimes causing the restructuring and downsizing of whole national industries. However, increasingly the global market affects sectors and businesses that were thought to be local, too. Large numbers of Americans now go abroad for medical services ranging from hip replacements to plastic surgery, specialty stores must compete with vast Internet shopping opportunities, low-cost stores must compete with incredible online deals, and even classy restaurants need to project an awareness of global cuisine trends as never before.

"Globality" is a term coined over fifty years ago that now describes an organization at the end-state of having achieved full globalization in a competitive world-wide society. Recently it is used to refer to a *hypercompetitive* condition after the process of globalization is mature. It is the new global reality. Globality brings continuous competition for customers and for talent from businesses everywhere for everything (Sirkin, Hemerling, and Bhattacharya 2008). Globality points to both the structural shifts in the flow of commerce and the power shifts away from traditional centers of international influence. Older, established geographic centers for particular industries disappear along with the current models for success.

Third, global awareness is *an understanding of global market opportunities*. Just as the emerging global market changes standards and increases competition, it also literally opens up a world of possibilities. But taking advantage of the blossoming global market takes an awareness of the global scene, and hence, specific global market competencies.

While globality can devastate old businesses that are not prepared to compete with new realities, it also can open up opportunities that were once ignored by the major global players and are now being mined by new players in the field. Bajaj Auto, a manufacturer and exporter of motor scooters, motorcycles, and auto rickshaws, is one such example of a new global player. Bajaj has captured the global market for small motorcycles with engines less than 200cc—a market that companies like Harley-Davidson passed over. In doing so, Bajaj expanded into fifty countries with a wide range of price points, including many on the lower end (Hoover's Inc.). Many new global challengers such as Bajaj are doing business in innovative ways that had been labeled as unimportant by established multinational corporations.

In addition to the leadership competencies that every successful entrepreneur needs (finding sufficient resources, for example), new global companies need additional competencies to assist them with their performance on the global stage. According to Isenberg (2008), those proficiencies are (1) articulating a global purpose that becomes integral to strategy, (2) building alliances even when the start-up is not initially negotiating from a position of strength, and (3) creating supply chains with sufficient oversight and quality, despite the lack of physical presence.

Let us look at an example of alliance-building in the emerging markets of aerospace, an industry that is developing much more slowly than others, such as consumer electronics. Both Boeing and Airbus already experience complex global design integration challenges, but research shows that globalization in aerospace is still in its infancy (Bédier, Vancauwenberghe, and vanSintern 2008). This is true despite the fact that emerging markets have already become major customers; for example, Chinese airlines were major patrons of Airbus as of mid-2009, having already placed orders for 600 A320 Family aircraft. According to Boeing, India is forecast to purchase 1,000 commercial aircraft valued at $100 billion over the next twenty years. As more and more sales materialize, emerging leaders in those consuming nations will also increasingly partner with the manufacturers, potentially securing opportunities to serve as a supplier or assembler. Chinese companies are already manufacturing some structural components, and Indian suppliers are providing engineering services and producing aircraft doors. There are many challenges to the manufacturer who develops new supplier alliances, such as increasing transportation costs, coordinating supply chains, and occasionally dealing with interruptions. If the company wanting to partner as a supplier is a start-up, its challenges of negotiating with Boeing or Airbus are even greater than an established company's. The start-up would need to prove its ability to meet safety requirements in a country environment that would naturally have standards different from its own. Start-up suppliers that find themselves facing obstacles such as these would benefit from their own internal government alliance, which could provide assistance when needed.

Fourth, global awareness is *an understanding of global business structures* when it is logical for the organization to either have branches in other countries or simply be organized as a multinational corporation. Such organizational structures have their strengths, such as their business reach, economies of scale, depth of expertise, cross-national idea-sharing, and diversification, among others. They also have enormous organizational challenges, such as cultural chaos, underutilization of scattered expertise, and communication obstacles, to name a few.

For example, companies that employ expatriates face challenges that extend beyond leadership attributes deep into their internal record-keeping systems; for example, keeping track of where employees are and what to tax where may prove extremely complex, particularly when the employee is paid in local currencies and the local language is used for record-keeping. Utilizing a single centralized data system in situations like this is recommended in an effort to "facilitate clear and accurate communication. A centralized system can circumscribe problems when negotiating expatriate compensation packages, helping the organization keep track of employees while ensuring they are paid accurately, avoiding compliance violations, and reducing the time and resources required for year-end tax processing" (Micciche 2009, 39). Internal record-keeping is not normally in the domain of discussions on leadership, but it is critical if not done well in the complex global environment, and it may well wreak sufficient havoc to interfere with leaders' focus. It might seem that established multinational corporations would perform better than start-ups in this regard; however, success is determined not by the size of the company, but instead by its savvy with database management.

Just because **multinational corporations (MNCs)** frequently have major advantages for prevailing in the global marketplace, it is not necessarily the rule that MNCs always prevail. In China, for example, multinational corporations tend to dominate in R&D knowledge-intensive and high-end brand-intensive businesses, but Chinese companies themselves tend to dominate when production and logistics matter most: "Being close to the market can make up for product-related weaknesses, especially if local customers have unique consumption habits" (Ghemawat and Hout 2008, 82). When MNCs can be most responsive to local customers by best meeting their needs, and by bundling services for products together with the products themselves, they can make up for the natural advantage that local companies might otherwise have.

Research suggests that the characteristics that successful global business leaders possess have been found to be shared. These characteristics, often referred to as "the big five," are extroversion, agreeableness, conscientiousness, emotional stability, and openness or intellect. Each of these characteristics in one way or another contributes to the leader's international success (Caligiuri 2000a, 2000b; Ones and Viswesvaran 1997). Given the high cost of developing global business leaders, firms that have employees who are invested in strong cross-cultural experiences will typically find the greatest return on their investment when the experience and the immersion are maximized. (Caligiuri and Tarique 2009). Selection systems that recognize these principles have great potential for promoting the correct and positive contacts between leaders in the multicultural setting.

Finally, while not all businesses must have global business structures, they certainly all should have *an understanding of global organizational networks*. Indeed, this becomes particularly important and challenging for smaller entrepreneurial companies seeking to take advantage of the burgeoning global market. Such challenges include the nuances of global marketing at a distance, the overcoming of a multitude of rules and regulations, and the coordination of simple technical issues such as time differences, currency exchange, and foreign representation when a critical business mass is achieved.

Thus far we have tended to focus on well-established companies with global activities. Because of the new global business model, start-up organizations that are innovative, agile, and daring can win in emerging markets as well. A start-up enterprise with an innovative product in the computer games industry, for example, might be remiss to limit itself to domestic activity when (1) U.S. consumers are not the primary market for computer games and (2) international firms in the industry could quickly take over the global market by executing whatever was unique about the new product. Nevertheless, the situation can prove different for a start-up venture that is born globally as opposed to the already mature MNC. Leaders of entrepreneurial start-ups must be especially adroit at building partnerships to help cover their areas of weakness, whether in the supply chain, global customer service, distribution, or production. New ventures deal with many of the same issues, such as distance and culture, with which every global enterprise deals. However, they most likely do not have the same infrastructure for tackling global issues, such as legal staff, country specialists, and so on. Even straightforward matters such as time differences can become challenging for a small company working with multiple firms that are open on different days, at different times of the day, and in different time zones.

While a mandate for "thinking global" is now a leadership imperative across industries, that is a far cry from saying that every organization must "go global." Globalizing the entire business or particular products at a given time is not always good or necessary. Rather, leaders should cultivate a global awareness in order to understand their industry and the overall business environment. Being able to understand and react appropriately to global issues is a fact of life, especially for those living in countries actively promoting lower trade barriers, increased "free trade," liberalized capital flows, more expert-worker exchanges, and similar global market objectives.

LEADING WITH CREATIVITY

We have talked throughout the book about numerous related traits, skills, and behaviors that leaders employ in keeping businesses current and providing a wholesome environment for change. Leaders need to be in a state of continual learning to be open to new ideas, and they must reflect personal integrity so that others will follow their path to change. Leaders need to be masters of different types of change, from problem-solving to organizational transformations. The specialized competencies necessary for the broader change initiatives include scanning the environment and strategic planning. Pulling these and related competencies together into an integrated approach to leadership involving both leaders and followers is our final leadership imperative, which we call leading with creativity.

Leading with creativity means being able to apply innovative processes, even in traditional situations or in organizations with traditional bureaucratic structures. Leading with creativity is related to the notion of **intrapreneurship** in corporate management, using entrepreneurial attitudes and behaviors such as risk-taking and innovation. Although we all have flashes of insight and some among us are simply a bit more creative by nature, creativity is largely learned and facilitated. Those who lead with creativity are able to know when creativity is needed, have the patience to achieve it, and have the discipline to harness it. For example, creativity is sometimes enhanced by a process known as benchmarking—visiting and studying the practices of other industries or other organizations within your own industry—or by discovering possible solutions in new technology applications and finding the organizational problem they can fix. Because creativity requires the mulling of ideas and allowing the mind to play with dozens or hundreds of combinations of ideas, it cannot be rushed or coerced. Creativity is coaxed by playfulness, analysis, and bouts of hard, intense thinking with periods of relaxation. Once a creative idea has been tentatively adopted, it may need the discipline of experimentation and vetting; after implementation, it may need substantial adaptation as technical flaws are uncovered. Although it is often said that necessity is the mother of invention, proactive creativity is an absolute requirement for success in today's fast-paced environment, and as we have seen, the complex creativity needed by today's businesses rarely can be forced by threats of organizational demise.

Leading with creativity has several formats in business. Sometimes it means developing entirely new products and services. Compare the Smith Corona Typewriter Company and the International Business Machines Corporation: one market sector leader stayed with its core business and ultimately became an obscure company that moved to Mexico, while the other became a global giant that constantly expanded into new markets. Leading with creativity can also mean expanding into new markets with existing products. Compare the newspaper industry, which, as we have already discussed, failed to diversify its market base, and the cable industry, which added Internet services using the same lines and right-of-way. The example presented here is primarily of the latter variety: rather than thinking of government as a regulator, business leaders in the private sector think innovatively of government in the public sector as a potential business collaborator.[2]

When we discussed collaborative leadership style in Chapter 2, it was established that business leaders today should be prepared to think in terms of possible participation in public-private partnerships that can serve to augment needed civic services while at the same time augment business' market base. Such partnerships present opportunities for substantial business growth, but they are not without their challenges. Government is interested in these arrangements in order to bring private investment into public infrastructure and services. A **public-private partnership (PPP)**, or public-private venture, is a contractual arrangement between public- and private-sector entities. Both parties share the responsibility for outcomes.

Typically, the arrangement involves a government agency contracting with a business or nonprofit entity in order to renovate, construct, operate, maintain, and/or manage a facility or system, in whole or in part, that provides a public service. In recent years, the term has acquired a broader meaning, defining any scenario under which private-sector business assumes a role in the planning, design, construction, operation, or maintenance of a public service, as compared to the more traditional procurement methods.

Typically, PPP projects are considered a public good because cost is handled in creative ways so as not to be borne entirely by the taxpayer; sometimes the business assumes risk in the project, sometimes capital investment is made by private groups because of contracts with the government to provide future services, and sometimes government provides a one-time grant in order to make investment more attractive to private firms.

Examples of PPPs are varied; they include economic development projects, running a public library or convention center, or even undertaking routine public functions such as waste collection.

Highways, ports, railways, and airports are frequently involved in the PPP arrangement. With stagnant state fiscal capabilities, there is renewed interest in the PPP. An increasing number of public transportation agencies are now outsourcing to private firms their former in-house maintenance and operations, program management, and strategic planning responsibilities. As of 2009, twenty-three states and one U.S. territory had enacted statutes to enable the use of various PPP approaches for the development of their transportation infrastructures.

In these contractual arrangements, the business partner usually makes a substantial cash, at-risk, equity investment in the project, while the public-sector partner gains access to a new revenue stream or service delivery capacity without having to make a substantial capital investment. The business then later obtains a steady return from the investment via an income stream from tolls, user charges, performance-based fees, and related real estate development. Therefore, benefits to the private firm can include a stable cash flow, welcome profit generation over the course of the concession, and various tax incentives. It is typical under such an arrangement for the government agency to retain ownership of the public facility or system, while each party shares in the income resulting from the newly formed partnership.

Benefits to the governmental entity are several: cost savings, sharing of risk, expediting projects, improving project certainty, leveraging expertise, and encouraging innovation.

The complexity of PPPs is substantial because of challenges for leadership in the legal, political, and financial arenas. Through experience, several guidelines for leaders in both the private and public arenas have emerged.

GUIDELINES FOR LEADERS IN PPPS

1. Understand the differences between the public and private sectors in the context of the arrangement. The institutional and organizational designs for the two sectors are significantly different. In the absence of market mechanisms, the public sector is governed by a system of restrictive rules and regulations. Business leaders need to understand the protocols of the public-sector procurement systems, as well as those for budget and financing, project approval and implementation. Leaders must grasp and take under advisement the different frameworks of public scrutiny and accountability. For those leaders in the public sector, it is critical to realize that the PPP arrangement is substantially different from the normal "buyer-seller" relationship in a standard procurement arrangement. They should be cautious about taking in the free-market rhetoric that typically surrounds privatization. In essence, the public sector is not so much "buying services" from a "competitive" market through such arrangement as it is seeking to merge with a capitalized partner who is willing to serve the public interest.

2. Balance the influence from each sector. PPPs often involve a relationship between the two sector partners for a long period of time. The interpersonal dynamics in any long-term relationship may fluctuate, such that one partner could exert a stronger influence than the other. It is critical for both parties to realize that a PPP entails not only collaboration and cooperation, but also competition and submission. It is often advocated that the public sector strive for a leadership role that defines the tenor of the partnership, because the project is ultimately for public purposes. However, excessive public-sector control and influence may suffocate the proactive creativity and productivity of the private sector. The public partner may assume the leadership role to ensure the approval and legitimacy of the partnership, respond to political pressure and public scrutiny, and monitor output in order to minimize performance errors or agent abuses. The private party may lead in market analysis, project design, construction, operation, and management, or wherever its expertise and experience may excel that of its public-sector counterpart.

3. Gain public acceptance of the project and the general nature of the PPP in advance. It is critical to the success of any PPP project to have public awareness and acceptance in advance. A project that enjoys broad public support can reduce not only the political risk for the public agency, but also the financial risk for the private partners. In contrast, a project that has been constantly questioned and disputed can easily drain a partner's interest and confidence. Because of the size and costs involved, PPP projects can easily generate attention from the public, media, local businesses, and local politicians. At times they are likely to stir opposition because of the physical, environmental, economic, and social impacts and, especially in economically conservative states, the expanded role of private corporations within the public sector.

4. Align partners' interests in order to achieve a sustained partnership. The conflicts between the public- and private-sector interests in PPP are probably inevitable. Advance alignment of partners' interests can mitigate litigation between the parties. Though some obvious matters can be considered in advance and dealt with in the contract, unexpected conflicts often occur during or after the contracted period. Good leaders must be adept at balancing and aligning competing public and private interests. In addition, large PPPs often involve a vast array of private and public institutions, each in pursuit of its own interest through the vehicle of the project. Leaders should not haphazardly treat either the public or private partner as a whole, but try to understand each individual party's view and interests. An effective communication network connecting every participant may reduce the risk of conflicting interests and achieve a sustainable partnership.

5. Build public agency organizational capacity to accommodate contractual relationships and contingencies. It takes courage and strong associate-building skills to enter into long-term contractual relationships knowing that associations can change because of unexpected events. The complexity and significance of transportation PPP projects often require a strong and capable public partner that is well staffed, well trained, and sound in institutional design. Public officials need knowledge of both sectors in project finance, construction, and operation. They also need skills in negotiating, evaluating, and monitoring contracts. Most importantly, they need to know how to communicate with their private partners, the press, and the public.

6. Embrace the entrepreneurial spirit that actively takes risks and seeks return on investment. When partnering with a private counterpart, public officials may need assistance in setting aside the traditional bureaucratic procurement mentality and embracing the spirit of entrepreneurship. However, being largely constrained by often excessive procurement rules and regulations, public procurement officials generally exhibit limited enthusiasm in pursuing an active economic agenda, as their business counterpart would normally do. The need for mutual respect is great, as in any partnership, and without mutual acceptance of an entrepreneurial approach, benefits of the PPP will be lost.

We know that with risk often comes profitability—on both sides of the public and private equation. It is not unusual in a transportation infrastructure project for the public sector to absorb the returns of the investment. Within a few years of operation, a project can accumulate a significant net asset and become a revenue source for public improvement of adjoining corridors.

Overall, willingness to investigate public-private partnerships is an excellent example of leading with creativity. It provides leaders with vision the opportunity to achieve business success and simultaneously make a difference in their communities. Leading with creativity requires hard work; PPPs require the understanding of both sectors and their different needs and demands. PPPs are fraught both with new prospects and uncommon pitfalls. But leaders with creativity master these challenges and emerge as business and social prototypes.

CONCLUSION

Leading ethically requires that all leaders must look inward to ensure their own right behavior. Because of the unethical and illegal behavior of some executives, leaders are scrutinized—and should be—for their ethics; if ethics are not clearly communicated and upheld, those individuals will lose their status as strong, moral leaders and will not be effective in inspiring change. After ethics scandals jolted the United States and the ensuing repercussions had financially destroyed countless people in the early 2000s, the nation was no longer willing to accept anything but ethical behavior in its leaders. An ethics-based approach to leadership assumes that leaders respect their own standards and principles and those of stakeholders as well. They must deemphasize their personal interests and potential gains in order to be effective over the long term, and their behavior must be based on social consciousness, self-discipline, and moral courage.

In order to inspire change, it is essential to lead wisely in the face of challenge, using a variety of different approaches depending upon the type of economic environment being faced. Blithely leading the same way in all external conditions does not work. Decline may be caused by at least three different kinds of factors that create different conditions: organizational atrophy when the organization becomes inefficient and inappropriately bureaucratic, vulnerability that reflects the organization's inability to prosper in its environment, and environmental decline when reduced resources are available to support an organization contained within a "shrinking pie."

Leading with global awareness is a prevailing imperative for all types of organizations ranging from service to production. Whether an organization has outsourced suppliers overseas, has international partners, or simply is affected by international competition, leading with global awareness is central to the approach to business. "Globality," a phenomenon that brings continuous competition from businesses everywhere in the world, introduces to the world stage newcomers that target lucrative global markets not previously sought by multinational corporations. Today all walks of business have to deal with global issues, and leaders must be aware of any new situations that call for additional strengths.

Finally, leading with creativity is a call for leaders to think innovatively. They must continually learn, master change, and consider alternative methods of business. Creative leadership may mean new products or services or it may mean partnering in new ways. A public-private partnership is a creative leveraging of private expertise for the public good, as well as a means to tap into a huge market. Leaders with vision will see these innovative opportunities as worth investigating. Benefits to the business can include stable cash flow, profit generation over the course of the concession, and various tax incentives.

KEY TERMS

benchmarking
boundary spanning
corporate social responsibility model
ego-boosting
environmental decline
ethically neutral
expatriate
globality
intrapreneurship

multinational corporation (MNC)
organizational atrophy
provocation-based selling
public-private partnership (PPP)
revenue stall
servant leaders
soft hands approach
value-for-money strategy
whistleblower

RESOURCES

In this reprint of Milton Friedman's famous 1970 *New York Times Magazine* article, "The Social Responsibility of Business Is to Increase Its Profits," he makes the case that if business emphasizes its social conscience, it is preaching socialism. After reading this article, explain Friedman's position relative to this chapter's discussion of ethics-based leadership.

- Milton Friedman, "The Social Responsibility of Business Is to Increase Its Profits," *New York Times Magazine*, September 13, 1970. www-rohan.sdsu.edu/faculty/dunnweb/rprnts.friedman.html.

Certain professions have a code of ethics. Read this code for engineers as an example and discuss whether business executives should be held to similar standards. How would such standards be established since there is not an educational degree or professional certification required for executives?

- National Society of Professional Engineers, "Code of Ethics for Engineers," Publication #1102, January 2003. www.mtengineers.org/pd/NSPECodeofEthics.pdf.

"Fifteen Strategies for Leading in a Down Economy" on the following blog by Richard Levick gives practical suggestions to leaders such as "run to the problems, not away from them." Which do you find most critical, and why?

- Richard Levick, "15 Strategies for Leading in a Down Economy," Bulletproof-Blog: The Blog on Crisis Communications, April 8, 2009. www.bulletproofblog. com/2009/04/08/15-strategies-for-leading-in-a-down-economy.

A diagnostic survey is available at the following site by the authors of the study on stalls. They identify fifty red flags that can help leaders wake up to the danger that lies ahead before a revenue stall hits hard and literally brings company growth to a halt. A revenue stall normally impedes the organization's growth, leading to what is then referred to as a growth stall. Over the passage of time, a return to organizational health becomes less likely.

- Corporate Executive Board, "The Stall Points Initiative: 'Red Flag' Diagnostic." http://stallpoints.executiveboard.com/redflag.html.

Bajaj Auto is not a new company per se, having been founded in 1926, but its entry onto the global stage is an interesting story. What about globalization makes it possible for a company that specializes in two-wheelers with very small engines to grow so rapidly? Be sure to visit the product line when on the website.

- Bajaj Auto Ltd., www.bajajauto.com.

DISCUSSION QUESTIONS

1. As a student, you are aware of business students' behavior of plagiarizing and cheating in the classroom. Some who cheat in school would say that after they have become a manager, they would put aside their cheating ways. Is that possible? Is it likely? What should be done about cheating in business classes?
2. One of the resources at the end of this chapter is a link to Milton Friedman's article on social responsibility in business. Do you accept his position that when the market is allowed to function freely, principled ethics will follow?
3. Reflect on your own ethics. Who do you think has influenced you the most in formulating your standards? Think about your standards relative to cheating in the classroom as discussed in question 1. Who has most influenced your standards in that regard?
4. Think about a specific organization that you have heard of that was affected by environmental decline before 2010. How did the organization's leaders attempt to combat the negative effects of the environment?
5. Levi Strauss was given as an example of a company that experienced a revenue stall in about 2000. Did this occur because of environmental decline? Explain why or why not.
6. What factors would you consider when trying to position a company well

for the period after environmental decline has run its course? Do the factors differ from those used in regular long-term planning?

7. Which influences do you think have the greater impact on international business today: psychological influences or geographical influences? Why?

8. In a successful business that does not have to gain additional revenue for survival, what might be reasons that corporate leadership would entertain public-private partnerships?

9. What are the respective benefits to government and to private business of negotiating a successful public-private partnership?

CLASSROOM ACTIVITIES

1. Consider your place of employment. Have you heard about or seen situations in which an ethical stand was taken or should have been taken? Describe the situation to the class, and invite discussion on how the situation should be handled.

2. At the website www.international-business-etiquette.com you will find descriptions of business etiquette in different countries and regions of the world. With different countries assigned to different members of the class, hold a discussion that contrasts appearance, behavior, and communication practices.

3. Many well-known companies disappeared from the American scene during 2008 and 2009, including Levitz Furniture (dating to 1910), Circuit City (dating to 1949), and Countrywide Financial (with assets of $200 billion and founded in 1969). Form three teams to research and report back to the class on these three organizations. Describe each company's leadership throughout its history. Can you determine the major reasons for its decline and dissolution? Tie your key points back to the chapter.

CASE STUDY: A CORPORATE WHISTLEBLOWER

Time magazine named three women as its 2002 Persons of the Year—the people who most affected events during the year. One was Cynthia Cooper, vice president of internal audit at WorldCom. How did a CPA gain so much notoriety? Cooper knew that what was occurring at WorldCom in 2002 was not right, so in June of that year she reported her findings to the board of directors, explaining the company's fraudulent accounting practices. Although her audit memos were released by a member of Congress, she had not intended to go public. Nevertheless, her actions ultimately brought down the twenty-fifth largest company in the United States and exposed an $11 billion fraud—the largest in accounting history at that time. Investors lost billions when the stock became suddenly worthless.

Cooper begins her book *Extraordinary Circumstances: The Life of a Corporate Whistleblower* by writing, "I never aspired to be a whistleblower. It wasn't how I envisioned my life. But life is full of unexpected turns." In her first eight years with the company, revenue grew from $1.5 billion to an astounding $38 billion, and the regional company grew into an enormous enterprise in sixty-five countries. CEO Bernie Ebbers became wealthy quickly in a rags-to-riches tale, donating millions of dollars to charity along the way. WorldCom made its state of Mississippi proud.

Unlike many whistleblowers who make one-time personal sacrifices to do what they feel is right, Ms. Cooper says she would blow the whistle again if she had it to live over. "I really found myself at a crossroads where there was only one right path to take" (Ripley 2008). Ethics was important to her, and at age thirty-seven she listened to the voice in her mind in order to do what she knew was the right thing. Cooper says that fraud starts small on its slippery slope and people rationalize their behavior, but it becomes big when those people can bypass normal controls because the fraud has spread to the highest levels of the company. When orders were given to adjust the books by hundreds of millions of dollars, three accountants reluctantly did so, methodically adjusting liabilities and expenses. The well-liked CFO reassured the accountants that in the future no bad entries would have to be made as the company reduced earnings guidance. Little by little, the slippery slope grew steeper and more employees rationalized their behavior. Cooper and two who worked with her in the auditing department became suspicious and started examining the integrity of the financial information that the company was reporting publicly. Working without detection, Cooper and her staff unearthed $3.8 billion in misallocated expenses and phony accounting entries and then made sure that the improprieties were understood by the new outside audit firm KPMG (Pullam and Solomon 2002).

DISCUSSION QUESTIONS

1. Do you consider Cynthia Cooper a leader? Why or why not?
2. Is there any situation when an accountant who senses wrongdoing should not dig through company records at night so as not to be detected?
3. Cooper's suspicions about corporate reporting resulted in considerable pressure from her supervisor. How can suspicious employees draw the line between serving as ethical leaders and being disloyal to the company?

NOTES

1. There is not a single definition of the "midmarket" company as opposed to a small or large company. There is variation depending on the industry, but in general, the midmarket company has fewer than 1,000 employees and revenue up to $50 million (although in the manufacturing industry, a midmarket organization may have sales approaching ten to twenty times that amount); many midmarket companies have a less formal structure than large companies and are often family owned.

2. This final section on public-private partnerships is adapted from a July 31, 2009, report, "Managing Public-Private Partnership of Transportation Infrastructure: Lessons Learned from California's SR-91," written by Anna Ya Ni, assistant professor of public administration at California State University, San Bernardino, with sponsorship from a seed grant awarded by the Leonard Transportation Center in the College of Business & Public Administration.

12 Leadership Development at Individual and Organizational Levels

Leadership development is not an event.
Leadership development is self-development.
—John G. Agno, 2009

In Chapter 1, we mentioned that great leaders often start with great talent, but these abilities rarely find expression without study, mentoring, and practice. In Chapter 4 we discussed continual learning as an essential leadership skill. It is an explicit purpose of this book to help readers become both better analysts of leadership as well as better practitioners in organizational settings. Leadership development is now explored in depth as the key to *self*-development, which motivates people to become better leaders. We present this chapter to encourage developing leaders to seek study and mentoring and to come to the realization that lifelong learning is indeed an essential leadership skill.

Learning new things and preparing for constant change is required in any true leadership role. If you hear classmates say that they cannot wait to graduate with their degree so they can "just have a job that pays a lot" in order to "stop studying forever," help them to understand that today's business is ever-changing and requires leaders who never stop learning about themselves and their environment.

In a world that is in constant flux, leaders must develop themselves in order to understand the changing environment and to inspire others for continuous improvement of the organization in its environment. **Leadership development** is a strategic endeavor for leaders' personal and professional growth so they can reach higher levels of effectiveness for the organization. Leadership development as examined in this chapter begins with *developing oneself*. The chapter then turns toward *evaluating oneself* for continuous self-improvement and *developing others* and planning for succession for continuing the organization's leadership.

It is appropriate for the final discussion of *The Business of Leadership* to end on leadership development, for that is what keeps leadership continually up-to-date on industry issues and keeps a leader personally refreshed and forward-thinking. Leadership is the ability to see the right choices clearly and then make them. In doing so, leaders can motivate others and inspire change as the organization strives with purpose and conviction to achieve the desired change.

DEVELOPING ONESELF FOR LEADERSHIP

Leadership development refers to any activity that enhances the abilities, attitudes, and quality of leadership. In order to be an effective leader for inspiring change, leaders must be respected for their ingenuity on many fronts, including subject- and industry-oriented information and financial, process, or people-oriented know-how, depending upon the situation at hand. Leadership development is continuously required in all these areas, for development is the self-evaluation that helps keep the mind ever creative.

Leadership in organizations has become more difficult in recent decades for a variety of reasons (Barzelay 1992).

1. First, the *rate of change* in organizations has increased substantially. Organizations are adjusting to the movement from a traditionally bureaucratic paradigm to a learning paradigm that emphasizes distributing power and systems thinking (Senge 1990). This makes the job of leadership more interesting, but also more confusing and risky (Kanter, Stein, and Jick 1992).
2. Second, the *range of leadership activities* required of leaders is simply greater. They need to master change-management skills—technical, organizational, and personnel change skills (Van Wart and Berman 1999). A dynamic environment in which resources are scarce requires leaders to accurately assess what is happening and to inspire change by mobilizing internal and external stakeholders to adopt practical plans. This is hard work.

The development of leadership occurs through *self-study, formal training and education,* and *structured experience.* Leaders should seek all three approaches because they vary in their means to development and offer different insights into leadership. By experiencing all modes of delivery, the learner will identify those approaches that are most comfortable and informative. At one point in a person's professional life, structured experiences may be preferred because of the presence of exciting mentors in the organization. At another point, the same individual may opt for formal online training because of the convenience of accessing it at odd hours. These modes of delivering leadership development are examined first. Then we turn to three important themes of leadership development to which leaders should expose themselves: integrative leadership, shared leadership, and leadership for self-directed teams.

SELF-STUDY

Self-study is important as a means of leadership development. **Self-study** is the raising of one's consciousness before, during, and after either development experiences or formal training and education. Reflect back upon the UPS executive cited in Chapter 8 who advises students to read at least a couple of books per month after they graduate in order to continuously refresh their insights for visionary leadership. That executive was leading those students to practice self-study. Reading to expand your thinking is part of the process of developing yourself for strong, ongoing leadership. Be certain to include books from a wide range of perspectives, including the classics and books about your industry and about management and leadership.

It can certainly be argued that without self-study—that is, without a fundamental recognition of the essential issues, skills, and nuances of leadership—no leadership development can occur. Sometimes the term "self-leadership" is used to describe the direction, support, achievement, and inspiration that emanate primarily from introspection, but also it may be sparked by the personal learning that comes from structured experiences and formal education. Self-study here refers to any type of learning, in addition to the development from reading that occurs outside formal training and structured experiences provided by the organization.

Many individuals begin preparing for leadership long before they assume management or leadership roles by engaging in both technical and broad education. Leaders from all undergraduate disciplines frequently pursue more formal education, such as a master's degree in business administration, at their own expense in order to ensure a deeper understanding of organizational and management practices. Individuals should also cultivate work-specific personal development plans based on their self-observations about what knowledge and competencies they need to enhance. Numerous attitudinal traits and skills described in Part II of this text on managerial leadership behaviors are complementary to self-study; important traits include resilience, energy, need for achievement, and emotional maturity, as well as both task-oriented and people-oriented behaviors.

FORMAL TRAINING AND EDUCATION

The second major mode of delivery for developing oneself is formal training and education. Sometimes people assume that *training* and *education* are identical terms, but they are not. Both are valuable, but they are different. You are likely to be engaged in education right now, investing four years or more in college to achieve a long-term, broad understanding of life. Perhaps you are enrolled in a graduate program to enhance your career mobility. The experience should implant a desire for continuous learning, and the knowledge that is learned should stimulate the mind. As an undergraduate business major gaining technical understanding about fields such as finance, you also have been experiencing a broad-based learning as your career path takes you through two years of general education. As a graduate student, you are refining your conceptual skills while at the same time deepening your understanding of the integration of those skills into the business context and experience. In contrast, training is designed to meet specific short-term operational objectives and improve performance in a specific area—how to process field loans, how to enter package information in a handheld device upon delivery, how to identify account balances for a particular unit in an integrated organizational database system such as People Soft Financials, how to operate and maintain the 595D duplicating machine, and so on.

Training in supervisory skills focuses on the supervisors' direct interaction with subordinates in order to motivate them and achieve results. Specific interpersonal skills and clearly identifiable personnel practices are important targets. Many of the topics focus on organizational procedures and policies that supervisors must master—procurement, ethics, equipment and facilities, hiring, training of employees, information management, privacy and security issues, and so forth. To the degree that leadership per se is an explicit topic, transactional and the basic contingency approaches are often used, such as Blake and Mouton's managerial grid (1964) and Hersey and Blanchard's classic situational leadership (1969). Here is an example of leadership development provided by structured experience:

BP (British Petroleum) Group invested more than a year and $1.5 million into a participatively designed, comprehensive formal training program for its 10,000 supervisors known as "first-level leaders." The program was begun in the early 2000s following mergers of British Petroleum, Amoco, ARCO, and several smaller companies, spurred initially by reports from frontline employees who were unhappy with their own supervisors (Priestland and Hanig 2005). Whereas other organizations typically used electronic media extensively in training its first-line supervisors, BP Group decided to use 250 senior BP executives to deliver much of the content in face-to-face settings. Briefings from senior executives stressed leadership, self-confidence, and self-awareness, as well as BP's strategy and its implications in the global structure.

BP's first-line supervisors were scattered all over the world, making program design a challenge. By pairing first-level leaders with more experienced colleagues in peer partnerships, BP placed strong emphasis on team dynamics and help for first-level leaders in understanding how corporate strategy and the drivers that enabled its delivery applied to their own activities.

BP's face-to-face leadership training initiative was deemed successful. Participation was good and results showed that attendees were consistently ranked higher in performance by both subordinates and bosses than those who had not yet attended the formal training sessions.

Despite funding and energy invested for a decade in the success of BP's structured experience for first-level leaders, by 2010 BP became equally well known for its absence of training with a different classification of employee and a different subject matter. As the magnitude of the tragic BP oil spill in the Gulf of Mexico became known, so did the magnitude of training failures for those involved in the attempted cleanup. Although a spokesperson for BP said that the company "was ensuring that cleanup workers are getting very rigorous training," the U.S. assistant secretary of labor for occupational safety and health pointed to one cleanup site in Biloxi, Mississippi, where more than 800 workers lacked the required training (Taylor and Bolstad 2010). The assistant secretary further pointed to BP's failures in both basic training (providing shade or cool drinks to workers who were cleaning the Alabama shoreline in temperatures reaching into the mid-1990s) and more advanced training (sampling air for toxicity when oil spill dispersants were in use).

There is irony that, within the same company, BP's effective use of structured experience for leadership development could have informed systematic training for BP employees to be prepared for emergency cleanup of the world's worst oil spill disaster. Leadership development certainly focuses on developing oneself as a leader, but does not end there; leaders also develop formal training and structured experiences for others in the organization to help ensure their strategic success.

Just as supervisory skills training focuses on interpersonal skills and specific group processes and procedures needed for motivating followers and achieving results, management development focuses on more complex interpersonal skills in an attempt to achieve organizational results within a changing and complicated environment. The focus shifts from individuals to groups and from the problems of a unit to the management of programs and divisions. For higher-level managers, there is often a focus on the improvement of general analytical skills (as opposed to applied skills of technical professionals) and the ability to make balanced judgments based on a variety of data sources.

To the degree that leadership is an explicit topic, it is more likely to use more sophisticated contingency models such as Vroom's normative-decision model or team and self-leadership theory. As pointed out in the previous section, individuals can seek advanced educational degrees on their own as a type of self-study. However, it is not uncommon for organizations to pay for all or a portion of work-related formal education.

In 2008 the staffing services firm Accountemps interviewed 150 senior executives from the nation's 1,000 largest companies and found that 94 percent said their firm offers tuition reimbursement benefits to its employees. The executives argued that their firm's practice made good sense from a human resources perspective and also for the long-term productivity of the organization. Some firms have expanded the offer of assistance to include part-time employees, although most do not. Some companies offer support for an employee's non-work-related education, but again, this is not the norm. (Employees should read their employee manual for details as often there are conditions that must be met—for example: Is more than one course covered at a time? Is a grade of C+ or better required for reimbursement? What are the accreditation requirements for the school attended? Are textbooks covered? Is a certain length of employment needed in order to have the benefit of tuition reimbursement?)

Exact numbers of employers who provide some form of tuition reimbursement varies, of course, by how the sample companies are chosen and the employee group that is referenced. The Society for Human Resource Management found in 2008 that 66 percent of companies offer undergraduate tuition assistance and 61 percent offer graduate tuition assistance. Another study by the Bureau of Labor Statistics found that in companies with over 100 employees, 72 percent offer tuition reimbursement for managers. Regardless of the precise number offering tuition assistance, formal education being offered by an employer is considered a desirable benefit, both for the employee and for the organization.

Executive development is the most conceptual, as well as the broadest and most externally oriented type of training. Programs for executives tend to focus on the organization in its environment and to facilitate the executives' skills in coping with external opportunities and threats. Typical courses for executives focus on media and public relations, public speaking and contact skills, multisource leader feedback, strategic planning, interorganizational contracts, policy analysis, political and social trends, and legislative and lobbying processes. Leadership is itself often a formal topic. More common approaches include transformational and visionary leadership. Executives are most likely to participate in programs outside the organization because

---

Exhibit 12.1

An Example of Executive Education: Harvard Business School's Program for Leadership Development

Universities frequently offer executive education, designed to attract high-potential leaders and to entice organizations to invest in their next generation of leaders. Harvard has been offering such programs successfully for many years. As an example, participants may sign up for a four-module Program for Leadership Development, set both off and on campus, over a six-month period. On-campus modules run for a couple of weeks.

Harvard's program prepares functional managers with about ten years of work experience for higher-level cross-functional responsibilities and integrated, multifaceted leadership. The business case method is one form of teaching used to instruct managers on how to better assess and analyze complex situations. Full-time faculty from the Harvard Business School teach all executive education courses. They have become known for their familiarity with business practices and their commitment not only to teaching, but also to their research.

Harvard's 2010 schedule of courses gives insight into the variety of educational offerings available just through this one institution: www.exed.hbs.edu/programs/portfolio2010.pdf.

---

of the specialized and high-quality resources required, confidentiality, and the small pool of participants from which to draw in all but the largest organizations. Exhibit 12.1 gives an overview of one university's executive education programs.

When executives or high-potential leaders return from an education or training program, a report on what they learned and its utility for the organization is helpful, both to the individual and to other employees who may be interested in such opportunities. The report can be verbal, as in a staff meeting, or written, as in a memorandum. A one-on-one meeting with the individual is particularly useful to review materials and identify applications or work improvements based on what was learned. Placing developmental accomplishments and goals in the annual work review demonstrates to subordinates the important correlation between these experiences and job evaluation functions. Indeed, it has been repeatedly demonstrated that even the confidence that the supervisor exhibits in a subordinate has a significant effect on behavior, better known as the Pygmalion effect (Exhibit 12.2 gives an example of such a study). The corollary is unfortunately true, too, in that busy supervisors who overlook such opportunities send an unintended message that leadership development is not as critical as are other functions.

STRUCTURED EXPERIENCE

The third type of delivery mode for leadership development is provided by structured experience. **Structured experience** is a large category that includes a host of defined activities that advance one's leadership potential and self-development. Experience is a powerful teacher, and on-the-job training (OJT) has long been recognized as an easy, cost-effective method to arrange on the job site, particularly for operative and repetitive work. Long-term mentoring is often fostered as a type of structured experience for supervisory and management positions.

Three elements have been identified as particularly important in enhancing the developmental opportunities that are actually embedded in a structured experience:

Exhibit 12.2

The Pygmalion Effect

Most people are not aware that trainees' abilities can be enhanced simply by using the right approach with the trainees. Enhancing ability through psychological means is called the Pygmalion effect. In George Bernard Shaw's play *Pygmalion* (and the musical show and movie based on it, *My Fair Lady*), Eliza Doolittle is a cockney flower vendor with low expectations of herself. To win a wager, Professor Henry Higgins agrees to teach her Oxford English so she can pass as a lady. In six months, his high expectations win out, and she passes as an aristocrat—indeed, a princess. Eden and Ravid (1982) documented this thesis in a classic training study. Two identical groups of trainees were given the same training program. However, one group was told by a highly credible source—a psychologist—of their tremendous ability. Even though the trainer was not informed about this experiment, the trainees in the experimental group performed dramatically better than the control group. Thus high expectations both affected the trainees' perceptions of their ability and increased their motivation.

1. First, experience is valuable when work *offers challenging but realistic assignments*. People report learning more and appreciating the experience when work offers some real challenges. Indeed, failures also offer valuable lessons. However, the realism of challenges must be kept in mind. Unrealistic goals are discouraging and produce frustration and anger (Locke and Latham 1990).
2. Second, *variety of experiences* is critical for optimal executive development. Those who are trained in a "silo" of experience and have never worked in different areas of the organization will have difficulty understanding the language, norms, and mind-set of many parts of the organization. Leaders who have served in only one functional area, such as accounting, might find it difficult to appreciate and communicate with the operational divisions, and therefore a structured experience for job rotation into additional functional areas can be useful. Similarly, leaders who are advanced from line operations may make poor use of staff divisions without benefit of structured experiences that expose them to staff divisions.
3. Third, the *quality of feedback* received makes an enormous difference as well. Suggestions about how things work, why success or failure is achieved, and how to do better are critical for optimal learning. This means that as leaders are developing, their supervisors must take the time to understand the quality of their work as well as to discuss it in detail. Top organizational leaders also continue to need quality feedback, but they must often design and analyze it themselves.

Because the best development relies on providing challenge, variety, and feedback, multiple types of activities may be needed to foster a strong leadership learning environment. Of course, the types of developmental activities will vary substantially based on the level in the organization. Although the following activities will be described as if the learner is always the recipient of development, this is not to say that providers of leadership development do not also gain from the experience as they structure it and provide feedback. Teaching requires people to take implicit or "gut" knowledge and make it explicit. It also requires people to refine their ideas and increase their overall sophistication about the relationships inherent in leadership.

Methods for Development Through Structured Experience

Five specific methods of structured experience will now be discussed: individual learning plans, job rotation, specialized developmental assignments, coaching, and mentoring.

Individual learning plans are a good means of providing oneself the parameters necessary for structured experiences. Leaders at all levels of the organization should encourage those reporting to them to submit individual development plans that map out future learning goals, as well as employee accomplishment reports that emphasize past training and development. A development plan requires a person to specify a strategy to improve skills, abilities, and knowledge—whatever her or his current level. The assumption behind development plans is that everybody can and should try to improve current capabilities. Employee accomplishment reports should include both production achievements and personal growth achievements. Such accomplishment reports ideally are connected to performance ratings, pay increases, and promotions over time. The most comprehensive strategy is an individual annual report that includes the annual accomplishment report (the past year's) and an individual development plan (next year's). It is a powerful tool for supervisors who wish to hold those reporting to them responsible for their own development while maintaining a say in the authorization and reward of training and developmental activities.

Consciously designed, fully articulated annual plans for development do not spring full-blown to paper once a year unless a less formal, ongoing assessment of development needs has occurred during the year. Leaders and their supervisors need to be on the lookout for special learning opportunities and new competency deficits created by new responsibilities. While many microlevel skills do not rise to the level of inclusion in an annual development plan, they can nonetheless be critical in optimizing job success. For example, leaders must often take time from busy schedules to learn about technical systems for approvals, relaying information, budgeting and finance, and so forth. Understanding the details of such systems may not be critical because subordinates can provide the needed information; however, a basic understanding of technical aspects of work being done can improve leaders' ability to oversee those skills being carried out and to shape their own requests for information more astutely.

Job rotation can elevate the vision of the learner by exposure to a variety of structured experiences. A high-level manager needs to understand the varied parts of the organization in order to see the big picture. Job rotation enriches both the organization and the employees involved. Traditionally, job rotation serves as a form of executive development for employees chosen early in their careers for promotion. Bright and motivated young employees engage in a number of assignments throughout the organization to ensure that they have an excellent firsthand grasp of a wide range of essential organizational components. After working at a series of jobs, the employees may rise more rapidly through the ranks.

While job rotation can always promote skill development, it also helps with managerial succession planning by identifying a pool of candidates who are capable of moving into anticipated openings. In a true job rotation, a trainee is given a series of different job assignments in various parts of the organization for specific periods of time and is exposed to a variety of tasks or decision-making situations. There are several types of modified job rotation that achieve different purposes, such as rotating jobs among employees who work together within a single unit. When the rotation takes place at the lower levels of an organization, especially within a unit, it spreads skills more evenly throughout the work group. Trainees can fill in for absentees. Employees appreciate each other's work more, and group problem-solving can be enhanced. It is especially useful for leaders-in-training to experience both line and staff positions. Job rotation can also be an excellent means of assisting employees in exploring career alternatives.

The benefits of job rotation for senior employees are slightly different. These employees generally move through a series of units or perhaps are exposed to the mechanics of the entire organization. They gain an overall perspective of the organization and can make decisions that better incorporate the perspectives and needs of all divisions.

Job rotation is not without its problems, particularly in the operational areas. If the work area or organization is struggling with large workloads, rotational assignments can initially decrease productivity and efficiency. When the workload is too pressing, the trainee may feel great stress and may not receive support in the training. Considerable one-on-one training is required to assist the trainee to learn the basic work requirements and to monitor progress. An unmotivated trainee can contribute little and may have a shallow learning experience. These and other potential problems only emphasize that job rotation cannot be conducted in a random, unstructured, or casual way if it is to be consistently successful.

Specialized developmental assignments are structured experiences that can offer a broader leadership perspective and an enhanced range of skills by a different means than job rotation. Special assignments can be scheduled not only apart from one's regular job, but concurrently with it as well. Managers can be asked, for example, to chair a problem-solving committee or task force, assume a new general management function such as budget preparation, start up a new operation, substitute at an important meeting, or manage and write an important study. Sometimes such assignments do not require being in charge, but just observing. Attending meetings and conferences, conducting site visits, and shadowing an executive are examples of useful observation experiences.

Special assignments have particular relevance in an organizational universe moving toward flattening, decentralizing, and multitasking. The proverbial final item at the end of everyone's job description—"and other work as assigned"—is an everyday reality for most managers and supervisors. Leaders need to be prepared to take on a variety of special tasks in addition to their normal line or staff work, and these challenging assignments are the opportunities for development. Of course, the downfall of special assignments is typical of many developmental problems—poor planning, excessive challenges without sufficient support in carrying out the assignment, and poor feedback from one's supervisor.

Coaching, the most commonly used developmental technique at all levels, is the backbone both in OJT of technical know-how and for feedback on the social intelligence skills needed for outstanding leadership. When coached, employees normally learn through structured experiences from an immediate supervisor or a coworker, and executive level employees learn from the top executive team or CEO. More than anyone else on the job, the coach is in closest contact with the employee and therefore knows the employee's skills and actual performance well. Coaching occurs on a one-to-one basis, uses the trainee's actual job experience as a source of learning, and is done on site. Coaching is used to train new employees and to maintain and upgrade the skills of current employees. In other words, coaching should really never stop. It offers the opportunity for employees to become leaders by learning from their own mistakes and successes instead of learning only from generalized examples. The technique is often casual, which helps the learner to relax, but the informality may lead to sloppy implementation.

While coaching frontline employees is often a major function for supervisors, in practice it is much less an expectation at all levels of management. The management group that generally receives the most coaching is the new supervisor because of the shift from a technical to a management position. Right or wrong, the assumption at other levels, even when managers are moving into new positions and to higher levels, is that the managers have the experience and background to figure out the job with the limited structured training that is provided.

Coaching on technical processes and background information is normally conducted by subordinates at the manager's request. In general, managers and executives who need coaching because they are new, inexperienced, or encountering a new or specialized problem may have to seek out their own coaching. This means that they must recognize the need, identify a competent source, and follow through on their own. Because most managers have hectic jobs with dozens of issues swirling about them at any given time (Mintzberg 1979), it is easy to see why managers often fail to seek out or provide coaching even when they clearly recognize the need to do so. Occasionally managers can sidestep the immediate need for coaching by assigning the task or issue to a competent subordinate. This can save the manager's time, allow the manager to learn by example, and provide a professional experience for the subordinate. However, it is not always appropriate or possible to delegate all tasks that the manager does not understand. Typical coaches for managers are subordinates, the boss, a colleague at the same level, human resource personnel, executive staff, and other specialists in the organization.

There has been an increase in the popularity of executive coaching with external coaches, compared to the first two methods discussed for leadership development. Executive coaches can be hired consultants from outside the organization or high-prestige trainers with special training from within the organization. Some of the advantages of executive coaching with an external coach are flexibility, confidentiality, and convenience. Because of the expense of a consultant, or time consumption of an internal consultant, such training may be reserved for senior managers. It is particularly useful when provided in conjunction with other programs in which the executive is receiving a wide array of management-style performance data (such as through leadership survey feedback) or when the executive is implementing a special project (a form of action learning).

Mentoring refers to a protégé relationship in which a senior, experienced individual shares information about the organizational culture, career opportunities, and networking aspects of a job. Unlike coaching, which focuses on specific learning goals such as fixing a technical problem or learning about a specific process, mentoring focuses on the big picture. Mentors are often from other areas in the organization. Having a mentor is considered a powerful way for emergent leaders to develop.

Mentoring for those new to the profession, but who have high potential, such as those from MBA programs, is often more generic and discipline-related. Students may be matched up with a business executive during the latter stages of the program of study while still in school. High-quality internships build mentoring into a structured experience. There is no consensus about whether formal or informal mentoring is more effective. However, there is little doubt that in order to be effective, the mentor has to be a true and dedicated role model who is sincerely interested in the relationship. Given that time is often a senior manager's most precious commodity, good intentions are often not equivalent to good follow-through.

Topics to Cover in Structured Leadership Development Programs

What topics should be covered in leadership development programs and sought by emergent leaders? We will discuss three that are especially important to today's leadership environment: integrative leadership, shared leadership, and self-directed teams. A manager who is not prepared in these areas would have a difficult time in motivating followers and taking on the executive leadership behaviors that achieve results.

First, **integrative leadership** is one major component of a leadership development program designed to build emergent leaders. If you have ever completed a course in accounting and another in marketing and wondered if they have anything to do with each other, you have hit upon the need for integration. Integrative leadership is the ability to see each of the parts that make up the big picture individually as well as the ability to see how those parts integrate with each other to make up the big picture. Only when we see the integration of those parts do we see the whole, and that perspective allows us to begin to think with vision. Leaders who understand integration are able to see the often subtle relationships among ideas and concepts. They are able to organize their thinking around themes and pull individual topics together. Leaders need to master change-management skills as discussed in the prior section, but also they must be able to step away from compartmentalized thinking and use an integrated approach to complex organizational activity. The ability to exhibit integrative leadership is a sign that an individual may well be ready for higher level organizational leadership. But it does not necessarily come naturally without explicit development.

After the transformational leadership movement had run its initial course by the early 1990s, researchers began to focus on how to integrate different foci, without diminishing the insights of various approaches. This seemed increasingly urgent because the number of fundamentally different approaches had grown so large and the field had become a bewildering forest of theories, specialized concepts, and terms. Rather than expanding a single theory to be more inclusive, as Bass (1985) had done with transformational leadership, there is now an interest in a more comprehensive, integrated approach that includes multiple types of leadership and substantially different contexts. It involves the leadership of both day-to-day transactional settings and situations involving major change, as well as the perspectives of frontline supervisors and chief executives. Those working on integrated models or frameworks have tried to show the complexity of relationships, understanding that this makes it difficult or impossible to validate them as empirically testable theories. Nor are theorists in this mode as interested in being specifically predictive because of the extensive number of relationships that they attempt to identify. Despite fewer claims on empirical validity, they do attempt to offer greater utility in other respects.

Reasons for the utility of an integrated approach are not hard to identify. First, there is always a need to coordinate diverse research agendas, and this is particularly important in leadership studies that are so vast. How can the insights of trait, management, transactional, charismatic, transformational, and distributed approaches be brought together? Second, integrated approaches often reveal where consensus has been achieved, which can lead to shared nomenclature and concepts. Confusion of terms and concepts in leadership studies is sometimes extreme. Third, an integrated approach can more holistically identify research gaps among the various approaches. What aspects of the phenomenon have yet to be adequately explained? Finally, an integrated approach is useful to students attempting to understand leadership as a whole. The diversity of perspectives and different foci in the leadership literature is great; comprehensive theories provide a context in order to maximize comprehension and utility.

Leaders first assess the organization, their own constraints, and their own abilities. Then leaders begin to set goals and determine priorities. Their actions or behaviors are molded by their strategic purposes as well as by the reservoir of talents that they bring, which they have acquired through experience, education, and natural talents. The success of their actions will affect their performance. A simplified model is presented in Exhibit 12.3.

Reconceptualizing this process as a causal chain, leaders act using a wide variety of styles. Eight pure styles and one combined style have been identified. The proper selection of style is based on three variables. First, different organizational and environmental needs will require different styles. The frontline leader may need to use a supportive style more frequently; a chief executive officer has to be more versed in an external style. Although all leaders need a variety of styles, the mix of styles will vary by factors such as the need for control, differential goals and performance expectations, types of motivators utilized, and the type of leader focus emphasized.

Second, leaders must examine the constraints they face in terms of resources, power, and personal skills. A leader taking over a division in a crisis mode may need to rely on a highly directive style, whereas a leader taking over a high-performing division may initially adopt a laissez-faire style and study the organization for subtle refinements.

Third, the leader's own sense of priorities will shape the selection of styles. A leader more interested in developing long-term capacity through an investment in human resources may emphasize supportive, participative, and delegative styles. A leader more interested in meeting immediate environmental demands for greater competitiveness and organizational change may rely more on achievement, inspirational, and external styles.

Exhibit 12.3 **An Overview of the Leadership Action Cycle**

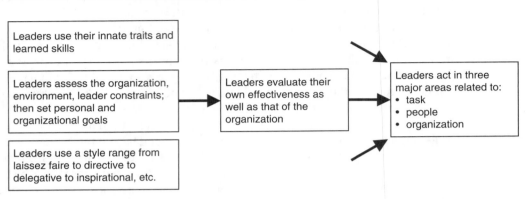

The degree of success of the various styles chosen is affected by leaders' characteristics and the quality of their behavioral skills. Have they had experience and practice in using various styles? Do they have a natural ability or talent for the styles that they are using? Do they have capabilities and the right attitudes for the tasks that they manage? Managers with high competence in operations but poor interpersonal and leadership skills will generally perform poorly overall. The same is generally true of managers who have good leadership skills but little operational experience because they will need to divert much time and attention to basic learning and may need to rely excessively on others for expert judgments in managerial decisions. As leadership skills and technical competence increase, quality in using various styles is also likely to improve along with overall performance.

Performance itself can be judged from radically different, although not mutually exclusive, perspectives. Technical efficiency requires cost efficiency, and program effectiveness requires fulfilling authorized goals through legitimate processes. Although a high level of follower or employee satisfaction and development may lead to higher efficiency and effectiveness, it need not necessarily do so. The "country club" mentality may maximize employee needs at the organization's expense. Emphasizing decision quality as a performance variable indirectly emphasizes a balance of various criteria through a thoughtful process. That is, the quality of the leadership process (quality decisions) is as important as any of the outcomes, such as productivity or employee satisfaction. Another performance outcome is the degree of alignment of the organization with the external environment. Poor alignment can occur because of internal dysfunctionality, such as organizational rigidity or apathy toward client needs, or it can occur because of a change in the environment itself, leading to a new mandate. Finally, performance can be assessed based on the organization's ability to change and be flexible. This type of performance factor becomes more important in a dynamic or turbulent environment. The **causal chain for the leadership action cycle** is illustrated in Exhibit 12.4.

Distributed or shared leadership is a second major component of a leadership development program that is designed to build emergent leaders. Most important leadership topics go well beyond *cognitive understanding*—that is, a mental process

Exhibit 12.4 **"Leadership Action Cycle" Causal Chain**

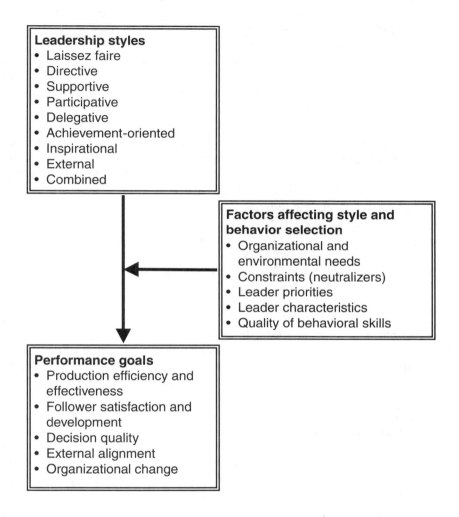

of knowing a topic through awareness, reasoning, and understanding. They typically include a behavioral element and sometimes a *willingness* factor. For example, a leader could mentally understand what "shared leadership" is without being willing to adopt shared leadership by letting go of appropriate power and authority. A leader could mentally grasp the notion of decentralization without becoming comfortable enough to trust others for a decentralized model to exist. Development for shared leadership therefore tackles not just the definition of shared leadership, but also issues of behavioral change toward shared leadership.

Distributed leadership emphasizes the sharing of functions through empowerment mechanisms such as participation and delegation. *Shared leadership* is one form of distributed leadership. It is based on the normative assumptions that various types of distributed leadership exist and are useful, and that a major role of traditional leadership is to enhance the capability and motivation to engage in distributed leadership. Shared leadership has strong parallels in other areas of the management literature, such as the literature on the learning organization (Senge 1990).

Distributed leadership is often contrasted with the traditional notion of the vertical hierarchy. Accountability, in fact, is traditionally perceived as being possible only through the traditional vertical hierarchy in which a specific individual or position is held accountable for particular results. With that notion, there are cascading levels of leadership authority. Yet the vertical structure is not the only means for achieving accountability; it also can be effective in some settings through mutual accountability. Becoming able to "let go" for shared leadership, or sharing of responsibilities through empowerment, is the subject of development. We know that normally an individual who has risen through the ranks is capable of doing things well and overseeing others to an equally high standard. That ability does not necessarily translate into willingness for shared leadership. Thus, if the organizational style favors decentralization, its leaders may need to participate in development for shared leadership in order to adopt this approach behaviorally.

The style proposed in shared leadership is actually a combined style based on both vertical and distributed forms of leadership occurring concurrently (Houghton, Neck, and Manz 2003). It is a multilevel model because different organizational members perform different types of leadership at the same time. Followers need to be developed also to accept the responsibilities and challenges of distributed leadership. Only when subordinates are prepared to accept responsibility does a robust form of shared leadership exist. Another important element of shared leadership is the empowered team, which not only carries out important management functions with relative autonomy, but also self-organizes and distributes leadership functions such as accountability and role assignments. In the ideal, shared leadership emphasizes that the best-run contemporary organizations need to maximize "bottom-up" or distributed leadership as much as possible (Locke 2003).

Overall, three factors determine the likelihood of success of shared leadership. The first factor is the capacity of the subordinates or members themselves. If turnover is high, education poor, training superficial, pay low, or recruitment sloppy, shared leadership has little chance of success. The second factor is the capability of leaders to develop and delegate. No matter how capable and committed subordinates may be, some leaders find it very difficult to teach others, much less share their power. The third factor is the general willingness of the organization, through its governing board, chief executive officer, and culture, to allow and encourage the use of distributed leadership models.

Why can shared leadership be powerful within an organization? First, it gives employees at multiple levels the opportunity to invest in the organization and serve in a leadership capacity. Increased commitment usually results. Second, nothing is sacrificed in terms of goals, and in fact, output may improve because of higher levels of commitment. The performance goals of shared leadership can be assumed to be similar to those of other leadership models. Production efficiency, follower satisfaction and development, decision quality, and external alignment are all significant outcomes.

Exhibit 12.5 **Shared Leadership Causal Chain**

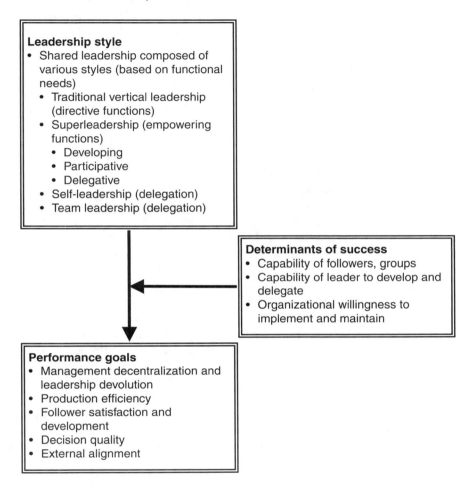

Leadership style
- Shared leadership composed of various styles (based on functional needs)
  - Traditional vertical leadership (directive functions)
  - Superleadership (empowering functions)
    - Developing
    - Participative
    - Delegative
  - Self-leadership (delegation)
  - Team leadership (delegation)

Determinants of success
- Capability of followers, groups
- Capability of leader to develop and delegate
- Organizational willingness to implement and maintain

Performance goals
- Management decentralization and leadership devolution
- Production efficiency
- Follower satisfaction and development
- Decision quality
- External alignment

Management decentralization and leadership devolution are also implied by the model. The implicit causal model for shared leadership is shown in Exhibit 12.5.

Building self-directed teams is a third component of developing oneself that should be sought by emergent leaders and covered in leadership development programs in order to prepare for today's leadership environment. A **self-directed team** is a natural work group that is cross-functional in nature and is fully empowered for a particular result—usually for production of a particular service or product. It is a form of organizational design that requires employees not only to do the work, but also to manage themselves in doing the work; it is a method that can be successful for achieving high-level results. Self-directed teams have been used in Europe since the 1950s, but generally the method did not migrate to the United States until the 1980s when major competition from Japan knocked down U.S. market share in the automotive and steel industries.

Everything discussed in the prior section regarding how shared leadership goes beyond *cognitive understanding* to also include a behavioral dimension and a *willingness* factor is true for participation in self-directed teams. Developing leadership for self-directed teams also requires that both dimensions be addressed.

Leaders who oversee areas in which self-directed teams function have to be comfortable giving employees direct access to budgetary and other information that allows them to take charge of their own operations. Higher-level managers then need to coach employees on the team about assuming full responsibility—what was previously reserved for management.

All members of self-directed teams need to participate as leaders. Leaders who oversee divisions or other units in which self-directed teams exist should be prepared to accept this approach to distributive leadership.

Leadership literature in the 1950s through the 1970s did focus on the emergence of leadership in leaderless groups, but the primary purpose was to study leadership formation rather than to encourage and support a form of distributed leadership of teams operating without a designated manager from among the members.

Social-exchange theory of the 1950s also offered a number of important social insights for work settings. The theory argued that behavior results from negotiated exchanges between parties in a sort of cost-benefit analysis in which people stay in a relationship when they match perceived benefits with costs of a relationship. Pay is traded for service and special consideration is exchanged for hard work. Emphasis today on high-performing teams can rely on exceptional efforts in the face of unusual demands, a deadline, or a crisis, but social-exchange theory was not used for analysis in a self-management context despite its other social insights.

In the 1980s great attention was paid to Japanese innovations in devolution, employee empowerment, quality circles, and similar measures. Almost overnight, interest in self-managed quality improvement teams, "empowered" project teams, and various types of self-managing employee groups mushroomed.

Formally managed and self-managed teams fall along a spectrum. The formally managed team has a strong leader who selects members or work assignments, monitors progress, encourages members, provides feedback for work deviations, sets goals, evaluates progress, and communicates organizational expectations to members while communicating team performance to the organization. In the extreme, the self-managed team selects its members; all members monitor progress; encouragement is provided by colleagues; goal-setting, evaluation, and work problems (including member expulsion) are handled communally; and external leadership is rotated or assigned by the group on an ad hoc basis.

Self-managed team theory advocates generally acknowledge that self-managed teams can thrive only under special conditions and that they should be considered a type of team leadership, not the type of team leadership. The single combined style of team leadership distributes the standard functions of leadership among the group or allows the group to assign leadership functions based on member talents and availability. Thus, direction, support, participation, achievement, inspiration, and external connectedness are mutually determined and executed. This practice is an appealing form of work democracy that, when functioning ideally, enhances identification with the work, task selection based on talent and interest, flexibility, and innovation. However, when self-managed teams are functioning poorly, they induce frustration, unresolved disputes, free riders (members who do not pull their weight), goal confusion, fuzzy accountability, excessive meetings, and other management pathologies.

Katzenbach and Smith (1993) provide a good example of the type of conditions that must exist for self-managed teams to perform well. They point to four ideal practices.

1. The first is a *common purpose and approach* by the team. Management theory holds that work done by groups must be organized to be efficient, which means that a major function of management is normally to divide and coordinate work (Mintzberg 1973). Under certain conditions, however, such division and coordination can be diffused and organic. Imagine a large, annual family gathering to which many members bring different dishes of food. There is an understanding that the meal will take place at a certain time, so self-selected members busy themselves with what seems necessary. After the meal, another self-appointed group starts to clean up. This self-organizing example highlights some of the factors contributing to a common purpose and approach: a history of cooperating and working together, a shared project and goal, and common interests.

In the organizational world, a common approach is enhanced by a strong culture and philosophy that in turn tends to rely on similar educational background. However, because of the multiple disciplinary perspectives represented in many teams and the complexity of technical functions to be executed, many organizations that want to encourage self-managed teams rely on extensive team training (Scholtes 1993).

2. Another principle of management theory is that without accountability, productivity will lag and quality will vary beyond permissible levels. As mentioned in the previous section, the classical management answer has been to provide cascading levels of leadership authority. Katzenbach and Smith are among those who assert that in many settings *mutual accountability* is as effective as or even more effective than traditional vertical accountability. For mutual accountability to work, mutual benefits must be freely and consistently exchanged and power relationships must be relatively equal.

3. A third principle of self-managed teams that function well is the need for *complementary skills*. The best role assignments on the team are based on individual skills and personality. Further, role differentiation becomes more important with task complexity. Complementary skills, then, are based on the natural talents of team members who are allowed to specialize for efficiency and coordination. However, the leadership role must also be distributed. Those in leadership roles are expected to be competent in basic social skills, have an appropriate demeanor, and be worthy of trust. While members can and should have different skill sets to contribute to team efforts, they must all have basic leadership competence for a diffused model of management to work well.

4. The last requirement for highly productive self-managed teams is to have an *appropriate number of team members*. As the group size increases, the pressure to formalize roles increases. Role formalization can enhance work uniformity, consistency of expectations, and complex accountability requirements, but also it can decrease

flexibility, common ownership of group products, creativity, and innovation. Self-managed teams avoid role formalization in order to take advantage of such potential virtues. A relatively small number of team members allows them to interact directly, get to know and trust each other, and develop a strong sense of community. A common approach is then more likely to be achieved and the purpose is less likely to become fragmented while mutual accountability can still be monitored informally.

The performance goals vary considerably in the self-managed team literature, from an emphasis on individual development through teams to an emphasis on high team productivity. Katzenbach and Smith (1993) emphasize the latter in their "high-performance organization." They also stress follower satisfaction, mutual development, and decision quality. The causal chain implicit in self-managed terms is illustrated in Exhibit 12.6.

Team theory acknowledges a powerful organizational mode and gives it the central attention it deserves. There is little doubt that teams with self-led features have had a substantial and growing impact in contemporary organizations. A second strength of this literature is its clear statement that high-quality, self-managing groups are neither easy to attain nor are they suited for all situations. In fact, self-managed teams take even more sociotechnical design than normal vertical leadership teams do. With the recent coalescence of the team literature and the increased popularity of team approaches, the connections between the reality and theory of teams has also been somewhat bridged.

Through development for self-managed teams, even if the organization opts for a more traditional vertical form than completely leaderless groups, good understanding is developed about what is possible on the continuum of distributive leadership.

LEADERSHIP EVALUATION

How is leadership evaluation done so that leaders may better gauge their development? Evaluation can be accomplished through a number of means and instruments. A key aspect of leadership development is self-assessment. The term "assessment" implies that data on leadership constructs are taken, evaluated, and acted upon by the leader to bring self-improvements; later the same constructs are re-measured to assess the extent of improvement actually achieved. One effective basis for continuous personal and professional improvement is 360-degree feedback obtained from all stakeholders. When taken seriously, the results of self-assessment serve as a kind of needs analysis for those wanting to build a personal learning plan around their development as a leader.

Self-assessment is known to be an important method of leadership evaluation. Peter Drucker (2005) wrote a classic article on managing oneself in which he stated unequivocally that the "only way" for leaders to discover their strengths is to utilize feedback analysis. He said it can be as simple as writing down what you expect will happen every time you take a key action and later comparing your prediction to actual results. Imagine Drucker learning through this process that he did not "really resonate with generalists" but rather had an intuitive understanding of technical people ranging from accountants to market researchers! Drucker challenged leaders

Exhibit 12.6   **Self-Managed Teams Causal Chain**

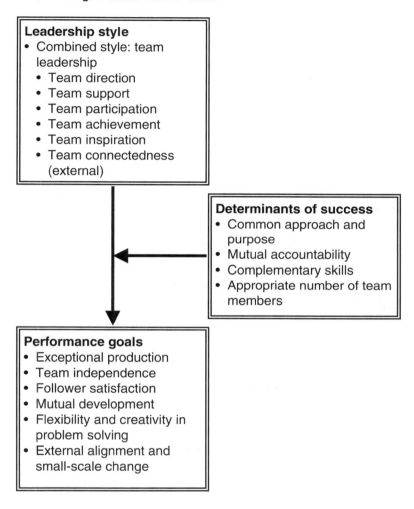

Leadership style
- Combined style: team leadership
  - Team direction
  - Team support
  - Team participation
  - Team achievement
  - Team inspiration
  - Team connectedness (external)

Determinants of success
- Common approach and purpose
- Mutual accountability
- Complementary skills
- Appropriate number of team members

Performance goals
- Exceptional production
- Team independence
- Follower satisfaction
- Mutual development
- Flexibility and creativity in problem solving
- External alignment and small-scale change

Source: Katzenbach and Smith (1993).

to evaluate themselves relative to how they learn, what their values are, and what they should contribute.

Another highly useful means of evaluating leaders for development is through information-gathering instruments, such as the sixty-item Leadership Assessment Questionnaire at the end of this chapter. Its questions guide leaders to consider many important dimensions of leadership that they might otherwise omit. The instrument is designed as a tool not to compare one leader against another, but rather to give extensive and meaningful feedback for development and improvement. Constraints, traits, skills, and other leadership dimensions are explored. The questionnaire could be used for self-assessment or included in a more structured evaluation of organizational leaders.

Which leaders should be evaluated? Simply put, everyone can benefit from evaluation. The method used can be a one-time instrument, given near the end of the initial probationary period, or an ongoing occurrence, such as an annual review for promotion. Leaders who skip evaluation, especially when they are new, or allow this function to atrophy may doom themselves to being, at best, second-rate.

Former CEO of Arrow Electronics Stephen Kaufman points out that it is traditional for midlevel organizational leaders to receive comprehensive performance evaluation, but it is not unusual for a CEO to receive only a perfunctory comment from the board of directors on just three or four financial measures that are important to the board (Kaufman 2008). To change this limited practice, Arrow Electronics instituted a system that required directors to spend time interviewing executives on the CEO's leadership, strategy, goals, people management, relationships with external constituencies, and yes, operating metrics. After each director met annually with three executives separately to discuss the designated topics of strategy, culture, competitive position, and operations, the directors were positioned to know the organization better and to give "real feedback" to the CEO. Kaufman, who became a senior lecturer at Harvard Business School, observes, "All the financial incentives in the world won't transform CEOs into better decision makers." Presumably, it is the detailed evaluation from experienced board directors, combined with the CEOs' communication back to the board on their understandings from the evaluation, that helps transform CEOs into better leaders.

What should be evaluated? In addition to each of the skill sets cited above, such as organizational strategy and operating metrics, interpersonal relationships and people management are important and should be evaluated as well.

The concept of *social intelligence* (Thorndike 1920)—interpersonal competencies that inspire others to be effective—is important in coaching and leadership development, so it should also emerge as part of leadership evaluation. In addition to permitting a glimpse into a leader's mastering of skill sets, evaluation can also reveal a leader's ability to inspire. When leading psychologist and science writer Daniel Goleman first wrote about what makes a leader, he focused on the role of empathy toward others combined with self-knowledge, and called it *emotional intelligence* (Goleman 1995). To miss this aspect of leadership in evaluation misses the characteristic that pulls leaders and followers together in cooperation and mutual support. Goleman has now developed a 360-degree assessment tool called the Emotional and Social Competency Inventory. The performance dimensions covered in this particular instrument are empathy, attunement, organizational awareness, influence, developing others, inspiration, and teamwork (Goleman and Boyatzis 2008).

DEVELOPING OTHERS FOR LEADERSHIP

Proper **succession planning** requires a systematic process for identifying future talent and developing it in order to supply the present and future leadership needs of the organization. What made the organization successful? However that question is answered serves as the base from which development should occur. Succession planning builds the organization from within by transitioning staff that have institutional knowledge and savvy through management levels. Executives review and support development of those in lower managerial levels to identify backups for senior positions and higher-level management positions. It typically takes years of grooming to develop employees because they need to respond favorably to content-oriented information at strategic levels of organizational activity as well as be a "fit" for the real leadership needed by the organization.

Succession planning programs literally keep the organization alive and vibrant without bringing unintended change. They are strategic in nature because they address the gaps between the leadership of today and the human resource needs of tomorrow.

Managers who are identified for development, usually at the entry to middle levels, are typically honored and respond favorably. The succession management process involves identifying competencies and participants for key positions within the organization, developing each potential successor in the competencies that were identified, and ultimately undertaking a search for applicants with internal candidates being encouraged to apply. When individuals are selected for a development program, it should be clear that they have been chosen to broadly enhance all leadership competencies, rather than focus on the competencies of a particular position.

Who will participate in the development necessary for succession planning? Most likely it will be those individuals identified as having high potential as opposed to those who are described as "good in their current job." Leadership continuity is the purpose of succession planning, so it is those employees with high potential who are singled out and invited to participate in leadership development.

Henri Fayol, when writing on the functions of management in the late nineteenth century, was concerned with the stability of tenure of personnel. If that specific issue was not addressed, he believed that the future organization would not be led by the very best candidates. Being "good" or average in one's current job does not necessarily lead to promotion, just as excellence in the skills required for higher-level positions does not necessarily guarantee advancement.

Planning prevents a leadership crisis. One of the many challenges affecting organizations today is the issue of age as the baby boom generation begins its exit from the workforce. Unfortunately, many companies have not completed a leadership profile by age of those in key positions, or they would realize the looming imperative for succession planning. The Age Discrimination in Employment Act of 1967 prohibits employment discrimination against persons forty years of age or older, so even though a company must not *discriminate* against workers in this group, company managers must *know* and plan precisely for the effects of this demographic over the next five to ten years. Demographic changes in the workforce require leadership development implementation. For a company to turn its back on the need to develop personnel who can step into leadership roles is to risk the success of the entire organization.

Succession planning, for example, was taken very seriously at General Electric. GE's board of directors spent thousands of hours over several years in the process of selecting a CEO to replace Jack Welch. This followed on the heels of GE's development in the 1970s of a series of operations called "leadership assimilation," a process designed to bring newly hired or newly promoted leaders into a strong positive relationship with their teams just a few months after assuming the new position. A facilitator guides the new leader to respond to key questions from the team over a period of several hours, realizing that the team expects the leader to be a good listener, but does not expect that expertise is fully developed on all questions. At the conclusion of the assimilation session, the leader writes a letter of thanks to team members for their help and attaches a copy of meeting notes. Collective achievement as a team is GE's focus through succession and assimilation.

It is possible to explore what competencies in a particular organization disappear as senior leaders retire and what implications that has for leadership development activities. One study, taken outside the confines of any particular organization, found large gaps in four competencies between senior- and mid-level manager populations, projecting that those competencies would decline because of retirements unless they were the focus of organizational leadership development (Wolff, Wageman, and Fontaine 2009). This research suggests that identifying applicable gaps within a particular organization would be helpful in refocusing where leadership development was most needed within that organization.

All the delivery modes for developing oneself are to be utilized in developing others for leadership, with special emphasis on *structured experiences*. Individual learning plans, job rotation, specialized developmental assignments, coaching, and mentoring will all be extraordinarily valuable manners of delivery. Again, a mix of such techniques is far better than utilizing just one method. In addition, future talent should be encouraged to participate in self-study and formal training and education. Potential leaders can be offered training and tuition reimbursement for appropriate job-related education.

In the same way that leadership development needs some organizational financing behind it to make it a serious priority of the organization, succession planning needs financing behind it to make it a serious priority of senior leadership. Leadership development is critical for the survival of business; it acts much like a river in that it keeps a successive body of leadership flowing through the organization at all times.

CONCLUSION

Enhancing leadership development is a responsibility of the well-managed organization. Ideally, organizations create multiple avenues for leadership development, including formal training, structured developmental opportunities, and incentives for self-study. Such diversity can provide a highly favorable environment and synergy among the types of training. Organizations can enhance leadership development by

- providing financial support for continuing education;
- providing an array of supervisory, management, and executive leadership programs;
- providing rewards and awards for those who create improvements and are innovative;
- providing rotational assignments;

- assigning pay increases partially based on skill development;
- allowing time for learning experiences and experimentation;
- including development as an explicit category in the annual evaluation for all employees;
- evaluating supervisors at all levels on their ability and success in providing management and leadership development (leadership succession);
- bringing in outside speakers and guests to stimulate new ideas;
- encouraging outside field trips to benchmark best practices;
- integrating "live" projects into formal training programs (action learning);
- providing multisource feedback on a standard schedule and with institutional support; and
- proactively establishing a "learning organization" that embraces new ideas and openness. (Senge 1990; Garvin 1993)

Whereas previous chapters have discussed the mechanics of leadership, this chapter has focused on how companies can consciously develop that leadership. The demands on leaders are greater today because the rate of change in organizations has substantially increased the skills necessary. At the same time, we have simultaneously entered an age more cynical about leaders themselves. Allowing leadership to develop haphazardly is likely to leave individuals with critical skill gaps and blind spots, and to leave organizations with succession deficits. Not taking the time to assess where one has been and where one needs next to go is to disregard the business of leadership.

There are three fundamental modes for delivering leadership development. Self-study is the raising of one's own consciousness by examining appropriate topics. For example, when a university goes through the accreditation process, it normally begins with an investigative self-study following a template of important areas to scrutinize about its results; self-study for leadership development may have some procedural elements in common or may be unstructured. The second mode of leadership development—formal education and training—is particularly important in executive education. The third leadership development method discussed involves providing structured experiences in the work setting, such as individual learning plans, job rotation, specialized developmental assignments, coaching, and mentoring.

Improving leadership development in an organization is most likely when there are multiple avenues for it to occur and when management takes the issue of leadership succession seriously. In the organizations best at supporting leadership development, supervisors at all levels engage in discussion of leadership development and work hard to provide the necessary resources, such as access to formal and informal opportunities, time to participate, and the monies they often require.

Evaluating oneself is done for continuous improvement and ongoing personal assessment. Assessment of leadership implies that data on leadership constructs are taken, analyzed, and acted upon by the leader to bring self-improvements; later the same constructs are remeasured to assess the extent of improvement actually achieved. Furthermore, organizations and individuals ensure that leaders are prepared with a broad set of perspectives—integrated leadership—and can cope and flourish in a shared power world with empowered and even self-managed teams.

Succession planning is yet another activity that involves substantial leadership development. It requires that organizations have a systematic process for identifying future talent and developing it to supply present and future leadership needs. Succession planning builds the organization from within by transitioning staff that have institutional knowledge and savvy through management levels.

Good succession planning ensures that the fundamental business of leadership will go on in the organization, even as it meets the new challenges of tomorrow. With the proper leadership development in place, an organization can be better assured that the inspiration that followers seek will be felt, that motivation among the organization's members will be stronger, and that the achievement of results will be a shared goal within reach.

KEY TERMS

causal chain for the leadership action cycle	leadership development
distributed or shared leadership	self-directed team
individual learning plans	self-study
integrative leadership	structured experiences
job rotation	succession planning

RESOURCES

Most universities and many private organizations offer executive training to provide leaders with a "safe environment" in which to think about how to inspire change in their firms. Look at this example of such an offering, and present to the class your concept of how the program could best be utilized. If you are currently working or have worked in the past, respond to the question through the eyes of your organization.

- Disney Institute. www.disneyinstitute.com/default.aspx?gclid=ckjk1pot45scfrf magodetn4-w.

Finding competitive advantage in self-managed work teams is not as common a push as it was in the 1980s, but it is regarded as an important concept for leaders to understand. This 2005 article from *Business Forum* gives a good overview of the contrast between traditional work design and self-managed work teams.

- Sandra L. Christensen, "Finding Competitive Advantage in Self-Managed Work Teams," *Business Forum*, December 22, 2005. www.allbusiness.com/human-resources/employee-development-team-building/620469-1.html.

Self-assessments form a good basis for determining professional development plans. Questionnaires, if taken honestly, can be helpful in evaluating areas to target. The following site has a good self-assessment for evaluating readiness for collaborative leadership.

- Turning Point, "Collaborative Leadership: Self-Assessment Questionnaires." www.turningpointprogram.org/toolkit/pdf/CL_selfassessments.pdf.

There is great similarity between public and private succession planning. The Office of Personnel Management (OPM) developed its Workforce Planning Model for governmental agencies to use in succession planning. All five steps of the planning model are explained. Anyone interested in federal employment will find links with interesting material on federal retirement patterns.

- U.S. Office of Personnel Management, "OPM's Workforce Planning Model," September 2005. www.opm.gov/hcaaf_resource_center/assets/sa_tool4.pdf.

DISCUSSION QUESTIONS

1. Describe the nature of executive education.
2. What kinds of structured experiences can contribute to leadership development?
3. Assume that you are speaking to a supervisor after having read this chapter. Now, explain to the supervisor his or her role in leadership development.
4. What is an example of a specialized developmental assignment? What kind of a developmental assignment do you feel would help to prepare you for your first supervisory role?
5. What elements are particularly important in enhancing structured experience as a developmental tool?
6. Give examples of different modes of delivering leadership development programs.
7. List leadership topics that should be covered in development content today that will help the emergent leader in today's environment.
8. Describe a succession management program and explain its purpose.

CLASSROOM ACTIVITIES

1. Interview a manager about the specific on-the-job education or training the manager received regarding ethics in the workplace. What topics were covered?
2. A powerful leadership development technique is a survey assessment in which a variety of raters evaluate your style and performance on the job. However, perhaps the most important assessor is you, assuming that you are honest and have self-insight. Complete the Leadership Assessment Questionnaire at the end of this chapter. What areas do you self-assess as your best? Which are your weakest areas? What might you do to strengthen your weak areas?

APPENDIX: LEADERSHIP ASSESSMENT QUESTIONNAIRE

Following is a sixty-item questionnaire that you are encouraged to administer for feedback about yourself if you are already in a leadership position.

BACKGROUND INFORMATION

You are being asked to contribute to an organizational and leader assessment. The instrument should take between twenty and twenty-five minutes to complete. A cover letter will stipulate the terms of confidentiality, the return address, and whether to use this form for your responses or a separate form that can be scanned. The survey has two parts. The questions regarding organizational effectiveness may or may not reflect a particular leader's effect on the organization. For example, leaders who are new or have a relatively small range of discretion may not have a major impact. Because leadership is ultimately about improving organizational effectiveness, however, these questions are vitally important no matter how great or small the leader's past role. The second part of the assessment focuses on the leader's traits, skills, and management behaviors. Leader traits are generally predispositions toward effectiveness, rather than guarantees of success. The leader skills selected here are those generalized capabilities that are used in many management behaviors. The leader behaviors are divided into those that are task-oriented, people-oriented, and change-oriented.

GUIDELINES FOR RESPONDENTS

- In nearly all cases, the organization, area, or unit being referred to is the area under the jurisdiction of the person being assessed, not the organization at large. The exception is when the person being evaluated is the chief executive officer.
- Reserve 5s for truly exceptional behavior. Most people are exceptional in a few things; almost no one is exceptional in all leadership areas.
- Reserve DK/NA (do not know/not applicable) for cases when you have no idea or the question seems completely inapplicable.
- Even though a number of the questions are broad or composite in scope, provide an average score for the range that you feel applies.

PART 1. ORGANIZATIONAL CONDITIONS

Unless a special scale is called for by a question, rate the following statements about organizational conditions using the following scale:

5 = strongly agree
4 = agree
3 = neither agree nor disagree
2 = disagree
1 = strongly disagree
DK/NA = do not know or not applicable

Overall Organizational Effectiveness (Organization-Wide)

		Disagree			Agree	
1.	The technical management of routine performance and problem-solving of the organizational area is optimal.	1	2	3	4	5
2.	The management of employees' needs—enhancing satisfaction and creativity—is optimal.	1	2	3	4	5
3.	The management of change—either to improve current systems significantly, replace processes altogether, or make changes in organizational culture—is optimal.	1	2	3	4	5
4.	Which of the three areas is most in need of attention in your opinion (technical management, employees' needs, management of change)? _____					

Organizational Factors Affecting Success

		Disagree			Agree		
5.	Task skills (as a result of recruitment, experience, and/or training) are generally excellent in the organizational area.	1	2	3	4	5	DK/ NA
6.	Role clarity—for individuals, teams, and entire units—is generally excellent in the organizational area.	1	2	3	4	5	DK/ NA
7.	The unit/organization is characterized by high levels of creativity and innovation.	1	2	3	4	5	DK/ NA
8.	Resources for the organizational area are generally optimal for employee pay, technology, facilities, support staff, training and development, travel, and so forth.	1	2	3	4	5	DK/ NA
9.	The level of subordinate effort (in terms of both well-managed time and subordinate enthusiasm) is generally excellent in the organizational area.	1	2	3	4	5	DK/ NA
10.	Formal groups/units and other teams are characterized by high levels of cooperation and mutual support in the organizational area.	1	2	3	4	5	DK/ NA
11.	The organization of work groups and the performance strategies they use to ensure high levels of productivity and quality are generally excellent in the organizational area.	1	2	3	4	5	DK/ NA
12.	The coordination of the organizational area with other external constituencies—other areas or agencies, legislative overseers, and public interest groups—is generally optimal.	1	2	3	4	5	DK/ NA

	Low				High	
13. Overall, how would you rate the level of organizational effectiveness, with 5 being high?	1	2	3	4	5	DK/ NA

Constraints on Leadership

	Few constraints				Many constraints	
14. Rate the degree of constraints placed on the leader by legal/contractual restrictions (such as legal limitations on rewarding and punishing employees, mandatory purchasing/ travel/process requirements, union contracts, etc). Many legal/contractual restrictions would be a 5; few legal/contractual restrictions would be a 1.	1	2	3	4	5	DK/ NA
15. Rate the degree of constraints placed on the leader by the level of the person's position in the organization. A chief executive position would be a 1; a frontline employee's position might be a 5 (but might also be lower depending on delegation and empowerment).	1	2	3	4	5	DK/ NA

	Few resources				Many resources	
16. Rate the constraints on leadership based on the level of resources. Few resources would be a 1; extremely lush resources would be a 5.	1	2	3	4	5	DK/ NA

PART 2. LEADER TRAITS, SKILLS, AND MANAGEMENT BEHAVIORS

Leader Traits

	Disagree				Agree	
17. The leader exhibits a high degree of appropriate self-confidence.	1	2	3	4	5	DK/ NA
18. The leader exhibits decisiveness in situations calling for decisive action.	1	2	3	4	5	DK/ NA
19. The leader is persistent in promoting long-term organizational goals and new projects that require time to provide results. The leader is persistent in keeping focus on organizational goals even when there are setbacks and disappointments.	1	2	3	4	5	DK/ NA
20. The leader generally exhibits high levels of energy.	1	2	3	4	5	DK/ NA
21. The leader demonstrates a high regard for excellence and forcefully motivates others to achieve excellence.	1	2	3	4	5	DK/ NA

22. The leader exhibits flexibility in responding to situations and also adapts his or her leadership style to the situation.　1　2　3　4　5　DK/NA

23. The leader generally demonstrates a public service mentality and a customer service orientation specifically.　1　2　3　4　5　DK/NA

24. The leader has very high standards of fairness, integrity, and honesty.　1　2　3　4　5　DK/NA

25. The leader's emotional maturity—self-control, responsibility for actions, lack of egotism—is consistent.　1　2　3　4　5　DK/NA

Leader Skills

	Disagree		Agree

26. The leader's oral communication skills are exceptional.　1　2　3　4　5　DK/NA

27. The leader's written communication skills are exceptional.　1　2　3　4　5　DK/NA

28. The leader's mastery of social and interpersonal skills (e.g., listening and empathy) is exceptional.　1　2　3　4　5　DK/NA

29. The leader is able to use influence and negotiation skills deftly for the good of the organization, without being perceived to be manipulative or excessively coercive.　1　2　3　4　5　DK/NA

30. The leader has the analytic skills—memory, ability to handle cognitive complexity, ability to make fine distinctions—necessary to do the job well.　1　2　3　4　5　DK/NA

31. The leader has technical credibility in the core responsibilities required by the unit.　1　2　3　4　5　DK/NA

32. The leader demonstrates continual learning on a personal level.　1　2　3　4　5　DK/NA

Leader Behaviors

Rate the leader in these behavior areas.

Task-oriented.

	Poor		Excellent

33. Monitoring and assessing tasks of subordinates.　1　2　3　4　5　DK/NA
34. Planning and organization of work processes.　1　2　3　4　5　DK/NA
35. Clarifying roles and objectives of subordinates.　1　2　3　4　5　DK/NA
36. Informing.　1　2　3　4　5　DK/NA

37. Delegating work appropriately.   1 2 3 4 5   DK/ NA
38. Problem-solving related to routine work issues.   1 2 3 4 5   DK/ NA
39. Managing technical innovation and creativity.   1 2 3 4 5   DK/ NA
40. Overall, how would you rate the leader's
    task-oriented behaviors?   1 2 3 4 5   DK/ NA

People-oriented.

	Poor			Excellent		

41. Consulting (with employees in their
    area of responsibility).   1 2 3 4 5   DK/ NA
42. Planning and organizing personnel (e.g.,
    deployment of the right people for the right jobs). 1 2 3 4 5   DK/ NA
43. Developing staff (e.g., training and mentoring).   1 2 3 4 5   DK/ NA
44. Motivating.   1 2 3 4 5   DK/ NA
45. Building and managing teams.   1 2 3 4 5   DK/ NA
46. Managing conflict.   1 2 3 4 5   DK/ NA
47. Managing personnel changes (e.g.,
    redeployment, getting personnel to
    adopt new standards).   1 2 3 4 5   DK/ NA
48. Overall, how would you rate the
    leader's people-oriented behaviors?   1 2 3 4 5   DK/ NA

Organization-oriented.

	Poor			Excellent		

49. Scanning the environment.   1 2 3 4 5   DK/ NA
50. Strategic planning and organizing issues related
    to organizational alignment (e.g., introducing a
    new service or taking steps to eliminate a service
    that is an inefficient use of resources).   1 2 3 4 5   DK/ NA
51. Articulating the mission and vision
    of the organization clearly.   1 2 3 4 5   DK/ NA
52. Networking and partnering (outside the organization). 1 2 3 4 5   DK/ NA
53. Performing general management functions (human
    resources, budget, information management,
    spokesperson responsibilities, etc.).   1 2 3 4 5   DK/ NA
54. Decision-making that is timely, effective, and
    well articulated (regarding major issues).   1 2 3 4 5   DK/ NA
55. Managing major organizational change and
    organizational culture over the long term.   1 2 3 4 5   DK/ NA
56. Overall, how would you rate the leader's
    change-oriented behaviors?   1 2 3 4 5   DK/ NA

Leader Style

57. How would you rate the leader's style range (whether that style is appropriate or not)? Does the leader change styles in different situations—sometimes being more participative, sometimes more consultative, and sometimes more directive? (The next question will consider style appropriateness.)

Limited   Broad

1 2 3 4 5 DK/ NA

58. How would you rate the leader's style appropriateness? For example, does the leader only use a directive style when speed or discipline are priorities and only use a participative or delegated style when subordinates are equipped and prepared to handle the responsibility?

Not appropriate   Appropriate

1 2 3 4 5 DK/ NA

Overall

59. What is the key leadership weakness or organizational issue that is especially important for the leader to deal with, in your opinion? _____

60. Finally, how would you rate the leader's overall performance, taking into consideration the current level of organizational performance and the leader's effect on it through his or her traits, skills, and management behaviors, and also taking into consideration the constraints the leader faces and his or her time in the position?

Poor   Excellent

1 2 3 4 5

References

Adler, N.J. 1996. "Global Women Political Leaders: An Invisible History, and Increasingly Important Future." *Leadership Quarterly* 7 (1): 133–161.

Aloft Group. 2009. "Americans Overwhelmingly Approve of Ford Not Accepting Government Bailout According to a Survey Conducted by Aloft Group." Reuters, April 30. www.reuters.com/article/idUS263429+30-Apr-2009+BW20090430.

American Institute of CPAs. 2010. *AICPA Code of Professional Conduct—Current and Historical Versions*. www.aicpa.org/Research/Standards/CodeofConduct/Pages/default.aspx.

American Management Association. 2005. "How Whirlpool's HR Department Got Strategic." *HR Focus* 82 (11): 7–10.

Angeles Insurance Company. 2009. Interview with K. Bowerman, Los Angeles, California, (Fictitious company name and anonymous at the request of president.) December 29.

Ansoff, I. 1980. "Strategic Issue Management." *Strategic Management Journal* 1 (2): 131–148.

Archer, D., and Cameron, A. 2008. *Collaborative Leadership: How to Succeed in an Interconnected World*. Oxford, UK: Butterworth Heinemann.

Argyris, C. 1957. *Personality and Organization*. New York: Harper.

———. 1993. *Knowledge for Action*. San Francisco: Jossey-Bass.

Aristotle. 1953. *The Ethics of Aristotle*, trans. J.A.K. Thomson. New York: Viking Penguin.

Armstrong, D., and Newcomb, P., eds. 2004. "The 400 Richest Americans." *Forbes*, Special Report, September 24. www.forbes.com/2004/09/22/rl04land.html.

Baker, D. 2009. Interview with K. Bowerman, San Bernardino, California, February 17.

Baldrige National Quality Program. 2008. "Criteria for Performance Excellence." www.baldrige.nist.gov/Business_Criteria.htm.

Ball, D. 2007. "After Buying Binge, Nestlé Goes on a Diet." *Wall Street Journal*, July 23.

Barrett, J. 2009. "Whirlpool Cleans Up Its Delivery Act." *Wall Street Journal*, September 24.

Barrie, J.M. 2006 [1902]. *The Admirable Crichton*. Lenox, MA: Hard Press.

Barzelay, M. 1992. *Breaking Through Bureaucracy: A New Vision for Managing in Government*. Berkeley: University of California Press.

Bass, B.M. 1985. *Leadership and Performance Beyond Expectations*. New York: Free Press.

———. 1990. *Bass and Stogdill's Handbook of Leadership*. 3rd ed. New York: Free Press.

———. 1996. *A New Paradigm of Leadership: An Inquiry Into Transformational Leadership*. Alexandria, VA: U.S. Army Research Institute for the Behavioral and Social Sciences.

Bass, B.M., and Avolio, B.J. 1990. "The Implications of Transactional and Transformational Leadership for Individual, Team, and Organizational Development." In *Research in Organizational*

Change and Development, ed. W. Pasmore and R.W. Woodman (4): 231–272. Greenwich, CT: JAI Press.

Bass, B.M., and Steidlmeier, P. 1999. "Ethics, Character, and Authentic Transformational Leadership." *Leadership Quarterly* 10: 181–217.

Bass, B.M., with Bass, R. 2008. *The Bass Handbook of Leadership*. 4th ed. New York: Free Press.

Bassie, L., Harrison, P., Ludwig, J., and McMurrer, D. 2001. "Human Capital Investments and Firm Performance." Bethesda, MD: Human Capital Dynamics, June.

Bates, K.G. 2006. "Jonestown: Portrait of a Disturbed Cult Leader." NPR, October 20. www.npr.org/templates/story/story.php?storyId=6353579.

Bauder, D. 2009. "Glenn Beck's Attack on Obama Riles Advertisers." *Press-Enterprise*, Riverside, CA, August 22.

Bédier, C., Vancauwenberghe, M., and vanSintern, W. 2008. "The Growing Role of Emerging Markets in Aerospace." *McKinsey Quarterly* 2: 114–126.

Ben & Jerry's *Social & Environmental Assessment 2006—A Letter From Our CEO*. www.benjerry.com/company/sear/2006/sear06_1.0.cfm.

Bennis, W., and Nanus, B. 1985. *Leaders: Strategies for Taking Charge*. New York: Harper and Row.

———. 2007. *Leaders: Strategies for Taking Charge*. 2nd ed. New York: Harper Collins.

Berner, Robert. 2007. "My Year at Wal-Mart." *Business Week*, February 12, 70–73.

Bertrand, M., Goldin, C., and Katz, L.F. 2008. "Dynamics of the Gender Gap for Young Professionals in the Financial and Corporate Sectors." September 30. http://emlab.berkeley.edu/~webfac/moretti/e251_f08/katz.pdf.

Bhatta, G. 2001. "Enabling the Cream to Rise to the Top: A Cross-Jurisdictional Comparison of Competencies for Senior Public Managers in the Public Sector." *Public Performance and Management Review* 25 (2): 194–207.

Blake, R.R., and Mouton, J.S. 1964. *The Managerial Grid*. Houston, TX: Gulf.

———. 1965. "A 9,9 Approach for Increasing Organizational Productivity." In *Personal and Organizational Change Through Group Methods*, ed. E.H. Schein and W.G. Bennis. New York: Wiley.

———. 1982. "Management by Grid Principles or Situationalism: Which?" *Group and Organization Studies* 7: 207–210.

———. 1985. *The Managerial Grid III*. Houston, TX: Gulf.

Blanchard, K., Fowler, S., and Hawkins, L. 2005. *Self-Leadership and the One Minute Manager: Increasing Effectiveness Through Situational Self-Leadership*. New York: William Morrow.

Block, P. 1993. *Stewardship: Choosing Service over Self-Interest*. San Francisco: Berrett-Koehler.

Boin, R.A., and Otten, M.H.P. 1996. "Beyond the Crisis Window of Reform: Some Ramifications for Implementation." *Journal of Contingencies and Crisis Management* 4 (3): 149–161.

Borins, S. 2000. "Loose Cannons and Rule Breakers? . . . Some Evidence About Innovative Public Managers." *Public Administration Review* 60 (6): 498–507.

Bowles, H., and Gintis, J. 2004. "Persistent Parochialism: Trust and Exclusion in Ethnic Networks." *Journal of Economic Behavior and Organization* 55: 1–23

Bowerman, K. 1995. "Organization Size, Life Cycle, and Decline." Instructor's Resource Guide to Accompany *Organization Theory and Design*, 5th ed., by R. Daft: 45.

Breen, B. 2005. "The Three Ways of Great Leaders." *Fast Company*, September 1. www.fastcompany.com/magazine/98/open_3ways.html.

Brown, J. 2010. Interviews with K. Bowerman, San Bernardino, California, January 21 and April 1.

Bryson, J.M., and Crosby, B.C. 1992. *Leadership for the Common Good: Tackling Problems in a Shared-Power World*. San Francisco: Jossey-Bass.

Buckingham, M., and Coffman, C. 1999. *First, Break All the Rules: What the World's Greatest Managers Do Differently*. New York: Simon & Schuster.

Burns, J.M. 1978. *Leadership*. New York: Harper and Row.

Caligiuri, P. 2000a. "The Big Five Personality Characteristics of Expatriate Success." *Personnel Psychology* 53: 67–88.

———. 2000b. "Selecting Expatriates for Personality Characteristics." *Management International Review* 40: 61–80.

Caligiuri, P., and Tarique, I. 2009. "Predicting Effectiveness in Global Leadership Activities." *Journal of World Business* 44 (3): 336–346.

Camerius, J. 1989. "Mary Kay Cosmetics, Inc.: Corporate Planning in an Era of Uncertainty." Midwest Society for Case Research Workshop, 989.

CareerBuilder.com. 2004. "Survey Reveals One-in-Three Workers Don't Think Their Bosses Are Getting the Job Done." August 5. www.careerbuilder.com/share/aboutus/pressreleasesdetail.aspx?id=pr135andsd=8%2f5%2f2004anded=12%2f31%2f2004andsiteid=cbprandsc_cmp1=cb_pr135_.

Carless, S. 2001. "Assessing the Discriminant Validity of the Leadership Practices Inventory." *Journal of Occupational and Organizational Psychology* 74: 233–239.

Carlino, B. 2010. "T100: The List Goes On." *Accounting Today*. March 15.

Carlyle, T. 1840. *On Heroes, Hero-Worship, and the Heroic in History.* Digitizing sponsor: Internet Archive, Book contributor: University of California Libraries www.archive.org/details/heroesheroworshi00carl.

Carnevale, A.P., Gainer, L.J., and Schulz, E.R. 1990. *Training the Technical Workforce.* San Francisco: Jossey-Bass.

Caro, R. 1975. *The Power Broker: Robert Moses and the Fall of New York.* New York: Random House.

Carroll, A.B. 1979. "A Three-Dimensional Conceptual Model of Corporate Performance." *Academy of Management Review* 4 (4): 497–505.

Carter, Adrienne. 2006. "Lighting a Fire Under Campbell: How Doug Conant's Quiet, Cerebral Style Got Things Bubbling Again." *Business Week*, December 4, 96–101.

Catalyst Inc. 1996. "Women in Corporate Leadership: Progress and Prospects." Research report, January. www.catalyst.org/publication/75/women-in-corporate-leadership-progress-prospects.

———. 2007. "2007 Catalyst Census of Women Board Directors of the Fortune 500." www.catalyst.org/publication/363/2007-catalyst-census-of-women-board-directors-of-the-fortune-500.

Cerdin, J-L., and LePargneux, M. 2009. "Career and International Assignment Fit: Toward an Integrative Model of Success." *Human Resource Management* 48 (1): 1, 5–25.

ChangingMinds.org. 1998. "Charismatic Leadership." www.changingminds.org/disciplines/leadership/styles/charismatic_leadership.html.

China CSR. 2009. "Johnson and Johnson China: No Recall for Baby Products." March 25. www.chinacsr.com/en/2009/03/25/4864-johnson-johnson-china-no-recall-for-baby-products.

Chrislip, D., and Larson, C. 1994. *Collaborative Leadership: How Citizens and Civic Leaders Can Make a Difference.* San Francisco: Jossey-Bass.

Ciulla, J.B. 2004. "Some Thoughts on the General Theory of Leadership Project." General Theory of Leadership Working Papers, Leadership Learning Community. www.leadershiplearning.org.

Clark, A. 2009. "Car Wars: How Alan Mulally Kept Ford Ahead of Its Rivals." *The Guardian*, May 11. www.guardian.co.uk/business/2009/may/11/ford-alan-mulally-interview-car-industry.

Cleveland, J.N., Stockdale, M., and Murphy, K.R. 2000. *Women and Men in Organizations: Sex and Gender Issues at Work.* Mahwah, NJ: Lawrence Erlbaum.

Cohen, M.D., March, J.G., and Olsen, J.P. 1972. "A Garbage Can Model of Organizational Choice." *Administrative Science Quarterly* 17 (2): 1–25.

Collins, Jim. 2001. *Good to Great: Why Some Companies Make the Leap . . . and Others Don't.* New York: HarperBusiness.

Conger, J.A. 1989. *The Charismatic Leader: Behind the Mystique of Exceptional Leadership.* San Francisco: Jossey-Bass.

Conger, J.A., and Kanungo, R.N. 1987. "Toward a Behavioral Theory of Charismatic Leadership in Organizational Settings." *Academy of Management Review* 12: 637–647.

Conger, J.A., and Kanungo, R.N. eds. 1998. *Charismatic Leadership in Organizations*. Thousand Oaks, CA: Sage.

Cooke, J. 2008. "The Greening of Whirlpool's Supply Chain." *Supply Chain Quarterly*, Quarter 2. Issue archives at www.supplychainquarterly.com/topics/Logistics/scq200802whirlpool.

Cooper, T.L. 1990. *The Responsible Administrator*. San Francisco: Jossey-Bass.

Corbett, S. 2009. "The Holy Grail of the Unconscious." *New York Magazine* (New York edition), September 20: MM34.

Costco Connection. 2005. "A Winning Recipe." 20 (7): 4–6.

Cottrell, D. 2002. *Monday Morning Leadership: 8 Mentoring Sessions You Can't Afford to Miss*. Dallas, TX: CornerStone Leadership Institute.

———. 2005. *12 Choices . . . That Lead to Your Success*. Dallas, TX: CornerStone Leadership Institute.

Couto, R.A. 1988. "TVA's Old and New Grass Roots: A Reexamination of Cooptation." *Administration and Society* 19 (4): 453–478.

Crockett, R. 2006. "Six Sigma Still Pays Off at Motorola." *Business Week*, December 4, 5.

Dahl, R.A. 1947. "The Science of Public Administration: Three Problems." *Public Administration Review* 7 (1): 1–11.

de Bono, E. 1985. *Six Thinking Hats*. Boston: Little, Brown.

Denhardt, R. 1992. *The Pursuit of Significance*. Belmont, CA: Wadsworth.

Denny's Corporation. 2008. Q2 earnings release. Adapted from conference call July 29, 2008.

DePree, M. 1989. *Leadership Is an Art*. New York: Doubleday.

Dotlich, D., Noel, J., and Walker, N. 2004. *Leadership Passages: The Personal and Professional Transitions That Make or Break a Leader*. San Francisco: Jossey-Bass.

Douglis, M.B. 1948. "Social Factors Influencing the Hierarchies of Small Flocks of the Domestic Hen." *Physiological Zoology* 21: 147–182.

Drucker, P. 1999. *Management Challenges for the 21st Century*. New York. HarperCollins.

———. 2001. *The Essential Drucker: The Best of Sixty Years of Peter Drucker's Essential Writings on Management*. New York: HarperCollins.

———. 2005. "Leadership Fundamentals—Managing Oneself: Best of HBR 1999." *Harvard Business Review* (January): 3–16.

Durbin, D., and Krishner, T. 2010. "Global Approach Gives Ford Lift." *Press Enterprise*, January 10.

Eagly, A.H., and Carli, L.L. 2007. "Women and the Labyrinth of Leadership." *Harvard Business Review* 85 (September): 62–71.

Earley, P.C., Wojnaroski, P., and Prest, W. 1987. "Task Planning and Energy Expended: Exploration of How Goals Influence Performance." *Journal of Applied Psychology* 72: 107–114.

Eden, D., and Ravid, G. 1982. "Pygmalion Versus Self-Expectancy: Effects of Instructor and Self-Expectancy on Trainee Performance." *Organizational Behavior and Human Performance* 30: 351–364.

Environmental Leader. 2009. "Whirlpool Redesigns Supply Chain." January 9. www.environmental-leader.com/2009/01/09/whirlpool-redesigns-supply-chain.

Etzioni, A. 1967. "Mixed Scanning: A Third Approach to Decision-Making." *Public Administration Review* 27: 385–392.

Evans, J.R., and Jack, E.P. 2003. "Validating Key Results Linkages in the Baldrige Performance Excellence Model." *Quality Management Journal* 10 (2): 7–24.

Fayol, Henri. 1984 [1917]. *General and Industrial Management*. Rev. by Irwin Gray. New York: Institute of Electrical and Electronics Engineers.

Fernandez, C.F., and Vecchio, R.P. 1997. "Situational Leadership Theory Revisited: A Test of an Across-Jobs Perspective." *Leadership Quarterly* 8 (1): 67–84.

Fiedler, F.E. 1967. *A Theory of Leadership Effectiveness*. New York: McGraw-Hill.

Fiedler, F.E., Chemers, M.M., and Mahar, L. 1976. *Improving Leadership Effectiveness: The Leader Match Concept*. New York: Wiley.

Fisher, R., and Ury, W. 1981. *Getting to Yes: Negotiating Agreement Without Giving In*. New York: Houghton Mifflin.

Fiol, C.M., Harris, D., and House, R. 1999. "Charismatic Leadership: Strategies for Effecting Social Change." *Leadership Quarterly* 10 (3): 449–482.

Fitzgerald, Elizabeth. 2007. "What It Takes to Make Happy Workers: Manufacturing Smiles to Win Talent 'War.'" *Star-Ledger* (New Jersey), June 24.

Fleishman, E.A. 1953. "The Description of Supervisory Behavior." *Journal of Applied Psychology* 37: 1–6.

Fleishman, E.A., Mumford, M.D., Zaccaro, S.J., Levin, K.Y., Korotkin, A.L., and Hein, M.B. 1991. "Taxonomic Efforts in the Description of Leader Behavior." *Leadership Quarterly* 2: 245–287.

Flessner, D. 2008. "TVA: Hospitality Costs Not Out of Line." *Chattanooga Times Free Press*, April 27. www.timesfreepress.com/news/2008/apr/27/tva-hospitality-costs-not-out-line.

Fortune. 2010. "100 Best Companies to Work For 2010." [From drop-down menu, obtain years of interest] http://money.cnn.com/magazines/fortune/bestcompanies/2009/index.html.

Freeman, K. 2009. "The Right Way to Close an Operation." *Harvard Business Review* 87 (5): 45–51.

Freeman, L. 1963. "The Feminine Mystique." *New York Times*, April 7.

French, J., and Raven, B.H. 1959. "The Bases of Social Power." In *Studies in Social Power*, ed. D. Cartwright, 150–167. Ann Arbor: University of Michigan.

Galinsky, E., Carter, N., and Bond, J.T. 2008. "Leaders in a Global Economy: Finding the Fit for Top Talent—An In-Depth Study of the Values and Engagement of Leaders in Multinational Companies." Research report for Families and Work Institute and Catalyst, May. www.catalyst.org/file/140/globaltalentmgmt.pdf.

Gantt, H.L. 1916. *Industrial Leadership*. New Haven, CT: Yale University Press.

Gardner, H. 2007. "The Ethical Mind." *Harvard Business Review* 85: 3, 51–56.

Gardner, J.W. 1989. *On Leadership*. New York: Free Press.

Garvin, D.A. 1993. "Building a Learning Organization." *Harvard Business Review* 71 (4): 78–91.

Gerstner, L. 2003. *Who Says Elephants Can't Dance?* New York: HarperBusiness.

Ghemawat, P., and Hout, T. 2008. "Tomorrow's Global Giants: Not the Usual Suspects." *Harvard Business Review* 86 (11): 80–88.

Gilbreth, F.B., and Gilbreth, L. 1917. *Applied Motion Study*. New York: Sturgis and Walton.

Gilder, G. 1981. *Wealth and Poverty*. New York: Basic Books.

Gilpin, K. 1997. "Harold S. Geneen, 87, Dies; Nurtured ITT." *New York Times*, November 23.

Glass Ceiling Commission. 1995. "Good for Business: Making Full Use of the Nation's Human Capital—The Environmental Scan." A Fact-Finding Report of the Federal Glass Ceiling Commission, U.S. Department of Labor, March.

Glassman, B. 1992. *Wilma Mankiller: Chief of the Cherokee Nation*. New York: Rosen.

GnanaDev, D. 2008. Interviews with K. Bowerman, Colton, California, February 20 and April 4.

Goleman, D. 1995. *Emotional Intelligence: Why It Can Matter More Than IQ*. New York: Bantam Books.

Goleman, D., and Boyatzis, R. 2008. "Social Intelligence and the Biology of Leadership." *Harvard Business Review* 86 (9): 74–81.

Graeff, C.L. 1997. "Evolution of Situational Leadership Theory: A Critical Review." *Leadership Quarterly* 8 (2): 153–170.

Graen, G., and Cashman, J.F. 1975. "A Role-Making Model of Leadership in Formal Organizations: A Developmental Approach." In *Leadership Frontiers*, ed. J.G. Hunt and L.L. Larson, 143–165. Kent, OH: Kent State University Press.

Graen, G., Cashman, J.F., Ginsburgh, S., and Schiemann, W. 1977. "Effects of Linking-Pin Quality on the Quality of Working Life of Lower Participants." *Administrative Science Quarterly* 22 (3): 491–504.

Graen, G., and Uhl-Bien, M. 1995. "Relationship-Based Approach to Leadership: Development of Leader-Member Exchange (LMX) Theory of Leadership over 25 Years: Applying a Multi-Level Multi-Domain Approach." *Leadership Quarterly* 6 (2): 219–247.

Greenleaf, R.K. 1977. *Servant Leadership: A Journey into the Nature of Legitimate Power and Greatness*. New York: Paulist Press.

Griswold, L. 2003. "President Bush Lands Ruiz Foods During Dinuba Visit." *Fresno Bee*, October 16. www.co.tulare.ca.us/news/displaynews.asp?NewsID=125&targetid=1.

Groysberg, B. 2008. "How Star Women Build Portable Skills." *Harvard Business Review* (February) 86 (2): 74–81.

Gulick, L. 1937. "Notes on the Theory of Organization." In *Papers on the Science of Administration*, ed. L. Gulick and L. Urwick. New York: Institute of Public Administration.

Gumbel, P. 2008. "Nestlé's CEO to Wall Street: I Did It My Way." *Fortune*, February 12.

Gupta, V. 2010. Interview with K. Bowerman, San Bernardino, California, February 21.

Gurley-Calvez, Harper, T.K., and Biehl, A. 2009. "Self-Employed Women and Time-Use." U.S. Small Business Administration Office of Advocacy No. 341, February, 1–50.

Haas, P.J. 2003. "The Use of Performance Indicators in State Administration." In *Encyclopedia of Public Administration and Public Policy*, ed. Jack Rabin, 898–900. New York: Marcel Dekker.

Halachmi, A. 2003. "Strategic Management and Productivity." In *Encyclopedia of Public Administration and Public Policy*, ed. Jack Rabin, 1157–1164. New York: Marcel Dekker.

Hambleton, R.K., and Gumpert, R. 1982. "The Validity of Hersey and Blanchard's Theory of Leader Effectiveness." *Group and Organization Studies* 7: 225–242.

Hammer, M., and Champy, J. 1993. *Reengineering the Corporation: A Manifesto for Business Revolution*. New York: HarperCollins.

Hart, D.K. 1992. "The Moral Exemplar in an Organizational Society." In *Exemplary Public Administrators: Character and Leadership in Government*, ed. T.L. Cooper and D.N. Wright, 9–29. San Francisco: Jossey-Bass.

Harvard Business Review: Leadership. 2009. "Great American Business Leaders of the Twentieth Century." www.hbs.edu/leadership/database/ethnicity.

Heifetz, R.A. 1994. *Leadership Without Easy Answers*. Cambridge, MA: Belknap Press.

Hejka-Ekins, A. 1992. "Marie Ragghianti: Moral Courage in Exposing Corruption." In *Exemplary Public Administrators: Character and Leadership in Government*, ed. T.L. Cooper and D.N. Wright, 304–323. San Francisco: Jossey-Bass.

Hempill, J.K. 1950. *Leader Behavior Description*. Columbus: Ohio State University, Personnel Research Board.

Hempill, J.K., and Coons, A.E. 1957. "Development of the Leader Behavior Questionnaire." In *Leader Behavior: Its Description and Measurement*, ed. R.M. Stogdill and A.E. Coons. Monograph No. 88. Columbus: Ohio State University, Bureau of Business Research.

Herring, C. 2009. "Does Diversity Pay? Race, Gender, and the Business Case for Diversity." *American Sociological Review* 74 (2): 208–224.

Hersey, P., and Blanchard, K.H. 1969. "Life Cycle Theory of Leadership." *Training and Development Journal* 23 (1): 26–34.

———. 1972. "The Management of Change." *Training and Development Journal* 26 (2): 20–24.

Hershberg, T. 1996. "Human Capital Development: America's Greatest Challenge." *Annals of the American Academy of Political and Social Science* 544 (March): 43–51.

Hindo, B. 2007. "At 3M, A Struggle Between Efficiency And Creativity." *Business Week*, June 11. www.businessweek.com/magazine/content/07_24/b4038406.htm.

Hofstede, G. 1980. *Culture's Consequences: International Differences in Work-Related Values*. Newbury Park, CA: Sage.

Hollander, E.P. 1958. "Conformity, Status, and Idiosyncrasy Credit." *Psychological Review* 65: 117–127.

Homans, G. 1958. "Social Behavior as Exchange." *American Journal of Sociology* 63: 597–606.

Hoover's Inc. "Bajaj Auto Limited, Pune, Maharashtra India." 2010. University library business databases by subscription.

Houghton, J.D., Neck, C.P., and Manz, C.C. 2003. "Self-Leadership and Superleadership: The Heart and Art of Creating Shared Leadership in Teams." In *Reframing the Hows and Whys of Leadership*, ed. C.L. Pearce and J.A. Conger, 123–140. Thousand Oaks, CA: Sage.

House, R.J. 1971. "A Path-Goal Theory of Leadership Effectiveness." *Administrative Science Quarterly* 16: 321–339.

———. 1977. "A 1976 Theory of Charismatic Leadership." In *Leadership: The Cutting Edge*, ed. J.G. Hunt and L.L. Larson, 189–207. Carbondale: Southern Illinois Press.

———. 1996. "Path-Goal Theory of Leadership: Lessons, Legacy, and a Reformulated Theory." *Leadership Quarterly* 7 (3): 323–352. Also available at http://knowledge.wharton.upenn.edu/paper.cfm?paperID=674.

House, R.J., and Aditya, R.N. 1997. "The Social Scientific Study of Leadership: Quo Vadis?" *Journal of Management* 23 (3): 409–473.

House, R.J., Hanges, P.J., Javidan, M., Dorfman, P.W., Gupta, V., and Associates. 2004. *Leadership, Culture, and Organizations: The GLOBE Study of 62 Societies*. Thousand Oaks, CA: Sage.

House, R.J., and Mitchell, T.R. 1974. "Path-Goal Theory of Leadership." *Contemporary Business* 3 (Fall): 81–98.

House, R.J., Spangler, W.D., and Woycke, J. 1991. "Personality and Charisma in the U.S. Presidency: A Psychological Theory of Leader Effectiveness." *Administrative Science Quarterly* 36 (September): 364–396.

Howard, A., and Bray, D.W. 1988. *Managerial Lives in Transition: Advancing Age and Changing Times*. New York: Guilford Press.

Hull, A., and Priest, D. 2007. "Hospital Officials Knew of Neglect: Complaints About Walter Reed Were Voiced for Years." *Washington Post*, March 1.

Humphreys, J., Ingram, K., Kernek, C., and Sadler, T. 2007. "The Nez Perce Leadership Council: A Historical Examination of Post-Industrial Leadership." *Journal of Management History* 13 (2): 135–152.

Hunt, J.G. 1996. *Leadership: A New Synthesis*. Newbury Park, CA: Sage.

Hurter, K. 2008. "INSPIRIS Acquires Care Level Management." Reuters, June 25. www.reuters.com/article/pressRelease/idUS123814+25-Jun-2008+PRN20080625.

Iacocca, L. 2007. *Where Have All the Leaders Gone?* New York: Scribner.

Ibarra, H., and Obodaru, O. 2009. "Women and the Vision Thing." *Harvard Business Review* 87 (1): 62–70.

Isaacson, Walter. 2009. "How to Save Your Newspaper." *Time,* February 5.

Isenberg, D. 2008. "The Global Entrepreneur." *Harvard Business Review* 86 (12): 107–111.

Ishikawa, K. 1990. *Introduction to Quality Control*. University Park, IL: Productivity Press.

Jackson, L. 2008. "This Isn't Like the 70s Oil Crisis. Spinning Wheels: A Community for Car Lovers." *Washington Times*, June 12.

Javidan, M., and House, R. 2001. "Cultural Acumen for the Global Manager: Lessons from Project GLOBE." *Organizational Dynamics* 29: 289–305.

Javidan, M., Dorfman, P., de Luque, S. and House, R. 1980. "Profile of a Black Executive." *World Book Report* (April): 28.

———. 2006. "In the Eye of the Beholder: Cross-cultural Lessons in Leadership from Project GLOBE." *Academy of Management Perspective* 20: 67–90.

Jennings, H.H. 1943. *Leadership and Isolation*. New York: Longmans, Green.

Johnson & Johnson. 2009. "How Our Credo Guides Our Actions." http://careers.jnj.com/careers/global/shared_values/guided_action/index.htm; jsessionid=PEMQCMYCBQPGSCQPCCFWU2YKB2IIWTT1.

Johnston, J. 1998. "Agency Mission." In *The International Encyclopedia of Public Policy and Administration,* ed. Jay Shafritz, 96–98. Boulder, CO: Westview.

Jones, R., Lasky, B., Russell-Gale, H., and le Fevre, M. 2004. "Leadership and the Development of Dominant and Countercultures: A Narcissistic Perspective." *Leadership and Organization Development Journal* 25 (2): 216–233.

Joshi, A., Liao, H., and Jackson, S. 2006. "Cross-Level Effects of Workplace Diversity on Sales Performance and Pay." *Academy of Management Journal* 29 (3): 459–481.

Journal of Blacks in Higher Education. 2006. "The Solid Progress of African Americans in Degree Attainment." Vol. 52 (Summer). www.jbhe.com/features/52_degree-attainments.html.

Kaiser, K., and Young, S. 2009. "Need Cash? Look Inside Your Company." *Harvard Business Review* 87 (5): 64–71.

Kamenou, N., and Fearfull, A. 2006. "Ethnic Minority Women: A Lost Voice in HRM." *Human Resource Management Journal* 16 (2): 154–172.

Kanter, R.M. 1983. *The Change Masters.* New York: Simon & Schuster.

———. 1994. "Collaborative Advantage: The Art of Alliances." *Harvard Business Review* 72 (4): 96–108.

Kanter, R.M., Stein, B.A., and Jick, T.D. 1992. *The Challenges of Organizational Change: How Companies Experience It and Leaders Guide It.* New York: Free Press.

Kaplan, R.E. 1984. "Trade Routes: The Manager's Network of Relationships." *Organizational Dynamics* 13 (Spring): 37–52.

Kaplan, R.S., and Norton, D.K. 1996. *The Balanced Scorecard.* Boston: Harvard Business School Press.

Karnani, A. 2010. "The Case Against Corporate Social Responsibility." *Wall Street Journal,* August 23: R1 and R4.

Katz, D., and Kahn, R.L. 1978. *The Social Psychology of Organizations.* 2nd ed. New York: Wiley.

Katz, R.L. 1955. "Skills of an Effective Administrator." *Harvard Business Review* 33 (1): 33–42.

Katzenbach, J.R., and Smith, D.K. 1993. *The Wisdom of Teams: Creating the High Performance Organization.* Boston: Harvard Business School Press.

Kaufman, S. 2008. "Evaluating the CEO." *Harvard Business Review* 86 (10): 53–57.

Kellerman, B. 2008. *Followership: How Followers Are Creating Change and Changing Leaders.* Boston: Harvard Business Press.

Kent, R.H. 2001. "You Can't Lead Without Managing." ManagerWise.com. www.managerwise.com/article.phtml?id=138.

Kerr, S., and Jermier, J.M. 1978. "Substitutes for Leadership: Their Meaning and Measurement." *Organizational Behavior and Human Performance* 22: 375–403.

Khan, A. 1998. "Strategic Budgeting." In *The International Encyclopedia of Public Policy and Administration,* ed. J. Shafritz, 2145–2150. Boulder, CO: Westview.

Khurana, R. 2002a. *Searching for a Corporate Savior: The Irrational Quest for Charismatic CEOs.* Princeton, NJ: Princeton University Press.

Khurana, R. 2002b. "The Curse of the Superstar CEO." *Harvard Business Review* (September): 60–66.

Kiley, D. 2006. "An Open Letter to Walmart, Julie Roehm and Draft/FCB." BusinessWeek.com, December 14.

———. 2009. "Ford Image Goes Way Up for Not Taking Taxpayer Money." BusinessWeek.com, May 1. http://nybw.businessweek.com/the_thread/brandnewday/archives/2009/05/ford_image_goes_way_up_for_not_taking_taxpayer_money.html.

Korn-Ferry Institute. 2008. "The 34th Annual Board of Directors Study." www.kornferry.com/Publication/9955.

Kotter, J.P. 1982. *The General Managers.* New York: Free Press.

———. 1990. *A Force for Change: How Leadership Differs from Management.* New York: Free Press.

———. 2007. "Leading Change: Why Transformation Efforts Fail." *Harvard Business Review,* Special Issue (The Tests of a Leader) January: 96–101. (Best of HBR, originally published in spring 1995).

Kouzes, J.M., and Posner, B.Z. 1987. *The Leadership Challenge: How to Get Extraordinary Things Done in Organizations.* San Francisco: Jossey-Bass.

————. 1993. *The Leadership Practices Inventory*. San Diego, CA: Pfeiffer.

Kurzman, D. 1987. *A Killing Wind: Inside Union Carbide and the Bhopal Catastrophe*. New York: McGraw-Hill.

Latham, G.P., and Yukl, G.A. 1975. "A Review of the Research on the Application of Goal Setting in Organizations." *Academy of Management Journal* 18 (4): 824–846.

Lay, P., Hewlin, T., and Moore, G. 2009. "In a Downturn, Provoke Your Customers." *Harvard Business Review* 87 (3): 48–56.

Leary, M. 2004. *The Curse of the Self: Self-Awareness, Egotism and the Quality of Human Life*. London: Oxford University Press.

Lehman, H.C. 1937. "The Creative Years in Science and Literature." *Science Monitor* 45: 65–75.

————. 1942. "Optimum Ages for Eminent Leadership." *Science Monitor* 54: 162–175.

————. 1953. *Age and Achievement*. Princeton, NJ: Princeton University Press.

Lewin, K. 1951. *Field Theory in Social Science*. New York: Harper.

Likert, R. 1959. "Motivational Approach to Management Development." *Harvard Business Review* 37: 75–82.

————. 1967. *The Human Organization: Its Management and Value*. New York: McGraw Hill.

————. 1981. "System 4: A Resource for Improving Public Administration." *Public Administration Review* 41 (6): 674–678.

Lindblom, C.E. 1959. "The Science of Muddling Through." *Public Administration Review* 19 (3): 79–88.

Lipman-Blumen, J. 2000. *Connective Leadership: Managing in a Changing World*. New York: Oxford University Press.

Locke, E.A. 2003. "Leadership: Starting at the Top." In *Shared Leadership: Reframing the Hows and Whys of Leadership*, ed. C.L. Pearce and J.A. Conger, 271–284. Thousand Oaks, CA: Sage.

Locke, E.A., and Latham, G.P. 1990. *A Theory of Goal Setting and Task Performance*. Englewood Cliffs, NJ: Prentice Hall.

Lombardi, Vince. 2007. "Quotes." BrainyQuote.com. www.brainyquote.com/quotes/authors/v/vince_lombardi.html.

Lombardo, M.M., and McCauley, C.D. 1988. *The Dynamics of Management Derailment*. Greensboro, NC: Center for Creative Leadership.

Lorange, P. 1980. *Corporate Planning: An Executive Viewpoint*. Englewood Cliffs, NJ: Prentice Hall.

MacMillan, D. 2008. "The Issue: Whirlpool Cleans Up Its Supply Chain." *Business Week*, October 24.

Manz, C.C. 1986. "Self-Leadership: Toward an Expanded Theory of Self-Influence Processes in Organizations." *Academy of Management Review* 11: 585–600.

Manz, C.C., Adsit, D., Dennis, J., Campbell, S., and Mathison-Hance, M. 1988. "Managerial Thought Patterns and Performance: A Study of Perceptual Patterns of Performance Hindrances for Higher and Lower Performing Managers." *Human Relations* 41: 447–465.

Manz, C.C., and Sims, H.P., Jr. 1980. "Self-Management as a Substitute for Leadership: A Social Learning Perspective." *Academy of Management Review* 5: 105–128.

————. 1987. "Leading Workers to Lead Themselves: The External Leadership of Self-Managing Work Teams." *Administrative Science Quarterly* 32: 106–128.

————. 1989. *Superleadership: Leading Others to Lead Themselves*. Englewood Cliffs, NJ: Prentice Hall.

————. 1991. "Superleadership: Beyond the Myth of Heroic Leadership." *Organizational Dynamics* 19 (4): 18–35.

Mason, J.C. 1992. "Leading the Way into the 21st Century." *Management Review* 81 (10) (October): 16–19.

Maslow, A.H. 1954. *Motivation and Personality*. New York: Harper.

————. 1967. *Eupsychian Management*. Homewood, IL: Dorsey.

Massie, N. 2008. Interview with K. Bowerman, Ontario, California, July 28.

Maxwell, J. 2008. *Encouragement Changes Everything: Bless and Be Blessed.* Nashville, TN: Thomas Nelson, Inc.

McCall, M., Lombardo, M.M., and Morrison, A.M. 1988. *The Lessons of Experience: How Successful Executives Develop on the Job.* New York: Lexington Books.

McClelland, D.C. 1965. "N-Achievement and Entrepreneurship: A Longitudinal Study." *Journal of Personality and Social Psychology* 1: 389–392.

———. 1985. *Human Motivation.* Glenview, IL: Scott Foresman.

McGregor, D. 1960. *The Human Side of Enterprise.* New York: McGraw-Hill.

McKenna, B., Rooney, D., and Boal, K. 2009. "Wisdom Principles as a Meta-theoretical Basis for Evaluating Leadership." *Leadership Quarterly* 20 (2): 177–190.

McKinney, M. 2010. "Business Reputation Isn't Just About Business." Leading Blog, January 6. www.leadershipnow.com/leadingblog/2010/01/business_reputation_isnt_just.html.

Micciche, T. 2009. "Preparation and Data Management Are Key for a Successful Expatriate Program." *Employment Relations Today* 36 (1): 35–39.

Miller, D., Kets de Vries, M.F.R., and Toulouse, J. 1982. "Locus of Control and Its Relationship to Strategy, Environment, and Structure." *Academy of Management Journal* 25: 237–253.

Miner, J.B. 1982. "The Uncertain Future of the Leadership Concept: Revisions and Clarifications." *Journal of Behavioral Science* 18: 293–307.

Mintzberg, H. 1973. *The Nature of Managerial Work.* New York: Harper and Row.

———. 1979. *The Structuring of Organizations.* Englewood Cliffs, NJ: Prentice Hall.

———. 1994. *The Rise and Fall of Strategic Planning.* New York: Free Press.

Mintzberg, H., and Quinn, J. 1991. *The Strategy Process.* 2nd ed. Englewood Cliffs, NJ: Prentice Hall.

Muczyk, J.P. 2008. "Toward a Cultural Contingency Model of Leadership." *Journal of Leadership and Organizational Studies* 14 (4): 277–286.

Mulder, M., deJong, R.D., Koppelaar, L., and Verhage, J. 1986. "Power, Situation, and Leader's Effectiveness: An Organizational Study." *Journal of Applied Psychology* 71: 566–570.

Mulder, M., and Stemerding, A. 1963. "Threat, Attraction to Group, and Need for Strong Leadership." *Human Relations* 16: 317–334.

Murchison, Carl. 1935. "A Social Behavior of Birds." In *A Handbook of Social Psychology*, ed. C. Murchison, 947–972. Worcester, MA: Clark University Press.

Myers and Briggs Foundation. 2010. "MBTI© Basics." www.myersbriggs.org.

National Center for Atmospheric Research. 2009. *NCAR Strategic Plan.* August 28. www.ncar.ucar.edu/publications/stratplan09.pdf.

Neck, C., et al. 2006. "Self-leadership—Special Issue." *Journal of Managerial Psychology* 21 (4): 270–388.

Newcomb, T.M. 1961. *The Acquaintance Process.* New York: Holt, Rinehart and Winston.

Newcomer, K.E. 1996. "Evaluating Public Programs." In *Handbook of Public Administration*, 2nd ed., ed. James L. Perry, 555–573. San Francisco: Jossey-Bass.

New York Times. 1991. "Chapter 11 for Taj Mahal." July 18. www.nytimes.com/1991/07/18/business/chapter-11-for-taj-mahal.html.

———. 2007. "The Wealthiest Americans Ever." July 15. www.nytimes.com/ref/business/20070715_GILDED_GRAPHIC.html.

Ng, E. 2008. "Why Organizations Choose to Manage Diversity? Toward a Leadership-Based Theoretical Framework." *Human Resource Development Review* 7 (1): 58–78.

Ni, A. 2009. "Managing Public-Private Partnerships of Transportation Infrastructure: Lessons Learned from California's SR91." July 21. White Report. Available from Leonard Transportation Center, Office of the Dean, California State University, San Bernardino, California.

Oakley, E., and Krug, D. 1991. *Enlightened Leadership: Getting to the Heart of Change.* New York: Simon & Schuster.

O'Connor, S.D. 2007. "Foreword." In *Women and Leadership*, ed. B. Kellerman and D.L. Rhode. San Francisco: Jossey-Bass.

Olson, M., vanBever, D., and Verry, S. 2008. "When Growth Stalls." *Harvard Business Review* 86 (3): 50–61.

Ones, D., and Viswesvaran, C. 1997. "Personality Determinants in the Prediction of Aspects of Expatriate Job Success." In *Expatriate Management: Theory and Practice*, vol. 4, ed. Z. Aycan, 63–92. Greenwich, CT: JAI Press.

Osborn, R.N., and Hunt, J.G. 2007. "Leadership and the Choice of Order: Complexity and Hierarchical Perspectives Near the Edge of Chaos." *Leadership Quarterly* 18: 319–340.

Ospina, S., and Su, C. 2009. "Weaving Color Lines: Race, Ethnicity, and the Work of Leadership in Social Change Organizations." *Leadership* 5 (2): 131–170.

O'Toole, J., and Bennis, W. 2009. "What's Needed Next: A Culture of Candor." *Harvard Business Review* 87 (6): 54–61.

Oxford English Dictionary, 2nd ed. 2008. "Ethnic, a. and n." www.oed.com.

Pavlo, W., Jr., and Weinberg, N. 2007. *Stolen Without a Gun: Confessions from Inside History's Biggest Accounting Fraud: The Collapse of MCI Worldcom*. Encino, CA: Etika Books.

Pellet, J. 2008. "We Need More Women Leaders. Now What?" *Chief Executive*, November 1.

Peters, T. 1992. *Liberation Management: Necessary Disorganization for the Nanosecond Nineties*. New York: Fawcett Columbine.

———. 1994. *The Pursuit of WOW! Every Person's Guide to Topsy-Turvey Times*. New York: Vintage Books.

Pettigrew, T. 1999. "Gordon Willard Allport: A Tribute." *Journal of Social Issues* 55 (3): 415–428.

Porter, J. 2008. "Using Ex-Cons to Scare MBAs Straight." *Business Week*, April 24.

Porter, M., and Kramer, M.R. 2002. "The Competitive Advantage of Corporate Philanthropy." *Harvard Business Review* 80 (12): 56–68.

Priem, R.L. 1990. "Top Management Team Group Factors, Consensus, and Firm Performance." *Strategic Management Journal* 11: 469–478.

Priestland, A., and Hanig, R. 2005. "Developing First-Level Leaders." *Harvard Business Review* 83 (6): 112–120.

Pullam, S., and Solomon, D. 2002. "Uncooking the Books: How Three Unlikely Sleuths Discovered Fraud at WorldCom Company's Own Employees Sniffed Out Cryptic Clues nnd Followed Hunches." *Wall Street Journal,* October 30: A1.

Quelch, J., and Jocz, K. 2009. "How to Market in a Downturn." *Harvard Business Review* 87 (4): 52–62.

Rahim, M.A. 1992. *Managing Conflict in Organizations*. Westport, CT: Praeger.

Ramanan, T. 1992. "The Bhopal Tragedy Revisited." *Risk Management* 39 (10): 62.

Rasmussen Reports. 2009. "46% More Likely to Buy Ford 'Cause It Didn't Get a Bailout." July 27. www.rasmussenreports.com/public_content/business/auto_industry/july_2009/46_more_likely_to_buy_ford_cause_it_didn_t_get_a_bailout.

Rauch, C.F., and Behling, O. 1984. "Functionalism: Basis for an Alternative Approach to the Study of Leadership." In *Leaders and Managers: International Perspectives on Managerial Behavior and Leadership*, ed. J.G. Hunt, D.J. Hosking, C.A. Schriesheim, and R. Stewart. Elmsford, NY: Pergamon Press.

Redwood, R. 1996. "The Findings and Recommendations of the Federal Glass Ceiling Commission." In *Motion Magazine*, October 2: 47–58. Also available at www.inmotionmagazine.com/glass.html.

Rhode, D.L., and Kellerman, B. 2007. "Women and Leadership: The State of Play." In *Women and Leadership*, ed. B. Kellerman and D.L. Rhode. San Francisco: Jossey-Bass.

Rigby, D., Gruver, K., and Allen, J. 2009. "Innovation in Turbulent Times." *Harvard Business Review* 87 (6): 79–86.

Ripley, A. 2008. "Q&A: Whistle-Blower Cynthia Cooper." *Time*, February 4.

Roberson, Q., and Park, H.J. 2007. "Diversity in Leadership Makes an Impact on the Bottom Line."

Cornell ILR School of Labor and Employment Law Program and the Cornell Law School panel discussion, New York City, June 28.

Romero, E.J. 2005. "The Effect of Hispanic Ethnicity on the Leadership Process." *International Journal of Leadership Studies* 1 (1): 28–43.

Rosenbloom, D.H. 1998. *Public Administration: Understanding Management, Politics, and Law in the Public Sector.* 4th ed. New York: McGraw-Hill.

———. 2000. *Building a Legislative-Centered Public Administration.* Tuscaloosa: University of Alabama Press.

Rost, J.C. 1991. *Leadership for the Twenty-First Century.* Westport, CT: Praeger.

Rotter, J.B. 1966. "Generalized Expectancies for Internal Versus External Control of Reinforcement." *Psychological Monographs* 80 (1): 1–28.

Ryan, L. 2007. "Leave Gen Y Alone." BusinessWeek.com, December 20. www.businessweek.com/managing/content/dec2007/ca20071218_909449.htm?campaign_id=rss_daily.

Sanders, M. 2005. "How Does Trump Repeatedly File for Bankruptcy and Still Stay on Top?" LegalZoom.com, October. www.legalzoom.com/legal-headlines/celebrity-lawsuits/how-does-trump-repeatedly-file.

Sandowsky, D. 1995. "The Charismatic Leader as Narcissist: Understanding the Abuse of Power." *Organizational Dynamics* 24 (4): 57–71.

Savvas, A. 2009. "IBM Cleans Up in Whirlpool Global IT Contract." ComputerWeekly.com, January 29. www.computerweekly.com/Articles/ 2009/01/29/234512/IBM-cleans-up-in-Whirlpool-global-IT-contract.html.

Schein, E.H. 1985. *Organizational Culture and Leadership: A Dynamic View.* San Francisco: Jossey-Bass.

Schmitt, B. 2010. "Prius Recall or Not? Toyota, a Mass Producer of Confusion." The Truth About Cars, February 7. www.thetruthaboutcars.com/prius-recall-or-not-toyota-a-mass-producer-of-confusion.

Schneider, M., and Somers, M. 2006. "Organizations as Complex Adaptive Systems: Implications of Complexity Theory for Leadership Research." *Leadership Quarterly* 17: 351–365.

Scholtes, P.R. 1993. *The Team Handbook: How to Use Teams to Improve Quality.* Madison, WI: Joiner.

Schultz, J.D. 1998. "Tennessee Valley Authority." In *A Historical Guide to the U.S. Government*, ed. G.T. Kurian, 567–569. New York: Oxford University Press.

Schultz, T. 1963. *The Economic Value of Education.* New York: Columbia University Press.

Selznick, P. 1949. *TVA and the Grass Roots.* Berkeley: University of California Press.

———. 1957. *Leadership in Administration.* New York: Row, Peterson.

Senge, P. 1990. *The Fifth Discipline: The Art and Practice of the Learning Organization.* New York: Doubleday Currency.

Shamir, B., House, R.J., and Arthur, M.B. 1993. "The Motivational Effects of Charismatic Leadership: A Self-Concept Based Theory." *Organizational Science* 4 (4): 577–594.

Sharp, L. 2009. Interview with K. Bowerman, San Bernardino, California, August 24.

Shartle, C.L. 1950. "Studies in Leadership by Interdisciplinary Methods." In *Leadership in American Education*, ed. A.G. Grace. Chicago: University of Chicago Press.

Shirouzu, N., and Linebaugh, K. 2008. "Toyota Shifts Gears to Build Prius in U.S." *Wall Street Journal*, July 11.

Simon, H.A. 1947. *Administrative Behavior: A Study of Decision-Making Processes in Administrative Organization.* New York: Macmillan.

Simonsen, W. 1998. "Municipal Bonds: Policy and Strategy." In *The International Encyclopedia of Public Policy and Administration*, ed. Jay Shafritz, 1453–1458. Boulder, CO: Westview.

Sirkin, H., Hemerling, J., and Bhattacharya, A. 2008. "Globality: Challenger Companies Are Radically Redefining the Competitive Landscape." *Strategy and Leadership* 36 (6): 36–45.

Skinner, B.F. 1953. *Science and Human Behavior.* New York: Macmillan.

————. 1971. *Beyond Freedom and Dignity*. New York: Knopf.

————. 1974. *About Behaviorism*. New York: Knopf.

Sorenson, T.C. 1963. *Decision Making in the White House*. New York: Columbia University Press.

Spear, S. 2010. "Learning from Toyota's Stumble." *Harvard Business Review* Online Blog—January 28. http://blogs.hbr.org/cs/2010/01/learning from toyotas stumble.html.

Spencer, B.F. 2007. "The Leadership Chain: McClelland and His Legacy." Spencer, Shenk, Capers and Associates. www.ssca.com/resources/articles/103.

Spencer, L.M., and Spencer, S.M. 1993. *Competence at Work: Models for Superior Performance*. New York: Wiley.

Steers, R.M., and Sanchez-Runde, C.J. 2002. "Culture, Motivation, and Work Behavior." In *The Blackwell Handbook of Cross-Cultural Management*, ed. M. Gannon and K. Newman. Oxford, UK: Blackwell.

Steiner, J. 1991. "The Second Tragedy of Bhopal." *Business Forum* 16 (3): 29–31.

Stephens, J. 2009. Adapted from email interviews with K. Bowerman, August.

Stodghill, R. 2007. "Room at the Top?" *New York Times*, November 1.

Stogdill, R.M. 1948. "Personal Factors Associated with Leadership: A Survey of the Literature." *Journal of Psychology* 25: 35–71.

————. 1974. *Handbook of Leadership: A Survey of Theory and Research*. New York: Free Press.

Stohl, C. 1986. "The Role of Memorable Messages in the Process of Organizational Socialization." *Communication Quarterly* 34: 231–249.

Stolberg, S.G. 2009. "Obama Signs Equal-Pay Legislation." *New York Times*, January 29.

Stone, D.C. 1945. "Notes on the Government Executive: His Role and His Methods." *Public Administration Review* 5 (3): 210–225.

Streufert, S., and Swezey, R.W. 1986. *Complexity, Managers, and Organizations*. Orlando, FL: Academic Press.

Sunseri, G., and Rottman, S. 2006. "Enron Verdict: Ken Lay Guilty on All Counts, Skilling on 19 Counts." ABC News, May 25. http://abcnews.go.com/Business/LegalCenter/story?id=2003728&&page=1.

Sutton, R. 2009. "How to Be a Good Boss in a Bad Economy." *Harvard Business Review* 87 (6): 42–50.

Taggart, A. 2007. "Beyond Diversity: Becoming a Culturally Competent Organization." *Ivey Business Journal* (September/October). www.ibj.ca/article.asp?intArticle_ID=712.

Taylor, F.W. 1911. *The Principles of Scientific Management*. New York: Harper and Row.

Taylor, M., and Bolstad, E. 2010. "BP 'Systemic Failure' Endangers Gulf Cleanup Workers." *McClatchy Newspapers*, May 28. http://news.yahoo.com/s/mcclatchy/20100529/pl_mcclatchy/3519831.

Terry, R. 1993. *Authentic Leadership: Courage in Action*. San Francisco: Jossey-Bass.

Thomas, K.W. 1992. "Conflict and Negotiation Processes in Organizations." In *Handbook of Industrial and Organizational Psychology*, 2nd ed., vol. 3, ed. M.D. Dunnette and L.M. Hough, 651–717. Palo Alto, CA: Consulting Psychologists Press.

Thorndike, E.L. 1920. "Intelligence and Its Use." *Harper's Magazine* 140: 221–235.

Tichy, N.M., and Devanna, M.A. 1990. *The Transformational Leader*. New York: Wiley.

Time. 2009. "The 10 Most Endangered Newspapers in America." March 9. www.time.com/time/business/article/0,8599,1883785,00.html

Tirrell, R. 2009. *The Wisdom of Resilience Builders: How Our Best Leaders Create the World's Most Enduring Enterprises*. Bloomington, Indiana: Author House.

Trevino, L.K., Weaver, R.G., and Reynolds, S.J. 2006. "Behavioral Ethics in Organizations: A Review." *Journal of Management* 32 (6): 951–990.

Trollope, A. 1883. *An Autobiography*. Edinburgh and London: Wm. Blackwood and Sons.

Trotter, R., Day, S., and Love, A. 1989. "Bhopal, India and Union Carbide: The Second Tragedy." *Journal of Business Ethics* 8 (6): 439–454.

Trudel, R., and Cotte, J. 2009. "Does It Pay to Be Good?" *MIT Sloan Management Review* 50 (2): 61–68.

Tsui, A., and O'Reilly, C. 1989. "Beyond Simple Demographic Effects: The Importance of Relational Demography in Superior-subordinate Dyads." *Academy of Management Journal* 32 (2): 402–423.

Uhl-Bien, M. 2006. "Relational Leadership Theory: Exploring the Social Processes of Leadership and Organizing." *Leadership Quarterly* 17: 654–676.

Ungar, B., ed. 1989. "Senior Executive Service: Training and Development of Senior Executives." Report to the Chairman, Subcommittee on Civil Service, Committee on Post Office and Civil Service, House of Representatives, September. GAO-GGD-89-127. Washington, DC: U.S. Government Accounting Office.

U.S. Bureau of Labor Statistics. 2005. *Women in the Labor Force: A Databook.* Report 985, May. Washington, DC: U.S. Department of Labor.

———. 2008. "Employment and Earnings, Annual Averages 2008 and the Current Population Survey, Annual Social Economic Tables." Washington, DC: U.S. Department of Labor. www.bls.gov/cps/cps_aa2008.htm.

———. 2009. "Employment Situation for July 2009." Economic News Release, August 7. www.bls.gov/schedule/news_release/2009_sched.htm.

U.S. Census Bureau. 1994. "Population Profile of the United States." www.census.gov/population/www/pop-profile/educattn.html.

———. 2010. "Educational Attainment of the Population." Current Population Survey, 2009 Annual Social and Economic Supplement. April. www.census.gov/hhes/socdemo/education/data/cps/2009/tables.html.

U.S. Office of Personnel Management (OPM). 1992a. "Dimensions of Effective Behavior: Executives, Managers, and Supervisors." Report no. PRD-92-05. Drafted by D. Corts and M. Gowing. Washington, DC: Office of Personnel Research and Development.

———. 1992b. "Occupational Study of Federal Executives, Managers, and Supervisors: An Application of the Multipurpose Occupational Systems Analysis Inventory—Closed Ended (MOSAIC)." Report no. PRD-92-21. Drafted by D.J. Gregory and R.K. Park. Washington, DC: Office of Personnel Research and Development.

———. 1999. "High Performance Leaders: A Competency Model." Report no. PRDC-99-02. Drafted by L.D. Eyde, D.J. Gregory, T.W. Muldrow, and P.D. Mergen. Washington, DC: Employment Service—Personnel Resources and Development Center.

Van Wart, M. 1995. "The First Step in the Reinvention Process: Assessment." *Public Administration Review* 55 (5): 429–438.

———. 1998. *Changing Public Sector Values.* New York: Garland.

———. 2004. "A Comprehensive Model of Organizational Leadership: The Leadership Action Cycle." *International Journal of Organization Theory and Behavior* 6 (4): 173–208.

———. 2005. *Dynamics of Leadership in Public Service.* Armonk, NY: M.E. Sharpe.

Van Wart, M., with Suino, P. 2008. *Leadership in Public Organizations.* Armonk, NY: M.E. Sharpe.

Van Wart, M., and Berman, E. 1999. "Contemporary Public Sector Productivity Values: Narrower Scope, Tougher Standards, and New Rules of the Game." *Public Productivity and Management Review* 22 (3): 326–347.

Vizard, M.M. 1999. "In the Region/Westchester; Trump Pushes 2 Golf Projects Long in Negotiation." *New York Times,* April 11.

Vroom, V.H. 1964. *Work and Motivation.* New York: Wiley.

Vroom, V.H., and Jago, A.G. 1988. *The New Leadership: Managing Participation in Organizations.* Englewood Cliffs, NJ: Prentice Hall.

Vroom, V.H., and Yetton, P.W. 1973. *Leadership and Decision-making.* Pittsburgh: University of Pittsburgh Press.

Waldo, D. 1948. *The Administrative State.* New York: Ronald.

Washington Post. 2007. "Walter Reed Reacts." February 20.

Weber, Max. 1968 [1921]. *Max Weber on Law in Economy and Society,* ed. Max Rheinstein, trans. E. Shils and M. Rheinstein. New York: Simon & Schuster.

Weed, S.E., Mitchell, T.R., and Moffitt, W. 1976. "Leadership Style, Subordinate Personality, and Task Type as Predictors of Performance and Satisfaction with Supervision." *Journal of Applied Psychology* 61: 58–66.

Weick, K.E., Sutcliffe, K.M., and Obstfeld, D. 1999. "Organizing for High Reliability: Processes of Collective Mindfulness." *Research in Organization Behavior* 21: 81–123.

Wheatley, M.J. 1992. *Leadership and the New Science: Learning About Organizations from an Orderly Universe*. San Francisco: Berrett-Koehler.

Williamson, P., and Zeng, M. 2009. "Value-for-Money Strategies." *Harvard Business Review* 87 (3): 66–74.

Wind, Y., and Mahajan, V. 1981. "Designing Product and Business Portfolios." *Harvard Business Review* 59 (1): 155–165.

Wolff, S., Wageman, R., and Fontaine, M. 2009. "The Coming Leadership Gap: An Exploration of Competencies That Will Be in Short Supply." *International Journal of Human Resources Development and Management* 9 (2–3): 250–274.

Wolfman, T.S. 2007. "The Face of Corporate Leadership: Finally Poised for Major Change?" *New England Journal of Public Policy* 22 (1–2): 37–72.

Woodward, H., and Bucholz, S. 1987. *Aftershock*. New York: Wiley.

Yukl, G. 2006. *Leadership in Organizations*. 6th ed. Upper Saddle River, NJ: Prentice Hall.

Zaleznik, A. 1977. "Managers and Leaders: Are They Different?" *Harvard Business Review* 55 (5): 67–78.

Zullow, H.M., Oettingen, G., Peterson, C., and Seligman, M.E.P. 1988. "Pessimistic Explanatory Style in the Historical Record." *American Psychologist* 43: 673–682.

Name Index

Subject Index

About the Authors

Karen Dill Bowerman recently retired as Dean of the College of Business and Public Administration at California State University, San Bernardino. Her service roles span from economic development to export issues. She has taught leadership in U.S. and Asian businesses, as well as in university management education courses. Her scholarly work is in the fields of strategic management, human resources, organization theory, and leadership. Before earning a doctorate at Texas A&M University, she led organizations in business and in state government.

Montgomery Van Wart is Interim Dean and Professor of the College of Business and Public Administration at California State University, San Bernardino. He received his PhD from Arizona State University. He has authored more than sixty publications, including seven books and a substantial number of articles in leading journals. *The Dynamics of Leadership in Public Service* (M.E. Sharpe 2005) was highly recommended in *Choice* and designated an Outstanding Academic Title for 2005. He is Associate Editor of *Public Performance and Management Review* and serves on numerous other editorial boards.